DATE DUE			

SOCIAL CHANGE IN TIKOPIA

by the same author
WE, THE TIKOPIA

RAYMOND FIRTH

F.B.A

Social Change
in Tikopia

RE-STUDY OF A POLYNESIAN COMMUNITY
AFTER A GENERATION

ILLUSTRATED

Ruskin House

GEORGE ALLEN & UNWIN LTD
MUSEUM STREET LONDON

PRINTED IN GREAT BRITAIN
in 10 on 11 pt. Times type
BY SIMSON SHAND LTD
LONDON, HERTFORD AND HARLOW

To

PA FENUATARA

'Where virtue has not the first place,
there aristocracy cannot be firmly established'

ARISTOTLE, *Politics*, (II, ii)

Ko taku foe taumuri voko
Ko taku foe
Mai mata vaka
Kua seke
Tanu i a vaerangi . . .
Te maveteveteranga o a tau
*   rima*
Soa E!

TIKOPIA SONG TO A BOND-FRIEND

Oh my paddle from the stern of the canoe
My paddle
From the bow
Has slipped away
Buried beneath far skies
The unfastening of our hands
My friend.

PREFACE

An anthropological field expedition to a remote island in the Western Pacific must be indebted to a variety of people and institutions for many services and kindnesses outside the ordinary run of professional relations. This was so with the Tikopia expedition of 1952/3 which I carried out with the help of my colleague, Mr James Spillius. It had been my wish since the war to make a re-study of Tikopia society. This became possible through the facilities afforded me by the Australian National University. After being for some time a member of the Academic Advisory Committee of the University during its formation, by leave of my College I was able to accept an invitation from the Vice-Chancellor and Council of the new University to serve for a year as the Acting Director of its Research School of Pacific Studies, not long after its establishment in Canberra. As part of this arrangement the University sponsored a re-study of Tikopia. I was able to spend from March to the beginning of August 1952 on the island and Mr Spillius, who accompanied me, stayed until July 1953. The various acknowledgments which I am glad to make here are primarily my own, though necessarily some of them relate also to our joint work.

I wish first to acknowledge my debt to the Director and the Governors of the London School of Economics and Political Science for the grant of leave which made the expedition possible. I am most deeply indebted to Sir Douglas Copland, (then) Vice-Chancellor of the Australian National University, to Mr R. A. Hohnen, Registrar, and to other members of the University staff for their very great help and untiring courtesy in all the arrangements for the expedition. To a generous travel grant from the British Dominions and Colonies Program of the Carnegie Corporation, and to further financial assistance from the Australian National University I owe the co-operation of Mr Spillius. To the late Professor S. F. Nadel, whose untimely death in 1956 was such a loss to the University, I am indebted for putting me in touch initially with Mr Spillius, and for much other assistance.

In preparing for the expedition we had the invaluable help and advice of Mr H. E. Maude, (then) Executive Officer for Social Development in the South Pacific Commission. We were also helped very greatly by Mrs Nancy Phelan of the Social Development Section of the Commission who even, at a critical moment, personally superintended the loading of some of our essential stores. We were indebted to the Social Development Section also for the loan of a tape recorder and generator which enabled Mr Spillius to secure some unique records of Tikopia speech and music. To Amalgamated Wireless of Australia Ltd we were most grateful for the loan of an Australophone which, operated by Mr Spillius, was invaluable in maintaining communication with our neighbours at Vanikoro, and at the seat of Government, 600 miles distant. Without this radio telephone communication we would have been greatly hampered in our work, and the Tikopia would have been even more gravely affected by the famine which developed during our stay.

We are very glad to acknowledge also the many facilities put at our disposal by the officials of the Western Pacific High Commission and the British Solomon Islands Protectorate Government. For much personal kindness in addition we were indebted to the Resident Commissioner, Mr H. G. Gregory Smith, to the Director of Medical Services, Dr W. H. McDonald, and to the various Government Officers in charge of the Eastern Solomons District. I myself owe a particular debt of gratitude to Mr H. G. Wallington, a generous host both ashore and afloat, who took us down to Tikopia in March 1952 and did much to assure the success of the expedition. To Sir Robert Stanley, High Commissioner for the Western Pacific, the expedition owed many kind services at a later period. To members of the staff of the Kauri Timber Company at Vanikoro we were also grateful for hospitality and help. The Melanesian Mission, as always, was most hospitable, and to the Bishop and other members of the Mission we were greatly indebted.

For consultation of material after my return to London I am indebted to the Librarian, India Office, and to the authorities of the Public Records Office, to whom I also owe permission to quote from the Logs of the ship *Barwell* and of HMS *Mohawk* respectively. I owe grateful thanks also to the Rev R. P. Garrity, General Secretary, and to Miss R. M. Palmer, Assistant Secretary, of the Home Organization of the Melanesian Mission for their help in giving me access to the published journals of the Mission library in London. I am also indebted to the authorities of the Mission for allowing me to quote from these journals.

For the writing up of the major results of my own work from the expedition I am greatly indebted to the Behavioral Sciences Division of the Ford Foundation. Through the use of part of personal research grants which the Division made available to me I have been able to have the further help of Mr Spillius and also other research assistance at various stages of my analysis of the data, as well as secretarial and photographic services. These have all proved most helpful to me in the preparation of this book, as of my other recent publications on Tikopia.

For various helpful items of information I am also indebted to Dr David Bonnet, Professor J. W. Davidson, Mr John Hearth, Mr James Tedder, and Mr G. B. Stigant.

For reading my draft manuscripts critically and making various and helpful suggestions I am much indebted to Mr Spillius, to my colleague Mrs Lorraine Lancaster, and to Dr Joan Metge, who formerly acted as my Research Assistant.

I must express my especial appreciation of the help received from Mr James Spillius. Much is demanded from a companion on a scientific expedition to a small isolated island with the prospect of being months together without relief from the outside world. I owe a very great deal to Mr. Spillius for the cheerful and unflagging way in which he maintained our own cordial relations, supervised the most vital practical tasks of the expedition and secured the friendship of the Tikopia, while devoting himself to the scientific objects of the expedition. The systematic records, especially of political affairs and of pagan religious ritual, which he continued to collect for a year after I had left the island, have been an invaluable contribution to our understanding of Tikopia social life. In the immediate context of writing this book I have been especially grateful for his draft reports, his supporting evidence for many of my conclusions and for his penetrating comment upon them. He is, of course, in no way responsible for the form in which they are finally expressed.

Lastly, the thanks of the expedition are due to those many Tikopia who helped us unwearyingly and most hospitably to observe and understand the ways of their society. Many of them have since died in the epidemic of 1955, but some day their descendants—including those of our friend Pa Fenuatara to whom this book is dedicated—may read of the debt which we are glad here to acknowledge.

RAYMOND FIRTH

London, September 1958

CONTENTS

DIAGRAMS

MAPS

CHART

PLANS

TABLES

GENEALOGIES

PLATES

CHAPTER I

Tikopia Re-studied

My intention in returning to Tikopia in 1952 was primarily to study the degree of change that had taken place in the structure of the society since I had left it in 1929. I also wanted to work out, by reference to the time-phase, some problems in social organization. In addition to making a contribution to Polynesian ethnography I hoped to be able to throw some further light on the analysis of the dynamics of small-scale integral social systems.

Return to the field of earlier anthropological analysis has now become almost a commonplace. But until fairly recently an anthropologist going back to the scene of his former research did so in order to fill gaps in his earlier record. He was searching not for change but for persistence, for further insight into the workings of a 'primitive' society, implicitly regarded as almost static in its condition. In this older style of work the lapse of a generation was a great disadvantage since many earlier informants might be dead, and contacts and confidence would have to be re-established. In modern work such a generation lapse has its difficulties; but it also offers a remarkable opportunity. It offers, even if only over a brief period, that truly historical comparison which is necessary for adequate investigation of social change.

I would emphasize that my Tikopia study was not simply one of 'acculturation'. I did study social change resulting from or intimately related to external contacts, broadly summarized under the head of 'Westernization' or 'modernization'. But the relative isolation of Tikopia gave an opportunity of estimating the effects of primarily internal movements too. Hence I considered the social changes associated with ecological change, including population movement on the one hand and hurricane and drought on the other. Of particular interest to me also were the changes associated with the process of generation replacement. Tikopia patterns of residence and marriage, and of lineage movement had been, as it were, constantly re-worked through the years to give small but appreciable differences in the social map of 1952 from that of 1929. Some differences in the social system then could be associated with the 'natural succession'—the emergence of new persons, new groups, new relationships on the social scene.

The problems examined in this book may be expressed from another point of view, in the following terms. During the generation that passed between my visits to Tikopia certain changes took place in the socio-economic environment. These changes demanded or were related to organizational responses. The action taken involved appreciation or evaluation of the situation, assumption of responsibility for mobilizing resources, direction and control

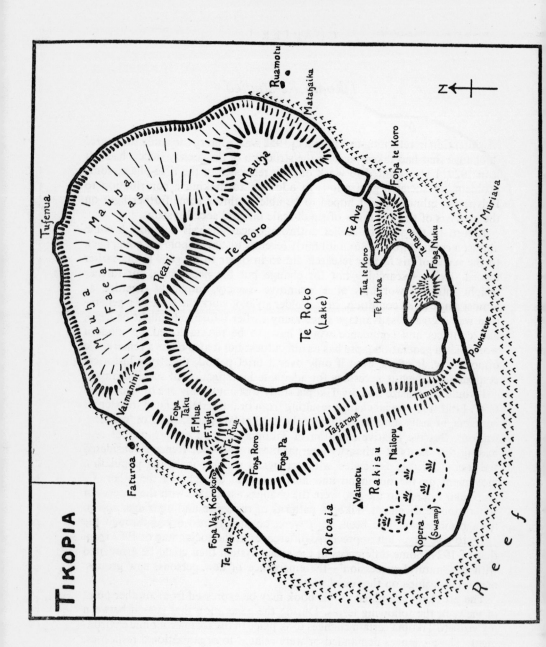

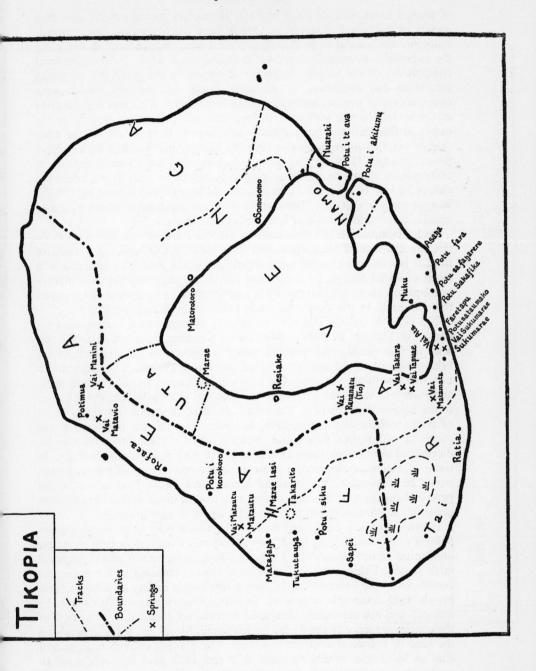

TIKOPIA

Tracks

Boundaries

× Springs

of factors concerned, decision between alternative procedures. Where, in a society of the type I observed in 1928/9, were the evaluation, the responsibility and the control to be found, and what were their nature? How far did the responses—necessarily expressed at an individual level—involve structural components of the society, implying alteration in the principles of group formation and operation, or of major social relationships, which were characteristic of Tikopia society as I knew it formerly? What was the character of the social change, looked at in long-term perspective? Almost from the outset of this analysis, but especially in Chapters II and V, it will be clear that in some easily recognizable respects Tikopia had by 1952 undergone a radical change. How far did such a development seem inevitable—or, in other words, what alternatives seemed to be open? To what degree could the change be said to have been cumulative, and how far did it seem by 1952 to be apparently irreversible? These are some of the questions to which it seemed feasible to try and provide at least tentative answers.

Such a comparison as I have made in Tikopia is, strictly speaking, no more than an estimate of similarities and differences at two separate periods of time. It is a *dual-synchronic*, not a strictly *diachronic* study. To interpret it in terms of social change, as trends and not simple differences, would involve assumptions about regularities in the interim period—or at least assumptions that any kinks in the movement could be disregarded as insignificant.

The possible trap in this may be seen by reference to a comparative example, in Malaya. In 1947 I returned to Kelantan, in north-east Malaya, after an interval of seven years in order to re-examine the structure of the fishing industry in the area where I had worked in 1939/40. The major structure was essentially the same. But prices of equipment and of fish had risen, and there had been some change in the relations of distribution, in the shares to the agents of production. There had also been alteration in the alignment of crews with specific net-masters, and some less efficient net-masters had gone out of business. One could interpret some of these other facts as indicative of continuous broader trends in the Kelantan fishing industry. In terms of major developmental process, such a consistency of interpretation would be reasonable. Yet it would ignore the episodic fluctuations of the period of Japanese occupation, during which some quite violent irregularities occurred, in production, in prices and in supply of equipment.

In other words, a dual-synchronic study, which is all most social anthropologists can manage, must not be interpreted as equivalent to a complete diachronic record. But while I regard this as a significant methodological qualification, I think that its importance varies according to the scale and conditions of the observation. In such a small-scale society as Tikopia, with people highly accessible to personal enquiry, preserving a record of events by memory and not constantly distracted by external contacts, a great deal of the interim sequence of events can be recovered. Moreover, much depends on the kind of collateral evidence available. For Tikopia enough independent data as to interim events between 1929 and 1952 have been collected to render the interpretation in terms of trends plausible.

In this study two methodological questions are relevant to the comparison of the results. The first concerns techniques used in the research. The second concerns personal relations of the investigators with the Tikopia, and our role in community affairs.

FIELD TECHNIQUES

On my first visit to Tikopia I worked alone. Considering the little that was then known of the society, the suspicion of the Tikopia towards an outsider, their reputation for wildness, and the need for personal responsibility in establishing confidence, this seemed sound procedure. On my second visit I took a research assistant, James Spillius, a Canadian anthropologist who had already some preliminary field experience on the north-west coast of the United States. Since the structure of Tikopia society was now known, as well as a great deal about the Tikopia language and custom, distinct advantage could be gained by joint work. We were able to cover a greater range; and to exchange data and interpretations as the research proceeded. In particular too, since I could only remain for about five months on the island, I had wished to have the help of a colleague in obtaining a record of events on Tikopia over at least a complete year. This was accomplished by Spillius, who remained on the island for nearly seventeen months in all, in very difficult conditions.

In any discussion of the validity of our findings in Tikopia in 1952/3, the question must be raised as to how far Spillius and I were making comparable observations. From this point of view, we took some elementary methodological precautions. At an early stage we made brief reliability assessment checks on each other's recording. We recorded the same ceremony independently, and checked for each other's omissions or variations of record. We found that these differences were slight, mostly to be explained by differences in our seating position. We also made a test of comparability of interpretation by giving independent accounts of the position of executives (*maru*) *vis-à-vis* their chiefs. Here the differences were wider, but neither then nor subsequently did they seem to be of major account.[1] We also, of course, continually discussed together our field records and interpretations. The immediate point of such checking was, as far as I was concerned, to ensure that as far as possible our empirical records could be equated and that, in particular, those of Spillius in the period after my departure could be properly compared closely with my own of 1952 and of 1929. I may not always agree with Spillius's interpretations, in matters of emphasis and attribution of motive. But after working together in the field for five months, and on the material in London for a year, I have been eminently satisfied as to the comparability of the empirical records made. Where, however, any specific issue is at all

[1] Cf. accounts of political structure in Raymond Firth 'Authority and Public Opinion in Tikopia' in *Social Structure*, ed. M. Fortes, 1949, pp. 168–88; James Spillius 'Natural Disaster and Political Crisis in a Polynesian Society: An Exploration of Operational Research', *Human Relations*, vol. X, 1957, pp. 3–27, 113–25, esp. 5–6, 11.

critical, I have indicated when material is drawn from Spillius's account. On the other hand, I have his authority to state that, for him, my 1929 picture of Tikopia society has seemed valid both in general and in detail, and that any differences of interpretation he found could be attributed primarily to post-1929 development.

Spillius and I used the ordinary intensive techniques of research common to British social anthropology. As regards language, I myself used the vernacular from the time of my arrival in Tikopia. I had remembered much of this through working over my Tikopia texts for many years. In talks with Tikopia in Honiara and on the voyage down I found that my command of the language was at first halting. But it turned out that over the years my grammatical control had actually improved so that in a few weeks I found that I tended to be more fluent than on my first visit. Spillius for some time used pidgin-English interspersed with a growing Tikopia vocabulary. But in the later months of his stay practically all his discussions were in the Tikopia language.

As in 1929, a great deal of information was obtained by interview with informants, either in their own houses or in ours. These were for the most part private conversations and frequently lasted an entire afternoon or evening. They were relatively unstructured interviews. While directed for the most part by us along channels to provide information on selected topics, apart from our census enquiries they were not concerned with any formal questionnaire and allowed free presentation of other topics. Some interviews were conducted in semi-secrecy, barring the door to outsiders. This was on Tikopia initiative, as, for example, by a spirit medium who knew he was being criticized by the officials of the Church, or by a man of rank wishing to discuss problems of public order with frankness. Observation of Tikopia behaviour in as many different contexts as possible was, of course, the necessary supplement to talking with informants. We both used freely the method of participant observation which, as I have described earlier,[1] is regarded as natural by the Tikopia. From fishing drives to funerals, from canoe chases of would-be suicides to Work of the Gods, Spillius and I, together or separately, took part in many Tikopia affairs. We also at times entered into situations in which from our point of view we were almost *dramatis personae*, being assigned specific roles to play in the ritual system. The ideology was one in which we did not believe. But for the Tikopia no question of belief was involved; they simply assumed our concurrence. Spillius bore offerings to a funeral; he also poured kava libations, carried ritual instruments; and anointed a sacred canoe in the Work of the Gods. I had a long series of discussions with spirit mediums in the trance state, made spirit offerings, and was myself involved in a system of family relationships on the 'spirit' plane. Here we were more than usual self-conscious actors on the social stage.

The qualitative information we obtained dealt with the main features of the social, political and economic system, with the prime objective of providing comparison with 1928/9. A special study was made of the religious

[1] *We, The Tikopia*, p. 11.

system, in particular of the 'Work of the Gods'. In 1928/9 I had made a very detailed investigation of this elaborate religious cycle. In 1952 I made a parallel study, strictly comparing the rituals item by item to see how far they were repeated precisely or what variation had occurred in them. This study was continued with great fidelity by Spillius after I left. Our joint observations provided the basis for a close estimate of change in the internal religious field.[1]

An important section of our work was quantitative in character. One of my main instruments of research in 1929 was a sociological census; this was repeated in 1952 with a similar schedule.[2] Spillius and I jointly also made a record of land use and ownership in the area of Rakisu, superimposing it in effect on the sketch map and records of that area made by me in 1929. Other comparative quantitative records included a village plan, a plan of fish weirs, and a property census—all by Spillius. I also made a canoe census more complete than in 1929 with help from Spillius. By such repetition of observation it was possible to get some quantitative estimate of change in significant social relationships over the generation. We recognized the general precautions in the use of quantification: that there was no point in accumulating figures for their own sake, in aiming at a false precision; that data had to be collected in view of their relevance to a definite problem; and that in the last resort it was not possible to define all trends in numerical terms. But we also saw that at a relatively gross level of interpretation of social material, comparison of quantified data could be very significant in correcting the errors of impressionism. Moreover, we hoped that by such aid it might be possible to present some indices of social change which could be used for comparative purposes. I relate this quantitative material to its appropriate context of problem later, and think that this type of study is of more general methodological interest.

In writing this book I have paid especial attention to the general principles of the responsibility of a field anthropologist for his material. It has become clear to me as the years have gone on that an anthropologist should be prepared to treat his field notebooks and diary as an historical source. He should use as factual data only what can be substantiated by reference to these contemporary records, with the minimum of memory links. He may well cite remembered impressions—provided they are so described. But memory is a treacherous guide and in the reworking of data it is easy to mistake the sequence of events, alter their emphasis and misrepresent the facts of an observed situation unless one can go back for check to an original record made at the time. As scientific social anthropology develops, interest in the validity of empirical generalization is likely to grow. With the long period of time which often elapses between making a field record and final analysis of the results, it is all the more necessary that the analysis should be capable of being related point by point to the record made at the time of observation.

[1] The results of this study will be published separately.
[2] See *We, The Tikopia*, p. 409; and 'The Population of Tikopia, 1929 and 1952' by W. D. Borrie, Raymond Firth and James Spillius, *Population Studies*, vol. X.

ROLE OF THE INVESTIGATORS

Participation in Tikopia social and ritual affairs depended upon and was an index of our rapport with the people. This rapport was obtained much more swiftly than in 1928. Then, when I arrived the Tikopia were outwardly friendly and hospitable, but in reality they were greatly disturbed over the presence of a European on the island.[1] I was fortunate in that the barriers of mistrust were breached and that memories of the first visit had remained lively and agreeable. Small details of my earlier visit had been vividly remembered. In 1952 stories were told in my presence of where I had sat in 1928/9, of what I had eaten and what I had said on occasions a generation before. In particular, gifts which I had made to people were remembered with warmth and some had even survived. A piece of calico given as a temple vestment had been carefully preserved and an adze presented to one of the chiefs had been consecrated and made into a sacred implement. Such objects and incidents were spoken about in Tikopia with a sentimentality which, while sometimes almost cloying, was nevertheless touching to me. From the scientific point of view this all meant that there was an atmosphere of receptivity and co-operation in our work. In 1952, as in 1928/9, the anthropologists were welcomed as being 'just like Tikopia', polite inclusions were still used in regard to 'our' canoe, 'our' orchard,[2] and 'our' kin group. Immediately on my arrival I was greeted by kinship terms appropriately readjusted to recognize advances of age and status. The new Ariki Tuamako, for example, son of the chief whom I had known and with whom I was on brotherly terms, greeted me outside his house when I arrived with '*E aue! Toku mana.*' 'Oh alas (how long since we met) my father!' Spillius too was rapidly absorbed into a wide kinship field, and speedily created other kin and friendship ties.

In 1952, then, the anthropologists were not feared and their general intentions towards the Tikopia were not suspect. In 1929 there had been some questions as to whether the taking of photographs might not be dangerous to the subjects; in 1952 no such questions arose and we were invited to photograph even the most sacred rites. Photographs were well-known and admired by all Tikopia. Indeed, one Tikopia, Vakasaumore, actually had a camera of his own with which he took photographs. In 1928/9 my private discussions were an object of great suspicion to the Tikopia at first because of the religious knowledge which they thought might be divulged. In 1952/3, while some of our private sessions were suspect for political reasons, because of local controversy over relations with Government and the Mission, in general they were accepted as part of the technique of the anthropologist. Again, when in 1952 meetings of chiefs were held privately, without inviting us, it was not for religious reasons but for political reasons. In the ritual sphere information, even when most esoteric, was freely given. It was expressly stated that all the essential facts had been revealed to me in 1928/9 and, therefore, there was no point in further concealment. The same attitude

[1] *We, The Tikopia*, p. 8.
[2] *We, The Tikopia*, p. 11.

applied to my colleague as to me. Moreover, the Tikopia had learned that all Europeans did not come with destructive intent. Hence, right from the outset not only were we allowed free access to the most sacred religious rituals, we were enthusiastically invited to participate.

In one respect, however, our approach varied from that which I adopted in 1929. Then, for the most part, I refrained from advising Tikopia in regard to their relations with Government and the Church. I had given them opinions when asked on the attitude of the Government about infanticide and similar questions, and endeavoured to clarify their minds on what were to them obscure issues, including the relations between Government and the Mission. I also discussed Tikopia problems with Government representatives and Melanesian Mission authorities, and tried to explain Tikopia attitudes to them. But, apart from such general consultations, I made no attempt to control Tikopia actions. The situation in 1952 was different. The hurricane and threat of famine on the one hand, and our possession of radio-telephonic communication on the other, made it almost impossible for us to hold aloof from the decisions of the Tikopia on practical problems. We reported to the Government on the situation, as it developed. We reported the intentions of the Government and transmitted the questions of Government to the Tikopia. This involved two things: it meant deciding on the most effective channel of communication and reply, in particular deciding on what subjects Tikopia should be asked for views to be transmitted to Government. It also meant assisting the Tikopia to put their point of view in terms most easily understood by Government. There was also a further development. When the Government decided to send relief supplies of food, they also decided that in the absence of a fully established local administrative system, we must supervise the distribution. This involved an active intervention in Tikopia affairs, which needs no justification by ordinary humanitarian standards, and is fully defensible on purely scientific grounds inasmuch as, without it, the continuance of our work would have been impossible. Such intervention was continued and extended by Spillius after I left, when the lessening of public order through widespread theft of food supplies seemed for a while to have imperilled the stability of Tikopia society, and when the Tikopia eagerly sought guidance on Government policy and actions.[1] But for the most part our role was that of prime consultants or social catalysts. We helped the Tikopia to explore the possibilities of a situation and decide for themselves what was best to be done in the light of the fuller knowledge we could give them. In the last resort, as Spillius has pointed out, even when the food situation was most desperate, and social order seemed most in danger, it was the Tikopia who eventually decided what should be done and carried out their decisions.

In other words, Tikopia society in 1952/3 was not one where radical changes occurred primarily through the presence of European residents. The presence of European social scientists, explaining and elucidating new external influences against the Tikopia background and concepts, in sympathetic

[1] See James Spillius, *op. cit.*

relation with leading Tikopia, allowed some local forces and potentialities to come to expression more effectively than might otherwise have been the case. But great sections of Tikopia life were carried on without reference to the presence of the anthropologists.

From some points of view, our work—especially that of Spillius—could be regarded as an essay in applied anthropology.[1] But even as such, it had to be distinguished very clearly from the type of active incorporation of an anthropological analysis in the developmental work of a community such as that envisaged in the conventional community development project or in the 'action anthropology' type of programme.[2]

---

[1] This is exemplified by the special commendation given in 1953 by the Secretary of State for the Colonies to Spillius for his efforts during the famine.

[2] Eg. Sol Tax, 'Action Anthropology'. *America Indigena*, vol. XII, 1952, pp. 103–9; papers in the journal *Applied Anthropology*, 1942, *et seq.*, etc.

CHAPTER II

On the Threshold of Modernity

Tikopia on my first visit was an isolated community, remote from anything that could be called civilization, primitive in its technology, and unsophisticated in its knowledge of the ways of the Western world. In 1952 these terms could still be applied, but their relative magnitude had decreased. Physically by improved communications, and ideologically by significant changes in attitude and comprehension, the Tikopia were more in touch with the forces of contemporary society elsewhere in the Pacific. In terms of social relationships, there was now less distance between them and their neighbours in the modern world. As a preface to the general analysis, therefore, I outline the position of Tikopia *vis-à-vis* these 'modernizing' influences, and trace their historical development.

FORCES OF MODERNIZATION

The forces of modernization have come mainly from outside the society. The processes whereby members of the Tikopia community have been brought to an appreciation of new forms and values, and conditioned to their use, may be looked at crudely in a tripartite frame, in terms of technical development, social development and ideological development.

Technically, Government officials and others abroad have been interested in assisting the Tikopia to make better use of their local resources, and also in making Tikopia resources—especially labour resources—more easily available to other parties. Socially, there has been interest in trying to get the Tikopia to conform to accepted Western standards of behaviour in matters of public order. Ideologically, there has been interest, even pressure, to get the Tikopia to accept new sets of political and religious concepts and beliefs.

These forces of development or controls have been applied with varying strength and success. On the whole, elements in each category have tended to reinforce one another. But sometimes they have operated neutrally or at variance, as when the Government officially has been indifferent to the religious condition of the Tikopia, or has found that the partisan interests of the Church have interfered with some administrative procedure.

As far as the Tikopia have been concerned, their reaction to these different types of forces has been selective. With any attempt—slight as it has been—to give them greater technical control over their own resources they have been in warm agreement, and they have accepted enthusiastically, as if solely for their benefit, any moves to utilize their labour abroad. With the moves for the institution of greater social control on the island they have been outwardly acquiescent, but internally they have pursued their own individual and group ends as far as possible without regard for the external forces. As regards ideological control, they have accepted a new system of ideas of political sovereignty—though understanding it in only the most sketchy way—but for long they resisted a new system of religious ideas. Unlike the people of Rennell Island, they did not oppose mission proselytization with violence. They restricted themselves to polite non-co-operation and, in their own circles, to argument, at first on the plane of material prosperity and then on the moral plane. But as difference of interest and opinion arose and crystallized among the Tikopia themselves, ultimately an ideological clash of some strength developed within the society itself.

Part of my task in this book is to trace the differential course of these developments in recent times. But in order to do this, it is necessary to examine the earlier history of Tikopia contact with the outside world.

The course of modernization and development in Tikopia hinges upon physical identifiable facilities of communication more obviously than with most other primitive communities undergoing social change. In the special situation of the island, isolated and remote from any major centre of civilization, means of transport have been critical. These have of necessity been almost completely by sea, and the number, frequency, duration and character of the communicating agents have been deeply affected by the nature of the oceanic environment. Vessels calling at Tikopia have been few in number and their visits widely spaced. Their stay has been of brief duration because of the inadequate shelter and anchorage.[1] Because of this and of the lack of any attractive resources for external exploitation on Tikopia the character of Western contact has been episodic[2] and for the most part superficial. This has been in marked contrast with the more pervasive character of contact and communication as they have affected, say, African tribes or peoples in other large land areas. Most of the more radical aspects of social change in Tikopia have been influenced by this episodic character of communication. Material goods have arrived in a staccato way. Powerful external forces have presented themselves for a brief period, then withdrawn, leaving their interpretation in the hands of Tikopia who have had only a partial knowledge of the external world from which these forces have come.

But social change in Tikopia has shown the pervasiveness of ideas. Technical control over resources by the Tikopia has tended to increase over the last century, but it has suffered considerable fluctuation. The amounts of goods coming in and replacing depreciated equipment have varied very

---

[1] In bad weather, approach to the coast is dangerous, and landing almost impossible. Even in quiet weather, a shift in the wind may cause trouble. In June 1952 a trading and recruiting schooner dragged anchor and went on the reef at Ringdove Anchorage; fortunately, since it was calm, she was got off again easily.

[2] Communication by radio telephone in 1952/3 may also be described as episodic because of the frequency of weather interruption and breakdown. Moreover, this was not communication direct with Tikopia people. Radio contact ceased altogether in July 1953 after the departure of Spillius from the island.

considerably. The onset of drought, hurricane or seismic sea wave have depressed the volume of resources on occasion suddenly and unexpectedly. But ideas once introduced have tended to be accepted and have proliferated. The value of knowledge of the outside world, the widening interest in alien material goods, the growth of desire to have new experiences abroad, the spread of the new ideology of Christianity, these things have seemed to be incremental, to have gained momentum as the years have gone on. Finally, in some respects a saturation point has been reached, as in the religious sphere when in 1955 the last pagans gave their formal allegiance to Christianity. But criteria of saturation are very difficult to accept—even more so, perhaps, in religious than in other spheres. For the most part a preferable concept is one of establishing levels of performance—situations in which a combination of elements seems at last viable, corresponding to the existing pattern of resources and demands upon them. Another example of this is the lodgement at last among the Tikopia of the concept of money as a medium of exchange (v.p. 147).

In much that I have written about the Tikopia I have described their culture as 'primitive', meaning by this no more than a relative lack of modern equipment and of knowledge of the techniques for using it. Their economy also could be described as primitive, since it was non-monetary; even by 1929 the people hardly knew how Western money was used. Because of its isolation and the infrequency of civilized visits to Tikopia, even recent visitors have sometimes gained the impression that the people are not only 'primitive' but also 'savage' and 'unknown', having had hardly any contact with the world outside until modern times. This view is wrong. What is characteristic about Tikopia is not the recent nature of its contacts with the West but their rarity and their irregularity, despite the long period since they first began.

Early Tikopia Contacts with the World Outside
A brief history of European communication with Tikopia—as far as it is known—will bring out both the infrequency and the force of the impact, especially on the economic side.[1] Even the earliest Western relationships, some very fleeting, are significant to students of Tikopia society.

The first recorded contact, by Quiros on April 22, 1606, illustrates that even 350 years ago some communication existed between Tikopia and neighbouring islands, for Quiros got his knowledge of Tikopia in the first place from a native of the Duff (Taumako) group, who included it in a list of islands named as being in the vicinity. The Spaniards made no attempt to land, and Tikopia natives took the initiative in the contact. As the ship lay in the offing a small canoe with only two men came out and 'gave a mantle of fine palm leaves and notice of other lands and bade farewell with great signs of regret.'[2]

[1] See also *We, The Tikopia*, p.32.
[2] *The Voyages of Pedro Fernandez de Quiros 1596 to 1606*, trans. Sir Clements Markham, vol. I, London, 1904, p. 233. J. Burney states that they presented Torres (sailing master to Quiros) with some coconuts and 'some bark of a tree which appeared like fine linen' (i.e. bark-cloth). *A Chronological History of the Discoveries in the South Sea or Pacific Ocean.*

After this Tikopia was not visited by Europeans again, apparently, for nearly 200 years. According to the Chevalier Peter Dillon, the *Barwell* in 1798 was the first ship the Tikopia had ever seen; people from her attempted to land but were driven off by brandished weapons, allegedly because the Tikopia thought they were evil spirits.[1] Dillon himself visited Tikopia in September 1813 (in the *Hunter*) and in May 1826 (in the *St Patrick*) and September 1827 (in the *Research*). On the first occasion he left there, at their own request, a Prussian sailor named Martin Bushart, his Fijian 'wife', and a lascar named Joe. In 1826, as is well-known, the clues which Dillon got at Tikopia from Bushart and Joe led to his discovery of the fate of La Pérouse on Vanikoro. In February 1828 Dumont D'Urville also called at Tikopia, seeking confirmation of Dillon's news of La Pérouse.

To Dillon and Dumont D'Urville we owe valuable ethnographic details—e.g. on population, residence, food production, chieftainship, tattooing, dancing, religious beliefs.[2] Several of these are especially relevant to our present analysis.

Firstly, their accounts bear out in various instances Tikopia traditional information I myself obtained independently a century later, and so give some indication of the trustworthiness of genealogical and other data bearing on social change. In particular, Dillon mentions 'Thamaca', one of the Tikopia chiefs, as having made ten voyages to 'Mannicolo' (Vanikoro), and 'some years ago' having been lost at sea on a voyage to 'Anutha'. By the Tikopia stories told to me in 1928, Matakai, Pu Veterei, an Ariki Taumako who lived four generations earlier, was said to have 'broken the ocean path ten times to Vanikoro', and to have been finally lost at sea, on a voyage to Anuta. My Tikopia informants said that Pu Veterei brought back from Vanikoro the *Canarium* almond, a piece of iron 2 feet long, a gouge (buried in a hurricane some time after 1900) and a glass decanter (seen by me in a temple in Tikopia in 1928). These European items had been acquired from Vanikoro people who had them from folk called the Mara, who had been shipwrecked there, and attacked, some of them being killed. Before this Tikopia had only shell adzes. Now Dumont D'Urville records that the Vanikorans gave to La Pérouse and his people the name of Mara, a name which the Tikopia also used in speaking to him of them. He also states that

II, p. 293, 1803–17. Cf. also H. B. Guppy, *The Solomon Islands and their Natives*, London, 1887, pp. 251–2, 277.

[1] The Log of the *Barwell* (India Office Library) for October 14, merely states 'At 6 a.m. saw an isle bearing NNW distance 10 Leagues. At noon this island bore S½ E 10 or 11 miles this island is not laid down in any of our Charts make its Situation to be Lat 12°14′S and Long 168°59′E until further information shall call it Barwell Island.'

[2] Chevalier P. Dillon, *Narrative and Successful Result of a Voyage in the South Seas . . .* 2 vols., London, 1829 (especially vol. I, pp. 28, 34; II, pp. 115–39, 168, 171); J. Dumont D'Urville, *Voyage de la Corvette L'Astrolabe exécuté par ordre du Roi pendant les années 1826–1827–1828–1829 . . .* tom. V, *Histoire du Voyage*, pp. 107–24, 304–15 etc. (including data by Gaimard, Quoy, Sainson), Paris, 1833. Cf. also Anon., *Voyage Pittoresque autour du Monde*, tom. II, Paris, 1835, pp. 124–6, (a fictional account, founded on fact, published under the direction of Dumont D'Urville). Cf. also Captain George Bayly, *Sea-Life Sixty Years Ago*, London, 1885, pp. 149–53, 170–2.

a Tikopia chief made a sojourn of fifteen months on Vanikoro prior to 1813, and brought back to Tikopia pieces of iron, of which various tools were made. (He thought this chief was the Ariki Kafika, whereas Tikopia tradition is quite specific that it was the Ariki Taumako; D'Urville almost certainly got this wrong, especially since there are a few other inconsistencies in his account of the chiefs.)

The second point illustrates the overseas relations of the Tikopia, within a fairly limited range. The knowledge demonstrated to Quiros two centuries earlier was shown to have been maintained, as by the canoe voyages already mentioned between Tikopia and Vanikoro.[1] Moreover, both Dillon and D'Urville took Tikopia guides to Vanikoro, and the latter was surprised to see how correct the Tikopia were in pointing the way by the stars. He noted also the 'very exact knowledge' the Tikopia had of the location of the islands that surrounded them to a considerable distance. These relations gave rise to only scanty trade; Dillon notes this consisted mainly in the export of bark-cloth and some fine mats from Tikopia in return for shell ornaments and bows and arrows from Vanikoro.

A third point is the indication that contacts of the Western world with Tikopia had effectively begun. An aged man, estimated to be almost 100 years old, told D'Urville that the *Astrolabe* was the eighth ship he had seen. The first, from which by his account the crew were not allowed by the Tikopia to land, may well have been the *Barwell*. Dillon's three visits and that of D'Urville, together with those of the whalers reported to Dillon by Joe the lascar as having called in about 1824 and 1825, make up six more. The remaining ship may have been the schooner *Governor Macquarie*, said by D'Urville to have returned Bushart to Tikopia after he had been left by Dillon in the Bay of Islands (New Zealand). But the old man mentioned the second vessel of his series as having given the Tikopia hoop iron (*cercles de bariques*), of which they made hatchets and knives, 'till then serving themselves with stones'. This vessel was probably the *Hunter* in 1813, but if any of the calls mentioned above was not in his list, then it was most likely an unknown vessel—at the beginning of the century. In any event, it is clear that including the *Bayonnaise*, Captain Le Goarant, which called in 1828, also in the search for Le Pérouse, Tikopia had at least six visits by European vessels in the five years between 1824 and 1828.

The fourth point, superficially a demographic one, has deeper implications for the history of contact. A major effect of Western contact, even so early, was transmission of disease. The Tikopia had suffered from malaria in Vanikoro, so they told D'Urville, and warned him against it; there was none then on their own island. Contagious epidemic disease was new to them, and they regarded it as supernaturally caused. They told D'Urville that fifteen to twenty days after Dillon left them in 1827 many of them were struck by an

---

[1] Dillon (*op. cit.* II, p. 168) states that after the loss of the Ariki Taumako, whose fleets numbered five to ten or even twelve canoes at a time, the intercourse between Vanikoro and Tikopia rapidly declined. Yet according to Joe the lascar, three visits had been made from Tikopia to Vanikoro by canoe between about 1820 and 1827.

C

epidemic cough ('? *grippe*' asks D'Urville). A year or so later the captain of the *Bayonnaise* reported to D'Urville himself, when both were in Mauritius, that a short time after D'Urville's own vessel had gone from Tikopia an epidemic malady had attacked the people and 115 of them had died. (If D'Urville's estimate had been correct, this meant between a fifth and a quarter of the population!) The unhappy Tikopia, it was alleged, attributed this epidemic to an evil spirit on D'Urville's vessel, and hence had received the *Bayonnaise* badly, not wishing her crew to land.[1]

From the material of Dillon and D'Urville two things especially stand out. On the one hand the social structure of Tikopia in the early part of the nineteenth century appeared to be essentially of the same order as I observed in 1928/9. On the other hand, by the end of the first quarter of the nineteenth century the Tikopia material culture had already suffered a revolution—the technologically crucial change from shell and stone tools to iron tools was well advanced. There is much mention of the desire for iron in those early accounts; there is no mention of shell or stone tools in use. The demand for iron tools had already arisen, though they were in bitterly short supply.

In the economic field, the accounts of Dillon and D'Urville may almost stand for the situation during my first stay on Tikopia, about a century later. Dillon remarked on the great scarcity of water supplies, and on the small food surplus offered for exchange. He noted the absence of pigs and poultry (alleged by the Tikopia to have existed formerly but to have been destroyed because of their depredations on the crops). In particular, Dillon gave evidence of the intense eagerness of the Tikopia to acquire Western goods, especially tools. In 1813, unarmed 'but very wild' Tikopia who came off to his vessel seized bars of iron, a frying pan, an axe, knives, saucepans, etc., and jumped overboard with them (which seems to indicate that they had put to quick use their previous experience of the value of iron from Vanikoro). In May 1827, he stated, five escaped convicts from New South Wales were robbed of all they possessed by the Tikopia and their longboat was broken up in order to procure the nails from her. In September 1827, Dillon's presents of axes, beads and other goods 'highly gratified' the chiefly recipients. D'Urville tells much the same factual tale, of poverty and of eagerness for Western goods. But he and his colleagues also stressed in a romantic way the simplicity, gaiety and innocence of the Tikopia, and so provided the first description of what has tended now to become a Tikopia stereotype—'the world is so small for them and life is so simple, they are so happy in the unknown corner of the earth which suffices for their needs. . . .' (Sainson, p. 314).

Even then the Tikopia had that fierce thirst for goods to meet needs not capable of satisfaction by their immediate resources. But from these and subsequent vessels the Tikopia did acquire iron enough to meet their most pressing demands without falling back on their traditional tools. They also began their practice of shipping abroad for goods and for experience. D'Urville took five Tikopia, unwilling, with him to Vanikoro, but later on

[1] Cf. *We, The Tikopia*, p. 413.

men appear to have shipped voluntarily on other vessels. A decade later, by such means, a few seem to have learned a modicum of English as a means of communication. On December 22, 1838, the whaler *Achilles* sighted Tikopia and the natives, appearing very friendly, came out and brought a little fruit which they sold. Those who came (or some of them) were said to have spoken English. They said that one of their number had been to Sydney in the *Alfred* and had returned in the *Wolf*, Captain Lewis. Cordial relations with the *Achilles* did not last. Two boats had gone ashore from the vessel and when the canoes returned to shore also a quarrel was seen to start. A third boat was sent in to the land but no news was obtained that evening. The next morning a boat approaching the shore was met with musket fire. Thus defied, the master apparently decided that some or most of the men on shore had been killed, and the ship then made off for Sydney to inform the Government.[1] It may well be to this and possibly other such incidents that the Tikopia owed their later reputation for ferocity.

Lack of known record makes it impossible to say exactly how much external commercial contact the Tikopia had in the nineteenth century. Captain John Mackay, a labour recruiter, states that in the early part of the century the island was 'frequently touched at' by some of the Hon. East India Company's ships on their voyages from Calcutta to Fiji,[2] but that later, with the exception of an occasional call from an American whale ship, it was seldom visited. Mackay himself called there in 1875, when he was returning plantation labourers from Queensland to the Western Pacific. When Tikopia canoes approached his vessel he ran out loaded carronades, but found that barter, not war, was their intention. Yams, taro and fish were offered him, and he had a conversation in Fijian with 'Sam', a 'young chief' who had been to Fiji. (I was told of 'Sam' in 1928. He was in reality a junior great-grandson of a Taumako chief and virtually a commoner.) Mackay does not mention that he recruited any labourers from Tikopia, and Wawn, another recruiter of long experience, does not mention having called at Tikopia on any of the score of voyages which he made in the Western Pacific between 1875 and

[1] *Sydney Gazette*, Jan. 22, 1839. (I owe these details to the kindness of Professor J. W. Davidson.) It would appear that no further action was taken.

[2] The *List of Marine Records of the late East India Company*, London, 1896, does not mention any voyages from Calcutta to Fiji. Between 1795 and 1834 (when the Company ceased to be traders and sold its merchant vessels to private firms) the *List* mentions five voyages from Port Jackson to Calcutta (or Bengal). Their courses seem to have run well to the west of Tikopia. But the *List* cites eighteen voyages during the same period from Port Jackson to the China coast (Whampoa, Macao, Canton). One of the earliest of these was that of the *Barwell*, which re-discovered Tikopia. But while my examination of their logs (in the India Office Library) shows that several of them sighted Mitre Island (reported by the *Pandora* in 1791) none but the *Barwell* seems to have sighted Tikopia. The course they followed in 12° to 10° S. latitude seems naturally enough to have taken them either between San Cristoval and Santa Cruz at about 163° E. long., or a little to the east of Mitre Island, at about 171° E. Unlike the whalers, who were continually looking for water and fresh provision, the East Indiamen seem to have been intent on their passage and on avoiding land wherever possible. On the whole, the logs seem to have been carefully kept, reporting sight of land (and in one case even of land birds) so it is unlikely that any call at Tikopia would have gone unreported.

1891.[1] After 1900 there was a little recruitment for plantations in the New Hebrides and Solomons,[2] but in any event such moves were blocked by Government Ordinance in 1923.

Information from the Tikopia themselves on nineteenth century commercial contacts with the West helps to fill in some of the picture. What I could learn even in 1928 was unsystematic and fragmentary, and probably distorted as regards European matters, but with more detail on the Tikopia side, especially in placing prominent personalities in their kinship position. From genealogical and other comparison I have made a summary which seems plausible.

The Tikopia distinguished broadly between whaling vessels (*vaka fai sinu tafora*) and labour recruiters (*vaka tari tangata*)—the 'whale-oil makers' and the 'carriers of men'. In the early years of white contact a number of whaling vessels (names and masters unknown or unremembered) called and took off Tikopia men. This was the 'fleet of old' (*fua ki mua*). But among the early whalers were 'Capn. Lee' and 'Capn. Cook' (though it is possible that the latter name has come from mission schoolboys' Pacific history, and wrongly refers to the great explorer—who did not even call at Tikopia). The earliest whaling master given some definite chronology was 'Capn. Van', who enlisted a Tikopia named Fareatai when he was still a youth with the conventional *sope* (lock of hair) on his head. This man returned with a beard to Tikopia, again went abroad, and a third time; then grew grey in Tikopia, and finally went to Anuta, where he died. A man born about 1870 told me that as a boy he had seen Fareatai, but other men of nearly the same age had not; hence he must have been first enlisted by 'Capn. Van' about 1845 at the latest. Fareatai was said to have brought back to Tikopia three guns, an adze and other goods, including the first European beads known there. Rather later, possibly about 1850, a whaler enlisted several Tikopia, who had an exciting adventure. One of them, about to lance a whale, fell into the creature's mouth, up to his waist—due to the machinations of spirits, the Tikopia thought. When the whale was about to close its jaws, the young man was pulled out by his uncle. Two others were in a boat when up went the tail of the whale, descended and cut the boat in two. Each survived in his own half and got back to the ship. It was one of these men, Pu Aneve, who brought back to Tikopia the name Niukaso (Newcastle), which survived as a house name in his lineage four generations later, in 1952. In a dance song composed by this same man (in annoyance at the boasting of later adventurers) occur the first Tikopia references to money which I have been able to discover.

By about 1870, by genealogical reckoning, whaling enlistment had ceased, and plantation recruitment had begun. About this date came 'Capn. Martin', who recruited twenty or thirty Tikopia, including the chiefs of Kafika and

---

[1] Captain John Mackay, 'Tucopia', *Proc. & Trans. Queensland Branch Royal Geographical Society of Australasia*, 2nd Session 1886–7, vol. II, pt. 2, pp. 81–5, Brisbane, 1887; W. T. Wawn, *The South Sea Islanders and the Labour Trade*, London, 1893.

[2] See *We, The Tikopia*, p. 42; cf. W. H. R. Rivers, *The History of Melanesian Society*, vol. I, p. 300, Cambridge, 1914.

Tafua, and some Anutans, for work in 'Somosomo' or 'Reipuka', i.e. Fiji. A little later, about 1875 on this scale, came 'Miss Makai', presumably Captain John Mackay, as cited earlier, but it seems uncertain if Tikopia men were recruited by him for labour on plantations in Queensland, though according to report some Tikopia definitely worked there.

MISSIONARY EFFORT

Until the middle of the nineteenth century, contact with Tikopia was purely exploratory and commercial, the latter element, however, being small. No elements of social or ideological control were involved. But soon after mid-century a Christian Mission made its approach. The first visit of the Melanesian Mission to Tikopia seemed to have been by Bishop Selwyn on September 7, 1858. It was then reported that the people had been visited by a number of whaling vessels and that several of them spoke a few words of English. Four years later the Melanesian Mission vessel called again and Bishop Patteson remarked 'Once we were there, five or six years ago. . . . It is a place visited by whalers but they never land there, and indeed the inhabitants are generally regarded as dangerous fellows to deal with.'[1]

Records of the first visit of the Mission confirmed the commercial nature of the earlier relations of the Tikopia with the outside world. Several muskets were seen in the house of the 'principal chief' and it is recorded rather sadly that the Tikopia all seemed to be little satisfied with strangers who did not make the purchase of pigs and yams the principal object of their visit.[2]

---

[1] *Report of the Melanesian Mission for 1858*; and *A Letter from the Rt Rev John Coleridge Patteson, DD*, 1862, pp. 8–9. (E. S. Armstrong, *The Melanesian Mission*, London, 1900, pp. 37, 67, and W. H. R. Rivers, *op. cit.*, p. 298, give the first date as 1857, and C. E. Fox repeats this, while crediting the visit to Patteson (*Lord of the Southern Isles*, London, 1958, p. 209). Tikopia and 'Oanuta' (i.e. Anuta) are mentioned in the 'list of islands visited' from 1849–57 in the *Report of the Melanesian Mission for 1858*, but the account of the visit of 1858 speaks of this as if it were the first.)

[2] The mention of pigs is curious. Dillon in 1827 and D'Urville in 1828 said there were no pigs on Tikopia. In 1910 and again in 1928–29 there were none either; people said to me, as their ancestors did a century earlier, that they objected to them because they rooted up cultivations. The reference to pigs in 1858 may have been erroneous—no mention is made of having seen any—or it may indicate that this was one of the periods of pig-keeping which gave the Tikopia their objections. Cf. also W. H. R. Rivers, *op. cit.* vol. I, p. 353.

In March 1952 there were two pigs, belonging to John Fararava—a black-and-white boar from Pawa, and a black sow. It was said that many other pigs had been kept recently, but had died in the hurricane.

In mid-June, 1952, when I was sitting in Kafika temple in Uta, chatting after a rite, I saw a pig jaw attached to the central post of the building; it was used to hang up a water-bottle. On asking its origin, I was told it came from the time of Nga Ravenga (? about 1750). I queried this (I did not remember to have seen it in 1929), whereupon the Ariki Kafika replied that both Nga Ravenga and Nga Faea—ancestral sharers of the land with the progenitors of the present Tikopia—kept pigs. They kept them in stone sties, of which traces have been seen. Then the chief told the following story:

Pu Kefu, head of the lineage of Rarovi, observed that the oven of the chiefs in Resiake had no good food. He went to Tai—the coastal area inhabited by Nga Ravanga—and saw a pig of the chief of Nga Ravenga in a pen. He grabbed it, took it to the lake and drowned it.

A characteristic of the Tikopia at this time, and one which endured for a logn period, was their reluctance to let any of their children go abroad. It had become Mission practice to induce people on the islands at which the Mission vessel called to let lads be taken away for instruction at a central Mission school, earlier at Auckland, then at Norfolk Island and later at Vureas on Vanua Lava, in the Banks Islands, and at other places. Many island communities soon succumbed to Mission pressure but not so the Tikopia. In 1858 women caught up their little ones when the Bishop asked them to allow some of their children to be taken away; again in 1862 it was reported that the Tikopia did not agree to their lads going on the vessel. This was in marked contrast to their interest in labour recruitment. They would allow men to go (i.e. for work, experience, and the goods they would bring back), but not boys, for instruction.

The next recorded visit of the Mission vessel was in 1888. The break of about a quarter of a century in the Mission visits had been due in part at least to the murder of Bishop Patteson in the Reef Islands in 1871, a distressing event which shook the Mission to its core and for some years restricted voyages to the minimum of stations. But in 1888 the *Southern Cross* went twice to Tikopia. A number of canoes had been blown away from Tikopia in a gale and three had found their way to the Banks Islands, where they were hospitably received by the people of Mota and Motlav. The Tikopia had spent fourteen terrible days at sea after they were blown away from the island until they made land; in addition to these privations they had contracted ague, i.e. malaria, in the Banks Islands. After five months their crews (numbering twenty-two, including two women) were taken home by the Bishop in his yacht.[1] Their return was greeted with great enthusiasm. Crowds of

Then he carried it to Tapukuru, near the orchard Samea, on a hillside overlooking the lake, and made an oven, secretly. The chiefs, sitting in their dwellings in Uta, saw the glow of the oven in the night and were alarmed. They wondered if it was an oven for cooking a man, and if they were about to be attacked. The chief of Tafua, Pu Tafuaroa, went up to see. Pu Kefu was absent, having gone to seek vegetables for his meat. Pu Tafua lifted the cover of the oven, expecting perhaps to see man, but there was the pig. He replaced the cover and returned. Then later Pu Kefu came down the hill, having put the head of the pig in one basket, and its body and legs in another basket. The narrator, the Ariki Kafika, said that he had forgotten whether the chiefs had a leg of pork apiece or not. But Pu Kefu gave the basket with the pig's head to the then Ariki Kafika. This old man crawled up to the basket fearfully, wondering also if there were a man's head inside—but it was only a pig's head.

I am dubious whether this tale is really good evidence for the antiquity of pigs in Tikopia. I heard nothing of it in 1929, and while this does not destroy its validity, since fresh incidents of quasi-historical kind continued to be produced during my later stay, I have no other records to substantiate it. Spillius reported that a pig's bone had been found in a deep hole, but it is doubtful if this could have survived 200 years in sandy, damp soil. I suspect the story to be a gloss, recited in good faith by the chief.

[1] According to Tikopia accounts to me in 1928, these canoes were on a voyage to Anuta and were struck by a storm in the night, sinking one of them, that of Korokoro. Canoes of Fangarere and Maniva, and an Anutan canoe returning home, reached the Banks Islands. That of Maniva, which made landfall on Mota, was nine nights at sea, and the crew, without food or fresh water, existed by drinking salt water in small quantities. Four men of this crew were still living at the time of my first visit.

canoes came off to the Mission vessel, the people aboard shouting and weeping. The Bishop was led with great ceremony to where three chiefs were sitting and observed the traditional greetings of the returned voyagers to the chiefs. Yet despite the hospitality given by the Tikopia to the missionaries they still refused to let any boys go away to Norfolk Island and they refused even to allow Mission teachers to stay among them. In this recalcitrance they were not unintelligent. They said that of those men who had gone away to Queensland few had come back. Moreover, they were afraid that if teachers were placed among them disease and death would follow. As the Bishop reported—' "No," said they. "If a missionary stays with us we shall all die." ' The Mission was hopeful that this hesitation could soon be overcome and that in the following year a station might be established 'on the island to which the path has been so providentially made clear'. But immediately after this the unseaworthiness of the *Southern Cross* and the illness of the Bishop seem to have delayed the attack upon this pagan stronghold.[1]

Visits to the Tikopia were resumed, however, not many years afterwards and soon after the turn of the century the Mission succeeded in establishing some Banks Islands teachers. Rivers states that Motlav teachers were placed there about 1905, but Captain Sinker, Master of the *Southern Cross*, reported that on the homeward voyage in 1903 there were some Banks Island teachers working on Tikopia, though he did not think much headway had been made there as yet. Sinker noted that the island was seldom visited, that the Mission vessel was overrun by swarms of Tikopia who had to be cleared off by force when the vessel sailed—(a situation which obtained until at any rate 1929).[2]

By 1908 there were five teachers from the Banks Islands working in Tikopia and by 1909 two large schools had been established on the island, taught by Motlav teachers, Denmet and Mikael Tagalad. Moreover, at last the Mission had gained another major objective. Early in 1909 the *Southern Cross* had carried back to the island four men who had been recruited unlawfully by a New Hebrides vessel and thrown ashore at Raga. A letter sent to the four chiefs asked them to accept this service as an expression of the Mission's desire to help them. It was warmly received and when the vessel returned in November they found the chiefs more friendly than ever before. 'We were further rewarded with permission to take two of their boys to Norfolk Island, these being the first fruits of this island.[3] It was about this time that anthropological visits to Tikopia began, on the *Southern Cross*. In 1908

[1] *Report of the Melanesian Mission for the year 1888*. Ludlow, 1889; *Bishop's Journal*, ibid., pp. 4–6. (Cf. Reports for 1889 and 1890.) Even as late as 1923 it was also stated that if taken from their homes the people sickened and died, and that boys taken to the Central Schools suffered most severely from homesickness, *v.* Note on p. 41.

[2] W. H. R. Rivers, *op. cit.*, p. 298, W. Sinker *By Reef and Shoal*, London, 1904, pp. 48, 59–61. The Bishop reported as of 1903 that two Motalava men with their wives made a beginning on Tikopia 'last year', and forty people, mostly young, attended the school. (*A Melanesian Mission Report issued by the English Committee*, 1903, p. 12; but cf. also C. E. Fox, *op. cit.*, p. 209, who speaks of an unsuccessful attempt in 1901.)

[3] *Annual Report of the Melanesian Mission, 1908* (Sydney 1909), p. 29; *idem 1909* (Auckland 1910) p. 7.

W. H. R. Rivers spent a day there, his record in combination with the later work of Durrad (see below), resulting in the first attempt at a systematic ethnography of the community. About four years later Felix Speiser made a similar call.[1]

In 1910 the Rev. J. W. Durrad spent two months on the island with a Maori companion Poata. Durrad noted that there were no pigs on Tikopia, so the villages were very clean, and he could not find any malaria, though mosquitoes were abundant. The island in general he thought was healthy. But this was one of the occasions which bore out in part the fears of the Tikopia. On June 6, 1910, Durrad wrote 'In one way my stay here has been calamitous, for the ship brought a cold & cough which have caused most shocking distress among the people. Robust as they appear to be in physique, they are really most delicate constitutionally & collapse at once in illness. They have no stamina and no reserve of force with which to fight a sickness. Over 30 of them have died in the last 6 weeks, some of them splendid men in the prime of life. They are a great loss to the community for though the people are numerous the death of even one important man is a disaster. They tell me they get ill every time the S.X. comes here and they look upon the Mission as a bringer of death & sickness. . . . They say they have never died in such numbers before, so I daresay they attribute the extra severity of the cough to the arrival of Poata and me! . . . A great many are still ill & a greater number still are living in retirement as their custom seems to be when a relation dies. Many also are busy cooking funeral feasts. The number that now attend prayers or school is very, very small and dwindles day by day as more deaths occur. . . . An old man said to me the other day "We shall soon all be dead. The Bishop has no pity for us." '[2] Such a sad account epitomizes the results of one aspect of contact of Tikopia with the outside world.

From this time may be dated the permanent establishment of the Melanesian Mission on Tikopia. It was reported in 1911 that 'the work on Tikopia is now in charge of Ellison (Tergatok), a Motalava boy, with two Tikopia boys as assistants, and the report of what they have been able to do is satisfactory.' It was also stated that Tikopia had recently been added to the district[3]—in other words, the community had at last become recognized as part of the Mission diocese. After that, for more than forty years the work of the Mission was carried on primarily by Ellison. From this time, ideological control of the Tikopia was promoted not only by having regular contact with the religious world overseas, but also by having the local Mission as a permanent centre of dispersion for new values.[4]

But to the Tikopia in general the Mission vessel was primarily an agent

---

[1] W. H. R. Rivers, *The History of Melanesian Society*, vol. I, ch. XII, Cambridge 1914; F. Speiser, *Two Years with the Natives in the Western Pacific*, pp. 287–91, London, 1913.

[2] From a copy of a private letter given me by Durrad in 1927. See also W. J. Durrad 'A Ticopean Wailing', *Southern Cross Log*, Oct. 20, 1910, pp. 70–3, Sydney; *idem*, 'A Ticopian Wailing', *Southern Cross Log*, April 11, vol. 17, No. 4, pp. 52–6, London.

[3] *Annual Report . . . for 1911*, pp. 8, 21.

[4] Analysis of the religious effects of the Mission work is contained in my 'Conflict and Adjustment in Tikopia Religious Systems', now awaiting publication.

of contact with the outside world and a purveyor of Western goods. The Bishop of Melanesia reported in 1923 that the Tikopia were a most interesting race of giants. . . . 'A new race about which no one knows anything.' When he wanted to buy some mats there his emissary returned with them but didn't know what they cost because the Tikopia took everything out of his pockets when he got ashore. Three years later the Bishop wrote that the ship was 'besieged by numbers of these strange-looking Polynesians; ours is the only ship apparently that visits them, our coming was obviously a great event'. And in 1937 it was reported that the ship received a riotous welcome at Tikopia; the people were anxious to trade mats, fans and other articles for knives, fishhooks and pipes, and a fair amount of business was done. The visits of the *Southern Cross* were interrupted by the war for more than four years, and when they were resumed in 1945, barter with the Tikopia was again keen.[1]

GOVERNMENT AND OTHER VISITORS

In relations with the Tikopia, the Government did not display an assiduity parallel to that of the Mission—at least until quite recently. No administrative action seems to have been taken on early reports of outrages committed either by or on Tikopia. In September and November 1894 very brief visits were paid to Tikopia by HMS *Ringdove*, from whom the European name for the anchorage was taken. In June 1898 HMS *Mohawk* visited the island and on the evening of June 6th landed a guard of honour, hoisted a British flag and assumed a protectorate over Tikopia.[2]

Occasional calls continued to be made by naval vessels on the Australian Station, including HMS *Melbourne* and HMS *Adelaide*. To celebrate the arrival of the latter, in 1927, and the salute she fired, a Tikopia composed a dance song, the translation of which shows the effect produced:

'*Ne rere mai ko te vaka*	'The ship sped here
Ne pa moi te fana	The gun crashed
Ruia te fenua	The land shook
Ngaruru ko Reoni	Reani (the mountain peak) quivered.

[1] The *Melanesian Mission Southern Cross Log*, vol. 29, March 1923, p. 39; April 1923, pp. 52–3; vol. 32, March 1926, p. 37; vol. 44, Feb., 1938, pp. 29–31; vol. 51, no. 4, Oct. 1945—Jan. 1946, pp. 54–5. London.

[2] It was on this occasion that the vessel grounded on the reef and lost two anchors in getting off. One was recovered two days later, the other in August of the same year. (I owe the details, extracted from the ship's log of HMS *Mohawk*, to the kindness of Mr G. B. Stigant, and I am indebted to the Public Record Office for permission to publish them.) This incident gives a test of the accuracy of Tikopia record. Just thirty years later, in 1928, I was told of the visit of the *Mohawk* (about which I had then not known) and of an anchor being lost and later recovered. The Tikopia had a clear grasp of the operations involved, including the employment of a man in diving dress and the lowering of the yards lest they break loose through the rolling of the vessel.

> *Ne soro atu ko tatou*   We importuned
> *Fakataurongosia.'*   Asking permission (to sail away
>   in her).'[1]

Visits were also paid by officers of the Solomon Islands administration irregularly until the outbreak of the war with Japan and the invasion of the Solomon Islands. In 1933, B. E. Crawfurd, the District Officer in Vanikoro, had visited Tikopia and remained there for a week. The British flag was flown ceremonially during this visit, apparently to the bewilderment of the Tikopia. On May 6, 1941, Sir Harry Luke, then High Commissioner for the Western Pacific, visited the island. In accordance with the practice now coming to be standard, a dance was put on for his enjoyment. Money was then still not in use, and a distribution of tobacco, fishhooks, knives, soap and blankets distracted the attention of all from the dancing. The impression made on the High Commissioner at this time was one of a very isolated community, cut off not only from the white man's world but also from the great Polynesian world of Maori, Tongans or Samoans.[2] These and other visits by Government officials were regarded by the people as primarily of a social kind, though they served to demonstrate European interest in the island and the concrete existence of a distant power. This power in Tikopia had two main aspects. One was its repeated disapproval of murder and other violence. The other was its refusal to allow recruiting vessels to take away Tikopia as labourers.[3]

The second world war was to the Tikopia a peripheral experience since the island was off the main path of the campaigns in the Solomons. Luckily for anthropology in one sense, the Tikopia were spared the traumatic experience of most other islands; neither the Japanese nor the Americans established a base there. A Japanese fishing vessel appeared off the coast, perhaps in 1941. But no warships landed at the island and with one exception contact with aircraft was limited solely to the daily patrol of a solitary American seaplane which dropped cigarettes, chewing gum and messages about the progress of the war. The exception was an American aircraft which crashed into the sea off the reef, some of its crew being rescued by the islanders. But the survivors were picked up on the same day by another aircraft—without any recompense to the Tikopia for their trouble, somewhat to their disgust.

In the preoccupation with the Japanese war no Government official—and indeed no ship—visited the island for three years. After the war communication between the outside administration and Tikopia increased appreciably. Visits of Government officials began to be made on the average more than once a year and relations between Tikopia and the Government altered radically (see Chapter IX).

Other types of communication also became significant. As a result of the shortage of labour supply the Solomon Islands Government removed the

---

[1] Shortly afterwards a Tikopia man named his new canoe after the *Adelaide*.
[2] Sir Harry Luke, *From a South Seas Diary 1938–1942*, pp. 189–92, London, 1945.
[3] *High Commissioner's Gazette*, Notice 99, Western Pacific, September 24, 1923.

restriction on recruitment of Polynesians, and both trading and labour recruiting vessels began to call once again. But a special type of visitor was the schooner *Yankee*, which has periodically included Tikopia in its round-the-world pleasure cruises since 1948. The visits of the *Yankee* illustrate a special feature of communication with Tikopia, that is, the interest of callers in its more picturesque, exotic aspects. The island is not only remote; it also has the lure of the unknown, the 'unspoilt'. Typical of this kind of interest are newspaper accounts of visits to Tikopia and Anuta.[1] Tikopia, like Anuta, has been invested with the romantic colour of an island paradise. Smiles, flowers, hospitality are bestowed upon the European visitors, who wade ashore hand-in-hand with their hosts or are carried up the beach. Invitations to meals are given freely and dancing is the usual entertainment. Tikopia canoes, thatched houses, bark-cloth and mats are seen as survivals of a primitive culture vanished elsewhere. The implication of this type of communication which, as I have noted, goes back more than a century, is that it places the onus of understanding their place in the modern world on the Tikopia themselves. The interest of the visitors tends to be in the more primitive aspects of the culture rather than in the development of the Tikopia and their current problems. If facilities improve, visits motivated by interest in the exotic or even sensational are likely to increase. In this respect one aspect of 'modernization' is partly in conflict with others, since its concern is in part with the preservation of 'primitive' custom. But of course in offering tobacco, etc., in reciprocity for entertainment, and in promoting displays of dancing, these visitors are developing an incipient tourist trade, which in itself is one aspect of modernization; they also provide for the Tikopia more models of how Europeans behave.

TIKOPIA SOCIETY COMPARED

From this brief historical sketch, summarizing the scanty materials available, only the barest indication can be gathered of the state of Tikopia *society* at the various periods. Mention of 'chiefs', of ceremonial greeting, of formal gift-making, indicates that some major features of Tikopia social life, including its apical political structure, apparently continued throughout the period of record. But otherwise, except for the early descriptions of Dillon and D'Urville, and the relatively sophisticated accounts of Rivers and Durrad eighty years later, the conduct of affairs by the Tikopia themselves over three and a half centuries of contact has taken place, as it were, behind a screen. An analytical study of the processes of social change in Tikopia,

[1] One such, under the head of 'How many people have heard of Anuda?' describes Anuta as 'Surely Great Britain's least known colonial possession', and goes on 'Its nearest neighbour is Tikopia, 100 miles away, and the world hasn't heard of that, either.' (*Auckland Star*, August 4, 1951; *New York Herald Tribune*, April 15, 1953.) Tikopia has been described as 'The Shangri-la of the Pacific' (*Australian Magazine*, December 22, 1953). Cf. 'Romantic Voyage on the "Varua" ', including coloured photographs of Tikopia girls smoking pipes and of the Ariki Tafua giving a medical blood sample. (*Life Magazine*, April 1957); *Yankee* visit (*Nat. Geogr. Magazine*, March 1951).

including those induced by Western contact, from the fullest materials available, those over the last generation or so, is necessary to understand what has
occurred. Such a recent study is especially relevant now that external contact
with the Tikopia and interest in them have become so much more intensive.

As a basis for the analysis, a general outline of the character of Tikopia
society in 1929 is necessary.

Tikopia Society in 1929

When I left Tikopia in 1929 the characteristics of its society could be summarized as those of a small-scale strongly patterned community of people
in a very isolated situation.

The community numbered about 1,300 and had communication with the
outside world on the average perhaps only once a year. Its members were
almost entirely concentrated on the island, none living outside it except for
the occasional residence of a few on the island of Anuta, seventy miles away.
There was unusual limitation of resources, there being no exportable surplus
from agriculture and no untapped wealth of any size by which to build up an
export trade. Government ordinance and commercial lack of interest had
inhibited the recruiting of Tikopia labour for plantation or other work for
Europeans.

The society maintained a series of conventional patterns of behaviour
accepted by all mature members. There was a very strong focus on kinship
ties as a primary basis for social relationships. Structurally, these ties were
expressed mainly through a strong patrilineal interest in the transmission of
kin group membership, rank and property; but they also had a pronounced
matrilateral aspect. They provided a firm structure of obligations which
tended to be regularly met. One concomitant of this system was the establishment of set equivalents or 'prices' for service of many disparate kinds. This
avoided the need, in a society of relatively limited resources and artifacts,
for a search among different kinds of goods to match the service rendered.
'Statutory' payments of bark-cloth supplemented in some circumstances by
a pandanus-leaf mat were the return for such varied services as a cure of
illness, support in an initiation ceremony, manufacture of a canoe and
paddles, participation in a funeral service. However disparate in kind and in
the amount of time, energy and skill they represented, standard returns had
been established.

The Tikopia society had also a strongly developed status system which,
expressed in political form, constituted a system of rank with chiefs at its
apex. The chiefs and their closer patrilineal kin did not constitute an entirely
separate social class. But there was some distinction maintained between
them and commoners. Tikopia social relationships linked closely together
economic and ritual elements. The religious system, both in its traditional
pagan form and in its new Christian form—each operated by about half the
population—was a very important focus of social activity. Yet despite
cleavages existing from traditional alliance in clan and district terms and
new forms of alliances created through Christian-pagan split, all Tikopia

still regarded themselves as definitely members of a common body, characterized by a unique language and customs and their highly inter-knit system of
kinship. Though their customs were seen by them in a deprecating way to be
perhaps relatively inferior to those of the West, they were regarded as having
a high value in their own right and worthy of support as being essentially
Tikopia.

These customs were well defined; they were freely verbalized and their
close sequences of operations could be precisely described. Intricate in
number and in their variation, they were closely inter-related: by recipro-
cities direct and indirect; by assimilation to major usages; by linkage with
the integrated politico-religious structure with the chiefs at its head; and by
the implication of all the members of the society in the unified kinship system
so that there were no 'outsiders'.

It might be expected that such a society would be of calm, even temper as
far as personal relations of the members were concerned—'innocent' and
'happy' in D'Urvillean terms—not a strongly 'individualistic' society. It
might be expected also that the people would be strongly resistant to new
influences—their attitude fortified by their position in a resilient network of
obligations, so that some sudden and even traumatic experience would be
needed to effect a radical change.

Neither of these was the case. Personal relations in many respects bore a
strong individualistic character. In their attitude to children the Tikopia
respected them as persons, treated them gravely, did not expect too much of
them in work or judgment, yet cursed them violently and threatened them
with fearful punishments—which, however, were rarely carried out. In their
attitude to society, the Tikopia appeared often to be prepared to throw away
their lives on a canoe voyage for a trifle—the attraction of an overseas
adventure, a momentary occasion of shame. Again, in contrast to their
elaborate framework of rules of politeness and their adherence to their major
customs, there was another level of personal relations—of suspicion, jealousy,
rumour-mongering, gossip and slander, and factional support. These were
recognized by a number of special terms in common use. Such behaviour was
structural in that it followed divisions by lineage, village and district and it
was cross-cut by kinship ties. But it occurred even within the structural
frame, as between brothers.

As regards reaction to change, the quality of Tikopia behaviour was
complex. There was enthusiastic interest in the arrival of strangers, who were
eagerly welcomed. Visiting vessels were greeted with whoops of interest and
pleasure, strangers were given hospitality and food and, if they came to live,
were brought into bond-friendship or quasi-kinship with Tikopia. There was
continued great eagerness for goods of the West—tobacco, matches, iron
tools, calico, kerosene. The Tikopia were willing, in surprisingly docile
fashion, to accept much foreign advice. They were anxious to raise their
level of sophistication. This level, crude in its world view, found expression
in their low actual level of living and low aspirational standard of living. The
simplicity of their implements, clothing and housing was linked with a sur-

prising lack of knowledge of the standards of comfort of peoples in the world outside. They were pathetically pleased with new Western goods. Yet there were elements of resistance to a European framework of behaviour. Western modes of gifts and services were not merely interpreted into Tikopia phraseology but also into Tikopia categories. The reaction was one of *incorporation* —to keep the fabric of the culture intact while using in it as many foreign elements as possible. 'We, the Tikopia,' wished to remain *Tikopia.* Their ethnographic knowledge of humanity in general was slight. They had to be assured that people in other communities too wept at funerals. When they displayed emotion on being shown photographs of dead kin, they wanted to know if in other countries too such memorials were cherished. But their analytical knowledge of humanity in particular was very considerable. Their comprehension of human relations in immediate situations, even when Westerners were involved with Tikopia, was subtle and considerable. Their intellectual curiosity and naïveté about behaviour of people in other lands was matched by an intellectual sophistication about the behaviour of people in their own environment. Their overt diplomacy when status interests had been offended was often very delicate; their covert penetration of intention was often very acute. Behind their more exotic forms of expression, in rumour-mongering and even in spirit mediumship, often lay a true appreciation of a basic human situation.[1]

Their reactions to new knowledge were very varied: acceptance without judgment; judgment by reference to their own intellectual inferiority; a mild embarrassment at their earlier ignorance; or again, a filtering of new knowledge to yield a useful residue. But the Tikopia did not have a free choice in their relations with the outside world. There were certain forces they could not exclude (except perhaps for a time by violent measures). These forces were: an increase in their numbers; a growing interest in their welfare and their affiliations on the part of an external government, which nevertheless was largely ignorant of their attitudes and experiences; and the persistence of the Christian Mission which, at first alien and sporadic, had finally come to settle in their midst.

What had been the general extent of any changes that occurred between 1929 when I first left the island and 1952 when I visited it again?

ADVANCE INFORMATION IN 1952

After I left Tikopia I had had practically no information about conditions on the island for more than twenty years. In planning my second expedition I tried to obtain as much information in advance as I could in order to prepare for more specific enquiry. But even indirect information was difficult to obtain. For example, my colleague and I could not be certain until we reached the Solomon Islands whether or not Tikopia had actually been occupied by the Japanese during the war. Again, estimates of Tikopia population collected

[1] See my 'Rumour in a Primitive Society' in 'Case Reports', *Journal of Abnormal and Social Psychology*, Vol. 53, 1956, pp. 122–32.

varied greatly, guesses ranging from 2,000 to 4,000.[1] But all accounts seemed to agree that there had been a very great increase, and that there was acute pressure on food supplies. It was thought that barter was still current, but it was uncertain how far this had been replaced by money exchange. On social structure there were practically no views, though by one source I was told that all Tikopia had become Christians. (This proved incorrect.) It was almost impossible, therefore, at the beginning of 1952, to come to any valid empirical conclusions about the contemporary state of Tikopia society.

Impressions en Route
But on our way down to Tikopia through the Solomon Islands it became clear that new experiences had in fact already come to the community. It turned out that since the war many Tikopia men had been abroad working for Europeans. We met half-a-dozen at Honiara, working at the hospital, as well as two trained as hospital dressers and another as a carpenter. We met about a score of others at Vanikoro, part of a group working as labourers for the Timber Company. From conversations I had with these men, including two of them who travelled down to Tikopia on the vessel with us, it was clear that traditional forms of Tikopia society were still in vogue. The system of chiefs still obtained; kin relations were still extremely important; dancing was still a prime recreation. Even the old Ariki Kafika, the primary chief who had been the leading performer of the ritual cycle of the Work of the Gods[2] in 1928 and 1929 was still alive and carrying out his traditional rites. But it was also clear that, while Christianity had not been adopted by all Tikopia, there had been significant changes in the religion of most of the people.

A factor of great importance in the immediate situation was obviously going to be the effect of the hurricane which had taken place at the end of January or beginning of February, 1952 shortly before we arrived in the Solomons. Its impact on Tikopia was not properly known, but the Tikopia men abroad were greatly alarmed as to what might have happened at home. The account received in the Solomons, 500 miles away, was grave. But although its effect might have been exaggerated, clearly the hurricane must have done damage and affected some aspects of Tikopia life. Accordingly, our attitude and that of the returning Tikopia was one of more than usual speculation and anxiety as we approached the island.

Impressions on Arrival
When the expedition arrived at Tikopia on March 13, 1952, it was quite obvious that the island had suffered terribly. The Tikopia young men aboard were greatly disturbed at its ravaged appearance. They said 'The land has been destroyed'. The deep green of the vegetation was interspersed by odd

[1] The actual population in 1952 turned out to be approximately 1,750. See W. D. Borrie, Raymond Firth and James Spillius, *op. cit.*

[2] *The Work of the Gods in Tikopia*, London School of Economics Monographs on Social Anthropology, vols. 1 and 2, 1940.

large patches of brown and red, indicating bare soil showing through in a most unusual way. Leafless trees along the strand indicated the destruction wrought by the wind. The crests of the island looked ragged. Many trees had disappeared altogether and coconut palms, formerly abundant on the hill slopes, stood, sparsely, with a few gaunt fronds at curious angles. When we later walked round the island we saw that the beaches of Faea were strewn with wreckage which had not yet been fully cleared away since the people had only just finished dealing with the debris in their orchards. Some houses had been broken down and even the solid walls of coral stones of a church had been torn apart. Practically all the canoes were intact, though rumours in the Solomons had said that they were all destroyed.[1] But sand lay thick all through the villages of Faea, covering the bases of the trees. No coconuts or bananas were to be seen; many large breadfruit trees were in ruins. Some of the low-lying areas were still flooded. Food shortage had already set in, and it was quite apparent to both Tikopia and Europeans that difficult times were ahead. The major question was, how difficult? When conversations began, both between Tikopia and government representatives and, less formally, between Tikopia and ourselves, the paramount topic was—what would be the degree of food stringency in the coming months and how long would the cultivations take to be reconstituted?

Yet in the cultural field the Tikopia seemed superficially to have preserved many of their former characteristics. When we arrived, fishing was in progress outside the coral reef in the traditional manner, by men hand-lining from canoes and also angling from floats, sitting up to their necks in the sea. When we anchored off Ravenga, outrigger canoes came round the vessel, most of their crews still clad in bark-cloth as in former days, with only a few wearing calico. There was the same horde of children, some swimming, some on sago leaf-stem rafts as before. There was still the same crowd of inquisitive, largely inarticulate Tikopia visitors all over the vessel, some merely curious, others offering items for trade. When we went ashore, our first meeting with the chiefs and their families followed very closely the pattern of a generation earlier. Their ceremoniousness, their courtesy and their hospitality were clearly part of what were still valued social roles. Food was offered—though not so abundantly, with apologies for its shortage. The terms of address and greeting put me at once on the old familiar footing of quasi-kinship. The seating arrangements we noted in the chiefs' houses also clearly indicated a persistence of traditional status relationships.

But there were observable changes. Among the canoes which came to meet us there were some paddled by crews of young women alone, with no men-folk aboard. To me this was a striking cultural novelty, indicating some loosening of the Tikopia rules about sexual division of labour, and access to and care of ritual property. Very few of the young men had the manes of tawny hair which I remembered; most wore their hair cut quite short. When we went ashore we were greeted not only in Tikopia but also in pidgin-English. (This pidgin-English was sometimes of uncertain accuracy. Around

[1] John C. Grover, *Geology ... In The British Solomon Islands Protectorate*, 1955, p. 61.

noon, Spillius was mildly surprised to be shaken warmly by the hand by a Tikopia man with the greeting 'Goodnight'!)

We soon had no doubt that since 1929 Tikopia experience of the external world had become much more extensive and much more realistic. In 1929, first-hand geographical knowledge of other islands than Anuta was restricted mainly to some old men who had once worked in Queensland or Fiji or who had reached the Banks Islands by canoe, and to very few young men who either had been to the Mission School in the New Hebrides or who had fetched up in the Solomons as castaways from an overseas voyage. From such wanderings, and from visits of a few natives of other islands either as castaways or as crew of vessels that called, the Tikopia had acquired a superficial knowledge of some of the Solomons, the Banks Islands and the Gilbert Islands, as well as of Uvea, Rotuma, Samoa, Tonga and Fiji. But in 1929 the Tikopia did not seem to have heard of Tahiti, or Hawaii, and barely knew of New Zealand, while many of the other islands mentioned above were hardly more than names to them. Anuta was the only island personally well known to many Tikopia, and Vanikoro the only other island of which they had a fairly clear idea.

The main regional distinction was between lands of the *atu runga* or *atu matangi*, the north and east (Polynesian outliers, Micronesia and the Ellice Islands), whose inhabitants were regarded as of the same order of culture as the Tikopia themselves—having 'grown up with clothing'—and the lands of the *atu raro*, the south and west (Banks Islands and New Hebrides), whose inhabitants, the Tikopia alleged, went naked and slept on the ground, not on mats. More specifically, the terms *Fasi* (New Hebrides) and *Raro* (Solomons) were terms used primarily to indicate directions and only secondarily places.

By 1952, Tikopia geographical knowledge had become more precise. Not only were more island names known, but more details about many islands. *Fasi* and *Raro* were terms in daily use. They were no longer simply directions or vague territories; they indicated important, well-known areas where Tikopia had recently worked and where some had recently died. News from these places was of interest not only when it concerned Tikopia but also when it referred to Europeans and Melanesians, many of whom were known to Tikopia. Interest in the outside world was active not only among young men who planned to voyage there, but also among older men as a matter of intellectual curiosity, which they could hope to have fairly easily satisfied.

In 1952 as in 1929 there was great interest in tales of travel and the lives of people in other lands far away. But though by 1952 standards of comparison through experience abroad had become more realistic, much Tikopia interest was still fairly naïve. It was realized that Tikopia was a small island, yet great was the stupefaction of a group of Tikopia on one occasion when Spillius showed them how tiny a dot represented Tikopia on a map of the Pacific. Again, while climatic differences in terms of cold weather were understood to be marked outside the tropics, and many Tikopia had heard of snow and ice, their implications were hardly realized: information, for example, that no coconut palms grew in Canada was greeted by them with startled bewilder-

D

ment. In 1952 it was still hard to convince the Tikopia that such different physical surroundings could really exist at home for people from the outside world whom they met in their own conventional atmosphere. On the other hand, they accepted for the most part fairly easily the explanation of seemingly much more abstruse matters, such as our radio-telephone. Not for a moment was there any suggestion of 'white man's magic'. Those of them who asked about the principles of its operation accepted easily an explanation given by analogy in terms of dropping a pebble in a pond and the consequent wave motion, or in terms of echoes.

These and other impressions indicated that the basic social structure of the Tikopia had remained intact over a generation. Their material circumstances had altered, in part very much for the worse—though presumably only temporarily—because of the hurricane. On the other hand, many Tikopia had acquired new material wealth and enlarged their cultural horizons. The system of economic co-operation, the kinship system, the system of descent groups, the major outlines of the political system, all seemed still current. It seemed that it was not clear at first sight how far the social system had altered in detail and what importance the Tikopia now assigned to its various parts. There were, for example, questions in regard to the structure of authority—how far the chiefs still represented the supreme power in the land? What was also not clear was how complete the ritual framework was, how far it had the same content as before? How far would it be found to be merely a formal framework, deprived of that personal, emotional adherence of belief which traditionally gave it meaning and ensured its continuity? It was also not at all clear how far the community of Tikopia was as relatively well-integrated as before. It was uncertain whether the conflicts of interest of a generation before had so deepened as to split the community effectively in its social activities as well as in its values.

There were some of the questions raised at the outset of our study. Before dealing with them in detail, however, I give some analysis of the social and economic effects of hurricane and famine, which it was necessary for us to understand before forming firm opinions on the wider issues.

CHAPTER III

Critical Pressures on Food Supply and their Economic Effects

Tikopia in 1952 was in a state of tension because of the threat of famine. This had arisen because of hurricane and drought and the effects became increasingly severe as the months went by. Sickness was common, the death rate increased and the social life of the people became governed very largely by the gnawing stringencies of their need to obtain and conserve food. It took more than a year before substantial fresh crops restored to the society its regular functions.

The implications of famine in social terms provide an interesting, if grim, example of the strength and weakness of a social system. Yet apart from Malinowski's brief examination of the concept of famine and of the reactions of the people to food shortage in the Trobriands, and observations by Richards, Fortes and others on African 'hunger periods', there are hardly any investigations by anthropologists of the sociology of such critical situations.[1] The test of social relations as a working system is the extent to which they can withstand the strain of competing demands upon their agents. At a period of general hunger such demands are apt to be raised to a high pitch. Here is an empirical test of the power of integration of the social system—a test not dependent merely upon the anthropologist's personal evaluation.

When I left Tikopia in 1929 the population appeared to be increasing significantly. On the side of subsistence, the community was not self-sufficient in that a very important section of producer's goods—its steel tools—were obtained by sporadic trade with the rare vessels that called. But there was no import of food, the people being entirely dependent upon their own agriculture and fishing, with the limitations of both being fairly clearly perceptible. They themselves realized this situation. From my observations in 1929 I reported that pressure of population on land resources was potential rather than actual; it was not acute nor might be for another generation. But if the then rate of increase persisted pressure would come and in the case of hurricane or drought there would be a threat of famine. As I was planning my second Tikopia expedition I had thought I might find a situation in Tikopia where anxiety about subsistence had become more marked through

[1] B. Malinowski, *Coral Gardens and Their Magic:* vol. 1, pp. 160 *et seq.*; (c.f. H. A. Powell, *An Analysis of Present-Day Social Structure in the Trobriand Islands*, Ph.D. thesis, University of London, 1957, pp. 1–3, 515, 516, 548); A. I. Richards, *Land Labour and Diet in Northern Rhodesia*, 1939, pp. 35–7, 50; M. & S. L. Fortes, 'Food in the Domestic Economy of the Tallensi,' *Africa*, vol. ix, 1937. A recent study by David M. Schneider, 'Typhoons on Yap', *Human Organization*, vol. 16, No. 2, pp. 10–15, offers especially interesting points for comparison with Tikopia.

population pressure on a *static* food supply. What I found was a rising population, and a severe intensification of pressure through the effects of hurricane in greatly *reducing* the food supply.[1]

[Where such a lowering of the food supply takes place fairly rapidly, the strains on the social system are not simply nutritional—belly-gnawing; they depend on recognitions, sentiments, moral evaluations and symbols of social relations. They involve emotional attitudes to the hunger of wife, children and kinsfolk, moral attitudes towards giving food to starving neighbours; social attitudes to the presentation of food as symbol of social status and social relationships. In earlier accounts I have given a description of the 'normal' workings of the Tikopia social and economic system; in 1952/3 we had to study as a major subject the 'abnormal' workings—the sociology of crisis and disaster.]

In this Chapter I consider the problem of crisis from the point of view of the organization which coped with problems of procurement and conservation of food. In the next Chapter I consider the other ways in which the famine affected the Tikopia social system.

But how far was the crisis really abnormal? Answer to this question must be rather speculative. But if accounts of senior Tikopia can be taken as a guide, it seems that this particular famine and its social implications were only part of a long-term process affecting the development of the Tikopia population and Tikopia society. Ordinary seasonal food shortage seems to have been well known in Tikopia. In May and June 1929, there was a marked scarcity of food of all kinds there, and I understood that such shortage was not uncommon at this period of the year, in an interval between main crops. Moreover, according to Tikopia tradition, it was not by any means the first time that more severe hunger periods had occurred, owing to exceptional drought or hurricane.

Tropical cyclones (known more popularly as hurricanes or typhoons, being closed low pressure systems with winds exceeding seventy-five miles an hour) occur with some frequency in the south-west Pacific, in the period mid-December to mid-April. They are especially prevalent in the region between 15 deg. S. and 30 deg. S., averaging three or four a year for the region as a whole. Tikopia, lying a couple of hundred miles to the north of this region, suffers infrequently, but occasionally feels the destructive force of such a cyclone. W. H. R. Rivers noted that 'a big hurricane' not long before 1908 was followed by 'a great scarcity of food'.[2] In 1929 I recorded from the Ariki Kafika and one of his elders that they had been through three severe

---

[1] See my detailed analysis *Primitive Polynesian Economy*, ch. 2, 'Food and Population in Tikopia', esp. pp. 46–8; and *We, The Tikopia*, p. 416. My earlier prediction was thus borne out in general, but I was wrong in one particular—I assumed that in time of crisis there would be no possibility of food imports from outside. In 1952/3, however, partly owing to improved communications after the war and partly owing to our coincidental presence on the island with a radio-telephone, when the famine did come after the hurricane and drought, relief imports of food were delivered. Even this relief could not avert a tragic crisis.

[2] W. H. R. Rivers, *History of Melanesian Society*, vol. I, p. 317, 1914. For notes on food shortage see *Primitive Polynesian Economy*, pp. 73–5.

hurricanes—i.e. on the average, one every twenty years—in which not a roof had been left on houses in Ravenga and Namo, and even large trees had been torn up. About 1937 Dr C. E. Fox wrote to me 'I was lately at Tikopia, where they had had a hurricane and were short of food; and still increasing' (i.e. their population). The Tikopia term *onge*, a word I often heard, was applied to such situations of devastating food stringency. Stories of the past told how in their hunger people ate the bark of trees, and in their despair put off in canoes to sea to face quick death in the ocean rather than a lingering death on shore.

At first sight it looks as if the famine apt to follow such a hurricane is a case of a simple Malthusian check on population. In 1929, the population of Tikopia was approximately 1,300 people. By 1952 it had risen to approximately 1,750—an increase of about 35 per cent. Already by 1929 the more responsible men had begun to view with disquiet the symptoms of population growth in terms of the limited food supply. The famine in 1952/3 may be regarded then as nature's way of cutting back the population to a manageable size in terms of the available resources.

But the situation was, of course, not so neat. In earlier times, with a greater degree of isolation than at present, the Tikopia demographic situation seems to have been characterized by an almost classical simplicity. A small but growing population[1] on a fertile but small island was singularly free (because of lack of contact with the outside world) from endemic diesase. With the expansion of the population, pressure upon food supply resulted, and war and expulsion of some section of the people was the obvious solution. Traditionally this is what occurred. But increasing contact with the outside world brought both new—or at least intensified—disease on the one hand, and a greater acquaintance with medical facilities on the other. In the countries which have had already a full quota of endemic 'killing' diseases, the introduction of Western medical facilities has stimulated the growth of population. This so far has not been the case in Tikopia; on the contrary, the introduced diseases have tended to check the growth of population and medical facilities have not been able, as yet, to alter this to any degree. Yet, even at the height of famine and epidemic disease, the population was not set back to the level of 1929.[2] The interrelation of factors was complex, but the expansion of population continued. Moreover, it was continuing as far as can be gathered at a rate greater than the expansion of the local food supply.

The situation was not a simple Malthusian one in other ways. At no time

[1] In 1828 D'Urville estimated the population at 400–500, and Gaimard at about 500. In 1862 Bishop Patteson said that it was probably not more than 300 or 400, and though this may well have been a gross underestimate even in view of the heavy mortality in the epidemic following D'Urville's visit, the true figure is unlikely to have been more than double. A figure of 1,100 people given by a missionary, apparently from the mission teacher, in November 1923, is very plausible (*M.M. Log*, June 1924, p. 85). A detailed examination of later figures is given by Borrie, Firth and Spillius, *op. cit.*

[2] The more severe epidemic of 1955 also does not seem to have been responsible for the deaths of more than about 200 people, leaving the population still about 20 per cent above the 1929 level.

did the Tikopia appear to have been concerned with a balance between population and food supply in terms of mere subsistence. They would seem to have been always interested in quality as well as quantity of food, and indeed their estimate of the prosperity of the land is basically affected by this. Moreover, during the last century at all events, they had been interested in raising their level of living in terms not only of food, but also of other types of consumer goods. Hence any disposal of their resources has had to take into consideration changing demands for goods other than food and the tools to produce food. (This was illustrated even at the height of the 1952/3 famine when there was a question as to how far the export of labour should be for food alone, or for other consumer goods as well.) Moreover, for more than half a century the increasing interest of the external government and of the Melanesian Mission in the social order of the Tikopia has meant that war and expulsion have not been 'free' solutions. However difficult it has been for these external agencies to help the Tikopia, they have been committed in the last resort to a search for methods of maintaining the community at some minimum level of health and comfort.

Speaking generally, then, one has the impression that though the famine of 1952/3 was abnormal in the short-run, in the long run it represented a movement in a pendulum swing of relations between Tikopia population and food supply that has been going on for at least a century, and probably much more. In my opinion, such changes in demographic pressure on subsistence are far more responsible for much of the structure of primitive societies than anthropologists have generally allowed.

But what was the intensity of the crisis in Tikopia at this time, in particular in its economic aspects? And what action was taken to meet it?

Immediate Measures of Organization after Hurricane

Two hurricanes affected the economic and social life of the Tikopia during the period studied by the expedition, the first (occurring in two phases) in January 1952, and the second of somewhat less force, in March 1953. Both were severe, breaking down houses and tall trees, and affecting even ground crops. In the first hurricane, said the Ariki Taumako, the wind was so violent that the leaves of the giant taro, large, fleshy and spadelike, were as if someone had rubbed them between his hands until only the bare stalk was left. In this hurricane waves at the high tide swept inland, broke down many houses near the beach in Faea and scattered and buried property. Low-lying areas of cultivation were flooded by salt water which broke into the swamp area where much taro was grown. In neither hurricane was there any loss of life, but recovery of the crops was long delayed, partly owing in the first case to drought succeeding the hurricane and partly in both cases to the effects of salt spray which had a caustic action and retarded the growth of new shoots. The immediate effect of each hurricane was to shock the people and inhibit their activity. But in both cases they soon rallied to the many tasks demanding their attention. As I have noted, they were not without experience in this.

Directly after each hurricane, contrary to what one might have expected, food was extremely plentiful. People tried to save as much as possible of the crop which had been damaged, and so collected it at once. They either consumed it almost immediately, as in the case of manioc, or laid it down as paste to ferment, as in the case of banana and breadfruit, to draw upon as required in the traditional way. All this necessitated considerable communal labour and domestic organization. Shortage of water impelled the organization of labour in another way. All drinking water is obtained from springs which flow into aqueducts down to the shore where the villages are located. These aqueducts, built of areca palm trunk, were almost completely destroyed, and for several days working parties were busy in reconstructing them and getting water flowing again. Housing was also affected seriously. Temporarily some people had to take refuge in the woods and others in shelters under the lee of cliffs, until their shattered dwellings could be rebuilt. But the repair and rebuilding of houses was inhibited owing to the shortage of sago fronds for thatch and of sinnet cord for lashing.[1] Because of shortage of materials although labour was available soon, at least a dozen houses damaged by hurricane or ensuing 'tidal' wave were not rebuilt for months, and others were reconstructed on a reduced scale. On the other hand, some dwellings—'houses of the famine'—were built anew on ancient sites to allow their owners to cultivate inland and guard their growing crops with greater ease. All this was apart from the routine work of clearing up the debris.

The emergency measures put into operation after the second hurricane, in 1953, were, by Spillius's account, rather more delayed. In the intervening year the people had suffered great privation and this second hurricane seemed to them the last drop in their bitter cup. There was much talk about putting off to sea on suicide voyages and about asking the Government to remove all the population to another island. But after two or three days their leaders began to rally them again. Executive officers talked sharply to men lounging on the beach or in their houses, asking them why did they sit there like thieves who had full bellies instead of getting to work. Public meetings were called and instructions given by the leaders. At first people were apathetic but soon responded to exhortations and threats. Village working parties were organized to clear up wreckage so that people could pass quickly and safely along the paths. Children were set to collect firewood and dry it on the beach. Young men were directed to repair the aqueducts and adolescents were assigned to cut down areca palms and scoop out the pithy trunks to make flumes for them. The people of Namo were instructed to open the channel leading from lake to sea, to lower the level of the lake and provide fish; they were to let the Ravenga people know when they were ready so that all could help and share in the fish supply.

Prospects of Famine

When a disaster such as a hurricane strikes a Pacific island community, the

[1] The shortage of sago leaf later involved us in paying what would have been in normal times a stupendous price for sheets of thatch—two fishhooks per sheet—for the small shed used to house our petrol engine. Moreover, we were unable to have built the new house which we had planned.

full effects are rarely perceived at once. Retrospectively, their course can be traced in an apparently logical sequence from the initial situations, but as the events unfold a number of variables have, in fact, been in operation, including local estimates of prospects and local action in the light of the estimates and the chances of external aid.

[One striking difference in the Tikopia situation from that of disaster in most Western or Oriental areas nowadays was the limitation which isolation set upon recovery. In the more accessible parts of the world there is almost immediate response from unaffected areas—goods and services flow in freely and speedily. But for a small isolated Pacific island community aid is distant and difficult to organize—it may be even difficult to finance. Hence all Tikopia planning for recovery had to be mainly local.]

It was, therefore, of prime importance to the people to make close estimates of the damage and its effects, not only as an immediate measure, but also to give a long-term framework. They had to get a proper basis for their planning, for months ahead. From the anthropological point of view it was of major interest to see how far the Tikopia seemed to look ahead, how accurate their forecast was, what steps they took to remedy the situation and how far they had to revise their estimates and alter their procedure as time went on.

The crux of the matter lay in the conditions of the local food supply. How long would the reduced food supplies remaining after the hurricane last? How long would growing crops and crops newly planted take to come to maturity? Would there be enough available supplies to bridge the gap?

[Normal vegetable food supplies in Tikopia were based on taro (*Colocasia antiquorum*—a ground crop) and breadfruit (*Artocarpus*, a tree fruit) as staples, with coconut as a regular emollient.[1] Supplemental to these were bananas, manioc, sago flour, yams and sweet potatoes. Pumpkin, Tahitian chestnut, aerial yam, cordyline roots and other foods were periodically drawn upon to eke out the menu. To all this food fish was regarded as a necessary supplement.]

In mid-March 1952, six weeks after the first hurricane, consultations with leading men such as the Ariki Kafika, Ariki Taumako and Pa Fenuatara, produced the following estimate of the time needed for food supplies to recover. Taro then in the ground was estimated to take up to three months to begin to yield sizeable corms, sweet potato and pumpkin would take about the same time, and banana (which had only two or three leaves beginning to show on most plants) about six months. Coconuts, it was thought, would bear in four to five months, but only where palms were alive—people had noticed some new shoots but few mature leaves had yet appeared and many palms had died. Breadfruit would take at least a year, possibly two years, to recover and fruit; no fruit at all was showing and trees had been so blasted that many would die. Some other foods such as sago, cordyline and aerial yam which had survived the hurricane were being consumed already, but they were coarse and unpalatable—'simply wood'.

[1] *Primitive Polynesian Economy*, pp. 48–53, 64–73; see also *We, The Tikopia*, pp. 103–111, for food recipes.

As regards the immediate prospects, the leaders thought in March that the community might maintain itself, though at a minimum level, for the next most critical three months. They were not much interested in government proposals for gifts of seedlings from abroad, except as a token of sympathy. They said that men who had plots in the swamp had ample taro seedlings and others could borrow from them. Some seedlings of manioc and sweet potato might be welcome, they agreed, but there were really plenty already in Tikopia. The future depended on the rainfall, they emphasized. If the rain fell adequately, the island should be in fair condition for survival after two or three months, though good food—that is food prepared with coconut cream—could not be available before about six months. 'Food is made palatable with coconut alone, as you know,' they said. But if rain did not fall normally in the next few weeks, then the situation would be very serious; actual famine might occur. They emphasized the gravity of the situation. At a later meeting of the chiefs in our house in an informal atmosphere the forcefulness and unanimity of their expressions were notable. They made much the same crop estimates as cited already, but stressed again that recovery would depend on the weather. For the ensuing couple of months, they said, conditions would be desperate. They wished a relief vessel to be sent immediately with food, but as a longer term measure they made suggestions for certain Tikopia men to recruit as labourers abroad, their wages to be paid in food to be sent to their families on the island.

Some weeks later the senior men revised their view; they put the period of recovery still further ahead. Taro, they reckoned now, would take six months to yield properly. Coconuts, coming on very slowly indeed, would need six months to a year to form, and even sweet potato would take some months to produce. They reckoned it would be a year at least before the island was on its feet again, and they talked of people putting off to sea in despair. This view was not unanimous. One very old man said rather cynically out of his previous experience 'They say they will die, but they will not die. They will dig for wild yam roots which will not be exhausted and they will go and search for early yams and for wild legume (*aka*).' But the more gloomy view was closer to what actually happened. (The old man himself died in the famine, though not specifically from hunger.)

Such early estimates show how the long-term concern of the Tikopia with their food supply manifested itself very quickly and in practical calculation. They needed no prompting from outside to survey their situation and judge its prospects. For the most part their appraisals were realistic. Polite about suggestions for help, they distinguished between them on grounds of their practicability. Moreover, the estimates of the most responsible Tikopia as to the gravity of the situation were proven in the upshot to have been more precise than those of Europeans, including the anthropologists, who judged with less experience.[1]

[1] The Tikopia attitude here seems to have been more realistic than that of the people of Yap, who seem to have exaggerated their food shortage after a typhoon, symbolizing in terms of famine their more general social anxieties. (See David M. Schneider, *op. cit.*).

Course of the Famine

In the trend towards famine or away from it were two major imponderables
—the weather as the months went by, and the behaviour of the mass of
Tikopia when faced by acute food stringency. Unfortunately, Tikopia fears
about the weather were realized. Though there was no marked drought at
any time there was definite shortage of rain in April and May 1952, prevent-
ing crops from maturing properly. Moreover, not even the Tikopia seemed
to have attached enough significance to the retarding effect of the salt spray
blown up by the hurricane. And an intensifying factor as time went on was
the growing prevalence of theft of immature crops in the ground, which still
further retarded the period of recovery.

Fortunately, fish from the sea, and in some periods from the lake, continued
to be available. There was an unprecedented length of run of mackerel off
Faea, lasting from July 1952 to the beginning of November 1952, and an
exceptional run of fingerlings in the lake in November and December 1952
and April and May 1953. Again, at the opening of the channel from the lake
in Namo for two nights in May 1953, large quantities of fish were caught on
their way to the sea. Apart from these bonuses, the regular seasonal fishing
for flying-fish and other types continued. But the amount of reef around
Tikopia is relatively small and is heavily worked daily and often by night as
well. It had been a first thought of the Government that the Tikopia could
make up by fishing the shortage of vegetable food caused by the hurricane.
But this was quite a mistake. The amount of fish ordinarily available just
suffices the Tikopia needs, and intensification of fishing by any existing
Tikopia methods would not necessarily have resulted in any significant
addition to the food supply.

But Tikopia was not completely cut off to work out its own fate. A factor
which encouraged the recovery of the community was the relief supplies from
the Government of the British Solomon Islands Protectorate. A shipment in
June 1952 consisted primarily of nine long tons of rice, and gave the community as a whole rather more than two weeks' rations. Another shipment
in the beginning of October 1952 consisted of eighteen tons of rice (including
about half a ton uneatable) and gave about four weeks' rations. A further
shipment at the end of March 1953 consisted of various foodstuffs such as
coconuts, rice and biscuits, as well as taro seedlings. These totalled about
sixteen tons or nearly one month's relief. These relief supplies, from Spillius's
account, cost the Government approximately £5,200. They were brought in
with considerable difficulty owing to rice shortage in the Western Pacific as
a whole; for instance, the second shipment was imported from Siam since
no rice was available in Australia at that time, and the third shipment had to
be gathered from the three territories of Fiji, New Hebrides and the Solomon
Islands. These shipments of food, amounting in all to about two-and-a-half
months' supply of the whole community, did not prevent the beginnings of a
famine. But they were crucial to the alleviation of the general stringency
because they gave food crops more opportunity to grow to maturity in the
fields instead of being drawn upon in an immature state, and so intensifying

the vicious circle. This extra time given by the relief food supplies made a great difference in the situation of many individual families. As it was, out of the total of eighty-nine deaths recorded by Spillius between March 1952 and March 1953, at least seventeen may be attributed to starvation; nearly all these cases were those of children under eighteen. But if it had not been for the relief supplies, undoubtedly the number of deaths directly attributable to starvation would have been greatly increased.

Receipt of these relief supplies in itself created some fresh problems. Many Tikopia, especially women and children, had not even tasted rice and foods prepared from flour. Contrary to what might have been expected, however, they all seemed to find these foods palatable[1] and, as far as we knew, there was no rejection of them. A serious problem, however, was how to cook them. The Tikopia ordinary methods of cooking were in earth ovens, in wooden bowls into which large red-hot stones were slid, and in leaf containers which were scorched over a fire. Most Tikopia then had no proper means of boiling rice or of making flour into bread. Consequently, immediately after the arrival of the relief supplies, we were besieged by requests for large containers to serve as boilers (see p. 110). Failing such utensils, the Tikopia, acting partly on our suggestions, partly on advice from their own young men who had been abroad, and partly using their own inventive talents, solved the problem in other ways. They managed to boil rice by borrowing and sharing utensils. But flour, which at first they hardly used, they began to treat like a Tikopia food. Some households prepared flour pudding (*susua felaoa*). A large amount of flour was put into a wooden bowl and baking powder mixed with it. Water was added and a thin paste prepared. Leaves of giant taro with banana on top were then filled with three or four handfuls of the dripping paste, tied up and cooked in the earth oven as for the Tikopia pudding (*kofu*). The result was a heavy, doughy mass, semi-cooked by European standards, which the Tikopia ate with apparent relish, convinced they were partaking of a Western food.

Yet as the months went by the situation became more acute. Fluctuations in food consumption between March 1952 and June 1953 can be followed from the Chart (p. 60). In this the waxing and waning of the main food supplies has been broadly indicated diagrammatically, summarizing our entries made in diary and notebook about the prevalence of the various foods. It will be seen from this how the famine mounted to a peak towards the end of 1952, so that for three months the only vegetable foods regularly available to the Tikopia from their own supplies were manioc, sweet potato and pumpkin, all nutritionally very poor, consisting of little else than carbohydrate and water. Even these were not available to all households.

A few examples of the straits to which the people were reduced, even before the famine had reached its peak, all indicate the strain upon their economy and the disturbance in their way of life through impoverishment of their resources both for domestic consumption and for hospitality and ceremonial

[1] The concentrated granular 'Bournvita' was found sweet by many Tikopia and they liked it neat. One man ate six tins in an evening before its use could be explained to him.

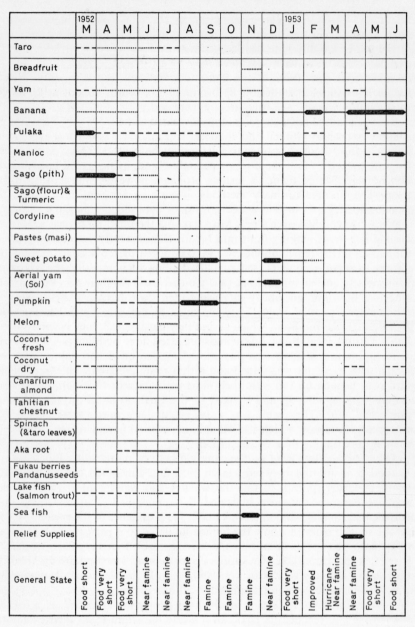

FOOD SUPPLIES IN TIKOPIA, 1952–53

presentation. After about two months from the first hurricane, that is by about the beginning of April, the finer foods had practically disappeared and even the stocks of paste of breadfruit, banana and taro, preserved in ground pits, had begun to run very low. Giant taro left standing in the ground as a general reserve had been heavily drawn upon and was beginning to be short. Fresh coconuts had practically disappeared and dried coconuts were becoming rare. A good index of stocks was given by the meals we recorded. In one of the more wealthy households (Vangatau) towards the end of April a meal offered to us consisted of salmon trout from the lake, yam pudding mixed with sago flour, breadfruit paste and manioc root. This was very adequate, but significantly the householder said that his manioc paste and his banana paste had been exhausted, and that he had breadfruit paste enough only for two more weeks. His yams and his sago flour were nearly exhausted and the salmon trout was a seasonal catch. This was the period when people began to cull their orchards for all the secondary food stuffs, e.g. aerial yam (*soi*, *Dioscorea bulbifera*), spinach and taro leaves, *fukau* berries (normally used as a funeral food because of their poor quality) and pandanus seeds (*fara*), which though standard articles of diet in the Gilbert Islands are a token of severe shortage when eaten in Tikopia. Some people foraged for a particularly hard root known as *aka*, looking like wood even when cooked.[1] Some children cut down aerial roots of a pandanus (*kie*) and chewed them like sugarcane —there is a certain sweetness in the sap. When I told a friend of mine that I had seen a child with a piece of such root he commented 'It is just the famine; they cut and gnaw. When the land is secure again in food they reject it.'

In conformity with the general Tikopia usage in times of food shortage, there was great resort to sago pith and cordyline. At such times sago palms are felled, the trunk chopped up into baulks and cooked in huge earth ovens.[2] Towards the end of April many of these sago ovens had been already prepared, so that in several villages all the sago of all the householders had been exhausted. In Nuku, for example, normally rich in sago palms, there was not a single palm remaining among any of the households. It takes five years for a sago palm to grow to a state ready for felling, and even then it is still small. So the drain upon resources can be seen. Into the oven with the baulks of sago the Tikopia put roots of *ti* (*Cordyline terminalis*), partly for flavour and partly to prepare from the roots a sweet thick syrupy liquid which they drink like soup. This liquid, known as *vai ti*, is prepared by hammering the roots between stones, putting the resultant juice into a bowl and mixing it with fresh water and turmeric flour (*tauo*). Then hot stones are slid in— steam-cooking the liquid. By May, few households had any turmeric flour left. As an alternative, manioc flour may be used, giving a more solid body.

[1] Possibly the tuber of a legume known in Fiji as *yaka* and identified as *Pueraria lobata* by E. Massal and J. Barrau, *Food Plants of the South Sea Islands*, South Pacific Commission, Technical Paper No. 94, Noumea 1956, p. 40; see also 'Pacific Subsistence Crops Cassava', *South Pacific Commission Quarterly Bulletin*, vol. 5, pp. 15–18, Noumea, 1955.

[2] See *Primitive Polynesian Economy*, Plate 3b, pp. 267; cf. my 'Economics and Ritual in Sago Extraction in Tikopia', *Mankind*, vol. 4, No. 4, 1950, pp. 131–42.

In famine times again the people may prepare *vai ti* with the turmeric pigment (*renga*), which they ordinarily use as dye or paint, but I did not see this done, presumably because the cordyline itself was exhausted soon. Some people, instead of drinking the cordyline liquor, extracted what extra nourishment they could from the root itself. The root was chopped into pieces, pulled apart by the fingers and chewed till the fibrous pith yielded no more sustenance. By the middle of the year households with few resources were already having a miserable diet in which some or all of the harsh foods mentioned were elements.

At the same time, the Tikopia were making strenuous efforts to restore agricultural production to normal levels. Almost immediately after the hurricane replanting of food supplies had begun and continued. By about May, the effects of this new planting were visible in the growing use of sweet potato and of manioc. But the growing prevalence of theft reduced the yield and prevented much of the crop from attaining full maturity. By August 1952, when real famine was close at hand, many families were eating sweet potato about the size of crab-apples and manioc about the size of carrots. (The usual length of a manioc root on Tikopia is about 2 feet.) The severity of the food shortage was by this time generally admitted. Towards the end of July, as we were sitting in a funeral gathering one day talking about the situation, Pa Fenuatara remarked 'There never was a famine on Tikopia like this one —the very posts in the middle of the orchards have been overturned.' He meant by this that the last standby, the final reserve, the enormous giant taro left to grow in the heart of the orchard for years, were being dug up and consumed—by thieves as well as by their legitimate owners. On another occasion the Ariki Kafika and the Ariki Fangarere, discussing the famine, emphasized that this one was particularly bad because in former periods of stress only tree crops were affected, but now ground crops were suffering too. As I was writing down the conversation, the old Ariki Kafika turned to me and remarked 'Paper of the famine on Tikopia—great is the famine, write it on your paper,' meaning that here was a record which should be carried to other lands and told there.

The period of most acute food shortage, properly to be described as famine, lasted approximately from some time in September until December 1952. For about three months the death rate on the island rose to three or two persons a week, or to about four times its normal level. Those most affected were the very old, and especially the very young, who were the least able to fend for themselves, in foraging for food scraps.

Towards the end of the year, according to Spillius's account, the situation showed some signs of improvement. Some breadfruit had matured by November and though the season was brief and not general, it inspired the people with hope of further crops soon. Coconuts had begun to appear in most orchards in Faea, though kept from consumption by a heavy taboo. Bananas were also showing. Theft had been much reduced by stern action by the men of rank, and the steady programme of planting ground crops had begun to have its effect. By February 1953 little manioc or sweet potato was now being drawn upon, and bananas had become a staple item of diet, with some giant taro and coconuts also being eaten. More fires were observable in the oven houses. Whereas the pattern had been that a household would prepare an oven only once every two or three days, now with the increasing quantities of food, some households had an oven every day. There were even some small surpluses of banana and manioc which were turned into paste (*masi*), and put down for storage.

Then came the hurricane of March 1953, which set back the food situation again for three months. Fallen fruits gave short-lived supplies, and the relief distribution of rice, biscuit and taro seedlings in April alleviated the worst distress. But the small stored surpluses were soon used up and theft again became rife. However, improvement was more rapid than before. By May, with bananas the staple food, there was also some manioc and giant taro, while by June some taro was being eaten and the breadfruit trees were budding everywhere. Coconuts were being used by most households, though sparingly, and again surpluses of banana and manioc were being made into paste for storage. Fish had continued to be fairly plentiful. By July, then, when the work of the expedition was closed and Spillius left Tikopia, the community was well on the way to recovery.

Organization for Food Procurement and Conservation
I have shown already how the Tikopia individually exercised considerable economic foresight in coping with the famine. They showed skill in searching out a range wide of food sources and in utilizing them. Some consumed their food carelessly and others did not plan adequately, but most husbanded their food supplies with great scrupulousness. When small surpluses became available, most at once began to lay down storage paste as reserves, and only a few indulged in gluttony, which would have been comprehensible after so long a period of privation. Without such individual care, the collective planning or centralized direction instituted by their leaders would have been ineffective. Such collective planning, too, showed a realistic appreciation of the situation and imaginative measures to meet it. In one respect, however, the Tikopia planners made some miscalculation. With the marginal yield of agricultural labour so low, they naturally wished to turn their labour power elsewhere and pursued most energetically requests for recruiting vessels to take large numbers of the male population to work on plantations in return for food to be consumed on Tikopia. But apart from practical difficulties of transport, the Tikopia did not work out carefully the ratio of monthly wages of unskilled labour to food costs of rice, etc., per family per month. With many families, if all the males had been away at work it would have been unlikely that the wages would have been adequate to support the women and children at home.

How far was such foresight narrow and individual in its application and how far did it envisage interests of a wider group? What was the assumption of responsibility and how did it operate? What was its relation to structural considerations? There was no doubt that in practically every case individual interests were subordinated to the interests of the elementary family or individual household. Men and women were concerned not merely for themselves, but especially for their children, and the careful planning in the use of resources was in nearly every case intended to safeguard family interests. On the other hand the range of calculation rarely went beyond this. The limitations of economic foresight were seen especially in the widespread theft of growing crops. Nearly everyone in Tikopia spoke hotly against theft and thieves. But only in a very few cases was this apparently accompanied by personal canons of responsibility. Before the organization to cope with theft had got into its stride, stealing of food from the cultivations had become rife, there being no visible distinction as regards offenders between districts, clans, villages, Christians or pagans, commoners or members of chiefly families. The main obvious exceptions were the chiefs themselves, a few of their close senior kinsmen, and the principal executants (*maru*). In other words, they were mostly the men whose traditional structural position demanded the most acute sense of community needs. Moreover, their restraint was correlated with the active leadership they assumed, with which known theft would have been incompatible. Losses of food and the threat to morale became such that personal foresight had, therefore, to be supplemented by the sanction of force.

Control of Manpower

Ultimate Tikopia success in coping with the famine was due to their mechanisms for control of manpower. As may be the case in coping with any disaster, this was manifested in two main ways: control of labour power and control of movement. Tikopia control of labour power was assumed by the most active of the executive officers (*maru*), acting in the name of the chiefs in the last resort—in structural term these executants are members of chiefs' lineages.[1] Initially these executants directed the labour power after the hurricane into clearing of paths, repairing of aqueducts and other essential tasks. Later they saw to it that a consistent planting policy was pursued and they followed the activities of individuals as well as those of the community at large. They reasoned thus: planting should be got under way at once after the hurricane and should be continued in order to replace foodstuffs drawn upon for subsistence. Moreover, they at once envisaged theft as probable and looked upon planting as one important means of later reducing it. There were many conversations about the necessity of the people planting new crops and enquiries were made about individuals not seen to plant. For instance, the Ariki Taumako asked about one member of his clan, 'Pa Tekara who lives there, is he not planting food?' 'No!' 'What will he do, go and steal? What will his children eat? Will they die of starvation?' In this case the man was feckless and a thief; in due course some of his children did die. But in general, largely as a result of the supervision and injunctions of the chiefs and executives, expressed through the public assemblies (*fono*), supplies of

[1] Raymond Firth—'Authority and Public Opinion in Tikopia', *Social Structure: Studies presented to A. R. Radcliffe-Brown*. Ed. M. Fortes, Oxford 1949. Pp. 168–88.

1 Village agriculture as famine approached. Sweet potatoes grown around the dwellings in Potu sa Taumako

Customary payment for building a canoe. Bundles of bark-cloth assembled outside house-eaves ceremonially before being carried off and presented to the workers

Traditional technique of turmeric extraction. A cylinder of turmeric (substituted by sand for photographic purposes) is blown from its wooden oven

2 House construction without nails. Timbers lashed together by coconut sinnet cord

sweet potato and manioc, the quick maturing bulk crops, became available as soon as feasible.

Control of movement was expressed in two main ways. One was to restrict economic opportunity in a sense by edicts to reduce the amount of fishing in favour of cultivation. It was thought that the most valuable use of labour was in the prime task of getting crops into the ground and for considerable periods sea fishing was discouraged for this reason. The edict was relaxed during the flying-fish season (October to December 1952 and March to June 1953), but in general a man met with severe disapproval if he went fishing instead of working on his land. (Fishing off the north coast of the island was also discouraged because from that area it was very easy to land and steal food undetected.)

The other control of movement was the whole elaborate series of restrictions governing resort to cultivations and orchards in order to try and eliminate theft. The objections of the Tikopia authorities to theft in this situation were threefold. They had a moral reaction against the impropriety of taking food belonging to another person. They also saw the economic disincentive: if some people's crops were systematically raided they would cease to plant and if other people were allowed to use theft as an alternative to cultivation then their productive labour would be lost. Finally, the Tikopia authorities saw clearly that theft, leading to dispute and violence, would be a threat to the social order on a scale far wider than the immediate property loss, and might affect their own ultimate position. Ultimately, quite an elaborate set of rules dealing with a whole range of activities from bird netting to lake fishing, use of cultivations and movements of people at dance festivals was introduced.[1] (Cf. pp. 322–4.)

Despite the efforts at control, however, stealing did become a very acute problem once the famine became severe. Some people, especially women whose husbands were away at work, or members of poorer commoner families, stole because they simply did not have enough food. But in some cases theft took place by people who, having just enough food to scrape along, feared that another catastrophe in the form of drought or hurricane would reduce them to a starving condition. Such people then stole in order to safeguard their own resources and accumulate a margin of safety. Spillius estimated that only about forty or fifty households (out of a total of nearly 300) were actually in a starving condition, but there is no doubt that many others were in very severe straits. Almost the only people who did not steal at the height of the famine were the chiefs and members of their families. Their restraint was primarily because on the one hand they were possessed of more land resources than most other people, and on the other because of the obligation still keenly felt that the people should support the chief. The slogan heard was 'The chiefs must be the last to die'. Yet, with typical human inconsistency, not even the orchards and gardens of the chiefs were respected by some thieves.

[1] For an account of the general type of control and the sanctions used to enforce it, see J. Spillius, *op. cit.*

E

There was a still further way in which, by what was in effect the direction of labour, the Tikopia authorities reinforced their attempts to deal with the famine. This was by using their influence in the selection of men who were recruited for labour in the plantations in the Solomons. In theory, presumably, recruiting should have been completely free for each individual. But the exigencies of the famine were such that it was only reasonable for recruitment to be related to the major food needs of the community. Some men, therefore, were discouraged from signing on so that they could continue to provide agricultural labour power at home. In a few cases men who were well known to be arrant thieves were given a very broad hint that they must recruit. This was equivalent to exile for a time and was much milder than the traditional Tikopia punishment of being sent off to sea. Again, after initial experience had given the plantation managers a very poor idea of the efficiency of Tikopia labour and threatened to imperil the recruitment, which was a major factor in the recovery of the island, the chiefs selected good labourers who turned out to be of excellent quality.[1]

In coping with the difficulties of the famine in manpower terms Tikopia initiative was not uniformly directed towards increasing productivity. There was much gloomy talk, some of it concerned with suicide risk voyages. One man of apparently equable temperament announced his determination to seek recruitment: but should he be barred, either by Government order or by his chief, he said he would *forau*—go on a suicide voyage. 'As it were I who sit here, I look on my children who are starving. I get my canoe ready to go. If a chief comes to block me I say "Shall I stay here to steal from your orchards? Or are you prepared to feed me?" Then he is silent and lets me go. . . .' This brings out the way in which the issues are conceptualized by the Tikopia in terms of choices: a man chooses between starvation on land and death at sea; his choice initially disallowed, he puts the situation in terms of a further choice by his chief. Note that the resolution is seen in a social compulsion—the chief, embarrassed at not having the wherewithal to feed his clansman, is compelled by shame to retract his ban on the suicide voyage. This conversation is patterned in type; it is the ideal mode. But the situation thus described is not merely an academic one. Voyages of this kind are said to have occurred in past famines. (Later the man quoted above *did* recruit.)

Migration Proposals

As an alternative to recruiting, or to possible suicide voyages, migration was also proposed.

Migration proposals for Tikopia have a long history. In 1934, 'in view of the increasing population of Tikopia', the *Southern Cross* mission vessel took to the Solomons several men who hoped to get governmental approval to a proposal to form a colony on Vanikoro or Santa Cruz.[2] In 1939 a memorandum by a Government officer discussed the problem with great care, and suggested various alternative homes for the emigrants—including the

[1] J. Spillius, *op. cit.*, p. 26.
[2] *The Melanesian Mission, Southern Cross Log*, London, vol. 41, May 1935, p. 70.

south end of Ndeni, Utupua, the south-east corner of Vanikoro, and the Treasurers' islands of the Duff Group. Later suggestions included Bellona, the south coast of San Cristoval, Ugi, and an island in the Tonga group. But though much was talked of, by Government and by the Tikopia, no recruits came. In July 1948, at a meeting of chiefs in the house of the Ariki Kafika, the subject was raised again by a Government officer 'and greeted with a refreshing laugh!', he reported. One difficulty on the Government side was to find a suitable home in which the Tikopia would not be immediately stricken with malaria. On the Tikopia side, while great enthusiasm was usually shown at the prospect of migration, when the time for action came, no one was actually willing to go. The Government in 1948 got the situation as far as to persuade the chiefs to allow a young Tikopia man to visit Ugi and report, and themselves persuaded the Ugi people to allocate land to the Tikopia who would go. But again, when it came to the point there were no emigrants offering.

In 1953 there was much debate publicly (in the *fono*) and privately about the possibility of migration. There was much discussion with representatives of Government and a commercial firm about plans for establishing a substantial number of Tikopia families in the Russell Islands. The Tikopia themselves, after one public discussion, expressed the wish to have a settlement near Kirakira, the Government station at San Cristoval, their prime motive here being apparently to be located near someone in authority in whose hands they could place their future. But by July 1953,[1] as food again began to be abundant, interest in migration began to decline and for three years no move took place. What were the reasons for this reluctance?

In 1929 there was no disposition of any Tikopia to go and reside abroad; they hardly regarded it as conceivable.[2] But by 1952 there were several Tikopia who were permanently in residence away from the island. One, aged about thirty-two years, had become a mission teacher and gone to work at Star Harbour (San Cristoval) where he had married and settled down. Another, aged forty to forty-five years, I met as a boatboy at the British Residency at Vila (New Hebrides). He was unmarried and had no wish to be married; he said he did not want to return to Tikopia; his parents were both dead, and his brother had married and raised a family to inherit the ancestral lands. It is clear that by 1952 some Tikopia, though few, regarded it as quite feasible to make a life for themselves in a foreign land. There were others, men with special skills useful in a European environment, who were willing to spend the greater part of their working life abroad, and who might well decide to settle away from Tikopia in the end.

This is relevant to migration prospects, in that it has already established a pattern of *emigré* Tikopia. The reasons for the prolonged lack of response to the Government's tentative moves must have lain elsewhere than in total disinclination to live abroad.

One reason why earlier migration plans did not proceed was that they did

[1] See J. Spillius, *op. cit.*, p. 21.
[2] *We, The Tikopia*, pp. 18, 21.

not seem to have always been fully understood by the Tikopia chiefs. Without
their support, the proposals withered. This was stated (by Robinson Vakasaumore to me) to have been the case with the proposed migration to Ugi.
Rongoiteava, son of a mission teacher, Pa Rongotau, had been chosen by
the *maru*, John Fararava, to survey the island and pick out a site. With him
went Marukimoana (Remon), a son of Pa Fenuatara, and Marutukukimoana
(Mark), a son of Pa Rangifakauvia. Despite the fact that both these young
men were of chiefly family, one of Kafika and the other of Tafua, the proposals of the party were not acted upon. It may have been partly because they
were too junior, but it was alleged that it was because the chiefs were ignorant
of what was involved. Remon thought his father had been informed, but
found that he had not. 'The chiefs objected: they objected to people going.
The root of their objection was that they did not know, and they objected to
the land being divided.'

A more basic reason was the highly integrated formal structure of Tikopia.
It was with difficulty that the Tikopia as a body could be brought to con-
template the dismemberment of their society. That unnamed individuals
should migrate was good. That a specific section of the community should go,
and disturb the intricate social relations with the rest, was another matter.
This was especially so when the proposed migrants would carry with them
any particular symbolic values of Tikopia society. For instance, for such a
migration to be successful, it was thought advisable for the migrants to have
a leader, who could act as headman *vis-à-vis* the Government, and as chief
according to the Tikopia pattern. One obvious suggestion would be that
one of the chiefs should lead the migration. But any such suggestion was
opposed flatly by the Tikopia.

There was also a third reason. Without the approval of the chiefs people
could not migrate. But on the other hand, the chiefs were not prepared to
indicate *who* should migrate. The reason for this is built upon the traditional
relations between Tikopia chiefs and commoners. No chief would wish it to
be thought that he was virtually expelling a commoner. (Cf. pp. 92–3.)
And however desirable the place of migration may be, such prolonged
absence is a form of exile from Tikopia. Hence there had to be a technique
of forming the migrating party by allowing people to nominate themselves
with the approval of the chiefs. A final set of reasons was quite simply the
great sentimental attachment the Tikopia had for their home and their specific
way of life.

Hence it had required the pressures such as the famine provided to give to
many people the final spur of decision to think of emigrating, and it was a
solution easily postponed when local prospects improved.

This analysis has been based on my own experience in Tikopia. More
recently some interesting details have become available of an actual resettle-
ment.[1] In 1956 a pilot scheme was got under way to establish thirty Tikopia
families in a village in the Russell Islands in association with Levers Pacific

---

[1] Colin H. Allan, *Customary Land Tenure in the British Solomon Islands Protectorate*
(Honiara, 1957, pp. 238–9).

Plantation Pty. Limited, a company which recently had had good experience with Tikopia labourers and was anxious to secure such a regular labour supply. About seventy-five acres of land were made available by the Government, the sub-division of the land being left to the Tikopia themselves. During 1956/7 an advance party of about twenty men, mostly single, was engaged in building houses, clearing and planting the land in preparation for the arrival of kinsfolk from Tikopia. After about a year approximately thirty to thirty-five acres were already under intensive cultivation with coconuts, taro, yam, manioc and European vegetables and fruit. The cultivations included group areas to feed new settlers as they arrived and individual plots for the support of each man and his family.

The new settlement has been named Nukufero, from an ancient name for Tikopia. By 1958 it had about sixty persons.

For the time being the settlement was intended to be only semi-permanent and to be built up to a total of thirty families of whom some, from time to time, were to return to Tikopia and be replaced by others. The explanation of this is significant. 'The reason is that when it came to the point, the settlers were reluctant to break all ties with Tikopia. They have insisted that social responsibilities require their periodic return to their homeland. Therefore, in the meantime, land interests in Tikopia will be used by close relatives but will not be extinguished. To this end the Tikopia chiefs have decided that in a family of four brothers, two will be allowed to settle in Nukufero. The two remaining in Tikopia will use the interests of the absentees which will be maintained alive. The passage of time and a steady development of Nukufero will perhaps result in the settlement being regarded as a new and permanent Tikopia. Any insistence on immediate extinction of land interests in Tikopia would have killed the settlement immediately. The compromise, unsatisfactory as it may be, offers a reasonable chance for its survival.'

An important feature of the new settlement is that in the event of a further famine in Tikopia it could probably be extended rapidly. The success of this experiment may well depend upon the ability with which satisfactory communication between it and Tikopia can be maintained.

Land Use

The economic effects of the famine as regards land use in Tikopia were of four main kinds: shortening or abandonment of fallow period; closer definition of cultivation rights in the lands of others; restriction of collecting rights on the land of others; and intensified demarcation of land boundaries.

(i) Shortening of fallow period. It had formerly been Tikopia agricultural practice to allow a piece of ground used for taro or other important ground crop to lie fallow for at least a season after use. The theory was that the height of the succeeding crop would be roughly proportional to the wild vegetation it replaced.[1] As a result of the famine, this practice was often abandoned. With abandonment of fallowing was associated the planting of short-term crops. In one of the major growing areas, Rakisu (see pp. 172–9), which was

[1] *We, The Tikopia*, pp. 403–4; *Primitive Polynesian Economy*, pp. 93–4.

formerly devoted almost entirely to taro, and of which for each season more than half was usually fallow, the fallow area practically disappeared as the famine developed. It was completely planted with sweet potato, manioc and pumpkin. This was so contrary to traditional use that it led Pa Fenuatara to shake his head sadly and say 'Pumpkin in Rakisu!' Owing presumably to lack of fallowing, the soil in this area after a year of intensive planting came to be regarded by the Tikopia as being in very poor condition.[1]

Pressure was put upon people with fallow land, even upon chiefs, to allow it to be cultivated. In November 1952 a great deal of pressure was put upon the Ariki Taumako by members of his clan to allow planting to be undertaken on a strip of land in Rakisu which he had been reserving for taro in preparation for the initiation ceremonies of his sons and one of his brother's sons. He finally gave way. But ceremonial and religious claims were not completely disregarded. Lands above Te Roro which belonged to the Ariki Taumako, despite the shortage of food and tobacco, remained uncultivated until June 1953 when clearing of them began, to grow taro for the initiation mentioned above. Similarly, lands in the same area owned by the Ariki Kafika remained in fallow for crops which would be used for religious ceremonies. There seemed to be no pressure put on either chief to open up these lands, the most sacred *mara* (*v.* p. 177), nor was any criticism of their policy heard by Spillius. In November 1952, however, the Ariki Taumako decided that other lands of his, near the peak of Reani, should be cleared and planted with manioc. Each lineage of his clan and others who requested permission were allowed to plant whatever ground they cleared. This decision was welcomed by the people since it made a great difference in food prospects to the households of commoners who had previously only very small patches of land.

(ii) Restriction of planting rights: At an early stage in the development of the food shortage after the hurricane, people began to impose restriction on the use of their land by others. One indication was a taboo sign—a coconut frond tied to a stick set up in a cultivation or orchard as a warning that the owner did not wish the land used or any of the crop taken or the wild fruits collected. Such signs, known as *pi* (barriers), were to be seen commonly between April and June 1952, as on hibiscus near Tufenua, on a coconut palm with a couple of nuts on it in Uta, on giant taro in the swamp of Ropera, on manioc in Rotoaia and on taro ground at Nailopu. (Cf. p. 179.)

But these were individual restrictions. As time went on they became less and less effective. Not only did thieves disregard them; close kinsfolk of the owners did so too, claiming that they had traditional right to do so. Indeed, these coconut frond signs came to be in the end protests after theft had occurred rather than warnings against it. Such individual signs came in time to be replaced by more general public rules supported by the chiefs and

---

[1] I have learned from Mr J. Tedder, District Commissioner at Vanikoro, that by mid-1956, while most of the area was still planted with manioc, there was no pumpkin and there were some taro gardens. It was stated that more taro would be planted again soon. Only a very small area was in fallow. By 1958 Rakisu was still under manioc.

executant officers instead of being left to the owners to implement.

Before the famine it was still customary, as in 1929, to plant a crop where one pleased without asking the permission of the owner of the land—provided of course that the land was not already in use or being cleared for cultivation.[1] Two significant changes took place in the course of the famine. First, it was declared in the rules laid down in public assembly that people would have to ask permission from owners to plant on land that was not under cultivation. Very few people asked for this permission since by this time it was apparent that hardly anyone would grant it. Some people attempted to plant in plots which had been cleared by close kin. But there was more than one instance where the owner of the land, on discovering in his plot seedlings not his own, tore them up fiercely and threw them out on the public path, tying a taboo sign on his land to warn off anyone else who had similar intentions. Secondly, it was proclaimed in the public assembly that no food should be destroyed wantonly in the course of a quarrel over land, and indeed that no land disputes should take place at all. This placed in an awkward position those people on whose land others had planted short-term crops before the famine. It became the practice of such croppers not to take out the entire crop of manioc or sweet potato at once, but to take only as much as was needed for a meal or so and replant seedlings. Thus the land never went out of cultivation and the owner was never able to get back the use of it during this period. Sometimes, however, pressure of public opinion forced the user of such land to send some food over to the owner in recompense. As can be imagined, several land disputes did in fact occur.

(iii) Restriction of collecting rights: One source of friction and accusation of thefts lay in the utilization of wild plants which had formerly been available to all, regardless of the ownership of the land on which they grew. In August and September of 1952, after such plants had assumed major importance as food or as material for nets and mats, quarrels about them had become increasingly frequent. Several rules were then made in the public assembly. It was agreed that the wild yam with aerial tubers (*soi*) which grew in each person's orchard should be his own and that no one else should take it. This rule took a long time to materialize. Even at the end of April Pa Ngarumea said that *soi* tubers had been gathered as was customary from orchards without distinction of ownership and that while owners of orchards had been angry it had been too late. Asked if he himself had taken *soi* from other people's orchards, he said 'No, because I give orders to others,' meaning that he felt he had to exercise restraint. It was decreed also that only one person (normally a woman) could go in to pick the *soi*. The idea behind this was that a woman could carry at the most two baskets of *soi*, which is about the maximum one could expect from the available crop in one orchard. If a woman were found with more than two baskets of *soi* she would be suspected of having raided other people's orchards. Similar rules applied to breadfruit.

The rule was also made in public assembly that no person could wander

[1] See *We, The Tikopia*, pp. 400–4; *Primitive Polynesian Economy*, p. 261.

about the cultivations looking for hibiscus bark for the manufacture of cord or nets. This was at a time when there was a taboo on fishing and it was argued, therefore, that no one needed hibiscus for nets or fishline; if people got in other gardens and said they were looking for hibiscus, they could only be using this as an excuse for stealing fruit. In addition to these changes in the customary rules for the use of land, it became suspect for an individual even to be seen near a plot of land away from his own.[1]

(iv) Demarcation of land boundaries: The increasing shortage of food made it imperative for most people to use to the full the amount of land available to them. It also intensified their interest in lands to which the title was in dispute or to which they could revive a claim. Another result was frequent quarrels between brothers, or other close agnatic kin holding a piece of land in common. In some cases land formerly used jointly by brothers was now divided and boundary marks set up to mark their respective properties. This process had been gaining ground in the intervening generation since my first visit (cf. pp. 161–8), but it was sharply accentuated by the famine. In some land disputes there was argument over precise boundaries. Every small margin in either food or land that could be gained was of vital importance to some people. Stones marking boundaries were even moved surreptitiously during the night to gain an extra bit of land, measuring say a yard wide by twenty or thirty yards long.

Effects on Exchange

By ordinary Western reckoning a famine should have seen the poorer Tikopia selling off their most prized possessions to the richer Tikopia for food, and the Tikopia as a whole selling off their other material possessions to buy food from outside. Neither of these happened on any scale.

As far as selling to outside suppliers was concerned the Tikopia would have been quite willing to have done so; the difficulty was that for the most part they did not have the appropriate media. Their mats, bark-cloth and other goods were not acceptable in general exchange. It is true that in default of cash a European trader took a quantity of Tikopia goods in exchange for food, hoping to dispose of them at a profit, but the experiment was not a success. For the Government relief supplies, partly to get some recompense and partly to impress upon the Tikopia that they should not expect charity, it was suggested that a contribution of pandanus mats and (on one occasion) wooden bowls should be given in return. This was done, but the market for these Tikopia products was small and inelastic, and in no case can the Tikopia be said to have conducted a normal economic transaction as far as relief supplies were concerned. But why did not the Tikopia conduct such exchanges internally? To a Tikopia an additional supply of bowls, mats and bark-cloth could always be absorbed through the mechanism of ceremonial exchange later. Why would a starving Tikopia not barter food for such things?

There was in fact a small amount of barter of Tikopia goods for rice, and one case is reported of a man who stripped his house of all his goods in a

[1] I owe information about all these rules to the observation of Spillius.

gluttonous frenzy. Twice it seems he had 'stolen' a pound or so of rice, leaving in its stead a knife or a hank of sinnet cord. But such cases were rare. The reason was essentially that the social norms did not provide for such kind of exchange. Probably not even the most wealthy Tikopia felt secure enough in the indeterminate conditions of the famine to barter away much food, and the poorer households may not have had much spare property. But the more wealthy Tikopia did dispense food—it went out in hospitality, support of kinsfolk and other dependants, and even in fulfilment of ceremonial obligations. Moreover, it would have been very difficult, and by convention impossible, for any ordinary Tikopia to acknowledge that he had taken a mat or other property specifically in direct exchange for a gift of food. Consequently, contrary to what outsiders might have expected, there was no significant flow of property in transactions involving transfer of food. I shall return to this in Chapter IV.

Exchange did take place, however, with one commodity, tobacco. The Tikopia tend to be obsessional about the use of masticants and about smoking. With the scarcity of areca nut, they had resort to various inferior substitutes—the inner bark of the breadfruit tree or of the *natu* (*Spondias dulcis*), or part of the coconut shoot near the flower bract (*roro niu*) or unripe *Calophyllum* berries. All these, however, unsatisfactory, were chewed with lime and betel leaf. In default of tobacco, the more ardent smokers were reduced to substitutes such as papaya leaf or the dried fibres of cordyline root after the food material had been extracted from it. In 1952/3, as in 1928/9, the Tikopia demand for tobacco was very keen. It intensified as with time a real shortage of locally grown tobacco developed. By May 1952 we had ceased to give out sticks or half-sticks of trade tobacco (save in exceptional circumstances, as to chiefs who themselves dispensed it) and were niggardly even with the tiny inch-long plugs into which we cut the sticks and which we took with us on daily routine calls for census-taking and ordinary observation. An illustration of the fierce demand for native-grown tobacco was the bitterness engendered when it was found that the Mission priest had cornered the Anuta supply.[1] Towards the middle of the year one man said, half-jokingly, 'Nowadays only chiefs smoke tobacco, others smoke leaves.' It was an exaggeration, but had some truth. Apart from resort to substitutes, there was also much theft of immature tobacco from cultivations. Yet it was interesting to note that despite the fierce competition for tobacco women were able to smoke nearly as much as men. The Tikopia men heard from us with astonishment of the Victorian ban on English women smoking and laughed heartily at the idea which I had put forward to them as a joke that they should forbid their womenfolk from smoking in order to conserve the tobacco for themselves. Later on, Spillius noted that a source of many domestic quarrels between husband and wife was tobacco, but he would have been a hardy man who tried consistently to stop his wife from smoking.

Later in 1952 the new tobacco crop matured. By August almost every

[1] Raymond Firth, 'Anuta and Tikopia', *Journal of Polynesian Society*, vol. 63, September 1954, pp. 118–19.

household had collected its tobacco and was preparing it in rolls for storage. The harvest had been meagre due to the hurricane and the supply began to run out about December 1952; by March of the following year the shortage was very acute indeed.[1] There was a famine not only in supplies for smoking but also in tobacco seedlings for replanting the future crop. Those people who had spare seedlings from their cultivations or who had bothered to plant them just outside their house, now demanded payment for them instead of giving them as before to kinsmen as an ordinary gesture of goodwill. They insisted not only on some equivalent at the time of handing over the seedlings, but also on a promise of tobacco when the harvest would have been reaped. A price asked was one stick of trade tobacco for twelve seedlings, or as a much larger quantity of seedlings was usually required, the equivalent demanded might be a piece of calico. In addition to this, the promise of at least one fathom of twist tobacco[2] was demanded against the time of harvest. If a person planted tobacco in another person's orchard, it was customary to give the owner a roll which came to fifteen or sixteen fathoms of twist tobacco. The Ariki Tafua, who owned the most productive land for tobacco, was the richest in this commodity and always had a supply on hand. To illustrate how great became the shortage of tobacco in the first few months of 1953, two exchanges may be cited: for half a fathom of tobacco, an axe or a knife; for a fathom of tobacco, a European blanket. There were no standard rates of exchange, but these examples—up to six times the normal rates—show how intense was the demand. By outside visitors a wide range of Tikopia goods was purchased with tobacco, e.g. the Captain of the sy *Southern Cross* bought many Tikopia war clubs as 'curios'.

From the growth of exchange rates for tobacco and not for food it might be argued that the quietening of their nervous excitation was more important to the Tikopia than the quietening of their pangs of hunger. But tobacco does not fit quite so closely into the Tikopia scheme of social conventions and ceremonial exchanges as does food, and therefore there was more freedom for direct exchange to develop for it.

Summary

From this analysis some general observations may be made on the economic

---

[1] It was pointed out at this time that the atmosphere round the villages was usually quite free from the taint of tobacco smoke. Some young men used to walk sniffing round the houses at night to smell if tobacco was being smoked. If so, they would enter and demand a draw at the pipe. When Europeans came ashore children were immediately set on their trail to pick up at once any cigarette butts they might drop; these were then stuffed into pipes.

[2] Local grown tobacco leaf is made up by the Tikopia into long lengths of twist about the thickness of one's finger, and these in turn are wound tightly into rolls about the thickness of one's arm. Measurement is as follows:

Te u paka na katoa, complete long roll;
Tutanga paka, large roll cut in half and re-wrapped;
Foi fetunga sokotasi, single arm-length of twist;
Ku rua ko foi fetunga, double arm-length, fathom;
Fetu paka sokotasi, a stick (trade tobacco);
Potu paka, a quid.

reactions of the Tikopia to the famine, and the light these throw on their conceptions of the nature of their society and the proper choices to be made in time of crisis. ⌐

Hurricane and drought severely reduced the Tikopia food income to a level at which their survival was threatened. Their accumulated stocks of food were inadequate to raise the level of subsistence appreciably for any period, or even fully to bridge the gap until agricultural production could recover a minimum level of comfort. This lack of reserves was due partly to the lack of more efficient techniques of food preservation, and partly to the practice of consuming food amply in times of plenty, using it as a social instrument in ceremonial procedures. Tikopia capital stocks in other goods were small, not sufficient to purchase any quantity of food abroad, and for the measure of relief they received from outside they had to depend in part upon Government philanthropy and in part upon the sale of some of their male labour, for work elsewhere. For the most part, they had to cope with the crisis themselves, with their own forms of organization.

Three considerations seem outstanding in their economic proceedings. The first was their maintenance of the social framework of their exchange system. Traditionally, food in Tikopia is transferred from one person or economic unit to another by gift, not by barter, and even in the stringency of famine this procedure applied. There was no sale of food to the highest bidder, no profit-taking on small food surpluses, and almost no transfer of non-food items for food by direct exchange. In particular, no capital transfers of land, or canoes or tools occurred, giving fortunate possessors of spare food any increase of productive control for the future. Both the complex system of rights of ownership over such items and the general conventions about the uses of wealth inhibited this.

The second consideration was development of control of manpower in the interests of the community at large. There was conscription of some people for public works, and direction of many towards private production which would result in public benefit. In the effort to intensify production, leadership in the community assumed a more overt and mandatory form than usual, and more rigorous sanctions than usual were applied.

The third consideration was the contrast between the tendency to increased communal control of manpower and the increased limitation of communal rights in food and associated consumer goods. While there was some pooling of labour, there was no pooling of food. The rights of families and households were more carefully demarcated and promulgated than in ordinary times. While they were often not respected, this breach was given no public justification. Moreover, in fields in which communal exercise of rights had been regarded as appropriate, such as the collection of aerial yams from any orchard, new restrictions were introduced. Thus, while the individual's labour power was held to be at the disposal of the community, his food resources were held to be his own property, irrespective of his neighbour's plight.

This last proposition had one modification, in the case of the chiefs. The formula that 'the chiefs must be the last to die' might seem from one point of view to be an archaic, feudal expression of inequality. In a sense this is true, in that the statement made for an intensification of unequal food distribution in two ways: it held that the food resources of chiefs ought to be inviolate; and that commoners, when both were in dire straits, should leave their food to the chiefs, and go out and perish that the chiefs should survive. It might even be argued that insofar as the Tikopia chiefs were richer in lands and food than commoners, the public insistence on private rights of consumption was an attitude fostered by the chiefs in their own interest. But this argument would ignore several points. One was that not every chief was so wealthy, certainly not richer than any commoner. Again, the public formula was not observed; theft from chiefs took place as much as from commoners. But the most important point is that a Tikopia chief is not simply a private person; he is also a symbol of the community and one of its acknowledged leaders. Hence the modification of the individualist rule—that each man was entitled to his own foodstuffs, without regard to the sufferings of others—in favour of the chiefs, was a real assertion in other terms, of the primacy of the community interest. The chiefs should survive, who else might perish, because they in the last resort were the representatives and directors of the community. Even though many people did not obey this rule, it was a factor in the choices of many, leading them to protect the interests of the chiefs on many occasions, to the possible detriment of their own. (For further discussion of this point see Chapter IV, pp. 92–3.)

CHAPTER IV

Tikopia Society in Famine

In the last chapter I showed how the Tikopia adapted their resources to cope with the famine. In this chapter I consider more specifically how the famine affected Tikopia society.

How far is it meaningful to talk of the reactions of Tikopia as a social system to the conditions of famine? Individuals clearly varied in their response to pressures on their food supply: some planned their consumption carefully, some ate heartily at the beginning and then drew in their belts, some stole, some tried to prevent stealing and to stimulate production of food. But to what extent did characteristic Tikopia attitudes in the use of food, dictated by social rather than economic considerations, still persist? How far did the food stringency affect their social behaviour? How far did institutions suffer? What general patterns were perceptible? Did the society tend to atomize, to disintegrate under the famine pressures, or to take on a special solidarity to meet the threat?

It will be clear from the last chapter that there is justification in speaking of Tikopia reactions as a whole, that some general patterns did emerge.

When the hurricane struck Tikopia and the food shortage began, no immediate resort to outside aid was possible; solutions had to be worked out on the spot and within the confines of Tikopia society. The presence of anthropologists provided the Tikopia with useful intermediaries, trusted by them, and able to communicate with ease between the people and the governmental source of aid. But though this gave them much help, the ultimate decisions lay with the Tikopia themselves. Their authority system of the traditional kind provided an anchor which prevented the Tikopia from being swept away in panic or despair if they had been so prone. Moreover, though they found it difficult at first to judge the magnitude of the disaster itself, its general type was already known from precedents and in many cases from personal knowledge. Hence the chiefs and other responsible men could give a speedy appreciation of the situation and their forecasts turned out to be fairly accurate.

The conduct of the Tikopia as a community was marked by contrasts of activity and of apathy. On the one hand they engaged in active measures to increase their food production and to preserve the foods they had left. But while they rationed themselves carefully with their local foods, they showed little self-restraint with the imported foods distributed to them from the Government. These they consumed rapidly as bonuses which did not need to enter their calculations. While co-operating with some energy in the institutional measures of public assembly, under the guidance of their leaders, they showed themselves irresponsible and lacking in restraint when it came to theft of food supplies from the growing crops. As with the sharpening of personal rights in land and in produce, this indicates attempts at individual or at least of family self-protection in the time of crisis. Yet throughout, the overt morality of distribution was preserved. Theft was universally stigmatized and in the long run it was countered by public action. Some people observed the rules, and in the distribution of relief supplies there was only one incident of disorder.

In more detail the questions involved may be epitomized as follows.

How far did the conventions about things normally used as food continue to operate, or cease to be observed? Was there resort to nutritionally useless and socially neglected substances, such as bark of trees, which nevertheless were belly-filling? Was there resort to nutritionally useful but ritually or morally forbidden objects, such as flesh of dogs, bats and taboo birds—or was there even finally cannibalism?

In the distribution of food, how did the various types of social relations fare? Domestically, how far was a man concerned with the needs of his wife and children; it someone had to go short, who was it? Were hungry neighbours and kinsfolk fed, when they asked for food—or when they did not ask, but it was thought they were short? How far did traditional conventions of hospitality carry in the feeding of visitors? How far did compliance with the ordinary rules of sharing go—to the point of disregarding long-term for immediate issues, and giving away food though household supplies would thereby be soon finished? What was the effect of the famine on relations with the chiefs? Did clansmen still bring in food for their chief, or was he left to fend for himself in his own orchards? Or did he in turn attempt to feed his people? Remembering that in Tikopia theory all orchards of the clan *are* the orchards of the chief, did he in straits levy toll upon them? What about ceremonial and ritual relations—were they weakened by the famine, considering that in so many ways traditionally they are maintained by food presentation?

In terms of social order, how did the competition for food work out? How far did the struggle sharpen to the point of using theft as the solution to extreme hunger? Was there violence, arising from discovery of theft, or as a direct means of wresting food from others? Or alternately, for some people did the social order simply dissolve to the point of abnegation of all social relations, either by sitting down in apathy to await death by starvation, or by seeking death in suicide by putting off to sea? Again, as the food situation became more acute, where was the imputation of responsibility, and did this involve any threat to the social order? In other words, was there murmuring against the chiefs and other men in authority—or against the gods—for not having averted the crisis? Finally, what measures of social control were adopted to deal with the crisis, both empirical and ideational, in the form of kava rite or Christian prayer?

Most of these points I had posed as field questions in April 1952; by

August, when I left the island, the answers to many of them had already been indicated, and by July 1953, thanks especially to the indefatigable work of Spillius, the basic effects of the famine upon the Tikopia social system had been made clear.

As regards conventions in the type of foods, most of the answers have been implied by the account in Chapter III. To some degree people did disregard the normal conventions of eating and fill their bellies with fibrous material such as *aka* and pandanus seed casing or roots. But they did not discard the ritual convention and ate no substances ordinarily forbidden them by religious or moral rule. Neither taboo birds nor bats seem to have been eaten by anyone, pagan or Christian, and as for cannibalism, there seems to have never been any question of it.

On the other hand, the social order was threatened in more concrete ways. Theft was rife (see pp. 314–24). Though there seem to have been no instances of food torn from the hands of others, there were cases of violence arising from discovery or alleged discovery of theft. There was an occasion indeed, when a threat of serious social disorder impelled Spillius to intervene in the Tikopia conduct of affairs.[1] And, if apathy and despair did not overcome some people to the extent of their letting themselves relapse into immobility, or going off to sea to die, this was primarily due to the alleviating, remedial effect of relief supplies of food.

I deal now with the social effects of the problems of responsibility for the famine, distribution of food and control of behaviour in famine conditions.

RESPONSIBILITY FOR THE FAMINE

The question of responsibility for the famine has for us both an intellectual and a moral side, each operating in more than one sphere of relationships. On the intellectual side, the famine was attributed by the Tikopia to a complex set of causes, beginning with the hurricane and drought as the natural forces primarily responsible, and going on to apathy and to lack of restraint in digging up immature crops, and especially in stealing food, as the human forces secondarily responsible. In this exoteric sphere, the moral judgement was restricted to stigmatizing laziness, lack of foresight, and theft. But there was also an esoteric sphere in which the imputation of responsibility took a rather different form. In the traditional Tikopia religious ideology, there is an elaborate set of links between chiefs, their clan gods, and the phenomena of wind, sunshine and rain, which can be controlled up to a point, by the direction of energy from chiefs and gods upon them. But on the one hand, competing interests may negate the ordinary bounty of nature; and on the other, the favour of the gods towards their representatives, the chiefs, may still further affect the issue. Hence the hurricane and drought could, in the view of the more traditionally minded Tikopia, be explicable in terms of competing religious forces (including perhaps those of Christianity), and the personal quality of specific chiefs. Here on the one side was a set of intellectual ex-

[1] Spillius, *op. cit.*, p. 18.

planations, and on the other the opportunity for the imputation of moral responsibility to human beings.

⌈It was assumed by Tikopia that this hurricane was the result of action by spirit powers. But this view was an inference from the capabilities generally ascribed to these powers rather than from any specific intention attributed to them. This aspect of spirit intervention was hardly discussed at all by the Tikopia. Hurricanes, like changing colours and forms of clouds in the sky, are part of the given structure of events in their universe. Hurricanes are sent by the gods, but men do not know why they send them—such might be a fair epitome of the Tikopia unspoken attitude.⌉

What did receive very clear expression on a number of occasions was the view that the famine in particular, though not specifically the hurricane itself, was due to the inadequacy of the human instruments who served gods, in other words, primarily the chiefs. This view was expressed by senior men, some pagan, others Christians by profession but still retaining the essentials of pagan belief; it was not apparently universally held. It took several forms. One was that prime responsibility rested on the Ariki Kafika, who was too aged to be a proper medium of communication with the gods and whose decrepitude was in particular an offence to his own major diety. He was deemed to be a weak link in the chain of powers making for fertility of the land. This view obtained among pagans even in his own clan and family.[1] Another form of the belief was that the famine was due to the malevolence of the chiefs who, in envy and jealousy of the wealth of others in food, destroyed their supplies by sorcery. I did not find this view widespread, but it had analogies with others I found in 1928/9 about the power of illwill directed against crops. A third form, to us the most sophisticated, was to regard famine as only an extreme instance of a more general lack of productivity, and to attribute it to the fundamental religious and social division in the land. To my Christian informants, who mainly championed this view, the pagan chiefs, recalcitrant as regards conversion, were responsible. On this view then, the 'infertility' of Tikopia in the natural sphere was the outcome of an infertility or ineffectiveness in the social sphere.

More abstractly, using terms more remote from the Tikopia forms of expression, their view of nature may be called *socio-centric*. For them, natural order and prosperity were related to social harmony. Disorder in nature, untoward events, lack of prosperity, were to be related to social defects such as the religious division of the society or the feebleness of its premier chief. Some people might regard these as specifically offensive to the gods, others might look upon them as merely disturbing in a more general sense. In both cases the association of natural event and social circumstance was one of indirect rather than direct causation—or perhaps hardly one of 'causation' at all. It was rather that the 'unnatural' condition of society was manifest in the abnormal conditions of nature.

The view of the crisis as man-made included, as I have mentioned earlier,

[1] See Raymond Firth, 'Some Principles of Social Organization', *Journal Royal Anthropological Institute*, vol. 85, 1955, pp. 8–10.

the attitude that famine was due to laziness and theft or to a combination of these. This view needs further examination. The Ariki Kafika and the Ariki Fangarere, discussing the food shortage when they were conducting the rites of Somosomo, said that it was 'a famine of man indeed' (*te onge te tangata na*). By this they meant that it was created through the wide and continual stealing. They said that there were only twenty or thirty men of the older generation who observed the proprieties and did not raid the orchards and gardens of others. This view that the famine was not so much the cause as the result of stealing seems exaggerated and unrealistic. But it was fairly widely expressed. 'We here are hungry from the famine of men, created in the heart of the woods,' said a woman once in a general gathering, and this received general assent. The Ariki Taumako argued that theft was due to men not planting at the right time. 'Does food grow of itself? Of course food is prepared by the hands of men,' he said. In all this, there was much truth. Lack of restraint had precipitated the crisis; the famine was certainly exacerbated greatly by the inconsiderate and irresponsible acts of people in stealing food before it was ready. Moreover, some planting had been late, and on too small a scale. It was a socially healthy attitude to lay the blame upon the human factor rather than on the vagaries of nature. Yet, this view may to some extent have been in defence against others. If much of the responsibility for the famine could be laid at the door of lazy, thieving human beings, then to that extent the responsibility was removed from the chiefs. It was perhaps significant that it was primarily among the Kafika-Taumako group of pagans that I found this attitude most strongly expressed. Holding as they did that human frailty was primarily responsible, the two pagan chiefs could intelligibly refrain from any special appeals to their gods and ancestors to mitigate the situation. This is a reconstruction of my own, and I had no specific confirmation of it from the Tikopia, but it does help to explain an otherwise rather puzzling feature of the religious aspects of the famine—that no special ritual appeals seem to have been made for relief. However, as with the Tikopia Christians, the regular appeals in the normal pagan rites could well be regarded as valid enough. If God—or the gods—wished to end the period of misery, they had had enough stimulus already.

DOMESTIC PROBLEMS OF DISTRIBUTION

In April 1952, though it was not yet famine, the food shortage was keenly felt and prospect of immediate relief was faint. But the norms of domestic conduct and of hospitality were being maintained. All the traditional ways of serving food politely in a household were carried out and manners were impeccable. Neighbours and kin were still being fed when they asked for food—as some had begun to do, going around from one house to another. The ordinary conventions of hospitality were still operative.

Despite our protests, men of rank—most of them old friends of mine—still insisted on serving us with meals when we visited them, in bringing baskets of food to our house and in issuing invitations to us to dine with them.

F

Whenever possible they prepared the food with coconut cream, on occasion using their last hoarded coconuts for the purpose. It was about this time that members of our host's family tended to eat different, poorer, food at the common meal with us, or occasionally, on one pretext or another, to eat little or nothing while we were there. At one meal with Pa Fenuatara, for instance, when about fifteen people were present, Spillius and I were given coconut pudding, taro and salmon trout, the Ariki Kafika was given coconut pudding, taro and flying fish, Pa Fenuatara himself had breadfruit paste, taro and salmon trout, his eldest son and his daughter-in-law had breadfruit paste, giant taro and flying fish and the young men and other juniors had giant taro and the remnants—altogether showing a very nice grading in food quality according to status. At the beginning I remonstrated strongly both against these meals given to us and against the traditional practice which still then obtained of sending back the surplus from the meal in a basket to our house. The reply was in some such form as 'It is all right as far as you are concerned, you are a Tikopia—that is the way we talk. But our friend James is a new visitor—a bird carried hither on a tree, and we would be ashamed not to feed him according to Tikopia custom.' When we first visited Pa Fenuatara in Uta (and made him a present of a knife and length of red calico), he ordered green coconuts to be plucked for our refreshment. When I protested, saying 'Leave them', he replied 'That does not matter', and plucked they were, almost to the last in the orchard. On many occasions we were told 'The land mourns and mourns over the two of you. No coconut. . . .' (This meant inadequate means for the preparation of fine food as hospitality demanded.)

As time went on the behaviour changed. During the first month or so invitations to attend a meal came to us on an average about one per day. Even towards the end of April I noted that on one afternoon we had three invitations from Taumako men of rank, none of which could be refused, and I noted at the time in my diary 'Powerful digestion again the anthropologist's best friend.' But later these invitations tapered off and as the food shortage grew worse we tended to have meals only at the houses of our close friends to whom, in one way or another, we could usually manage to make up for the food they expended on us. In the earlier days my arguments that the surplus from a meal given for us should be allowed to remain in the house and not sent back with us were not listened to; later they were acquiesced in, although usually after formal protest.

New themes, too, came to the fore in discussion. One of our neighbours expressed himself as being ashamed at seeing food carried to our house by others and not being able himself to invite us to a meal or bring food to us. This slur on his status appeared to have made him angry. Some of our visitors said that he was spreading scandalous stories about them—saying that they came to our house only to eat at our expense. It began to be increasingly clear that the famine was putting a strain on social relations. People felt themselves to be in difficulty through not being able to fulfil obligations demanded of them by custom and some tended to compensate for this by aggressive behaviour. In other words, cultural demands added an extra strain to nutritional demands.

In general it can be said, however, that while morals degenerated under the strain of famine, manners remained. At the times of greatest food shortage the ordinary modes of serving food were kept up. People waited to see that others had their portions before beginning on their own, and many shifts were resorted to by some members of households when food was insufficient to allow others to share it. Even children never lost their good behaviour at meals, and did not grab or beg for food. But they were not trusted with much responsibility. Very few children were given the job of carrying food from one part of the island to another, as had been the practice before the famine since, as the food situation became acute, there had been too many cases in which food baskets had been tampered with en route. But while in matters of hospitality all the *forms* of etiquette continued to be maintained throughout the period of the famine, its *substance* radically altered. No longer was food actually shared with visitors. Moreover, after food had been cooked it was not hung up in the traditional way in the ordinary small open baskets from the rafters, but it was concealed—sometimes even locked up in a box. Instead of being offered food immediately he entered a house, a visitor was immediately given an apology for its absence.

In this development kinship ties were affected, though not quite in the same way as the more general rules of hospitality. Kin who called in were treated as ordinary visitors; food was not shared with them. In some cases the kinsman would suspect that there was food in his host's house; he would sit and chat and wait, hoping that the host would give way and serve it. But nearly always the host would hold out until the guest had gone before unlocking the box and taking out the food. On two occasions a neighbour of ours came over to our engine house early in the morning and sat there with a couple of pieces of giant taro, eating them. He said that people had dropped into his house and he would have felt too much ashamed to have consumed food in front of them, yet having none to offer; if he had eaten, he would have had to share the food and there was simply not enough for them. He said that on many mornings he had had to go hungry to work in his orchard even although there was a piece of manioc or giant taro in the house, because someone had arrived at the time the household were going to have food. He could not possibly eat in the presence of the visitors without inviting them to share, yet he could not afford to give them any food. In many cases if food was left in a house a member of the household remained behind to guard it. Here, it was stated to Spillius, the inmates were often not so much afraid of theft by strangers but of the inroads of kin who normally would have been welcome to come and take what they pleased.

In the definition of kin interests that took place under the stress of famine there was some atomization of the larger kin groups on the consumption side and a closer integration of the individual household group. (This normally meant elementary family but often included other kin.) Even at the height of the famine it appeared that within an elementary family full sharing

of food continued to be the norm. The atomization tended to be most strong
where food was most desperately short—and it must be remembered that
supplies varied considerably in different groups, depending on their size and
their wealth in land. But in one respect the strength of kin ties was manifested, in the common practice of pooling supplies, especially where food—
though scarce—was not desperately short. Closely related households 'linked
ovens' (*tau umu*) by each drawing upon its own stock of food and then sharing
in the work of the oven and in a common meal. Sometimes this arrangement
even involved shifting residence. One man, when the food shortage began,
moved with his wife and children about a quarter of a mile to his mother's
dwelling—'We joined, we have one oven, there isn't any food.' In another
case two men who were not siblings but closely related agnatic kin of the
same small lineage joined forces and lived with their families in the one household. In some cases, too, kinship ties continued to be implemented fully
despite the food shortage. Thus, a son of the sister of Pa Samoa's late wife
continued throughout the famine to live with Pa Samoa, his adoptive father,
since his own father, of different lineage and different clan, was miserably
short of food. In other cases too, claims of the 'adhering child' were treated
as binding even at such a stringent time. There was at least one case where
the real father told the child many times to return home but she refused and
continued to be fed by her adoptive parent. In other words, the Tikopia
avoided where possible their general responsibility or undefined responsibility for kin during the famine, but showed no disposition to reject responsibility which had been specifically defined by undertaking. What the
famine did was to reveal the solidarity of the elementary family. But it
also brought out the strength of other kin ties personally assumed, as in a
household.

Problems of Distribution in Ceremonial and Ritual
What now did the Tikopia do about their ceremonial and ritual obligations
to furnish food (apart from hospitality to casual visitors)? Food ordinarily
is vital to the Tikopia in any kind of ceremony, no matter how small. As
regards major functions, during the year of the more severe food shortage no
initiation ceremonies or marriages took place and funeral performances were
drastically shortened. The Tikopia stressed in all these cases that lack of food
was the chief reason for not carrying them out or for curtailing them. Spillius
reported that repeatedly in the *fono* it was shouted that 'Tikopia does not
exist without food. . . . It is nothing. . . . There is no life on the island without
food.' These expressions alluded not so much to biological survival as to
sociological survival.

Lack of food, resulting in lack of ceremony, doubly affected the morale of
the Tikopia. It was not until nearly June 1953 that any marriages took place,
but even then the two which occurred lacked important foods such as breadfruit, taro and banana. This was criticized as being unseemly, in particular
because there was not enough food of the type proper to be sent to the chief
as an acknowledgement of the wedding. The curtailment of funeral ceremony

was of greater impact. Because of the large number of deaths practically every household at some time or another was affected by the lack of food to perform fully the appropriate ceremonial presentations or exchanges. In some cases of people of rank this tended to involve them in shame and a threat to their status.

Some details of funeral ceremony will illustrate the complexities introduced into the social situation by the famine.

In normal Tikopia funerals there are traditionally four main types of food presentation associated with reciprocal obligation: (a) *vai*—food given to family mourners in general by friends and kinsmen, (b) *kupukupu* (with *kava*)—food given to chief mourners by their mothers' patrilineal kin, (c) *punefu*—food (with valuables) given by deceased's patrilineal kin to burial party, i.e. deceased's mother's patrilineal kin, as material and symbolic acknowledgement of their task, (d) *moringa tangata* (with *ara manongi*) —food (with valuables) given by deceased's patrilineal kin as a second presentation to the burial group, symbolizing the transfer of the soul of the deceased person to its ancestral home.[1] The problem which faced any household involved in a funeral by ties of kinship or friendship was how to use their sparse supplies to the best advantage, whether by lessening the quantities of food given out at each transaction or by omitting the response to some obligations altogether. In normal times there has been always of course an economic problem, but not usually an acute one. What the food shortage did was to enforce a closer calculation of output-input relations. Behaviour on such occasions provided an index to the intensity with which obligations were felt. Certain general patterns emerged. In the early stages there was a reduction in the *size* of contributions to ceremonial and in their quality rather than in their *number:* as the crisis developed there was, however, a sharp falling away in the number of contributions to a particular funeral, i.e. some contributors failed to appear. For a time this affected the organization but not the *structure* of the funerary ceremonial. While individual household contributors cut out some of their contributions, enough were supplied by other contributors to maintain each type of ceremonial intact. As the famine developed, however, certain types of ceremonial performances were merged with others or simply omitted until at the height of the famine there were occasions on which even basic elements were abandoned.

An illustration of reduction in number of contributions at a fairly early stage of the food shortage was at the funeral of the son of Pa Nuikaso in April 1952. Only two *vai* were presented to the mourners instead of half-a-dozen or so which would have been normal, and only one *kupukupu* basket of food was presented jointly to the chief mourners, Pa Nuikaso and his brothers. This was specifically 'because the land is in bad condition through the famine; if the land had been well, there would have been a *kupukupu* for each of them.' Reduction in quality of the contribution was common. On this occasion the *kupukupu* food consisted of a paste, giant taro, manioc roots and aerial yams, with one sea fish of medium size; the food of the *vai* was

[1] See my *Primitive Polynesian Economy*, pp. 324–30.

similar. In neither was any pudding made with coconut cream, as would
have been essential in normal times.

But at such an early stage, every effort was made to fulfil traditional
obligations. At the funeral of Pa Nukutauriri in mid-May 1952, there was
much talk of the difficulties of the period: 'For the things that are performed,
where will the food come from? Because of the famine we are straining to
our utmost. . . .' and so on. Nevertheless, though the food provided was mainly
breadfruit paste, giant taro and aerial yams, about two dozen baskets were
made up and sent out as the *punefu*, the principal presentation. At the Nuikaso
funeral, no food was taken along by well-wishers after the initial period to
feed the mourners. But at least one such gesture was made for the funeral
of Pa Nukutauriri. I saw a woman carry a basket of manioc and aerial yams
there 'to feed those dwelling in the house'. The reason for her gift was that
the mother of her husband's mother was sister of the mother of the widow
who was principal mourner. This food was taken without recompense in
either food or other goods being given, and was for general consumption.
The basis of the presentation was a specific kin obligation but the food was
not presented to a specific individual. But the woman's husband explained
to me that while there was no direct reciprocation, there might come a time
when the recipients, conversely, would bring food to mourners in his household. This illustrates how in the economic calculations that went on a person
might deliberately continue to maintain what we would regard as a fairly
remote kin obligation because of its long term value. He could argue that
when such a future funeral would occur the land might have recovered and
in such case it would be precisely such a distant kinsman whom he would
wish to swell the funeral contributions. (I have no evidence that this man
neglected his nearer kin obligations, but he could argue that near kin would
almost inevitably assist him anyway.)

As the famine developed, however, obligations to the more remote kin of
necessity had to be abandoned by many people. When I asked Pa Ngatotiu
of Taumako if he went to the funeral of Pa Niuaru of Kafika, he said 'No'.
I said 'Was he not your kinsman?' The reply was 'Indeed, he is kin but it is
a bad time'—meaning that he could not afford the food gifts which he would
have had to take.

It is important to note that the essential link between food presentation
and attendance at a funeral as outside mourner continued to be maintained
throughout. It was not the practice to acknowledge kin obligation by presence
at a funeral without food. For preference a person would ignore the kin
obligation by staying away from the funeral altogether. In other words, the
Tikopia continued where possible to maintain the formal *structure* of response to obligation. What they did was to curtail the *sphere* of their obligations, to make organizational, not structural, change.

The famine had, at times, unexpected effects. The need to substitute one
food for another because of shortage did not always operate only in the
direction of inferiority. I noted one instance of this. Towards the end of May
Pa Ngarumea and his wife made a food presentation to the family of his

father's brother's son, from which a member had gone off in a recruiting vessel. Since the family was in mourning at the departure, the appropriate food should have been of the poorer variety. But because of the difficulty in finding the foods of austerity the presentation included at least one food, giant taro, ordinarily deemed too rich. 'In the times when food is plentiful, giant taro and taro must not be taken; papaya, pumpkin, manioc, sweet potato, *futu*, *nonu*, *poupou* (fruits) should be taken. Nowadays, because the famine has descended, giant taro is included.' So in a sense the rigours of mourning were abated by the rigours of famine. But this depended upon the socially recognized intensity of obligation. Shortly afterwards at the funeral of the son of Pa Siamano, a discussion arose about food presentation. It was stated that there would be no *vai* because of the famine. Likewise, there would be no company of young men and women as would normally assemble to farewell the deceased—there was nothing for them to eat since there were no *fukau* and other wild fruits available. Bearing in mind the previous case, I asked if giant taro would not do. I was told 'No,' that the mourners were prohibited from eating it. But if giant taro could be taken in the early case, why not here? 'Because when a person goes off on a voyage the mourning for him is mild; people dwell inside only for a short time—it is called an easy abiding, that for a voyage.' But for a funeral the obligation was more stringent and the requirement of poverty in the quality of food allowed no revision upwards—at least at that early stage of the famine.

In strong contrast to this maintenance of the spirit of ceremonial obligation was the denudation that occurred about two months later. By this time food was getting exceedingly short, and people in some households faced starvation. There had been thirteen deaths in fifteen days, and for some funerals there had been minimal provision of food. When, for instance, a girl of Fenumera died, aged twelve years, all the food for the oven which was prepared was about five small *pulaka* (giant taro) split into halves, making one small basketful for presentation to the mother's brothers' group, who were responsible for the burial. At this time it was customary in the poorest households to restrict the ceremonial to: wailing; burial; one small oven to feed the mourners and allow of acknowledgement to the burial party; and a few goods for the *punefu* to accompany the food.

In normal times, some days after the burial, ceremonies known as *moringa tangata* and *ara manongi* take place. Among pagans, these were often separate, even until 1952; Christians, under pressure from their teachers, had merged these ceremonies about ten years before. But during the famine—owing specifically to shortage of supplies—the pagan practice too was to merge these ceremonies on a single day.

The more elaborate aspects of ceremonial were among the first to suffer in the famine, those which were linked with special status-symbols. Pa Fenuatara and I were discussing the funeral ceremonies of a child from Resiake, his own grandchild, and also grandchild of the late Ariki Taumako. He said 'That one in Resiake, if the land had been well, its property would have been lifted'

—meaning that even though it was a child its chiefly ancestry would have merited a special funeral[1] with much greater quantities of food and property changing hands than usual. He said 'When a funeral is one which "lifts property" we know it is weighty; weighty things are to be done.' He mentioned that a ritual elder (*pure*) is also a proper subject for such a special funeral. I gave as an instance to the contrary the funeral of Pa Maniva, the recently deceased ritual elder of Taumako. Pa Fenuatara replied 'The oven of the elder is not just kindled as a commoner—but here is a lineage without food, because the famine is great.'

At a later date, however, one saw even normal basic funeral obligations tending to be omitted. At the funeral of Pa Niuaru in July no food contributions (*vai*) were brought by sympathizers from outside. Until the onset of the famine this would have been quite abnormal. A question was also asked about cooks, by a member of the funeral party. 'I don't know if there are any cooks or not,' said Pa Fenuatara. But someone replied: 'Ah! There is one only'—a man whose wife was the daughter of Pa Niuaru's brother. The absence of a group of cooks was a most significant change, since this service to wife's lineage by affinal men was normally one of the most regular in a man's whole life. The theme was pursued by the party among themselves. 'They just haven't got enough basis for attendance', was the explanation— meaning that they couldn't muster the contribution of green food which tradition dictated they should bring. A discordant note was introduced by one cynic who said 'The cooks are in full force when it is a funeral that "lifts property" '—meaning, they come for the share-out. But he was immediately taken to task by Pa Fenuatara, who rebuked him with a sharp 'What are you saying!' It was further explained to me that formerly the immediate filial kin (*fare tama*) did not go to do the work of the oven. They left that to the cooks. Now in the famine such differences between the specific functions of agnatic and affinal kin, with all their emotional and symbolic loading of status and obligation, tended to be minimized. Even the son's mourning for his father was abbreviated on this occasion. Pa Muriava, the son and chief mourner, began at one point to say rather apologetically to the assembled kinsfolk that he intended to keep fairly light (*fakamama*) mourning. The kin group agreed at once. 'Is the land in a good condition? The land is in a bad condition—bad indeed! If a man just sits in the house he will get ill. It is better to cut short the mourning and go and get food. No one will laugh at you. . . .' and more to the same effect. The normal period of mourning might well have been three months. But 'You stay three days in mourning only,' said Pa Taramoa to him—and as a son of the Ariki Kafika and a classificatory brother of the chief mourner, this man's words carried great weight. Thus, the mourner was reassured on all sides.

To sum up, the famine thus resulted in, and was regarded as morally justifying a range of modifications in ceremonial funeral behaviour: contraction of the participant group; reduction in size and in general in the quality of food transactions; merging of phases of ceremony; lopping off of 'extras'

[1] For explanation see *Primitive Polynesian Economy*, pp. 327, 330–1.

as status indices; dropping of structural differences in task-work; curtailment of obligation-period.⟩

It is noteworthy, however, that while greatly attenuated, the 'bare bones' of the funeral ceremonial still persisted with almost no exception. There was even at the height of the famine, some solemnization of a death. There was *some* mourning, *some* preparation of food, *some* transfer of property, *some* assembly of kin along structural lines. The skeleton of the social order was preserved, however attenuated the content. And it should be noted that though ties of remote kinship tended to atrophy under the pressure, and even close affinal ties tended to be intermitted, close agnatic ties and also close matrilateral ones tended to remain. The father's kin and the mother's kin of the deceased were represented by *some* of their members.

This norm is illustrated by an exception of a very striking kind. It occurred in the lineage of Maniva. In one week the head of the lineage, old Pa Maniva, and three of his grandchildren died, and the funeral organization finally broke down. The three children were those of Pa Tekara, the idler mentioned earlier (p. 64), who had by now been taken off to the Solomons as a labourer. For the first of his children to die, a girl of three years, there was wailing, but no oven was prepared. For the second, a boy of five years, there was wailing, but no special oven, though a small basket of food was separated off from the oven prepared for the funeral of his grandfather, who died the same day. For the last, a girl of twelve years, there was no oven; there was not even any wailing; and—an extraordinary circumstance—no kinsfolk were at the burial. These were all shocking circumstances to most Tikopia, even in their stricken state. I had noted that in 1928 there were no ceremonies for the burial of a stillborn child. But in this case it was a well-grown girl. The mother's brothers of the girl did not come according to custom, to bury her. They were occupied with the funeral of their own father, who had died three days before, in another village, and moreover they apparently were registering objection to the thieving habits of their absent brother-in-law. The mother herself, seemingly half-crazed with grief, was wandering abroad, without initiative. Even the father's brothers and other agnatic kin did not appear, though they lived close by. The burial was actually done by some young girls of the village, not direct kin. They had no pandanus mat in which to wrap the body, as custom dictated, so it was buried in a coconut leaf floor mat— 'like a cat' said one of our attendants, laughing, in a rather horrified way. (The comment of an elderly man of rank on this was 'She was wrapped up in a floor mat? They hadn't a sleeping mat—the poverty of commoners.') No Mission teacher was at the burial—one who lived near said that afternoon that he had not been asked to attend, but that he would probably go and give a brief prayer over the grave in the evening.

When I asked about the non-attendance of the father's kin, in particular, my informants professed ignorance—'their own idea'. But it seemed pretty clear that two sets of circumstances were behind their abstention: resentment at Pa Tekara's lazy, thieving propensities, which had involved his family in this disaster; and extreme shortage of food and other property for ceremonial obligations, aggravated by the drain on their already scant supplies by the earlier deaths, including that of the head of their lineage. Resentment, shame and apathy all together seemed evident in the lack of response to such a fundamental canon of Tikopia custom as wailing over a dead child of one's own lineage. This was the most acute example I met of the effects of the cumulative impact of a reduction in resources on fulfilment of ceremonial obligation.

I have described the state of obligations towards kin produced by the famine. What was the state of the obligations of the people towards their chiefs? Here the situation developed in a more complex way.

Relations between Chiefs and People

In normal times there are reciprocal obligations between Tikopia chiefs and people—each is expected to provide food for the other, according to occasion. How did the famine affect this? In the early stage of the shortage of food these obligations were maintained—all the customary tokens of acknowledgement to the chiefs were given, and they in turn did their best to carry out the traditional forms and in so doing to preserve the canons of hospitality and support to their people.

In mid-March, after the Ariki Taumako returned from a trip to Anuta (in the Government vessel) he held his *pungaumu*[1] at his house Motuata, in Ravenga. At mid-morning of the appointed day there were about two dozen men and half-a-dozen women at work preparing food, and contributions were being brought in by representatives of all the major groups in his clan, and by other related groups. By mid-day, more than fifty people had assembled. The cooks included several men of high rank, attending because of their affinal connections with the chief. The food included taro, giant taro, breadfruit paste. Two days later a feast (*anga*) was held—not one of a series, but according to custom. 'The feast of the chief who has jumped aboard to go to sea, who has voyaged; just a feast—a custom of this land.' (*Te anga te ariki ne sopo ki te moana, ne forau: te anga fuere—tukutukunga o fenua nei.*) For this about 100 men and women assembled with contributions—including four men of Faea who had not come to the *pungaumu*. The food included sixty-five bundles of taro, forty-seven giant taro (several of these 4 feet long, taking two persons to carry), seventeen coconuts, two bunches of yams, seven baskets of breadfruit paste and one basket of taro paste. At a conservative estimate, there were 1,000 lb. of food. Its composition was significant, since at this time already the main foods in the island were beginning to be sago and cordyline. People had put their best resources into the support of their chief.

---

[1] In *We, The Tikopia*, p. 423, I discussed the *pungaumu* as a category of celebration referring to the social significance of the 'injury' or 'death' of a person. The concept should, strictly speaking, be widened to include the *risk* of injury or death, e.g. the Ariki went to Anuta and returned safely. But there was social disturbance owing to his departure; the risk of his death was an injury to the land. In this sense a *pungaumu* in celebration of his return is a rite of social reintegration.

Such support continued. Towards the end of April, for instance, the Ariki Taumako was given three salmon-trout from the lake, by a man who had a good catch; the chief had caught only two. When I asked about this, the reply was 'A token of respect to the chief; a custom of this land.'

Yet the expenditure of food on the chief's feast in March was not without its critics. Some of the people of Potu sa Taumako, the chief's own village, were annoyed with Pa Motuata for having organized the *anga*:[1] they thought food too scarce. 'If it's made, where will the food come from?' For this reason there were no *raurau* presentations to the assembled crowd at the morning kava; only *roi* for chiefs and visitors. The absence of a general food distribution was in effect because the clan might have gone on strike. When I asked about the chief's view, I was told 'He wanted one, but he was ashamed to ask, because the clan had objected'.

It was in the light of this that Pa Motuata later composed a dance song, of the *mako lasi* type, likening the feast to a *mori* dance, and jeering at the objectors.

> *Tafito:*   *Ie fakanaia tino*
>   *Naia ki te mori E!*
> *Kupu Toto:*   *Te roto ra fetukoke*
>   *Na ku verea te voe*
>   *Saua rei te voe*
> *Safe:*   *Mako nevaia*
>   *Ku nevaia ko te roto.*
>   'Rejoicing of the body
>   Rejoicing in the *mori* O!
>   The mind is vacillating
>   But now the legs have splayed
>   The legs have been caught up.
>   Dance of rejoicing
>   The mind rejoices.'

The net effect of this is to say that once people were engaged in the feast they enjoyed it greatly, just as when one gets caught up in a dance, and they ought to have been ashamed of their grumbling.

But as the famine developed both parties found it difficult, and often impossible, to keep up mutual food presentation. One effect of the famine also was to reduce the gap in wealth between chiefs and commoners. One man, a commoner, said to me that because of the hurricane the chiefs were no better off than other people. Illustrating the lack of contact between them —at that time he remarked that he didn't know how his own chief, the Ariki Taumako, was situated for food supplies. (In fact, the Tafua and Taumako chiefs were in rather better case for food than most people; the Ariki Kafika and the Ariki Fangarere were much worse off.) There were several results of this. Firstly, the normal role of the chief as channel for inflow and disburse-

[1] For details of an *anga v. Primitive Polynesian Economy*, pp. 222, *et seq.*

ment of food supplies for his village and clan became impossible. Secondly,
though for months the conventional gifts of *monotanga*[1] acknowledgment
to a chief, as at a funeral, were kept up, they had to be abandoned in a number of cases, as with the children in the family of Pa Tekara. Thirdly, even
the fulfilment of a customary norm could mean social difficulty. By Spillius's
report, on one occasion it was embarrassing to the Ariki Taumako to receive
from a senior man of Kafika, Pa Raroifi, a great basket of food. This man
was probably at the time the richest in food on the island, and the chief was
hardly able to reciprocate in kind for many months. Finally, there were
occasions on which support to a chiefly family was totally lacking. Things
got so bad that, according to Spillius again, when a son of Pa Fenuatara,
heir-apparent to the Ariki Kafika, died, there was no one to bring the father
the *vai* of mourning—a circumstance which was a shock to the whole community.

In another way also the position of the chief degenerated as the famine
drew on—in the growing incidence of theft from his cultivations and orchards.
Despite stock statements about the sacredness of chiefs and their property,
the food supplies of chiefs have not in practice been free from thieves.[2] But
the famine exacerbated this greatly. Stealing from the chiefs became almost
barefaced. I remember the Ariki Taumako standing outside his house
Korofau one morning, looking ruefully at his sweet potatoes, which had
been raided (probably by children living nearby), and realizing that there was
little he could do about it. He made no public objection. The conventional
reaction to discovery of a theft of one's property is the *forua*—the high-
pitched yell of protest. As time went on, this yelling was discouraged by the
executive officials—on the grounds that as nearly everyone seemed to have
been stealing it was mere hypocrisy to yell about one's own losses; 'with one's
mouth full of someone else's food, maybe!' But with chiefs the reason was
different; they tended to refrain lest it be thought that they were anxious to
maintain themselves at everyone else's expense; they were ashamed to protest
when all others were also suffering. Pa Ngarumea said in general terms, 'the
territories of the chief stand without interference only so long as the land is
in good condition. But let things develop like this, they are thieved from.
When the land is firm (food is plentiful) people pay respect to the things of
the chiefs, but when there's a famine people go and make sport of them.'

Yet in strong contrast to this was the view, fostered by the *maru*, but
expressed also by commoners, that if the situation really became one of life
and death for the community as a whole, then whoever might die, the chiefs
must live. This was repeated in public assembly—at which the chiefs were
rarely present. But it also came out on other occasions, especially in times
of crisis. Some of this was the sententious type of expression which the Tikopia
are very fond of putting out as the ideal rule. But there was more behind it.
In part it was the keen wish to preserve the chieftainship, one of the most
important symbols of their communal integrity, intact. (Cf. behaviour in

[1] Cf. *Primitive Polynesian Economy*, p. 221; *Work of the Gods*, pp. 70–2.
[2] Cf. *Primitive Polynesian Economy*, pp. 260, 270–1.

the hurricane, pp. 76, 264.) In part it had a strong element of anxiety, of traditional kind. When I told a commoner of Faea, Pa Rarosingano, of the death of Pa Niuaru, he commented 'There you are! He died of starving himself.' He said this was the result of the words of the *maru* Pa Pike, who on the day of rice distribution said that ordinary people should abandon their entreating of food from the chiefs, so that the chiefs should have plenty. I asked him if this was a proper attitude to have taken up. He replied 'It's quite correct, friend, it is right that the chiefs should be satisfied with food.' Then he went on 'Here is the root of it—the expression—the water-bottles of the chief should be kept full, lest the land be slain.'

This revealing statement referred to the ancient tales of the sweeping out of some sections of the early Tikopia population by the ancestors of the present chiefs, in order, it is said, to cope with pressure of population on food supplies. Pa Rarosingano went on in fact to tell me the story which I had heard many times before, in 1928/9 as well, of the expulsion and extermination of Nga Ravenga of old. This moral is, if the food of the chiefs be not kept ample, they may again rise and expel the commoners from Tikopia. About this two further points may be noted. One is that this fear is always expressed in terms of the chiefs (and their lineages) driving out the commoners, and never vice versa; the supremacy of the chiefs, and indeed their right, up to a degree, to act thus are never questioned. The other point is that though in the circumstances of 1952 this might seem a very nebulous prospect, it was not conceived as such by many commoners—though I think it was regarded as absurd by the chiefs themselves. One incident in fact provoked unwittingly a mobilization of commoners of Faea to resist expulsion.

In sum, as far as social obligations of a ceremonial kind were concerned, the spirit of the social order was preserved except in a few isolated instances; the institutions continued. There was reduction in quality and in quantity of performance, severely so in many cases, as the famine became acute. There was also widespread evasion or rather omission of obligation. But there was no radical denial of obligation.

Moreover, as the apex of the social order, the chiefs were still held in their places. There was absolutely no questioning of their right to privileged survival. Although it bared some of the underlying tension between chiefly groups and commoners, the famine revealed the degree of the strength as well as weakness of the Tikopia social structure.

MODIFICATIONS IN RELIGIOUS RITUAL

Obligations in the specifically religious sphere present a question of great interest, since one might expect that the sanctions for performance of the ritual of the ancient gods would be stronger, and the denudation owing to famine less, than with simple kinship obligations or obligations to chiefs. In fact, this was not the case. For the Tikopia Christians, now by far the greater proportion of the population, the issue of course did not arise, except that a few of the more zealous would have rejoiced to see the pagan rites fail, and the majority would have had a nostalgic regret at their disappearance. But for the hard core of pagans, the chiefs and their entourage, the issue did not seem to present any great problem. There was some worry, lest food shortage interfere too drastically with the rituals. But diminution in quality and quantity of food were accepted with fair equanimity, and even cuts in the sequence of events, so long as there was a minimal amount of food for *some* celebration. The chiefs and other responsible pagan senior men were far more gloomy and concerned at the general state of malnutrition and shaken public order than they were with the threat to the specifically religious aspects of their obligations. It is noticeable too, as mentioned earlier, that no special kava seems to have been performed by the Ariki Kafika or other chief to try and alleviate the famine; specially emphatic appeals were made simply in the ordinary kava rites.

The following set of omissions and abbreviations of ritual in the Work of the Gods in the middle of 1952, recorded by myself and Spillius, illustrates the way in which the famine affected the performance of this great cycle.[1] Throughout the whole of the ritual, including the very weighty celebration of the yam harvest in Kafika temple, wherever the sequence called for pouring of libations from green coconuts, these were lacking. This part of the rite was simply omitted; there was no attempt to simulate it, as by pouring extra libations of kava, or of water from coconut water-bottles. The general Tikopia principle seemed to be that one could substitute for food, but not for drink; in this they adopted an attitude of literalism. For a number of minor kava rites, however, there was no food offered to the gods and none eaten by the participants afterwards. 'Some kava has food prepared, other kava are made without food—there's lacking the wherewithal to make it.' So for the first day of Somosomo (at the beginning of July) there was no *roi* prepared—the chief gave no word to prepare it, since food was so scarce. For a later rite he ordered *roi* to be made—but instead of being prepared with sago flour and coconut cream, as is habitual, it was simply made of giant taro, wrapped up and cooked overnight in the oven. No bunches of bananas were formally stood up at Somosomo—there were none available, and the early morning kava was consequently lacking in them. Neither was the basket of mixed food known as the *tua popora* prepared—there was no pudding for the offerings to the gods, and therefore nothing for the *tua popora* to accompany. 'No food', was the reason simply given for the omission of both. This implies also the omission of the ceremonial presentation and exchange of food gifts at this time, between the principal participants. Again, there was no provision of areca nut by the representative of the house of Tavi—none was available. Because of the shortage of coconut frond, the sacred mats of Ama and Katea were not plaited at Somosomo, and the special little platters of coconut leaf known as *lingilingi* were not made for Takerekere; *pulaka* leaf was used instead. Concerning these Karangatiaite-forau, son of Pa Fenuatara, who was doing most of the work at these rites

[1] See my *Work of the Gods in Tikopia*, London, 1940, I, 98; II, 309, 316, 324–5; I, 10, 107, 70–72, 334 *et seq.*, 59–60.

said 'There are only long coconut fronds (old and high); I am tired of climbing; if there had been any low fronds I would have plaited *lingilingi*.'

The food shortage also affected the ritual of the sacred canoes. When I discussed with Pa Fenuatara the programme for the Work of the Gods of the *tonga* of 1952 he referred to the order of events for the *taumauri*, the prime vessels. He said 'Vakamanongi (the sacred canoe of the Ariki Fangarere) will not fall singly because, friend, the famine is great; they will be aggregated.' In other words, food shortage necessitated the celebration of a number of vessels together. Moreover, in the *fainga vaka* some vessels were omitted. For example, Karoata, one of the sacred vessels of Kafika, was not re-sacralized; the lineage of Torofakatonga, in whose charge the vessel was, said that they had no food for the ritual basket over which the kava would be performed, and which would be sent to the chief. It was left to the discretion of the owners of the canoes as to whether they made such celebrations or not that season. The rites of the canoes that were re-sacralized raised some problems. Whereas those of Kafika chiefly lineage were normally supported by food contributions from various clan members, on this occasion the Kafika house had to supply these alone. In other words, the ties between chief and those who owed him allegiance tended to be weakened by the lack of food. This was shown in another way by a dramatic incident—one of the sacred baskets of food for one of the Taumako most sacred canoes was rifled as it lay overnight in the oven. This was an unheard-of outrage, and the news was received by the Kafika family, with whom I happened to be, with shocked surprise. The Ariki Taumako and his supporters were also much disturbed, and there was great speculation as to who might be the thief—gossip pointed towards a member of Kafika household.

As a final example, the *nuanga* may be mentioned. This turmeric manufacture was undertaken on a greatly reduced scale because of the famine. A couple of months ahead of the time one of the experts told me that because of the food shortage the only *nuanga* would be that of the Ariki Kafika—the turmeric-making of the other chiefs could be abandoned, but not his—because of his prime god, whose special care and symbol is the turmeric. 'The Akoako—the primary turmeric—is never abandoned,' said my informant, himself a Christian. In later discussion about prospects, the Ariki Kafika commented 'There is turmeric growing, but there's no food for its preparation.' And after the manufacture of the Kafika turmeric had begun (it was indeed not abandoned, and it was the only one) various people said that if there had been no famine there would have been a large *nuanga*, with plenty of participant groups, since there was plenty of turmeric in the ground.

This last example stresses how to the Tikopia a technical process such as turmeric-making, if it takes place in a ritual setting, must have food celebrations to implement it.

Apart from a certain hard core of rites, then, in Tikopia the proposition was—no food, no ritual. Sociologically speaking, for the anthropologist, the famine separated out those performances which were judged by the Tikopia to be the kernel of their pagan religion. The less essential were omitted, the more essential were retained, and food was saved or scraped up for them, or whatever food was available for ordinary consumption was oriented towards them—directed into ritual channels before being eaten. The proposition was not quite without exception: in some circumstances lesser kava rites could be performed without food offerings. Moreover, certain key rites including kava required that they be performed by persons holding specific offices, primarily that of chief, and many of these were the role of the Ariki Kafika. If he was unavailable, as through illness, then the rite could not be fully performed. As it happens, he *was* ill during part of the Work of the Gods in 1952, hence various rites were omitted completely; this had nothing to do with the famine.

It has been pointed out that performance of certain rites in the famine period, as in the Work of the Gods, definitely demanded a break with tradition in that inferior foodstuffs had to be substituted for those normally regarded as necessary. Yams, for instance, had to be eked out with other token vegetables in celebration of the yam harvest. Again, the quantities normally demanded simply could not be provided. How did the gods take all this? Were they not believed to be angry? The Tikopia view here was essentially a rational one—they attributed to the gods and ancestors an understanding spirit. There was an expression which covered such a situation: '*Tatou e sakasaka ora fuere*', 'We are just seeking welfare', meaning that the rite was performed with minimal offerings, the procedure in itself being the offering to the gods. All that was asked was just to be allowed to 'keep going' as it were. No special benefit was requested, and so no special amount of food was needed.

A point of theoretical interest is why an almost infinite regress of substitutions was apparently possible for at least some major rituals, and not for ceremonies as, for example, marriage. One reason would seem to be that ritual performances to a high degree involve immediately circular or self-contained transactions. The food offering is made, then withdrawn by the people who make it, and put into an ordinary meal. If the level of offering is symbolically determined a small offering is still significant; practically the level is almost irrelevant. This is not the case with *exchanges* between different social units, and here it is important to notice that in 1952 such ritual exchanges tended to drop out. When one turns to marriage again, though some of the transfers are symbolic, or partly so, much of the set of transactions is regarded in grossly material terms. Their satisfaction cannot be given by a minimal level of transfer. This is so at least in short term. In long term, if marriage is to take place at all, *some* solution must be found. In the case of funerals some solution *must* be found even in short term, since death is not a matter of decision and burial cannot be delayed. In other words, the optional or non-optional character of the social relation is also significant.

This attitude of treating fulfilment of the religious rituals as a matter of intelligent appreciation by the gods and ancestors rather than an attempt to get them to ameliorate conditions, would seem to be linked with views as to the causes of the famine. (Cf. pp. 79–81.)

3 Fish drive on the reef. Traditional nets of various styles are in use

A Tikopia oven. Stones are being heated in a pit, and banana and other large leaves are being prepared for the wrapping of the food

A chief at work. The Ariki Taumako planting taro. He is clad in bark-cloth, has a shell arm-ring, is wearing his hair long and loose, and is using a wooden digging-stick of ten li's and two

4 Carrying off a food gift for a canoe builder. The women is wearing a head-ring of human hair, from the hair-cutting of her male kinsmen

Institutional Developments from the Famine

For the most part, the effects of the famine on Tikopia institutions were in the direction of curtailment and limitation. But in two institutions, those of organized dancing, and of organized public assembly, the effect was the opposite—they were stimulated by the crisis.

Dancing

It might seem that a time of stringency and strain, of malnutrition and death, would be most unsuitable for the promotion of dancing. This point was particularly significant in a society such as Tikopia, where not merely good taste but specific restrictions impeded mourners from appearing in public, and above all from participating in a dance. Yet there was much dancing during the famine period, even when the deaths were at their height. This apparently macabre situation was in strong contrast to Tikopia in normal food conditions; a couple of deaths of persons of rank had then meant that no dancing took place in the community for months. Tikopia resort to dancing in the crisis was not due to irresponsibility or despair; it was the result of deliberate policy. The more responsible Tikopia argued thus; dancing is one of the major pleasures of the Tikopia, a characteristic feature of their life. It warms the heart of man, and takes his mind off his cares. Therefore, it is good to get people up on their feet, dancing, instead of lying down to mope, get ill and die. The expression was 'the dance makes the land good' (*te fakalaui o fenua te mako*).

But certain major questions had to be met as a result of this attitude: what should the form and content of the dance be? What about mourning obligations? What should be done if the people did not respond?

The first major question, involving a number of subsidiary ones about place for the dance, type of song to be used, degree of formality, accompaniment of performance by meal or not, was settled fairly easily, in terms of the existing mechanisms. Dancing took place on the usual grounds, depending on whom the organizers happened to be. Some songs were composed specially for the occasion, in particular when it was given a formal shape as a festival; other songs used were well-known favourites. In the early stages of the food shortage, some of the dances, held in festival form, with bodily decoration and ceremonial, acknowledgements of composers and dance-leaders, had a meal as accompaniment. For one at Asanga at the end of April, *masi* paste, aerial yam and giant taro were brought, and for one in mid-May, aerial yams only. Later, meals were omitted, as food became really scarce. Some of the new dance songs made specific reference to the disasters which had overtaken Tikopia. Thus, at an Easter dance festival a *foi mako lasi* composed by Pa Vangatau was chanted:

Tafito:	*Ruru fenua*
	Ne oko mai i tokerou
Kupu:	*Fepokai ko tatou*
	Afa rei ku repuo

G

    Safe: *Mako nivaia*
               Ne oko mai ki oi E!
               Shaking of the land
               Arrived here from the north-west
               Startled we arose
               The cyclone then had struck
               Dance with abandon
               It arrived upon us O!

The 'shaking' of the land refers to the terrific pressures and whipping effects of the hurricane, and the song in general expresses people's dismay. The term I have translated as 'with abandon' (*nivaia*, or in other songs, *nevaia*) is a conventional expression of an empathic kind; in other contexts it might be rendered as 'Rejoice'. It has an ironical connotation here—somewhat equivalent to 'dance in your disaster; there's not much else you can do!'
    Another song was a *foi lau*, composed to the famine itself:

    Tafito: *Tou kakatakina*
               Te onge roa
               Te matangi ne au
               Nai sorosoroia
               Te fenua kua pa rei ki te kere
    Kupu: *Tou ofo oke fetokoki*
               E furi te roto
               Pe nia ia ka popo ki oi.
               We are hungry
               In the long famine
               The wind came
               Afflicted by it
               Things in our land have crashed to the ground
               We go off to make ends meet
               We turn over in our minds
               As to what indeed we shall lay hands on.

    Such 'songs of disaster' indicate an interesting aspect of Tikopia behaviour. It is obvious that they tend to emphasize the social significance—dare one say 'social value'—of the events. But to what point? On the one hand they show an objectivity about distressing circumstances which is rather unexpected —a conquest over depressing fears. On the other they may be held to offer some kind of cathartic activity by facing the disaster, emphasizing its public and common character, its shared character, and the ability of Tikopia to turn it into material for a roaring chorus. It becomes thus part of the cultural furniture, and does not remain a vague impersonal phenomenon. This view, somewhat speculative, does bear out the strength of the 'social digestion' of the Tikopia to which I have made reference earlier.[1]

    [1] *We, The Tikopia*, p. 11.

As regards mourning obligations, these were kept, but at a diminished level. Thus in mid-April, the dancing ground at Raropukapuka was still out of use because of two deaths of young men which had occurred some months previously. But dancing was taking place on other grounds in Ravenga, though the deceased were of relatively high social status. By the first week in May the former ground again was in use by young people for their nightly dances. The personal interdiction on 'rising to dance' shortly after a near kinsman had died or gone on a voyage still held. Pa Panapa, who had lost a son some months before we arrived, was in seclusion from public affairs for several months after, and first attended a dance in mid-May. (His wife still stayed in retreat.) The village of Asanga, from which two prominent members went off to work in Honiara in mid-May, stopped dancing completely for some weeks, and their closer kin were absent from a dance festival in early June. And after a large recruitment of labourers had gone in early June, I noted three weeks later that no dancing had begun in Ravenga as yet— though Pa Ngarumea asked me to request it, on the grounds that the land would benefit. But the shortening of the mourning period (cf. p. 88) allowed attendance at a dance sooner than usual. Moreover, there was a tendency to restrict the burdens of keeping mourning taboos to a single member of a family as its representative, and permit the others to follow their usual pursuits. Thus, Pa Fenuatara took a very active part in a dance festival at the beginning of June, while one of his sons, Kavasiko, stayed away to mourn for his son of one of their close kinsmen who had died from a fall from a cliff only ten days previously. This constriction of the field of mourning had a double effect: not only did it allow people to get back into the less gloomy social life and keep up their spirits; it also lightened the burdens of keeping them supplied with mourning food, and let them use their labour fully in food production almost at once instead of keeping it idle, in the house.

As regards attendance, at a late stage it seems from Spillius that some compulsion was applied to get people to the dance. But in general participation was voluntary.

This was demonstrated by a dance festival originally sponsored by the Ariki Fangarere in June 1952. It is the custom when a chief or other man of rank has given a dance or other festival (i.e. taken the main responsibility for provision of food) so that people have eaten at his expense, for the guests to go the next day and *sanga*—clear the ground and plant food for him. He in turn makes an oven and gives them a meal in recognition of their reciprocation. In the case of this dance festival, while there were about fifty people dancing, only about seven people turned up to work. When I asked why, the reply was simply 'Were they tired, perhaps?' A couple of nights later there was a sequel. Tikopia dancing involves singing, and a dance was put on in order to perform songs which had not been used earlier. About thirty people turned up, of whom about fifteen danced, including the Ariki Taumako and the Ariki Fangarere. Later the Ariki Tafua came and sat on a coconut grating stool to watch, and finally the Ariki Kafika came and sat on the outrigger of a nearby canoe. But the dancers dwindled. Pa Rarovi, a keen dancer, came, stood for a while then went off, objecting to the dance beat. And there were no young people, ordinarily the mainstay of a dance. Finally, the dance was abandoned. It was significant that with all four chiefs present, giving their patronage, so to speak, there was not enough support to make the dance viable. References were made by them and others to *te au pariki* —the wretched younger generation—who lacked public spirit. But no attempt was made by their elders to rout them out on that occasion. 'The right to absent oneself', as it might be termed, is a well-marked feature of normal Tikopia social relations, which in such matters are very permissive. I asked later of one young man why he and his companions did not attend. He said 'It was held that it was a lazy kind of dance—a *tusoko*. They like their bodies to swing in a dance—what they like is the *matavaka*. They hold that they are not skilled—the bachelors and the maidens; they hold that they are skilled in the *matavaka*, and so they like it.' In actual fact, they could do the *tusoko* quite well. But they objected to it as not lively enough; what they wanted was an energetic dance with plenty of vigorous rhythm, so they did not join in.

In other words, dancing may be medicine for the soul, but the Tikopia attitude is that even when in a parlous condition the patient should be given some latitude of choice in the medicine he takes. But there are limits. The *matavaka* is in fact more than any other the stock dance of the Tikopia,[1] and for this compulsion later was applied.

Organized Public Assembly
One of the most marked social developments of the famine was the way in which the organized public assembly (*fono*) became a regular part of Tikopia life. In normal times an occasional public assembly might be called by a man of rank in an emergency. But traditionally, the only regular *fono* was the sacred assembly at Rarokoka as part of the Work of the Gods. Here annually, in a ritual setting, a formal proclamation was made by the Ariki Tafua enjoining upon the people norms of public conduct. One of its functions was to set out and reannounce periodically some of the major preoccupations of the leaders of Tikopia society about social order.[2] In this formal address theft and thieves were reprobated and control of population advocated.

The secular *fono* might touch upon much the same themes.

It would seem that development of *fono* is part of a recognized procedure in Tikopia to cope with famine. My old friend Pa Maneve explained to me the reason why one of his cousins had changed his residence in the generation since I was in Tikopia before. The house Nukuro stood in Potu sa Kafika. But Pa Nukuro fought with his brothers over land and when he died his wife took her children to live in a house in Tai controlled by Pa Maneve, whose father's sister she was. 'They dwelt in it and then my aunt died and while they continued to live there the famine fell. When the famine fell her

[1] See *We, The Tikopia*, p. 504.
[2] See *The Work of the Gods in Tikopia*; vol. II, ch. VII; *Primitive Polynesian Economy*; p. 44.

son began to steal. But in this land when the famine falls the *fono* is set up. Then they seek for the thieves. They sought and sought the thief and found him. I was angry and I drove him away. So he left and went to dwell there— in his present house.' Mention of this famine, which probably occurred in the late '30's, illustrates the *fono* as a device for the identification of thieves. It will be noted that action was taken not by the aggrieved losers of food but by another citizen, a kinsman, who deemed himself to have some responsi- bility after the *fono* had elucidated the facts.

The setting, the procedure and the treatment of the secular *fono* were very different from those of the ritual *fono*. The assembly took place not in the ritual district of Uta inland, but in whatever village on the coast was appro- priate, and the addresses were made not by a chief but by executant officers. The procedure was for one or more executant officers (*maru*) to summon the local population to attend a meeting place on a certain day at a certain position of the sun. The meeting, which was informal as far as seating and attention went, was then addressed in a mixture of argument and injunction, punctuated sometimes by threats, on a chosen theme. This was commonly the need to reduce theft, though some other subject for common action was sometimes raised. The essential procedure of the *fono* was to give an occasion for discussion of a public crisis or event. But it also allowed some expression of personal grievances. It allowed the officials not only to give vent to their own views and intentions; it also allowed them to obtain some idea of public feeling and the amount of support that they could command. For the most part the *fono* did not take very specific decisions. As a rule conclusions were expressed in the form of rather vague affirmations of broad questions of principle, such as for example that people should stop stealing. Sometimes the assembly broke up with no general expression of view at all. At times decisions were taken to control actions of individuals. But the efficiency of the *fono* as an instrument of public policy and the public court of appeal was governed to a considerable degree by the fact that it was expected to be summoned by *maru*. If a man of no influence attempted to call a *fono* he would get no assembly of people. On the other hand, an assembly called to listen to a man of influence tended on the whole to subscribe, on the spot at least, to his arguments. Thus, to some extent, the *fono* could be an instru- ment for the achievement of personal power as well as public policy.

The *fono* in 1952/3 followed this pattern. An interesting account of its political aspects has been given by Spillius,[1] and I accordingly give here only an outline of the development of the institution, particularly as I saw it in 1952.

Calling a public assembly to cope with problems of food shortage began before we arrived in Tikopia in 1952. At the end of February or in early

---

[1] *Op. cit.* esp. pp. 6, 12–13, 18–20, 22. My account of the *fono* here is based upon my own observations. But I have been greatly helped in my understanding of the general develop- ment of the *fono* by a narrative account of the events after my departure which Spillius, at my request, wrote up from his notes immediately on his return to England in 1954. This forms part of the basis of a further comparative study of the *fono* by him.

March 1952 a *fono* was summoned in Potu sa Kafika by my namesake Remon, a son of Pa Fenuatara. As a young man of rank he was entitled to call such a gathering in his own village. But since the organization of executive officials by Tikopia tradition has been for some generations primarily in the hands of the Taumako *maru*, the young man asked that these men should assist him. Accordingly, the speakers in the assembly were Remon himself, Pa Ngarumea, Pa Rangiuvia (brothers of the Ariki Taumako), Pa Vangatau and Pa Nukutapu (brother's son and son's son respectively of Pu Avakofe, whose name was revered as the great *maru* of all time).

The first *fono* we recorded was about a month after our arrival. This was called by Robinson Vakasaumore, a son's son of Pu Avakofe, and who emerged as time went on as the most powerful active political force in Tikopia. In response to this, his first summons, to discuss problems of theft, people failed to attend in impressive numbers. It was said that some of them objected to the young man's attitude. Angry at this, Robinson summoned a second meeting the next day for about 8 a.m. About 125 men, women and children were present, mainly local residents of the Taumako clan. They sat around in a rough oval group, leaving the centre clear. Up and down this space Robinson moved addressing the crowd, his main subject being fulmination against theft, and reference to the efforts of the *maru* to safeguard the property of the people. About a fortnight later another *fono* which he called was better attended, by about 150 people. Again the subject was theft with particular reference to two recent incidents. The main themes stressed were: evils of theft; that all people of Tikopia were in a bad plight together; that the people should go and plant food, not steal it; that restriction might have to be put on general access to the central planting area of Rotoaia, including the swamp; that people should prepare their ovens during the day when their actions and the food they used could be observed by others; and that it was a matter of public shame that the anthropologists' food stores, which were equivalent to their orchard, were being raided. Here then was an amalgam of statements of general values, specific instructions and comments, and a reminder of their public common interest. The speakers on this occasion were Robinson himself, followed by three other Taumako *maru* and then by two Kafika speakers, one a member of a chiefly house and the other being Pa Rarovi, the principal elder of the clan. The first two speakers strode up and down the whole length of the assembly. The others addressed parts of the assembly only and at times two speakers were operating in different areas of the gathering. The assembly broke up after about three-quarters of an hour to begin a dance festival.

Other *fono* took place at intervals as, for example, one called by Pa Ngarumea three weeks later and at which nearly 100 people were present. At this meeting the main theme was the injunction not to steal but to go and plant food; to leave aside the planting of taro and concentrate on putting in the quickly maturing crops, sweet potato, manioc, spinach.

Three points in particular were noticeable about these meetings. Firstly, there began a practice which later became standard, of the Sunday *fono*.

In the early stages the *fono* was irregular, but as the famine developed it became a regular Sunday assembly with mandatory attendance for everyone on the side of the island on which it was held. (Some village *fono* were also held during the week at a later stage to discuss theft and the plan of work for the next few days). Secondly, it became clear that while in theory any *maru* could call a *fono* and address it, the tendency was for only those *maru* of strong personality to take the initiative. Some who by the closeness of their relationship to the chiefly house were most entitled in theory to arrange and address meetings did not do so, whereas others with no better entitlement took a forceful lead. This was partly because (as one *maru* told me) according to convention when a *fono* takes place, only the *maru* of the locality will address it. (This is not an invariable rule but is generally kept.) Again, some *maru* it was recognized were not skilled in the art of speaking. ('Its basis is here in the belly. Thought comes up from the belly.') Hence, some men who felt their own inability, never addressed a public gathering. Moreover, not all *maru* who addressed a gathering were listened to with equal respect. From this point of view then, the *fono* became a means whereby men could test out and develop their influence in the society. The outstandingly successful organizer of *fono* and speaker in the assembly was Robinson Vakasaumore. He had, however, in the beginning an adventitious aid. Since he had just returned from Honiara, the centre of administration, and spoke with an air of great authority, it was widely imagined that he spoke in the name of Government, or at least that what he said was an expression of Government's views. In one discussion I had with a fairly typical family this point came out specifically. They said of Vakasaumore and his influence, 'Certainly when he addresses the assembly he "speaks Government", he follows the speech of the chief of the Government.' They added that 'The Tikopia listen to anyone who has gone abroad and heard the talk of Government. They will listen to such a one but not to any old talk, to any foolish rambling.' In fact, of course, Robinson, in much of his general policy of food conservation and in his fulminations against theft, was stating what would have been the views of Government. But he had no official status and in fact had had no contacts with administrative officials. Moreover, much of the implementation he proposed was entirely his own opinion. But the Tikopia could not distinguish clearly between these. Thirdly, the reference made to the possibility of imposing restrictions on access to and use of cultivation areas foreshadowed the later institution of specific rules for public behaviour and punishment for those who disobeyed. Towards the end of July residence in Rotoaia was in fact barred, but by the Ariki Tafua, not by the *fono* as such, though the *fono* took measures to restrict access to the area. According to the records of Spillius later, more than a dozen different kinds of rules were set up in the public assembly between about December 1952 and May 1953. Though at first these rules tended to be disregarded or evaded, as time went on control became more and more stringent and punishment for breach of them more and more severe (see also pp. 71–2).

What was important in this development especially was the recognition that whereas in times of relative abundance of food theft could be treated as an offence against individuals, in times of great scarcity theft imperilled not only individual relations but the whole basis of the social order and check upon it became then a matter of public policy. It was the function of the *maru* as executants to crystallize public opinion and to mobilize the resources of the community to meet the emergency.

Apart from the main type of *fono* described, there were variants. In Faea, Spillius recorded, the Ariki Tafua did not follow the custom of chiefs in general, but personally attended the *fono* and addressed it. This gave somewhat more formality to the proceedings though the *fono* operated essentially in the same way. A special type of *fono* in Ravenga in 1952 was that of the women. They did not speak at all in the ordinary *fono*. But as the famine developed the wife of the Ariki Taumako and some other women of rank called together rather irregularly an assembly of women at Potu sa Taumako. This, though well attended, lacked the crispness and force which later developed in the major *fono*. Discussions were on the same main themes, in particular the avoidance of theft. But no very specific action resulted from the women's deliberations and the men treated the female *fono* with some amusement. Yet here was an interesting development, non-traditional, under the stress of crisis, by members of the society having no formal channels of collective expression.

What emerges from a comparative consideration of the *fono* at different times is that its functions for the Tikopia were not fixed. They developed according to the gravity of the situation and the force and precision with which public action could be organized by men of rank. This explains why it would be a mistake to rely upon the mechanism of the *fono* alone, without strengthening, to serve as a regular legislative and judicial body for the Tikopia. Its structure in its traditional form is too amorphous to allow public action except after a crisis has been well under way. It is significant that once the famine came to an end in Tikopia and food became really plentiful again, the *fono* lapsed. By November 1954 ill-feeling between the Ariki Tafua and the pagan chiefs had resulted in the cessation of all meetings of the *fono*, and a visiting Government officer was asked by Tikopia to try and persuade the Ariki Tafua to collaborate again. Apparently this overture was successful, and in April 1955 it appeared that the *fono* had been meeting again regularly. But by mid-1956 it seems to have ceased again. Even the epidemic had failed to induce people to mobilize in public assembly—though perhaps this was because so many were sick. By 1958 it was still not functioning.[1]

Since the *fono* in Tikopia in 1952/3 was called into being to deal with the crisis of food supply, the major subjects it dealt with were naturally food conservation, theft, and work to remedy the situation. Much of the discussion, by standards of Western debate, was violent, rambling and inconclusive. Few formal resolutions were taken, and there was a great deal of what would appear to be futile accusation and recrimination, as well as moral injunction

[1] I am indebted for this information to Mr John Hearth, and Mr James Tedder, who successively served as District Commissioner, Eastern District, Solomon Islands.

Everyone joined in reprobating theft—even those who had committed it. (From the point of view of self-protection, this was to be expected.) It might seem that one of the most important functions of the *fono* was to give occasion to let off public steam at a time of great emotional crisis. But although it did seem to provide such function, as the situation worsened, and the need for more substantial restraint became obvious, the technique of the *fono* crystallized, and more specific rules took the place of most of the diffuse, general fulmination. The institutional structure became firmer in response to the crisis.

Conclusion

It is evident that Tikopia social reactions to the famine involved elaborate adjustment. As a community they did not lose their identity and dissolve into a set of fiercely competing individuals struggling for food; they retained their corporate character, including elaborate interconnected series of ceremonial transactions. Conceding a great deal to the force of circumstances, they nevertheless managed to keep the greater part of the structure of their institutions unimpaired; they made many organizational but few structural adaptations. But they did not act as an undifferentiated group. There was great variation in their ability to meet their difficulties, and their corporate survival owed much to the sense of responsibility of some of their leaders, for the most part those who by ascribed status were expected to be in positions of command. In the sphere of convention, they retained their manners; throughout the famine they followed out in practice their code of etiquette. Their morality suffered more. Their morality of action as regards theft was in many respects deplorable, a widespread breach of the rule. But the moral ideals themselves survived, given lip service to by all, though pursued in practice by only a few. The width of the gap between precept and practice might be attributed, in the case of the pagans, to the lack of moral judgment associated with their gods save in circumstances immediately affecting these gods. This religious disinterest in theft did not exist in the moral code of the Christians, who yet seem to have stolen just as much as the pagans did. But what the retention of the moral ideal did was to allow of a more rapid return than otherwise to a state of comparative honesty when sanctions of force were introduced; there was the backing for conformity when the organization for it was worked out. This moral continuity was very important for the survival of Tikopia social life in its systematic form.

From the point of view of a more general study of social change in the community, one is entitled then to continue to talk of Tikopia society as an entity.

CHAPTER V

Economic Resources and Influence of the External Market

The crisis of the famine illustrated most vividly for the anthropologists one of the major pressures upon present-day Tikopia—that of maintaining their food supply. But by its dramatic urgency the famine threat tended to obscure more ordinary social developments, especially in the economic sphere.

Since 1929 there has been a definite enlargement of the economic horizon of the Tikopia. By 1952 this was evident in the greater scale of their wants, especially in consumer's goods; in the much greater range of experience in employment on the part of many of their men; in an improvement in their capital possessions; and in their greater familiarity with the use of money.

Alteration in Tikopia Standard and Level of Living

Even in 1929 Tikopia, though it could be described as primitive, was not in the Stone Age or in its north-west Polynesian analogue, the Shell Age. Two traditional forms of wealth, adze blades (Tridacna shell and stone) and wooden fish hooks, had been discarded as useless.[1] For many years, as indicated in Chapter II, the people had used iron or steel tools, though they did not possess by any means enough to satisfy their wants, and were avid to acquire more. But in other respects in 1929 Tikopia material culture was simple, with few European tools and consumer goods.

A generation later things were different. Through the earnings of their labourers abroad they had acquired a wide range of Western items, and an appreciation of what aid and comfort could be obtained from them. The threshold of their economic expectations was, therefore, much higher in 1952 than in 1929.[2]

In such a discussion one may distinguish between *standard* and *level* of living. The former indicates an ideal, a frame of consumption which people aspire to; the latter, the actual condition attained.[3] A raising of standards may be normally thought to precede a raising of the level of living. While for the Tikopia of 1952 this was generally true, there were cases in which the new

[1] The stone adze blades and some of the larger shell adze blades were conserved as sacred objects, but the smaller shell blades were looked upon simply as antiques of no special interest. But in 1928/29 and again in 1952/3, learning of European interest in these objects, their owners willingly sold them as *toki na mua* (adzes of olden times) for fishhooks (or if children, for sweets.) Some people kept a look-out for them when digging in the cultivations. What I think was the last antique wooden shark hook was acquired by us in 1952.

[2] See my *Primitive Polynesian Economy*, p. 48.

[3] *Report on International Definition and Measurement of Standards and Levels of Living.* U.N., New York, 1954, esp. p. 2.

goods came to them in concrete form—brought back by their young men from abroad—before they had realized effectively that such goods were indeed attainable by them, or sometimes before they even knew their use. But the most notable characteristic of 1952 as contrasted with 1929 was the Tikopia internalization of standards which previously they had regarded as appropriate only to others—Europeans—and not to themselves.

To illustrate this consider first their homes. Tikopia architecture had not changed much by 1952. (A few houses differed in walling and had more height.) In particular, foreign materials such as corrugated iron and sawn timber which became so common in many other places in the Solomons owing to the war, were lacking in Tikopia. The absence of troops, and heavy transport costs, had prevented their introduction. Even the use of iron nails had been minimal and the traditional techniques of house construction were still current. There were no wooden floors. Coconut-leaf floor mats and pandanus-leaf sleeping mats were plaited as before, and the technique was as widespread with apparently as much skill.

But in furniture and household equipment there were new objects, new drives towards their acquisition, and a diminution in the use of several articles of native manufacture. As an example of the range of interest in Western goods, in about a fortnight after we landed in 1952, we had requests from various Tikopia for the following articles: scissors, lamp, kerosene, torch battery, spoon, mosquito net, writing paper, toilet soap, chewing gum, cigarettes, biscuit, meat, rice. Whereas in 1929 few European household items were to be seen, our observations in 1952 revealed a wide range of them. A property census (taken by J. Spillius) indicated the relative frequency of the major items. Whereas in 1929 no household except that of the Mission teacher had a mosquito net, by mid-1952 there were over a hundred mosquito nets in Tikopia, on the average almost one for every three households. In 1929 a wooden box with a lock was a much prized and very rare item; by 1952, though still greatly prized, there were more than 200 of these in Tikopia, on the average roughly two to every three households. Kerosene storm lanterns, formerly regarded as out of the range of any ordinary Tikopia, were becoming quite common by 1952, and it was expected that every young man returning from work abroad would bring back a four-gallon drum of kerosene for such a 'light'. Gallon jugs and large bottles were coming into fairly common use as water containers, tending to substitute for the traditional coconut water bottles which were almost ceasing to be made, though the sinnet cord holder was still in use. Galvanized pails were coming into demand not only for carrying water but also for holding vegetables.

Technical equipment had not undergone such changes. The Tikopia form of canoe with paddles was still fully in vogue. Sailing was rare, but there was no indication of any turnover to a Western type of boat. Ordinary Western tools had become more common. In 1929, while nearly every household had a bush knife, there were few axes and very few adzes indeed. In 1952 nearly every household had two or more bush knives and axes were common— so much so that they were rarely borrowed. Adzes, however, were still relatively scarce and were still prestige laden; they tended to cost more and, in any case, were not usually stocked by the stores frequented by Tikopia overseas. Even in 1952 they were still largely in the hands of the chiefs and their close kin, and the present of an adze was, as a generation before, one of the high points of gift-making during our stay. In 1929 saws were coming into use by craftsmen, and brace-and-bits were keenly borrowed for boring holes for lashing in canoe-building. There were only a couple of these instruments in Tikopia, and the loan of one was reciprocated by a basket of food. But no other Western tools were in demand. By 1952 hammers, planes and some other carpenter's tools were in some request, though they were still on the luxury list. In agriculture, the traditional wooden digging sticks (see *We, The Tikopia*, Plate XXV) had been nearly abandoned, the Ariki Taumako being almost the only man who still used one. Crowbars and other iron rods were keenly in demand, for their weight, piercing power and compactness, and women showed themselves not at all conservative in their use, being if anything more clamorous for them than the men. Among men our spade became popular after a time and was continually on loan; one man took the precaution to bespeak it as a gift a year in advance of the end of the expedition.

Yet the use of some tools, even in 1952, was not always fully understood. One elderly man asked me for a carpenter's plane, but it turned out that he wished it merely for the plane-iron in order to haft it as an adze. Electric torches were tending to become common, but there were hardly any batteries to keep them in use, and the purchasers had not really considered the problem of re-charging. There were no sewing-machines or bicycles. Fairly rare still were blankets, European clothing, suitcases and knapsacks, camp beds, domestic china, tins cups and plates, and Western toys for children. The possession of such items, as with others already mentioned, was a sign of prestige though they also served utilitarian purposes. The integration of such items into Tikopia usage was shown by the choice of a camp bed as a bier for the dead father of a labourer recently returned from the Solomon Islands, who had brought the bed back with him.

In 1952, as in 1929, bark-cloth was still regarded as normal Tikopia dress. When the anthropologists wore Tikopia dress, the Tikopia took it as a compliment but also as a natural way to behave. The first hint of a tendency to regard it as old-fashioned or 'native' came from Robinson Vakasaumore, in some ways the most advanced of all Tikopia, who expressed himself as being ashamed when he saw photographs of Tikopia so dressed. But this was before he returned to the island. After his return he wore European clothing for a long time, but finally took up bark-cloth dress as regular wear. For the Tikopia in general, calico and other items of Western clothing had become much more common by 1952 than in 1929, though as before they retained considerable prestige value. By 1952 a calico kilt was almost *sine qua non* for a young man, red being the 'proper' colour, with green and white less desirable. By 1952 all young men endeavoured to acquire short trousers (preferably white) and a shirt to wear at dances or other formal occasions.

Over this was worn the calico kilt; a handkerchief was commonly worn round the neck or head. Older men wore either calico or, more rarely now, the traditional *kie*.[1]

Another article which had acquired prestige value and entered into the standard of living since 1929 was the chair. In 1929 nearly all the Tikopia felt that sitting on a chair was a strange and awkward proceeding, characteristic of Europeans. A coconut-grating stool had been the traditional seat offered to a Tikopia chief at audiences or on other ceremonial occasions, but its use had never been very common. For comfort the floor had been the preference of all Tikopia, though a few—including the Ariki Kafika—liked the novelty and status of a chair. But by 1952, when it had been observed abroad that Europeans regularly sat on chairs and when the chiefs had had some practice in using chairs or stools, such articles became objects of demand. They were asked for greatly by chiefs and other men of rank when the expedition's furniture was being distributed at the end of our stay, and some prudent men established a lien on such items months in advance. Deck chairs were preferred, but a camp stool was welcome if nothing else was available. The use of a chair by a Tikopia chief had a double function. It gave him a seat of status and some comfort; it also facilitated the traditional custom of commoners moving around in the chief's vicinity at a level lower than his head. Commoners did not ask for chairs. They knew our supplies were small, and were content that they should go to men of rank.

There had been a great increase also in Western items of personal adornment. By 1952 mirrors, razors and scissors for shaving and hair cutting had become common, as also combs of European style. Beads still retained their former appeal though they were now much more common. Almost the only items of Western goods in which the Tikopia no longer showed interest were the plastic tooth-brush handles which, in 1929, were eagerly taken to work up as imitation turtle-shell earrings. By 1952, no more interest was displayed in these, because of the vastly improved import of ordinary ornaments.

The range of new objects available for the young Tikopia man or woman had changed the concept of what constituted an attractive person. Talcum powder and eau-de-cologne or other scent were in demand for attendance at dances or for lovers' meetings. European rings and bracelets were now commonly exchanged between lovers, signifying serious sentimental intent. Perfumed soap, expensive and disappearing quickly, was also a valued gift. In 1929 some of these articles were known but were not at all in common use by the younger generation. By 1952 they had come to be the accepted thing. Among the unmarried men and women a radical change had also occurred in hair style. The efforts of the Church against the pagan dances, coupled with an interest in imitating European and Melanesian style, had led most

---

[1] The number of women who could make *kie* mats was now very small and these articles were rare. The technique was still the same, as I saw by comparing two mats made by the same woman, one in 1929 and the other in 1952. The technique is Anutan, and when Tikopia went in 1952 to Anuta there was great competition to trade for *kie*. There were no new dyes for either these or bark-cloth.

men to cut their hair short. By 1952 it was very rare to see the long bleached manes of the men in the dance, as had been common in 1929. Conversely, the young women in 1952 were tending in some cases to let their hair grow longer, though they all still conformed to the traditional custom of shaving after marriage. Decoration of the body by tattooing had also become a matter of some self-consciousness. By some young men who had been abroad it was thought that only 'bushmen'—a derogatory pidgin-English term for unsophisticated Melanesian natives—marked their bodies so and that it was a token of savagery. Some young men, therefore, led a campaign to reduce or eliminate the tattooing custom. The faces and wrists of young people tended to be tattooed but less heavily than before and it seemed likely that the chests and backs of the young men, for example, would be left unmarked, contrary to traditional custom.[1]

[In the use of new articles and in the formation of new tastes great influence was exercised by fellow labourers from other Solomon islands and from the New Hebrides whom the Tikopia had met at work, and who were much more sophisticated in their knowledge of Western ways. In Melanesia, as in Africa, a great deal of what is termed 'westernization' generally is in fact the influence of other non-European people of broadly similar background.]

[The introduction of new Western items led to a modification of traditional behaviour.] One of the major tasks of any Tikopia household is the preparation of food, which is traditionally done jointly by men and women. Cooking in Tikopia often involves not only collecting large pieces of firewood in considerable quantity, but also strenuous pushing about of hot stones and covering and uncovering the oven, using large pads of leaves. When rice became fairly common during the famine, cooking utensils for it were at a premium since the Tikopia had no appropriate vessels of their own which they could use for boiling. There was a keen demand for saucepans and pots. There were also eager claimants for any empty large tin cans from our household and quite a waiting-list for them developed. One man offered two shillings in cash for a tin. The scarcity of utensils forced some households to combine their cooking activities, but ignorance of techniques sometimes led to the same procedure. At first many Tikopia put in too little water with the rice or did not cook it long enough and it was hard. Pa Fenuatara, realizing this, invited a clansman of his from Faea—who had been abroad—to come over and show his family how to cook rice. The new knowledge soon spread. The saucepan or tin broadened the labour basis for cooking. Since twigs instead of branches could be used for the fire, the demand for heavy firewood was cut down. Since the fire was small and needed no hot stones, its care could be left to children and it rapidly became the children's job at this time to cook the rice. Sweet potatoes, manioc and local spinach soon also began to be cooked by means of a saucepan. Fish were usually cooked in leaves resting on an open fire in the traditional manner, but boiled fish began to be more common. Returning labourers later introduced a new dish called *supsup* (soup), a sort of vegetable stew strongly laced with coconut cream.

[1] Cf. Raymond Firth, 'Tattooing in Tikopia', *Man*, 1936, No. 236.

When on one occasion fish was thrown in as an experiment, the taste was approved by the young returned labourers who cooked the dish. (But portions were not offered to the older people nor did they ask for a share.)

[Another use for Western cooking utensils was to make tea.] In 1929, the anthropologist's house and that of the Melanesian Mission Deacon were the only two places in Tikopia where tea was brewed. In 1952/3 there were at least eighteen houses where tea was made and offered on social occasions. It became especially in demand at parties in some bachelors' houses late at night. While then in 1952 rice and tea were still prestige foods, they were becoming more acceptable and in regular demand by all who held cash earned abroad.

Some of the new items introduced, by acting as substitutes, reduced the amount of labour involved. This was so with cooking utensils and also with the large glass containers which replaced the traditional coconut water bottles. These containers saved work in two ways. They obviated the laborious process of scooping out the interior of each coconut with a special tool made for the purpose and they reduced the frequency of journeys to the spring for water. On the other hand, they increased the dependence of Tikopia upon the external market, since they were goods which could not be made locally and could only be acquired by money.

Some of the most useful introductions in the field of production were goggles and rubber thongs used for under-water fishing. The Tikopia were used to diving down to as much as ten fathoms after large greensnail (*alili*, a species of large *Turbo*), but they previously had not had any form of under-water shooting. With rubber thongs cut from a motor tyre and a steel arrow obtained from old war-time submarine netting in Tulagi harbour (in the Central Solomons, near the former capital of the Protectorate) they were able to get fish. Goggles which increased their clarity of vision were either imported or were made locally from pieces of glass set into wooden frames. In 1929 this form of fishing was quite unknown. It was introduced only after the war, and by 1952 had become very popular with the young men.

[It will be clear that by 1952 the Tikopia had incorporated into their lives a number of new Western items partly as consumer goods and partly to improve their production. These new items had already begun in various small ways to affect their traditional technology and their traditional patterns of work. Moreover, while a generation before their interest in such new kinds of goods had been keen, their attitude then was one of curiosity and haphazard acquisition rather than of systematic demand. Now their standards of comparison were much more realistic and by many young men in particular it was realized that a variety of these new goods might be installed permanently as features of their island life.]

[The process of incorporation was uneven.] For a few individuals the standards expanded very greatly. In 1952, the ownership by Robinson Vakasaumore of a camera, and the possession of a shotgun by Pa Fenuatara, were unique for Tikopia. Even then these were beyond the wildest dreams of most Tikopia and there was no assurance that they would continue to be serviced with films and cartridges respectively. But while for most Tikopia standards had been raised to a much less extent, in some particulars, for instance mosquito nets, hurricane lamps, hair combs and rice, the community as a whole accepted the new items and presumably hoped to perpetuate them. The more direct and personal appraisal of consumption standards during the last generation had meant a considerable 'raising of sights' for the Tikopia community. How far it is a realistic appraisal depends upon the degree to which the Tikopia can continue to provide themselves with media of exchange in the open market. This means considerable expansion of their resources.

Expansion of Resources
It will be clear that by 1952 intensified agriculture and fishing alone had not been able to meet the enlarged demands of the modern Tikopia created by their rising population, let alone the expansion in their wants as they became more familiar with Western goods.

Critical in the Tikopia attempt to enlarge their resources was the factor of communication. From the point of view internal communication was not very significant and over a generation Tikopia had undergone no development. In 1952, as in 1929, there were no roads, no vehicles, not even bicycles. The old paths and the beaches were used for foot traffic as before, and inland I observed few variations from the beaten tracks and hedged paths of a previous generation. On the lake or the reef waters no outboard motor disturbed the silence; only canoes plied as before. As regards external communication, which is vital to Tikopia development, there had been no changes in substance. No air transport had developed. Tentative enquiries of mine about possibly having a seaplane land on the lake produced the official reply that the lake was too small and too surrounded by hills to be safe. As regards land planes, there was no economic inducement to construct an air strip—even if enough level ground could have been found and if the Tikopia had been willing to spare it from their cultivation.

Shipping is the only key to the Tikopia economic situation. Here there was a marked alteration from 1929, although in degree rather than in kind. During the year of my first residence the only vessel that called at Tikopia was the *Southern Cross*, the Melanesian Mission yacht, and that only once. Only two other vessels appeared on the horizon. In 1952/3, during the whole period of the expedition sixteen vessels called, an average of nearly one a month. This was mainly because of the famine; but if the famine had not occurred, by Spillius's estimate at least six vessels would have called on other business. (Ten unknown vessels which did not call were seen on the horizon.) The isolation of Tikopia had now been lessened. The hills still resounded to the cries of '*Ieful Te vaka!*' (Ho! A vessel!) when a ship appeared on the horizon. But no longer did canoes chase the vessels and attempt to bring them in to shore or pursue them at sea with offers of trade. Vessels were indeed so frequent in 1952/3 that many Tikopia became blasé about them. Fewer canoes set out to meet incoming craft and some people from Ravenga did not even bother to visit the anchorage side of the island at Faea to see them.

Shipping in the generation until 1952/3 comprised primarily the Mission yacht and vessels of traders, recruiters and the Government. For the most part these were quite small craft—the Government motor vessels were ordinarily only about 60 feet long and a recruiting launch from Vanikoro was only half this size. Normally these vessels did not come primarily for purposes of trade, and only a small amount of exchange usually took place between them and the Tikopia. For several years before and after the war until 1950 a trader from Vanikoro paid visits to the island, but specifically trading vessels were rare because the volume of Tikopia goods available for trade was so small. Trade in souvenirs took place with the yacht *Yankee*, which exchanged lengths of calico, knives, fishhooks and tobacco for dance bats, spears, cowrie shells and other objects. But the tendency has always been for Tikopia to seek gifts from visiting vessels, not only commercial exchange, and from craft such as the *Yankee* the Tikopia received sizeable disbursements of tobacco and fishhooks as gifts. The increase of shipping was associated not so much with developments in trade as with the provision of important new avenues of employment for labour.

Changes in the Employment Situation

In 1952, the general forms of occupation in Tikopia in agriculture, fishing and craft work were still as in 1929, but some of the traditional techniques had begun to lose ground markedly. One of these was the pursuit of bonito, which seemed to have become much less regular in its shoal appearances and for the capture of which the skills of lure-lashing and trolling seemed to have become much less widely known. (In fishing generally there seemed to have been a secularization of the pursuit by the abandonment of many ritual formulae.)[1] Apart from underwater fishing with goggles, rubber thong and steel arrow, hardly any new techniques of production had been introduced. Inlay in pearl shell or in greensnail shell, an importation of style from the Central Solomons, was practiced by one Tikopia craftsman, Pa Maneve, on walking sticks. He also was one of the first 'curio' makers in Tikopia. By 1952 he was making bonito-hook barbs of greensnail shell simply for exchange with ships that called; occasionally he strung some of these into a necklace. Technically these barbs were not adequate, the material being far too breakable; but they seem to have been fairly popular with visitors. (There was also a little manufacture of clubs, and of model canoes, for sale.) Another minor craft practised by some of the young men was the construction of their own ukuleles from local wood and imported strings. I saw two in 1952, each with four strings of piano wire, but in 1953, after their manufacture developed as a craze with the return of labourers from abroad, Spillius saw more than a dozen of them being made, all using imported gut for string.

In 1952 traditional forms and conditions of labour still operated with small modifications. Women had begun to take a limited share in the handling of

[1] Raymond Firth, 'The Sociology of "Magic" in Tikopia', *Sociologus*, N.S. vol. 4, pp. 97–116, 1954.

H

canoes, as I saw when we first came to anchor. Spillius noted later that one or two young women acted as paddlers in the arduous work of manoeuvring canoes in the flying fishing season at night. This, however, was definitely in response to the shortage of male labour through recruitment abroad. At no time did a woman appear as a crew member in one of the sacred canoes; this would still have been regarded as ritually very dangerous to her. A more marked, though temporary, modification in traditional pattern was the direction of labour by the *maru* towards the end of 1952 in order to cope with the exigencies of famine. Apart from the control of the time of works, labour was directed in particular from fishing into agriculture. Though possibly uneconomic in the case of a fishing specialist, this was in conformity with the prevailing Tikopia code, which stressed the primary importance of continuing work in the cultivations without respite.

In the period immediately after the war it would seem that there was considerable under-employment of labour resources in Tikopia. Land resources and technical methods were practically static and the population was increasing. Tikopia young men grew very restless and had no regular opportunity of voyaging abroad. Hence for a period of five years or so there were many escape voyages. Young men, nearly all unmarried, took canoes and, occasionally with the knowledge of their kin, but more often secretly, set out for the New Hebrides, Vanikoro or the Reef Islands. As was usual with those voyages, they were nearly always inadequately provisioned and their sailing equipment was rudimentary. Despite the fact that Tikopia are superb seamen and extremely tough and enduring at sea, many of these young men perished through storm or exposure. By checking through my censuses, and from other information obtained from Tikopia and from Government reports, it would seem that at least thirty such escape voyages took place in the post-war period. Through these about eighty men died (a few, on landing, by disease or exposure, but over seventy lost at sea); only about twenty survived.

Those who were fortunate enough to make land stayed in the Solomons or the New Hebrides for upwards of two years before being returned to Tikopia. The experiences of these men gave them some knowledge of the Western world, though rather an idiosyncratic one. The limitations of shipping space prevented the transport to Tikopia of most of the personal belongings and gifts which these men had wanted to bring back, but after their return in 1950 these young men tended to present themselves to their fellow Tikopia as sophisticated in the ways of the European, more proficient in pidgin-English and more knowledgeable about the direction in which the best interests of the island community lay. Later, some of them assumed significance in negotiations with the Solomon Islands Protectorate Government (pp. 272–3).

The almost obsessional interest of the young Tikopia men in going abroad after the war did not at first coincide with provision for their recruitment. But the Protectorate Government soon realized their interest. In earlier years recruitment from Polynesian outlying islands had been prohibited. Now a labour scarcity had developed in the Solomons, partly through general changes brought about by the war and partly through specific disturbances on Malaita—the 'Marching Rule', which had resulted in a substantial withdrawal of the largest and best labour supply of the Central and Eastern Solomons. This fell fortunately for the Tikopia in one way. The Government allowed recruiting once again and between October 1948 and the middle of 1952 four recruiting vessels had called and taken men away to work for Lever Bros. plantations in the Russell Islands and for the Timber Company at Vanikoro. In addition, Tikopia men had been taken into Government service as police and as hospital dressers and hospital gardeners. Others were working aboard the Mission vessel *Southern Cross* or other European craft, and several lads had been taken away to the Mission School at Pawa. From the postwar regular recruitment in October 1948 fifty-nine labourers were returned after six months with a poor working record, many having suffered severely from illness on the plantations; other batches of labourers were returned as their contracts ran out. But by the middle of 1952 we counted 175 men away from Tikopia. Further returns of labour from Vanikoro[1] reduced this number, but upwards of 140 men were absent until the middle of the following year.

By the middle of 1952 the proportion of male labour absent from Tikopia was serious. It amounted at the maximum to about 40 per cent of the effective working males and for most of the time was rather more than 30 per cent.[2] The Tikopia situation was thus in an analogous position to those so often described from Central and South Africa.[3] The figure which Spillius reports as that which the Government decided to take as the optimum for men away at work from Tikopia was approximately 110 or about one-quarter of the effective working males.

In considering this question of Tikopia labour supply abroad, the motives of the men are important. They may be said to seek three things: (a) income, expressed in money but regarded by them as representing food and other goods; (b) opportunity to see and acquire specific types of goods not obtainable from vessels that call; (c) adventure and experience of foreign travel and the status to be obtained at home through such experience. Here I would judge that there has been a significant change in the motivations in recent years. In 1929 the desire for Western goods as such and for adventure and

---

[1] In 1952 Vanikoro employers decided to replace Tikopia labour with labour from the Santa Cruz and Reef Islands because these men were regarded as more efficient. It was held that it was difficult to get the Tikopia to understand technical work partly because of their lack of 'intelligence', partly because of their unfamiliarity with pidgin-English. Orders and explanations had to be transmitted through the boss-boy and this wasted time. On the other hand, it was admitted that much of the difficulty in handling Tikopia labour was due to the Europeans in charge. Moreover, Tikopia labourers had the reputation for living quietly and causing no trouble. When food shortage threatened through lack of shipping the Tikopia accepted the situation whereas the Santa Cruz and other labourers protested and refused to co-operate. The Tikopia, it was held, were 'loyal' to Europeans.

[2] Taking the age-period of effective working males as between about eighteen to fifty-seven years, the total number by my census in 1952 was 428. See W. D. Borrie *et al.*, *loc. cit.*

[3] E.g. Margaret Read, 'Migrant Labour in Africa', *International Labour Review*, XLV, 1942, pp. 605–31: I. Schapera, *Migrant Labour and Tribal Life*, 1947, pp. 33–9.

the status accruing from it were most prominent in all the Tikopia who had been abroad or who wished to go. They did not look upon labour abroad as periodic, or a regular means of obtaining or enlarging the incomes of themselves and their families. By 1952, although several kinds of motivation were definitely present, on the whole labour abroad was looked upon as repeatable and primarily as a means of income enlargement or of maintaining economic stability.

While the labour recruitment represented a significant drain upon Tikopia productive capacity on the island, the incomes earned abroad were a very substantial contribution to the economic wellbeing of the community. But in 1952 and 1953, because of shortage of food in Tikopia, labour recruitment was regarded quite concretely by the chiefs and other responsible men as a means of securing food for the community. Measures were proposed by Tikopia themselves for advance payments in food either to a man's kinsfolk or to his chief for distribution to them. In 1929, Tikopia talking to me about work abroad had very vague notions about details of payment, and treated earnings as of the order of gifts made at the discretion of the employer in return for labour services. By 1952, many Tikopia had a very clear idea of the nature of wages and of the sanctions operating on employers. Their ideas about relative wages in different occupations and different areas—as between the Solomons and the New Hebrides, for example—were much vaguer. Relying upon the experiences of the few men who had worked in the New Hebrides at a period when copra prices were very high and wages corresponded, they were apt to exaggerate the average wage level there. Moreover, when they expressed their strong preference for work in the New Hebrides, they found it difficult if not impossible to grasp the District Commissioner's argument that the prosperity of the New Hebrides might be only temporary in the absence of a guaranteed price for copra, such as obtained in the Solomons. But, significantly, for the first time in my experience, these Tikopia were using a wage differential as argument—previously in reference to recruitment in bygone years they had referred to general non-wage conditions of labour when they expressed preference, or to the amiability of an employer in making them generous gifts.

What was the relative independence of these labourers or the degree of control which their community exercised over them? Even in 1952, the would-be labourer did not dispose freely of his own services. There were three main controls here:

(1) *Kin interest and sentiment.* Very commonly when a young man wished to go abroad either by canoe voyage or by ordinary recruitment, his father or some other elder kinsman tried to dissuade him and very often succeeded. The argument was often economic, that his labour was needed at home, but it was frequently also on sentimental grounds. As much as anything else it was the desire to avoid the claims of family sentiment which led, in the earlier post-war period, to secret canoe voyages made without permission from father or other senior kinsman. (But when a person set out on a voyage either

by recruitment or in a canoe, his immediate kin wailed for him in formal style, whether he had gone secretly or not.)

(2) *Control by chief.* Each chief was regarded as having powers of disposal over the labour resources of members of his clan. This did not mean he normally interfered with their daily work or choice of occupation. But it did mean that he was regarded by all Tikopia as having a legitimate veto over recruitment of his clansmen for labour abroad. His reasons might be partly those of kin attachment, but they usually included some political or economic elements. A chief tended, especially, to restrain his sons and his brothers from going away. He lost their economic support and their general backing for the time being; he also ran the risk of their dying abroad. It was particularly because of such risk of loss of life abroad that a chief, for his own reputation, tended always rather to restrain than to encourage recruitment of any specific person, quite apart from his own immediate interest in that person's services at home.

(3) *Public policy.* In the actions just described there are distinct elements of public policy. The chief, if pressed, could always justify his control of recruitment on the grounds of clan and community interest. The proof of this is in the converse case when in 1952 and 1953 chiefs deliberately encouraged the recruitment of men known to be incorrigible thieves, and in certain cases gave specific orders that such men were to sign on for work abroad in order to remove them for the time being from the community. In traditional Tikopia situations, then, social policy in the use of labour is consistent in the last resort with the attitude of chiefs. But as contact with the governmental administration and Western views has grown, this coincidence has no longer tended to be taken for granted. Now there has tended to be an assumption that a chief, in exercising control of labour power in recruitment, as elsewhere, will not be arbitrarily governed by his own personal wishes alone, but will have some obvious justification in acknowledged community interest. This is an instance of a more general process of translation of the personal rule of the chief into a rule which is an expression and instrument of public policy (see pp. 297–8). Moreover, in determination of this public policy the external administration has begun to take an increasing share.

This is illustrated by one incident recorded by Spillius in 1953 when a maximum figure for recruitment of labour from Tikopia was fixed by the Government and agreed to by the chiefs. It was agreed also among the chiefs that any recruitment should take place only with the consent of them all. But the Ariki Tafua, ignoring the agreed plan, without consultation allowed twelve men from the district under his control to be recruited for work in Vanikoro. When this became known the men were returned forthwith by the employing Timber Company, at Government instance.

As a means of gaining employment abroad, the personal initiative by canoe voyage has already been mentioned. This is unorganized, likely to lead to loss of life, or alternatively likely to make the voyagers a public charge through the need for care for them and return of them to the island. Hence, the Solomon Islands Protectorate Government, as may be expected, once the implications of these canoe voyages were realized, has taken a discouraging view of them. But obviously their discouragement can only be effective if alternative avenues for seeking employment are open. Of these other means, Government vessels, trading vessels, and the Mission vessel, the *Southern Cross*, offer occasional avenues of employment to Tikopia, as seamen or in the work of the organization ashore. These, however, are too sporadic to offer any reliable outlet for individual Tikopia ambitions, or a general solution of the economic problem. Government employment as police or workers in connection with hospital or other official institutions offers more prospect; but, on the whole, recruitment under Government sanction for private commercial enterprise offers the best prospect for Tikopia employment under adequate conditions. This is the policy which has been followed since the lifting of the ban upon Polynesian recruitment.

The procedure has been for commercial concerns to have sent recruiting vessels or to have chartered recruiting vessels to Tikopia; these have been usually powered schooners which have anchored off Tikopia for a day or so. Three methods of recruitment have been followed. The earliest one was for the recruiter to let it be known that he wished to embark labour and then to sign on men as they offered themselves, without distinction except for rejection of those obviously unfit to the eye. The second method, followed later by one recruiter, was to use a Tikopia employee as agent, giving him some payment as a commission for his trouble. Since there were more applicants than were required, in these conditions the Tikopia intermediary who had no inducement to keep agricultural labour at home, tended to exercise some bias in the direction of men from his own kin and his own district. By this method relatively no attention was paid to Tikopia domestic requirements. The third method, which may be described generally as agreed recruitment, began when responsible Tikopia themselves had had occasion to consult about what men should go in the light of the recruiter's requirements and of the local situation, and had been able to get their point of view accepted by the recruiter and Government.[1] Clearly, if satisfactory labour rules are to be maintained between employers, Government and Tikopia, some form of the last method is desirable.

In recruitment, as with labour at work, the usual safeguards insisted upon by the Government appear to have been applied. There were, however, two special practices outside this which have some sociological interest.

It has been customary in recent years for the recruiter to make some advance payment, usually to the labourers themselves. One recruiting agent early in 1952 was said by the Tikopia to have paid £2 per man on recruitment. Since this would be normally handed over by the man to the kin he was leaving behind, and they would almost certainly spend the money at once in the ship's store on tobacco, calico, knives and other goods, this was a shrewd as well as a generous gesture. Another recruiter in early 1952 gave no money in advance but a bag of rice and a case of tinned meat to be divided among the

[1] In these discussions Spillius took a considerable part in 1952/3. See J. Spillius, *op. cit.*, p. 26.

men recruited, and this was regarded by the Tikopia as quite a good disbursement. In mid-1952 a recruiter advanced up to £4 to each labourer, but again in the form of food to his family, mostly in meat and flour. It will be noted that since all of these food supplies came from the recruiter's own store, he was able to take ordinary trading profit upon them.

The second 'extra-curricular' practice was that of a recruiter giving a douceur to the chief whose men were being recruited. The Ariki Tafua in 1952 told us of one occasion when he had been given a shirt, a knife and an axe by a recruiter in order to induce him to consent to his young men going away. (The recruiter had apparently been told that the chief had objected to their going.) Another version reported to us was that when £2 per man was proposed by the recruiter as an advance—to go to kinsmen or chief—the Ariki Tafua had protested that the sum should be £5 or £6—without, we gathered, stipulating that he himself necessarily should receive it. He and the recruiting agent argued, and at last the chief gave way. Then he was given an axe, knife and biscuit, and the recruiter took forty men.

Such a present to a chief as acknowledgment of his interest and as a preliminary to entering into negotiations with his people, was quite in accord with Tikopia etiquette, and followed a long-standing custom in recruitment. As in many parts of Africa and the Orient, such a gift must not be regarded, from the Tikopia point of view, simply as a bribe. It is on the one hand an acknowledgement of status, and on the other a recognition that a contract with a Tikopia is not a purely individual matter, but has elements of public interest. From a Western point of view, such a practice is obviously open to abuse. But the issue turns partly on who takes the initiative, and the jurisdiction that is assumed by the chief. If the person wishing to do business first marks his recognition of the status of the chief by a gift, this is appropriate; it does not commit the chief. But if the chief puts impediments in the way of business, or lets it be known that he will do so, until a gift is made, then his motives must be suspect. He may put unfair pressures on labourers to recruit, or he may withdraw quite valid objections to their going. Yet to the Tikopia this would be still an incomplete interpretation. A gift to the chief is indirectly in some sense a gift to the community; by insisting on it for whatever reason, the chief has increased the general income of the labourers. Moreover, his insistence on a gift before letting them go, though it may be primarily for his own benefit, is to some degree an earnest to them that he is concerned about them. If he let the recruiter bargain with them individually, and did not enter the transaction himself, then from one point of view he would be showing a lack of interest in their fate. In the case cited a mixture of elements was apparently present, and though the Ariki Tafua was undoubtedly motivated partly by private gain both he and members of the community regarded his action as proper, and contributory to the general interest.

Now it is necessary to consider how the labour force of Tikopia was in fact composed. What kind of manpower did the Tikopia lose by recruitment? In general, those recruited tended to be relatively young unmarried men. This was naturally because of their lack of family responsibilities. On the other hand, there was the desire to recruit by some young married men who, in the period since the war, had not been able to go abroad and felt a lack of sophistication by comparison with their unmarried kinsmen. In the early recruitment there were only a couple of married men in each batch of labourers. But in the recruitment of June 1952 a high proportion of older married men signed on simply because they felt they had inadequate resources at home to keep their families from suffering. This recruitment consisted of twenty-nine married men and thirty-six unmarried men, and its unusual composition caused it to be known colloquially and jokingly by the Tikopia as the 'voyage of the married men' (*te forau nga pure*). As regards the clan and lineage distribution, as also district distribution, in the long run this became fairly even. Most families with young men had one or two away at work, and from some all the sons were away together. So also in regard to status grouping. The proportion of men of chiefly lineage away was broadly equivalent to that of the total males abroad from the population as a whole. Recruitment was not an instrument of policy used by the chiefs to promote their own interests or those of any particular descent group.

Working conditions for the Tikopia were those ordinarily found in the various parts of the Solomons. In general, they lived in labour lines, they were responsible for cooking their own food, the basic items of which (rice, biscuit, meat, tea and sugar) were part of their total payment and were issued as rations by the employer together with certain other amenities. They did not always have easy opportunities to cultivate food for themselves—but the practice of having small private gardens of their own developed. Medical care, hours of work, etc., were laid down by Government regulation in the same way as were wages and rations.

In one respect the conditions of labourers had improved very greatly since 1929. Then, as for the whole period of pre-war labouring, Tikopia suffered very heavily from the incidence of disease in the place of employment, particularly from malaria. The combined effects of such diseases, aggravated by nostalgic depression, caused heavy mortality. By 1952, however, modern anti-malarial and other anti-biotic drugs and improved medical skill were adequate to ward off the worst effects of disease at work. This meant that the Tikopia, who previously were at a disadvantage owing to their relative lack of immunity from disease, could now be maintained in the open labour market.[1]

The Tikopia now are directly comparable with labourers from other parts of the Solomons in terms of the quality of their labour. In 1929 the only resource which they could hope to use abroad was unskilled manual labour. By 1952 the range of skills open to them had widened considerably as in-

[1] On the other hand, there seems no doubt that the liability of the island community itself to disease has been now greatly increased. Epidemic disease, originating from visiting vessels, has been responsible again in recent years for serious illness and death, while in particular malaria—introduced by returning labourers—appears to have now become endemic in the island. (I understand from Dr David Bonnet of Honolulu that Anopheline mosquitoes are present on the island and are capable of acting as vectors of malaria.) (Cf. *We, The Tikopia*, pp. 411–12.)

creased communication and new opportunities had allowed them to develop their energy and initiative in various technical fields. By 1952 their occupations had become fairly diversified within the unskilled and semi-skilled range.]

For the most part they were general labourers. In this respect, by Solomon Islands standards, which in themselves were not high, their skill and industry were very variable and of indifferent quality. Opinions did differ about them. The wife of a European carpenter at Vanikoro characterized the Tikopia there as faithful and good workers, interested also in fishing. But the general opinion at Vanikoro was that Tikopia labour was very poor in quality. Although at boat-repairing they were interested and useful and at jetty-building they were good but not conspicuous for their industry, at timber work in the bush they were said to have no sense of responsibility. In the copra plantations in the Russell Islands the general judgment, on the basis of their output, was at first very adverse. Some of this opinion seems to have been due to European misconception. In Vanikoro one idea was that the Tikopia were unused to labour. 'In their own home they do not need to work.' But more enlightened opinion realized that the problem lay rather in lack of stamina for persistent work of novel character than in inability to work hard at all. It was thought that with sympathetic European oversight Tikopia might do well. This was borne out by one special Tikopia contingent of young men who showed high productivity and earned substantial bonuses.[1] As police and hospital dressers they seemed competent. As gardeners they seemed interested and gave good service.[2]

A few Tikopia have shown special skills, one as a plantation foreman and another in charge of a motor launch. A third has been boatswain of a recruiting trading steamer, and as master has taken it on trading voyages alone. Another, Robinson Vakasaumore, was a good, careful carpenter at the hospital at Honiara and gave great satisfaction. (It may be noted that he was a member of the great craftsman family of Avakofe.)

The upshot of all this seems to be that in their raw state without special selection or oversight the Tikopia give a poor quality of labour when the ordinary demands of the external production mechanism are put upon them. In this, unfamiliarity, timidity, and lack of simple understanding of what is required are all involved, as well as the lack of habit of consistent work over a stated period of hours. The effects of all this are exaggerated when they are debilitated by illness. On the other hand, Tikopia respond with much greater efficiency to work which presents them with problems with which they are relatively familiar or in which they have been guided by sympathetic consideration. Moreover, there are among them some individuals capable of a fairly high degree of technical skill and industry that compare very favourably with the best workers from other Western Pacific areas. On the whole

[1] See J. Spillius, *op. cit.*, p. 26. Tikopia efficiency in appropriate conditions seems to be borne out by further information, in 1955.
[2] Several Tikopia in 1955 had taken charge of motor scythes on the Government Station at Honiara, and did their work satisfactorily.

then, the central problem of stamina appears to be resolvable in social rather than in physiological terms.

[As regards payment, in 1929 the minimum wage for unskilled labour in the Solomons was £1 per month with rations, etc., in addition.] Probably no Tikopia employed at an earlier period had ever earned more than this. By 1952 the minimum wage for unskilled labour had become £2 per month with rations, etc. Workers of semi-skilled capacity, such as cooks, received for the most part £3 per month with rations, or £6 without rations (which they had to buy themselves). The hospital carpenter was receiving £6 10s 0d per month, without rations. The hospital dresser received £90 per annum but had to provide his own rations. For really highly skilled work such as tractor driving in the Timber Company a man might earn £20 per month, but no Tikopia there was in such a position.[1] The boatswain (sometimes captain) of the trading vessel received £15 per month wages, and got a commission on the trade store sales he made; his employer estimated that he received on the average about £25 per month, easily the highest remuneration of any Tikopia. But by reference to local prices of consumer goods (e.g. a 70 lb. bag of sugar for £3 4s 2d) hardly any of these wage rates, especially the rate for unskilled labour, could be regarded as high, even by comparison with the relatively low demand schedule of the Tikopia.[2]

For the most part the labourers spent their wages on food and tobacco to supplement their rations and on articles of clothing and trade goods to take back to their kin at home. The Tikopia boatswain mentioned above spent about £40 on goods for his kin in Tikopia on one trip. When the hospital carpenter went ashore with a friend, a Tikopia policeman, in Vanikoro, he bought three tins of scented talcum powder, a trade knife, a fathom of Hong Kong blue calico (of very poor quality) and ten sticks of tobacco, the lot costing rather more than £2. The police constable wanted to buy two trade knives but had spent all his money earlier; he tried, without success, to borrow. This incident illustrates two patterns of Tikopia spending habits.

More precisely, one can cite an average expenditure in terms of a rough analysis, made by Spillius in 1953, of the contents of some boxes of goods brought home by labourers from a coconut plantation who had been away for about a year. The total income of slightly over £30 was distributed as in Table I on p. 123.

In one recruitment by Lever Bros. in 1953, however, a decision was made affecting this list. After conferring with the chiefs, the manager of Lever Bros. agreed to withhold the first six months' wages (at £2 10s 0d per month) of each labourer, except for 10s 0d per month, and this £12 was to be used for the purchase of rice which Lever Bros. procured and issued at wholesale price to the Tikopia. This was a deliberate measure to cope with the abnormal food shortage on the island.

---

[1] But I understand that in 1955 there was at least one Tikopia tractor and lorry driver on Lever Bros. estates.

[2] A Tikopia who served as boatboy to the British Resident Commissioner in the New Hebrides received £13 per month in 1952, but said the cost of living there was very high.

TABLE I

CONTENTS OF LABOURER'S BOX

	£	s.	d.
Kerosene—4 gal. drum	1	10	0
Hurricane lamp		12	0
Wicks		3	0
Beads	3	0	0
Calico—nine fathoms	5	0	0
Tobacco	1	0	0
Cosmetics	1	0	0
Torch and batteries	1	0	0
Fishhooks		10	0
Shorts		15	0
Singlets	1	10	0
Jewellery	1	0	0
Saucepans	1	0	0
Combs		9	0
Pipes		10	0
Mirror		8	0
Scissors		15	0
Belt		10	0
TOTAL	£20	12	0
Contribution to chief's 'box'		10	0
Food bought on trip		8	0
Expenses while working (tobacco, sweets, snacks, etc.)	9	0	0
	£30	10	0

One of the first uses of wage payments in 1952/3 was recognition of the status of the chiefs. When a contingent of labourers went abroad each, as was customary, contributed a portion of his earnings to make up a chest of goods for the chief of the clan to which he belonged. In this chest were normally calico and tools. Since the wooden chest was known by the Tikopia as *bokis*, the gift itself came to be known as the *bokis*. Moreover, in Tikopia style each man contributed not only to the gift for his own clan chief but assisted (*soaki*) the members of other clans so that the *bokis* for each chief was of approximately equivalent value. The custom is said to have arisen in this way. In olden days when a man went away to work, on his return he gave a case of knives, pipe tobacco, fish hooks, to his chief. He paid his chief a visit, taking the gifts, made formal obeisance to him and presented them. But recruiting was in fewer numbers and these were individual acts of loyalty. Mass presentation was initiated by the first recruitment after the war. This included about twenty men from sa Tafua, who, helped by men from other clans, made a *bokis* for the Ariki Tafua. The chest contained many fathoms of calico, forty knives and many fishhooks. A similar box was then prepared for each of the other chiefs. Each chief distributed the contents among the various lineages of his clan. Moreover, the initial 'headmoney' (*tauvi nga tangata*, exchange for men) given as an advance was £3. Of this, £1 was given by each man to his clan chief. This first postwar recruitment has become known as 'the voyage which set up presentation chests' (*forau fakatubokis*).

In more recent cases the *bokis* has not necessarily involved an actual chest. The labourers returning from Vanikoro in 1952 did not include their goods in a wooden box but made analogous presentations. For example, ten fathoms of red calico were given to the Ariki Kafika, all the labourers irrespective of clan subscribing to it. The Ariki Taumako, in a comment, said that such a gift was termed 'A first offering for the chiefs' (*a muako nga Ariki*). He likened it to the first presentations of calico which I made when I arrived in 1928. He said that the calico given by Vanikoro labourers to the Ariki Kafika was divided among the chief's sons: four fathoms to Pa Fenuatara, three to Pa Taramoa and three to Pa Fenuafuri. The chief added further 'My own money was prepared by them and broken down into an adze.' By this, he explained, he was given six fathoms only of red calico and the rest of the equivalent sum was made up by a small adze since it was known that he wanted one. The first thought of the labourers had been to give him a large adze but the only one which they could muster had already been used in work and, as he put it, it was appropriate that anything of the kind given to a chief should be new. The calico for the other three chiefs was bought in Vanikoro and announced ritually to their respective gods. 'Then,' said the Ariki Taumako, 'one of the leading labourers, a Kafika clansman, dreamed that night of the supreme Taumako god.' He awoke, made ritual offering to the god from a piece of calico in his own box, and the next morning they went and purchased the things for the Ariki Taumako. Was it perhaps the deity of the reef, the sea eel, was angry that the gods of the other clans had received presents and he had not? 'Perhaps this was not so,' replied the Ariki Taumako to his own question—but the implication obviously was in his mind.

The significance of these gifts is clear. They are in the first place an acknowledgment of the right of the clan chief to part of the product of his clansmen's labour. Secondly, they are also recognition of the status of all Tikopia chiefs. In this sense, then, the Tikopia labourers abroad, like the men at home, must also support the existing social structure. Is this exploitation? Not in the Tikopia idiom. To the Tikopia the chief is their senior or their protector, a symbol of their clan and community, and as such he merits gifts.[1] Again, it is believed that (if a pagan) he does whatever he can by intercession with the spiritual powers to protect them while they are away. Further, they expect him to have some care for their families. Moreover, these gifts do not by any means benefit only the chief or his immediate family. They percolate by secondary gift and by borrowing widely throughout the community.

---

[1] Spillius reported that the labourers returning from coconut plantations in the Central Solomons in 1953 brought back a *bokis* of rather less magnitude to each chief. The chiefs were somewhat dissatisfied. It is possible that as time goes on such gifts may tend to assume a more perfunctory character.

The distribution of rewards for wage labour also affects the kin of the labourer over a wide range. Fishhooks, tobacco, lamp oil and other goods speedily find their way out through bilateral kin ties. Moreover, durable tools such as axes and knives are regarded as property to be borrowed by a man's kin. Not only this, such goods have come to be expected by them as a legitimate import by other returning Tikopia. One common complaint against a young man who returned very ill before the expiry of his contract was that he brought back no such durable goods, no axe, not even a knife! In other words, the present state of Tikopia society is such that those who go to work abroad are regarded as doing so for the community as much as for themselves.

In terms of future prospects, if annually the average number of labourers away at work from Tikopia is to be in the region of 100, then a quantity of goods to the value of probably £2,000 to £2,500 per annum will flow into the Tikopia economy. It is difficult to compare this situation with that of 1929. Although the putative value of Tikopia labour services abroad in relation to their indigenous goods had doubled by 1952, the rise in price of Western goods had more than doubled. But considering that in 1929 Tikopia had no employment abroad, the general enlargement of their income through labour abroad in 1952 changed the whole balance of advantage in their favour. This may well be only temporary. It is probably correct to say that the enlargement of the Tikopia demand schedule plus changes in the value of money have tended to keep many Tikopia in the long run still further away than before from the possibilities of attaining their desired standard of living. On the other hand, for a few men who can attain specialist skills it has become more possible than before to match their wants. However, the possibility of curtailing their luxury expenditure and rendering a high proportion of their earnings into rice and other food supplies can act as a buffer against conditions of shortage, caused by hurricane and other disaster. Hence, the upshot may be firstly to secure a considerable expansion in the amount of Western goods in the possession of Tikopia—although not perhaps to the degree which the Tikopia would wish; and secondly to provide an insurance against the worst effects of hurricane and famine.

The Tikopia demand for money by 1952 was almost solely to facilitate the purchase of goods from the external market. There was not at that date any demand for money in order to meet tax obligations, as has been the case in many other Western Pacific communities. In 1952 the Tikopia had not seemed at all to envisage a liability to taxation as one feature of their growing participation in the Western monetary system. Unlike nearly every other area of the Solomons then, they paid no tax. This in the past had been reasonable since no social services were provided for them by the Government. But now that the Government has begun to make provision for some medical services for them, and is spending time on plans for Tikopia betterment, the question of taxation must obviously loom ahead. By native tax regulation in the Eastern District, adult males between sixteen and sixty years of age are liable to tax. In 1952 'single men' (a category including widowers) paid 6s 0d per annum and married men 3s 0d. On the other hand, there were provisions for various exemptions at the discretion of the District Commissioner—for blind persons, persons unable to work through illness and persons with many dependent family kin. Moreover, if a community, that is, a sub-district, because of failure of food supplies or because they were without social services, could show cause for exemption, the Central Government might remit their tax. Assuming that in due course the Tikopia become subject to taxation, this may reduce their net community income by upwards of £50 per annum. This would not be a heavy drain on their income provided that the market for their labour be maintained. If, however, this market seriously contracts, with lack of any sizeable resources for export, they could find themselves in serious difficulty.

What have been the general social effects on Tikopia of these movements of labour and their new income sources? On the whole local production and techniques did not seem to have suffered, the amount and range of food and other goods increased, and much new information about the outside world was gained. For those who stayed at home, life proceeded much as before. The structure of the society was not obviously affected, and in particular, as we have seen, there was no fundamental challenge to the authority of elders and chiefs as has arisen from returned labourers in some other parts of the world.

But while the formal structure of Tikopia society remained the same, a subtle process of infiltration and permeation of new ideas was at work. One result was a wish to return to the field of labour. Most men who had been abroad to whom we spoke said they wanted to return for work, partly to taste its exciting experiences again and partly to amplify once again the range of their consumer goods. A typical answer was by a man who said he would like to return to work for Europeans because 'I want money to buy things I wish, and then to come back'. But in a few cases the desire to go back to wage labour was not in order to buy more goods and return to Tikopia but to continue to enjoy a more interesting life abroad. In three cases in 1952/3 labourers returned to work in the Solomons and took with them their wives and one or more of their children—leaving others behind in Tikopia. This readiness to accept a family life abroad was a new phenomenon for the Tikopia. It appears likely to become more general as time goes on, and may become a real threat to the integrity of the society. Moreover, as more young men went away, the appetite of those who stayed at home was whetted more keenly. Although restrained in many cases by their elders, who did not want to lose their prime cultivators and fishermen, young men showed the greatest eagerness to be away, and few very could be kept indefinitely on the island. Nearly every member of the group between about fifteen and thirty-five had had experience abroad by 1953 or was on the point of seeking it. This tended to some extent to slow down the marriage rate. But in the long run the desire of young men to take wives with them to their place of work abroad, and even settle there, may solve the migration question by degrees.

Apart from this, even the most conservative Tikopia are aware of Western standards and realize their need to comply with them if they wish to participate more fully in the benefits they want to obtain from Western contact.

THE LEARNING OF ENGLISH

For example, this has been markedly so with language. The inevitable pre-requisite to any large scale acquisition of new knowledge and skills by the Tikopia is a broadening of their basis of communication. Since Tikopia is so small there is practically no incentive for any visitor—except an anthro-pologist—to learn the language. Hence for important communication the Tikopia must learn another tongue. Traditionally, in the history of the Melanesian Mission, this was Mota which in the past has been very useful in enabling missionized Tikopia to have social intercourse with European clergy and Melanesians from other islands. But in recent years, to cope more adequately with modern conditions, the Mission has had to teach in English in the Solomons. Moreover, as the divergence between the role of the Mission as proselytizer and the role of non-Mission European in commerce and Government has become more clear to the Tikopia, their need for English as a language of communication has become more obvious to them. This is quite essential when Tikopia work as labourers abroad. Very largely the English they have come to use is in the form of 'pidgin-English', which is still current throughout the Solomons and New Hebrides.

In 1929 the knowledge of English in any form in Tikopia was very limited indeed and most Tikopia had no thought of trying to learn it. One of the aims of travel among younger men, it is true, had been the acquisition of status and influence back home on the island through a knowledge of pidgin-English so that they could act as interpreters to visitors and intermediaries in trade. They could thereby also gain some material reward. But until about 1950 there would seem to have been only three or four reliable interpreters on the island. By 1952, after many young men had worked abroad, most of them could communicate with visitors in indifferent 'pidgin' and the number of reliable interpreters had increased to about ten. The importance of these interpreters in the formation of Tikopia opinion became considerable. More-over, many boys and young men who had not been abroad were ardent in trying to learn pidgin-English to fit themselves for work overseas. Most of them knew a few phrases and even some of the girls had mastered a few words.

The Tikopia themselves took some initiative in acquiring this lingua franca in an earlier period in which all pidgin-English was obtained on an individual basis, in a work situation with Europeans and Melanesians or by getting deliberate instruction from a Tikopia who knew something of it.[1] Even by 1952 there was still no Government school on the island and the Mission school, the teaching of which was very elementary, taught only in Mota.

---

[1] *We, The Tikopia*, p. 40. Even by 1952 there were current words of English in Tikopia style, as in 1929, and some new ones, e.g. *te atamole* (watermelon); *napauani* (number one)— of leading quality.

Since ordinary facilities were lacking, some years after the war several Tikopia men who had been abroad set up 'bush' schools of their own. Apart from the economic benefit of the gifts received in exchange for their teaching, they wished for the status acquired through setting up as a teacher.[1]

The teaching varied considerably in skill and verve. John Fararava attracted a large audience at his school; he was said to have had as many as a hundred pupils on a single night. He sat up on a box and taught by asking questions in English of individuals in the crowd. If the answer, also expected in English, was wrong he hit the unfortunate pupil on the head with a stick in the best school-mastering tradition. The people apparently did not resent this but regarded it as appropriate treatment for stupidity. But it must be remembered that he was a *maru* (cf. p. 294) and so licensed to strike people. The other teachers seem to have had from thirty to forty pupils apiece. Judging by the very imperfect command of correct English but fairly fluent pidgin-English we heard, it must have been the latter rather than the former which composed the curriculum.

What is particularly remarkable about these schools is that they were spontaneous developments of the people themselves. Though they were informal and, from the point of view of efficiency, clearly of very low grade, they did serve to lay a slight foundation of familiarity with the commercial lingua franca of the Solomons. Moreover, they demonstrated the avidity with which the Tikopia seek, if not education, a facility of putting themselves into communication with the outside world.

The Capital Position in Tikopia after a Generation

I wish now to discuss the wealth of the Tikopia in 1952 as compared with 1929, as capital from the point of view of its economic aspects. It is very difficult, particularly after the effects of the hurricane, to discuss with precision the degree of economic growth that has taken place in Tikopia since 1929. But some general indication can be given of changes in the capital position.

[1] These schools were, of course, quite unofficial. They all taught reading and writing in English and the speaking of English, though one, (v), later switched to Mota. They were as follows:

(i) John Fararava had a school for one year in Ravenga in his family house of Mapusanga and then moved to Rofaea where he operated for two years in another house of his lineage Papaivaru. He taught at night. He had been to the Melanesian Mission School at Pawa and learned his English there.

(ii) Philip Pangisi taught for one year in a house specially built in Faea. He also taught at night and, like Fararava, had learned English at Pawa. His school ended in 1952 when the hurricane came.

(iii) Pa Rangimarepe taught for one year in Namo at the invitation of the people there in the house Nukumaru. He had learned English by working in the New Hebrides.

(iv) Pa Tuarangi, elder brother of Philip Pangisi, taught for a while in a house, Te Niu, in Ravenga (afterwards the anthropologists' home). He too had learned English in the New Hebrides.

(v) Pa Rongotau, a Mission teacher, otherwise known as Mark, and his son, began to teach English in Asanga, but later turned to Mota. In all they taught for three to four years.

Pa Fenuatara represents his father. The Ariki Kafika was ill, and Pa Fenuatara performed a simple canoe rite in his stead; not being a chief, he wore no necklet

5 The Ariki Kafika in 1952. The coconut frond necklet indicates that he has just performed a religious rite.

A modernist chief. The Ariki Tafua in shirt and calico kilt at an official meeting. (He sometimes wore Tikopia costume—as in plate 8—and he kept his hair long)

6 A traditionalist chief. The Ariki Fangarere in a new bark-cloth garment during a religious rite in the Work of the Gods

The first question to consider here is the Tikopia attitude towards capital conservation. In general terms the Tikopia have been very careful about the preservation of their more durable wealth. Sinnet cord, pandanus mats and such perishable property is usually wrapped up carefully if it is to be kept and they also look after their tools. The life of traditional Tikopia goods of wood seems to be fairly long, there being quite a number of ancestral bowls, turmeric ovens and head rests still in use. Most of the Western tools which I had introduced in 1929 were worn out, broken or lost. But of the seven adzes which I had given to the chiefs, to Pa Fenuatara, Pa Rangifuri and Pae Sao in 1929, three at least—those of the Ariki Kafika, Ariki Taumako and Ariki Fangarere were still extant. The present Ariki Taumako told me that he kept as an heirloom the adze which I had given to his father. It was short in the blade but still serviceable and he did not allow it to be used in everyday work in case it wore out. He had set it aside as ritual property.[1] In general, it would seem that there has been no rapid capital replacement of Western goods by the Tikopia.

Until at least 1952 there was a very strong unsatisfied demand for Western capital goods such as axes, knives and, above all, adzes. It remains to be seen whether the influx of wealth as labourers continue to go abroad will satisfy this demand and make for the more rapid replacement of such goods. To some degree this would mean a more efficient technology by saving time in sharpening and rehafting.

As against this very careful conservation must be put some destruction of capital over a generation. On the one hand there is the random destruction wrought periodically by hurricane and seismic sea waves. In January 1952 the people of Faea in particular lost a considerable amount of capital buried in the sand or washed out to sea by high waves which followed the hurricane. Apart from this, there is a certain amount of calculated ritual destruction. When the late Ariki Taumako died, a small saw which I had given him was buried with him. When the late Ariki Tafua (Pa Rangifuri) died in 1951, into his grave went a large number of valuable objects including beads, calico and knives and, I believe, the adze which I had given his father twenty-two years before.

Three points may be noted about this ritual destruction at burial. Firstly, it involves no change of custom. It is a continuation of practices I saw in 1929. Secondly, it includes the destruction of capital goods and in this way can have some effect on future productivity. There is no evidence that canoe building or house building was held up specifically for want of the adze that was buried. But the chief's son was most keen to have a replacement for it in addition to one which we presented to him on our arrival in 1952. Thirdly, the practice of ritual destruction is closely linked with that of conservation. Both can depend upon the high value which attached to the object, and to

---

[1] An example of the way in which the Tikopia conserve goods was an ancient axe blade, in 1952 almost worn out, which was kept by Fakasingetevasa. This, he said, had been brought to Tikopia by Fareatai, a man of Rarovi, in the time of his grandfather (i.e. about the middle of the 19th century) (cf. p. 36).

I

some degree it is ritual destruction which makes long conservation of the
remainder necessary. On the other hand, the number of available producers'
capital goods actually destroyed in any given year is not large and there is
always the possibility that the high value attaching even to old tools allows
the more worn ones to be thrown into the grave without loss of prestige.

Such ritual destruction occurs also in the case of goods of Tikopia manufacture, especially canoes. I noted cases of this in 1929,[1] and others occurred
in 1952/3. Pa Niukaso left his large Anuta canoe to decay after the death of
his son and later broke it up; Pa Nukuro, a poor man, gave away his canoe
to kinsfolk in Namo on news of his father's death abroad; the large canoe of
Pa Porima was broken up by his son for a house wall and dance sounding
board when his father died. Such a destruction of canoe working capital
affects the family concerned even more severely than the loss of knife or
adze since it is more valuable than one and more frequently used than the
other. In Tikopia it is usually durable goods that are so destroyed, not
growing trees as in some other parts of Oceania. But soon after the death
of the son of Pa Niukaso I found him felling coconut palms—a most unusual
occupation for a Tikopia. Asked what he was about he said 'Those which he
(his son) planted are left to stand as a token of affection from which to take
food. But those which I planted with my own hands, those I am destroying.
That is the custom. This is the completion of my love.' By this he meant that
this was the last of the formal acts whereby he expressed his mourning. Such
a rejection of one's own and attachment to that of the other person is in line
with other Tikopia attitudes. When I saw this man he had felled five palms
already, and had destined five more for destruction. This represented a
serious loss, and was especially remarkable in view of the prospect of famine!

In comparing the community capital position in 1952 with that of 1929
it must be remembered that many Tikopia items which would be classed
initially as consumer goods can also be used as producers' capital to pay for
the construction of a canoe, a house or a net. Such items are sinnet cord,
bark-cloth, pandanus mats and wooden bowls. In 1929 I estimated as closely
as I could the amounts of these goods in Tikopia. In 1952 Spillius made a
count of these items (except bark-cloth) as part of a more general census of
Tikopia property. My estimate was very rough indeed, but Spillius's count
for the items cited may be taken as having much more accuracy. The comparative figures are approximately as follows:

	Pandanus Mats	Sinnet Cord	Wooden Bowls
1929 (est. round figures) ..	1,000	1,125	1,120
1952 (count)	2,150	860	1,007

For pandanus mats the figure for 1952 is greater than might have been
expected in proportion to population growth. Moreover, due to the hurricane
one might have expected lower figures through lack of raw materials. It is
possible that my original estimate was too low. On the other hand there has

[1] *Primitive Polynesian Economy*, pp. 344–7.

been a growing demand for such mats for export from Tikopia since they are of exceptionally hard-wearing quality and are liked by even the most sophisticated Melanesian Solomon Islanders as sleeping mats, and are also in demand by Europeans as local floor mats and as curios. But this demand is one which seems to be soon saturated. On the whole it would seem that there has been some growth of capital in respect of this item over a generation.[1] As regards sinnet cord, the amounts held in the middle of 1952 were considerably less than those in 1929. This to a large extent must have been due to the devastation of the hurricane which had reduced the amount of coconut husk available for sinnet production at the same time as it had made a very heavy drain upon supplies for repair of houses and canoes. Hence the 1952 figure cannot be regarded as normal. But for sinnet cord there was practically no external demand and it may well be that capital in this item had not increased very greatly since 1929. As regards wooden bowls, losses due to the hurricane and seismic sea waves were probably considerable, but here also it would appear that the rise in accumulation had hardly been proportionate to the rise in population.

One inference from this could be that even allowing for the hurricane there had not been any great amount of economic growth in the accumulation of traditional Tikopia capital over a generation. If so, it would be explicable on several grounds. Firstly, that the increase in population as yet had not demanded a corresponding increase in producers' goods but only in consumer goods; secondly, that there may have been some diminution of interest in Tikopia capital as against acquiring capital of Western form; and thirdly, that the absence of numbers of young men abroad had taken away from the community a considerable amount of working time which would have been put in on the production of such traditional types of goods. The items mentioned are among those which have particular value in the ceremonial exchanges at initiation, marriage, funeral. It does seem that in common with shortage of food, shortage of such items and of bark-cloth did have some depressive effect upon ceremonial. Marriages were inhibited, only two occurring in the whole sixteen months, towards the end of the expedition's stay, and there were no initiation ceremonies at all. Funerals could not be put off, but the capital goods applied to them in some cases were drastically reduced. One result of this was that for a number of years to come there would tend to be some curtailment of subsequent ceremonies because of the lack of initial services demanding reciprocity.

But what of other forms of capital goods? A man's wooden headrest is a significant traditional item. Apart from its daily use as a pillow, it may be buried with a man or kept by one of his children as a sentimental heirloom. It is even said that it is part of a man's defence—if a thief comes in to steal, the householder, awakening, snatches the headrest from under his head and hurls it at the intruder. According to Spillius's account, in 1952 there were about 450 headrests in Tikopia or about one for every adult male. Of turmeric

---

[1] Subsequent to the property census about 600 mats were sent from the island as a gesture of acknowledgment of Government relief food supplies.

pigment cylinders, among the most valued objects in Tikopia, he counted approximately 270, of turmeric ovens approximately 100 and of grating staves nearly 70. All these represented a fairly high level of capital in turmeric production. Certain types of traditional productive equipment had become rare in 1952. With the decline in bonito fishing the equipment for it almost disappeared, although the pursuit itself was held in high respect. The classical types of wooden agricultural implement had almost disappeared by 1952. In other traditional Tikopia capital items the level seemed high. About 200 flying fish nets, nearly 100 seine nets and approximately 330 scoop nets (used by women) seemed an adequate amount of equipment.

Another item of fixed capital of some importance was the fish corral. In 1929 I noted a set of fish corrals on the Ravenga reef.[1] In the latter half of 1952 at my request Spillius prepared a similar diagram for the same area (see Plan 2). Comparison of this shows that over a generation there had been more extensive utilization of the reef for fish corralling and some alteration in the dispositions of the corrals. The question of community and individual rights in this is of some interest. Each fish corral was built and maintained by one or two men. As in 1929 so in 1952, they owned the constructions but they did not necessarily own the product. The builders resorted to the corrals they constructed, but so also did other people in general. Here differences of view arose. Some builders made no objection to use of their corrals by the general public, and laid no claim to any share in the produce. Others freely admitted the right of the general public to fish there, but thought that they should receive some *tufanga*, some share of the fish. Others again objected to the presence of women sweeping the reef there or of boys diving for fish because they overturned stones in their search for their prey. Hence, most owners chased away women and boys seen fishing within the corrals. A few other owners again, if they saw men putting a net at the exit from the corral, went themselves and set their own net at the mouth of the exit, partly in protest and partly to trap any fish first. But whatever be the attitude of the builders towards shares of the product, it seemed clear that in hardly any case did they ever get such. Hence they tended to nurse a grievance—that they put in time and energy on repair and maintenance of the corrals for the public benefit, with no recompense beyond that from their own personal netting.

The general position in regard to this capital item was, therefore, that over a generation the number of corrals had been almost doubled, that is, there had tended to be higher individual uses of the reef waters. But the principles of capital use had not altered. The reef was still regarded as communal property on which individual corrals were allowed but not to a degree that they infringed communal rights. Communal interest was still pushed so far that it ignored in nearly every case any recompense to the corral builder for his work and care. This has probably to be correlated with the particular character of the fishing yield. The use of a fish corral by one person does not inhibit its use by another on the next tide. Short of setting fixed traps—which do not exist in Tikopia and would probably not pay owing to the frequent

[1] *Primitive Polynesian Economy*, p. 62, Fig. 1.

Plan 1. STRUCTURE OF A FISH CORRAL

a) *Outlets*
b) *Rock pile*
c) *Natural rock wall*
d) *Artificial rock wall*

Plan 2. FISH CORRALS ON RAVENGA REEF

rough seas—it is impossible for the builder of a fish corral to use it continually. When others are using it there is no loss to him. Therefore, there is no
particular reason from their point of view why they should pay him rent. As
a capital investment by a man then, a fish corral is primarily a means of using
his own labour most efficiently. He employs himself over a period when the
reef is dry and he cannot fish in building walls which will increase his catch
when he can fish. In that sense the entry of other people at other times is
irrelevant. To give him a share of fish caught is rather then in the sphere of
ex gratia payment than economic rent. In this respect, by 1952 the Tikopia
do not seem to have moved in the direction of sharpening personal rights
any further than they had in 1929.

Another comparison with 1929 is given by canoes, which are the most
valuable individual capital held by Tikopia. In April and May 1952 I took
a canoe census for the whole island. Contrary to expectation, canoes had
suffered very little in the hurricane. The general figures were as follows:

TABLE II
CANOE CAPITAL

	Sacred canoes Vaka tapu	Ordinary canoes			
		Paopao large	Tovi		
			Sea	Lake	Total
Ravenga	21	31	16	13	81
Namo	4	12	3	7	26
Faea	–	50	7	2	59
	25	93	26	22	166

In 1929, I took a census of canoes in Ravenga and Namo. In this I aggregated
paopao (large seagoing craft) and seagoing *tovi* (small inferior craft). Comparison of the two sets of figures is as follows:

Canoes in Ravenga and Namo 1929–1952

	Vaka tapu	Ordinary seagoing craft	Total
1929	28	31	59
1952	25	62	87

Comparing these totals, we see that if all the seagoing canoes are taken
together the total change is an increase of about 47 per cent over a generation.
This represents an advance in the capital position of Ravenga and Namo
considerably more than the proportionate increase in the general population.
By 1952, the number of sacred canoes dedicated to gods and ancestors and

for which annual dedication rites are performed, had been reduced by three. Naturally, there had been no such canoes in Faea since the district became Christian about 1924. This diminution of ritualized craft was not proportionate to the advance of Christianity over the period, but since sacred canoes are used for all ordinary fishing purposes and indeed often lead the way in the fishing fleet, a diminution in their number was of economic as well as religious significance. On the other hand, the number of ordinary seagoing canoes had been doubled and the number of large craft (*paopao*) in this category had itself become larger than all the seagoing craft in 1929. (With regard to Faea, no exact comparison with 1929 is possible, but it would seem from the 1952 figures that either the capital position had not improved so much here, or that my original guess at its parity with Ravenga and Namo was an over-estimate.)

As regards the use of this capital equipment, observations made by me in 1929 were valid also for the situation in 1952.[1] In particular in 1952, as in 1929, a considerable number of households were without canoes. However, many of the men of these were specific sharers by right in the canoe of elder brother or other close kinsman. Of 250 households, for example, nearly a half rated as possessors of one or more canoes and nearly one-third specifically shared the craft of kinsfolk in these canoe-possessing households. Of the remainder, rather more than one-sixth of the total laid claim to no rights in canoes. As in 1929, approximately 15 per cent of the effective male population were non-owners. However, those households with working males had for the most part fairly permanent arrangements with neighbours or kin of various kinds to serve as crew. In 1929, the crew ratio of working males to canoes in the canoe-owning groups was an average of 3.2 males per vessel. Including working males from groups without canoes of their own, the average for Ravenga and Namo as a whole was 3.8 males per vessel. The corresponding ratios in 1952 were 3.3 and 3.85. In other words, it seems that in 1952, as in 1929, there were adequate capital resources in canoes to meet the sea fishing requirements on the existing level of technology. The same may be said about lake fishing, which was a significant feature for the Tikopia, although the number of canoes involved (used for setting nets) was small. The capital position here seemed to be much the same after a generation. Naturally nearly all the lake canoes were owned by Ravenga people since they live around the shores.

In canoe equipment Tikopia may be described as having a static economy. It would seem that they had tended to maintain their level of fixed capital in this most important item of equipment at a level proportionate to the number of workers able to use the equipment. They had not accumulated any large reserves of canoe capital. Nor on the other hand had they taken any measures to reconstitute the raw materials upon which they have drawn. In 1929, the number of *Callophyllum* trees available for large canoes was very limited, and by 1952 it seemed that there was a definite shortage. But although these trees are very slow-growing, the Tikopia had not attempted any planting of

[1] *Primitive Polynesian Economy*, pp. 246–50.

them. It may well be then that over the next generation or so the shortage of good canoe timber may restrict or lower the level of canoe holding.

Although in this respect Tikopia economy may be regarded as static in general level, there had been considerable movement within it. Differential population increase and differential canoe building had led to a marked improvement in the position of some groups and a marked depreciation in that of others.

The table which I constructed from my 1929 figures, showing canoe ownership by kinship groups in villages, when matched by a similar arrangement from the 1952 figures showed no great change. A few kin groups not previously named had emerged by 1952 as significant canoe owners. A few others had a change of residence. A few also had dropped out of the canoe-owning category. But all these changes were relatively small. As regards the households not owning canoes, in some cases this was due to basic poverty of resources and in others to the fact that young men of the community had taken the family craft for overseas voyages and they had been lost. This was markedly the case with the groups of Rarovi and Vangatau, both of which were wealthy in land and manpower, but had been deprived of their canoes in this way, and had not yet built others.

But of those groups owning canoes, it is interesting to compare clans and chiefly lineages.

The figures for clan ownership of canoes in Ravenga and Namo in 1929 and 1952 are as follows:

TABLE III
CLAN OWNERSHIP OF CANOES

	Vaka tapu		Ordinary Seagoing craft		Totals	
	1929	1952	1929	1952	1929	1952
Kafika	7	7	9	14	16	21
Tafua	(3)	–	7	11	10	11
Taumako	13	14	14	30	27	44
Fangarere	5	4	1	7	6	11
Totals	28	25	31	62	59	87

It will be seen, then, that as regards sacred canoes the clan position was much the same as in 1929, save that the nominal interest of the Ariki Tafua in such craft in 1929 had disappeared altogether by 1952. But in ordinary seagoing craft there had been a very great change. Proportionately this was greatest in the case of Fangarere, but the numbers involved were small. In the case of Taumako, however, the increase by 1952 was very great. By comparison with Kafika and Tafua, each of which had increased their ordinary craft by only about 50 per cent, Taumako had increased theirs by more than 100 per cent and were far ahead of any other clan as canoe owners. Much the same was true when the lineages of the chiefs themselves were compared from this point of view. Whereas in 1929 the Ariki Kafika and his closely related kin had six canoes among twenty-three males, in 1952 they had six canoes among forty-two males. The Ariki Fangarere and his kin, who had in 1929 three canoes among four males, in 1952 had three canoes among ten males. On the other hand, the Ariki Taumako and his close kin, who had in 1929 six canoes among eighteen males, had by 1952 thirteen canoes among thirty-one males. This chief and his close kin, therefore, alone had improved their position materially in this respect over a generation. In 1929 I pointed out that the then Ariki Taumako, as far as canoe equipment was concerned, was in the most favourable position; a generation later his son was in a still better position relative to the other chiefly groups. If Tikopia transport had any significance for the outside market, one might look to the emergence of the Ariki Taumako as a semi-monopolist in this field. But considering the general character of the Tikopia economy, such a radical change is unlikely.

The static character of the Tikopia traditional economy over a generation has not, of course, been matched by a similar condition as regards Western capital goods. Here there had been a very great enlargement by 1952. Since I made no systematic count of Western goods in Tikopia in 1929, this cannot be given quantitative documentation. But from all the evidence of my observations in many households and from the views of the Tikopia themselves, this capital growth is undoubted. By 1952 the number of knives, axes and adzes in Tikopia seemed adequate for all ordinary work. From the material obtained by Spillius on expenditure by labourers, it would seem that the amount of capital expenditure on producers' goods by one contingent at least was only about 5 per cent of their total income, and it appeared that by mid-1953 the demand for ordinary working tools of Western type had been for the time being nearly satisfied. At the present technological level of the Tikopia there should be no great difficulty in maintaining their working tools at an appropriate level, provided that the external market for their labour continues and that they are willing to make some sacrifice of desirable consumer goods in favour of working equipment. If, however, they develop interests in more skilled employment locally, such as carpentry or metal work, then they may have to devote a higher proportion of their resources to new capital equipment.

In summary it may be said that by 1952, as compared with 1929, the Tikopia, though they had suffered some depression of their capital through the hurricane, had on the whole improved their position substantially. Not only had they maintained the traditional types and values of their capital goods relatively intact, they had also added to them a considerable volume of Western goods, including some new types. But despite this overall improvement, the threatened growth of population may make their choice between capital goods and consumption goods more keen than before. Moreover, greater inequalities between individuals and groups are likely to emerge in the new conditions.

Old and New Exchange Situations

In comparing exchange situations in Tikopia after a generation, there are three major kinds of problem. How far have the traditional forms of exchange in Tikopia custom persisted after a generation of intensified Western contact and what changes, if any, have taken place in the volume of transactions and the rates of exchange? In the transactions analogous to barter between Tikopia and visitors to the island, has there been any radical alteration? Finally, has there been any change in the attitude towards the use of money, regarding which in 1929 many Tikopia were ignorant?

[*Persistence in Traditional Forms of Exchange.* The traditional Tikopia system of exchange involved considerable matching directly of goods and services against one another. These exchanges have several attributes:

(i) This matching or reciprocation of one item for another was often long delayed, making it difficult to decide for any given transaction whether it should be classed as a simple transfer from A to B or part of an exchange between A and B. But since most transfers ultimately involved reciprocation, they may be best treated in general in the category of exchange or initiation of quasi-exchange.

(ii) While there was a fair range of transactions of a utilitarian kind, including repayment of loans in goods and services, there were many trans-actions with a ceremonial component, forming part of a series of ceremonial acts.

(iii) The line between what we would regard as a gift and the Tikopia describe as a *sorimori*, and what we regard as a purchase and which the Tikopia speak of as a *tauvi*, was not clearly drawn. Both might involve reciprocation (*fakapenu*). In distinguishing between them, reference was rather to a somewhat vague sympathetic initiative in the first case: the giver of *sorimori* does so in theory from *arofa*, affection; the proposer of *tauvi* does so because he wants the object. Hence, to the Tikopia the social context is different though the final result may be the same. To us, at least in theory, the difference in the final result is an indication of the social context.

(iv) In reciprocation no exact set of equivalents obtained; there were equivalents, but they were of general rather than specific order.

(v) In respect of these general equivalents there was a set of different spheres or circuits of exchange. Each contained a series of articles not easily or directly translatable into terms of those in another series. These series could be expressed, for illustration, in terms of food; mats and bark-cloth; turmeric and bonito hooks respectively.

(vi) From this it follows that there was traditionally no general medium of exchange in Tikopia.

(vii) In the considerable volume of exchange in the ceremonial field, some of the items exchanged, e.g. food, were of straightforward economic and social order, giving support to the economy as a whole and repaying services rendered in carrying out enterprises. But some of the items exchanged bore a symbolic quality, standing for an expression of kinship sentiment or ritual offering to a god or ancestor. The article presented and exchanged carried a significance beyond itself, representing a whole class of such articles or some aspect of nature or of the human spirit. What is to be remarked in particular is that the series of bark-cloth, pandanus mats, turmeric and bonito hooks was not correlated with an increasing symbolic quality in transactions in which these were used. The symbolic value did not coincide with the economic value. Some transfers of objects of low or medium utilitarian value such as food, bark-cloth, mats, had a high symbolic quality.

In discussing Tikopia traditional exchange transactions, one may distinguish between their *form*, their *volume*, their *type* and their *rates*. In theory it is possible for each of these to vary independently.

As regards the form of exchange transactions, this was maintained in 1952 as in 1929. The same general basis of treating an economic transaction as essentially a social transaction, with rules of etiquette, was in operation.[1]

The various linguistic categories of transactions I recorded in 1929,[2] were still all recognized and operational. For example, in 1929 I recorded the reciprocation of canoe builders in two cases, with payment to skilled and unskilled labour in the form of *maro* and food. In 1952, I recorded a similar case (see Plates I and IV).

In March 1952 two men, Pa Maneve and a son of the Ariki Fangarere, built a canoe for Pa Maneve's brother, Pa Fenuafou. They were assisted by several other men of less skill. The craft's hull was hewn from a *Callophyllum* tree which had been overturned in the hurricane and the craftsmen used mainly adzes of European type. They were reciprocated for their craftsmanship by the conventional Tikopia *maro*. The senior builder was the canoe owner's brother. When the time for reciprocation came, he said to his kinsfolk 'Now look, of the adzes which are superior there is one, and of those which are inferior there are two.' By this he meant that though, in fact, he was a leading craftsman, in the same technical category as the son of the Ariki Fangarere, by virtue of his close relationship and of the status of the chief's son, he himself wished to be treated as a junior worker. Consequently, he was arguing that when the *maro* were prepared he should not receive one. The son of the Ariki Fangarere was given a *maro* containing one pandanus mat and two pieces of bark-cloth, one of these being a sheet of the more valuable rectangular kind known as *mami*. A neighbour who had given particular help—the other 'inferior adze'—was given a *maro* of five pieces of bark-cloth, including one *mami*. Another helper received four pieces including one *mami* and two other helpers received two pieces of bark-cloth but without any *mami*. However, Pa Maneve was not overlooked; his kin disregarded his injunction. They provided for him too a *maro* of six pieces of bark-cloth (the number indicating his seniority) including one piece of *mami*. Each *maro* was accompanied by a basket of cooked food, that for the senior builder being

---

[1] For example, Pa Fenuatara made a new dance bat for the use of Pa Fenuafou. This was treated as a gift. It was *sorimori* only, not *tauvi* 'because he was the true mother's brother of the lad in this house'. Yet the wife of Pa Fenuafou was not Pa Fenuatara's own sister, although she was from the chiefly house of Kafika.

[2] *Primitive Polynesian Economy*, Appendix 2.

very large. It is significant to note that reward in such cases is by no means interpreted strictly in status terms. One of the two helpers who received the minimal *maro* was Pa Taramoa, a son of the Ariki Kafika and a very senior man in Tikopia society, but who had not done much of the work. As usual in such cases, the materials for the *maro* were assembled by the household of the canoe owner, but were in fact contributed not only by them but also by a range of other people because of various kinship ties. Comparison with the material from 1929 shows that the amounts of goods in the *maro* were of the same kind and approximately of the same amount as the generation before. In this respect the form, the type and the rates of exchange of goods for services had not varied significantly—there had been no inflation here.

In one respect, however, there had been an alteration. In discussion of the *maro* with me, the ordinary lengths of bark-cloth were described as the *foi mane nga Tikopia*, the 'money' of Tikopia. This expression, which I do not think would have been used in 1929, indicates how the Tikopia, even in their ordinary transactions, had advanced some way towards Western concepts. They did not, of course, mean to be exact in their identification. They were referring to the use of bark-cloth as a payment for services, equivalent to the way in which their own labour services abroad were reciprocated by money. They did not mean that bark-cloth in Tikopia had all the functions of money in a Western system. Moreover, the Tikopia had not themselves adopted money of Western type as providing an acceptable equivalent for building a canoe. In the Tikopia scheme, by 1952 calico would have been acceptable as a substitute for bark-cloth in the *maro*. But money or other types of goods would not have been acceptable, even although by ordinary economic reckoning they would be of equivalent value. In other words, there was in 1952 still a traditional association between the work of canoe building and the specific kind and rate of reciprocation in customary goods.

An important question to consider is whether by 1952 the increase in Westernization of the Tikopia had led to any tendency to a restriction of credit. It may be thought that with the greater opportunities for Tikopia to be absent abroad, and therefore unable to fulfil ceremonial obligations on the occasions of funerals, etc., or to give ordinary economic co-operation, givers of services might have become wary. Fearing a lack of reciprocation they might have refused to part with their goods or give their services, or might have insisted on more prompt repayment. But this situation did not seem to have arisen. The reasons for this are probably three-fold. Firstly, the social urge to give still remained very strong. Participation in exchange was often a moral obligation and was still part of the general fabric of Tikopia values. Secondly, since so few Tikopia had gone to live permanently abroad, it was still envisaged that all Tikopia who went away would return again within a reasonable period. Thirdly, the principle of kin responsibility was still strong and, therefore, repayment of obligation could be expected from some close kinsman of the debtor.

As regards the volume of transactions, it is difficult to give any precise comparison. Because of the implications of the famine and the shortage of materials owing to the hurricane, there was in 1952 undoubtedly some reduction in the volume of food exchanges and other transactions, including hospitality and its repayment. But my impression was that, as compared with 1929, the magnitude of individual transactions in normal times would have been of the same general order. It appeared that there had been no serious attempt to reduce the size of food gifts or the quality of a service actually given. Norms as regards volume seemed to have remained though their actual fulfilment was a function of the resources of the time.

But while the *volume* of any specific transaction did not seem to have radically altered, there had been a distinct reduction in the *types* of transactions. This was so especially in the ceremonial and ritual fields. In 1929 the custom was still operative of presenting to the Ariki Kafika the *peni roi* annually in reciprocation of a marriage of a woman from Kafika. The Ariki Kafika said this was abandoned when Christianity was established in Ravenga —apparently during the '30s. But clearly unbaptized pagans as well as baptized Christians seized the opportunity to get rid of burdensome economic obligations. Again, the *ara manongi* had been greatly reduced in scope and had been often omitted from the funeral ceremonies. Where Christians still prepared the gifts of food they omitted the presentation of bark-cloth and other goods. The setting out of the *putu* offering, bundles of fresh food on a person's grave, had also been given up. This was at the instance of Christians who said that it was a waste. Yet comparison of marriage presentations and exchanges in 1929 with a similar set recorded by Spillius in 1953 shows that out of approximately twenty-five different types of transactions, including counter presentation, only about seven can be definitely said to have been omitted by 1953. All the main presentations recorded a generation before were made at approximately the same level of wealth. Nearly all the items omitted were of minimal importance—the most significant being the 'oven of mats' which was dropped out from the major feast known as *anga*.[1]

In summary then, the general patterns of Tikopia exchange relationships and, broadly speaking, their volume had remained the same over the generation. But there had been some attrition in the sphere of ceremonial exchanges, with a tendency to eliminate the minor or ancillary exchanges and concentrate on those of major importance, which were regarded as the core of the ceremony. Again, there had been some tendency to shorten the time schedule in exchanges—not by a reduction of the credit period and a demand for quicker reciprocation, but by lopping off those items which were most removed in time from the central event. With the advance of Westernization, then, the intricacy of pattern of ceremonial exchanges had been reduced while the main lines had been retained. This general tendency was to be correlated in part with the recognition of alternative uses for the time and the goods of the participants.

Exchanges with Foreigners
The Tikopia have carried on exchanges with foreigners for well over a century.

[1] Cf. *We, The Tikopia*, pp. 550–63; *Primitive Polynesian Economics*, p. 323.

For the greater part of this time these exchanges have taken place at sea when the Tikopia have boarded visiting vessels from their canoes, or in brief, casual contacts on shore. Until quite recently, these exchanges have been conducted by quasi-barter, goods being exchanged for goods. Owing to the mutual ignorance of the parties of each other's language, in general the exchange took place with little or no haggling about prices. Up till 1952 this process was still continuing as in 1929. Crews of Government vessels, the *Southern Cross* and the American pleasure-cruising schooner *Yankee* all bartered European clothing, calico, knives, fishhooks, and tobacco for pandanus mats, fans, spears, dance bats, cowrie shells and other Tikopia products.

A considerable amount of barter took place in 1952/3, as in 1928/9, with the anthropologists resident on the island. This embraced transactions in both goods and services. The anthropologists were in a different position from other traders in several respects:

(1) They had been much more catholic in their demands for Tikopia goods since they required specimens of Tikopia workmanship of as varied a range as possible, covering all aspects of the culture.[1] Other European visitors have been interested usually in a very narrow set of objects, mainly weapons, pandanus mats, model canoes, fans and shell adze blades.

(2) The anthropologists have been much more selective as regards the quality of the objects they took.

(3) They entered into the barter situation much more carefully, bearing in mind their limited stocks of trade goods and their need to establish exchange rates which would allow of continued trade throughout their stay.

(4) Through their command of the vernacular they were in a position to interpret Tikopia wishes in exchange closely and to discuss margins in the quality of objects. Because of the intense Tikopia demand for Western goods all foreign visitors occupy a semi-monopolistic position since they can find competing sellers among the Tikopia, whereas the market for the latter is for the time being highly restricted. Yet the relations of the anthropologists with the Tikopia allowed them to fix exchange rates for some types of goods fairly firmly, while providing for full discussion of such rates and avoiding marked inequality as between individual Tikopia sellers. This was in contrast with barter by the Tikopia with visiting vessels when a man either tended to obtain a windfall gain in his exchange, through European ignorance, or parted with his object at a loss through lack of adequate explanation.

Apart from casual purchases of specimens, barter as a matter of convenience in 1952/3, as in 1928/9, was arranged to take place on given evenings in our house. The occasion was treated by the Tikopia as public entertainment. The house was packed by those who came to watch as well as to trade. Men of rank attended and each transaction and object were freely commented upon by the audience. For the most part trading was carried out in an atmosphere

[1] A collection of ethnographical specimens from Tikopia was deposited by Raymond Firth in 1929 in the Department of Anthropology, University of Sydney; and by Raymond Firth and James Spillius in the Department of Anthropology, Australian National University, in 1952–53. The former collection has now been joined to the latter in Canberra.

of sociability and badinage, and much ethnographical information was also accumulated.

From the barter of 1928/9 I published a table of equivalents for a wide range of Tikopia items. It is interesting to compare the prices paid then with those paid in 1952. See Table IV, p. 144.

These prices, a generation apart, are by no means always comparable since different trade objects were often given. But the general pattern in both cases was much the same: (*a*) the relative value of different kinds of Tikopia objects had remained for the Tikopia much the same as a generation earlier; (*b*) while the general level of exchange prices had remained fairly level for some objects, many, e.g. adze blades, net gauges, darts, fans, headrests, bonito hooks, turmeric cylinders, had advanced in trade value in the meantime. Prices expressed in fishhooks, for instance, had risen to double, treble or even four times their earlier level, and those in calico now often required a supplement.

From one point of view a fall in prices might have been expected. With inflation in recent years the price of Western goods on the external market had risen very greatly whereas the amount of labour required by the Tikopia to manufacture their local articles had remained the same. However, the increased Tikopia contact with the outside world had introduced additional factors. It made them familiar with the notion of a general increase in prices, including the price of labour in the open market, so they were predisposed to some extent to ask for higher rates for their products. Moreover, their recent experiences in trading with European vessels had been to secure for them on the whole higher rates than those obtaining in pre-war days. In particular, by 1952, Western goods had become less scarce for them, and hence they wanted more of them for a given Tikopia article. Finally, our position as traders was less monopolistic than mine had been a generation before; if the Tikopia did not sell to us, they knew they would have an opportunity to sell to someone else later. Hence, the ordinary rules of supply and demand applied; by the time we arrived in 1952, the base level tended to be set higher than in 1929.

In addition to our barter for specimens we made a number of payments of an agreed kind for specific services.[1] These were generally known as *tauvi*. For example, we paid two fishhooks for each sheet of sago-leaf thatch used in building a small engine-house for the generator of our radio-telephone. This rate was set by one of our Tikopia advisers when we asked him for his view. Later he said 'If folk won't part with their thatch for two fishhooks, would you be willing to pay three?' I said 'No.' He agreed that this was reasonable and we did in fact get all the thatch we wanted at the rate quoted. For labour we were invited to pay five fishhooks per man, irrespective of the amount of

---

[1] Presents of knives, axes, calico, etc., to informants were exchanges of a very different kind. They were discussed solely in terms of *sorimori*, not *tauvi*. They were gifts for assistance in recording ethnographic material and were calculated with reference to the wishes of the informant for a particular item, the period over which sustained discussions had taken place, the uniqueness and secret character of the information given, the status of the informant, the general assistance he gave to anthropological work, etc.

TABLE **IV**
COMPARATIVE EXCHANGE RATES 1929–1952

Article	*1929 Rate*	*1952 Rate*
Clam shell adze blades (obsolete)	1 fishhook	4–5 fishhooks
Net gauge	2 fishhooks	8 fishhooks
Sinnet beater	3–4 fishhooks	2 sticks tobacco/ 10 fishhooks
Shell wrist ornament	1–3 fishhooks	6 fishhooks/1 stick tobacco/ 1 small beads
Dart	3 fishhooks	8–15 fishhooks/1 fathom red calico (for ancestral specimen)
Wooden hook	4 fishhooks	1 stick/3–6 fishhooks
Arrow	4 fishhooks	10 fishhooks/1 stick tobacco
Wooden top (toy)	4 fishhooks	Comb and small mirror
Coconut leaf fan	4 fishhooks	12 fishhooks/3 sticks tobacco
Stone adze blades (obsolete)	4–6–7 fishhooks/1 clay pipe	2–3–4 fishhooks/2 sweets or (for a fine one) 10 fishhooks
Bow	6 fishhooks	1 comb and 5 fishhooks
Bag net (*kuani*)	6 fishhooks	1 fathom white calico
Net shuttle (*sika*)	6 fishhooks	6 fishhooks
Betel mortar	7 fishhooks/1 pipe (for two)	1 pipe/1 fathom calico/6 sticks tobacco
Neck ornament (*pa*)	3–4/8/12 fishhooks	Mirror/1 comb/1 handkerchief/5 sticks tobacco/ 1 small knife
Neck ornament (*tavi*)	6–10/20 fishhooks/1 fathom white calico	12 fishhooks/1 fathom calico /1 small bush knife/1 small knife and beads
Bark-cloth beater	7–9 fishhooks	3 sticks tobacco/20 fishhooks /1 spoon
Dance bat	7–8 fishhooks/1 pipe/1 fathom red calico	1 fathom patterned calico and 4 fishhooks/1 small bushknife/4 sticks tobacco
Wooden headrest	8–9/10 fishhooks/ 1 pipe/1 cotton belt/ 1 plane-iron	1 plane-iron and 10 fishhooks/1 fathom calico and 1 bush knife (for 3 headrests)/25–30 fishhooks/ 4 sticks tobacco
Short club (*tuki*)	10 fishhooks	1 knife/1 plane-iron/5 sticks tobacco/40 fishhooks
Taro grater	10–12 fishhooks	15–20 fishhooks/1 stick tobacco
Wooden shark hook	11/20 fishhooks	1 fathom green calico
Man's sinnet belt	15 fishhooks	1 small bushknife/5 sticks tobacco
Wooden slab for grating hibiscus	1 pipe	10 fishhooks

Article	1929 Rate	1952 Rate
Coconut waterbottle	1 pipe and 1 stick tobacco	5 fishhooks
Tattooer's equipment	1 pipe and 6 fishhooks	1 fathom white calico
Bark-cloth sheet (*mami*)	2 pipes and 5 fishhooks	1 large bushknife
Whalebone pestle	5 fishhooks/3 strings beads	1 fathom red calico
Coconut-shell beads	3 strings/6 strings small beads	1 fathom white calico
Turmeric grater	16 fishhooks/3 strings small beads	30 fishhooks/1 string red beads and 4 fishhooks
Spear	9 strings small beads/1 fathom white calico	30 fishhooks/1 fishline/ 1 fathom calico and 2 sticks tobacco/1 1-gal. tin (for cooking rice)
Club	3–4 strings beads/1 fathom calico white or red/1 plane-iron and 1 string beads (ancestral specimen)	1 fathom red calico/1 small bush knife/8 sticks tobacco /1 string beads
Kava bowl	15 fishhooks/40 fishhooks/ 1 pipe and 1 fathom calico	1 plane-iron/1 bush knife and 1 string small beads/1 plane-iron
Food bowl (small)	11/12/15 fishhooks/2 pipes and 5 fishhooks	1 small bush knife/10 sticks tobacco/50 fishhooks/1 handkerchief/1 string beads/1 hone
Food bowl (large)	1 plane-iron/1 fathom white calico, 1 fathom red calico and 3–5 fish-hooks	1 plane-iron/1 fathom red calico/1 bush knife/ 1 fathom red calico and 1 bush knife/10 sticks tobacco and 20 fishhooks (for trough)
Bonito hook	2 pipes and small beads/1 fathom white calico/ 1 fathom red calico/ 1 sheath knife, 1 12 in. knife	2 strings beads/1 bush knife/ 1 fathom calico and beads /1 small knife and hone
Fish line	1 sheath knife/1 12 in. knife	1 fathom white calico/1 handkerchief, 5 sticks tobacco
Kilt (*Kie*)	4 strings beads/1 12 in. knife	1 bush knife/1 fathom white calico/1 string beads/1 small bush knife
Pandanus mat	3 strings beads/1 pipe and 1 string beads/1 fathom calico and 12 in. knife	1 bush knife/1 fathom red calico
Turmeric cylinder	1 12 in. knife/1 14 in. knife	10 sticks tobacco/1 hatchet/ 1 bushknife and 1 fathom calico
Shell adze blade (sacred)	1 14 in. knife	1 saucepan

K

work done. When I asked our adviser should we pay five fishhooks or ten fishhooks per man, the reply was five. But although fishhooks were desirable, especially because food was getting scarce, many men wanted to be paid in tobacco
instead. Again, two men bespoke pipes in advance, one for ten sheets of thatch
and another for his labour alone. When fishhooks or tobacco were suggested as
remuneration for the labour of another, he asked for fish line—he wanted
large gauge but took small gauge willingly. This was roughly equivalent to one
stick of tobacco. Two other men then followed his lead. In other words, there
was then a fairly clear notion about what rates of payment for labour should
be in terms of Western goods. But it was considered that the labourer should
be allowed to exercise some choice as to what goods he would accept as
remuneration.

Even when no specific contract was entered into, a standard rate for services
tended to establish itself. In 1929, when I was taken in a canoe over the lake
no reciprocation was usually required. But in 1952, as tobacco grew scarce,
we began to be asked for some whenever we went in a canoe; the practice
grew of giving two small plugs as a routine payment for this service. Intensity
of demand could even create a marketable service. In our census operations
normally we entered a house as guests for conversation, and in 1929 food
was always offered to me. In 1952, food was offered rarely because of the
shortage. On the other hand, in order to stimulate goodwill Spillius and I
used to take a small plug of tobacco to each household. When the famine of
tobacco set in and the desire for it became very acute these plugs came to be
looked for as our regular contribution whenever we visited a house. On a few
occasions too, the people clearly regarded the tobacco as payment for the
service of their information, though this was an interpretation which we did
our best to discourage.

As compared with 1929, trading facilities open to the Tikopia resident on
the island had been substantially enlarged. One result of this trade was to
stimulate slightly the production of 'curios' such as model canoes, clubs,
bonito hook barbs, elaborately decorated mats; but the change in this respect
was small. More significant was the considerable knowledge of English
gained by the Tikopia, resulting in much keener discussion about prices and
their greater sensitivity to the market.

Another feature of the post-war years has been trade with the Tikopia in
monetary terms. Not only the schooner which came occasionally for trade,
but also the labour recruiting vessels have sold Western goods to the Tikopia
for the money which the Tikopia have earned abroad. This for the first time
gave the Tikopia an opportunity of direct comparative estimation of the
value of their own goods in monetary terms.

Development in the Use of Money
The outstanding feature in the Tikopia exchange system in 1952, as compared with 1929, was the development of the use of money. Since records of
the introduction of money to a non-monetary economy are rare, I discuss
this process in detail.

A generation before, the few pieces of money which the Tikopia possessed or had seen were regarded as items valued by Europeans and possibly exchangeable by them for goods and services, but not usable by the Tikopia. Pa Fenuatara gave me a florin as he might have given me a shell disc of the same size as a wrist ornament; it was something he recognized as valuable to me. What happened in the intervening generation was that the notion of money as a medium of exchange which the Tikopia could use with the outside world was recognized by the whole Tikopia community. Has this involved a revolution in their economic thinking?

It may be said at the outset that the Tikopia seem to have made this innovation in their economic operations with little difficulty. It has not dislocated their ordinary system of exchange and it has entered only certain sectors of it, running parallel to it for the most part. The Tikopia have, as it were, slid money into their economic scheme.

They have done this in several ways. In the first place they have tended to regard money as a currency for international trade but not for domestic trade. They have isolated conceptually the kinds of transactions which take place in the outside world. This is to them the economic sphere of the white man. Just as in the Tikopia sphere bark-cloth and similar goods are necessary for exchanges, so in the white man's sphere money is necessary for exchanges. It is the business of Tikopia going abroad to secure money by work, and to learn how to use it effectively enough to buy with it the goods the Tikopia want. Since these goods are not produced on Tikopia and can be distributed almost entirely through local processes of gift and other forms of transfer to kin and to chiefs, there is practically no need for Tikopia to use money at home. Nor do they need in their own community to make any set of monetary equivalents between Tikopia goods and Western goods. In fact, for very many years calico and European trade tobacco have been incorporated into Tikopia ceremonial exchanges and equated with Tikopia goods and services without taking into account their monetary value.

The sphere where the monetary equation is to some extent forced upon the Tikopia is in trade with a foreign vessel which calls at the island. Since at one time they may be offered or calico or fishhooks for a pandanus mat and at another time they may be offered money, of necessity they have tended to construct some rough equivalence between the values in money of these various items. The Western system is, so to speak, brought to their door. But this is a recent phenomenon. In 1928, when I first went to the island, the Tikopia were known to accept only goods in exchange. Even in 1952/3 the situation was still uncertain; the vessels that called were still so impressed by the primitive simplicity of the Tikopia that for the most part they brought along tobacco, calico, fishhooks and knives to trade for articles of Tikopia workmanship, which they would hardly have done for any other island in the Western Pacific. Hence, a Tikopia who wanted such goods and who found difficulty in handling monetary concepts even then did not need at that economic stage to be much concerned with such concepts. In many cases, as with many peasant market transactions, the money received for an article was at once spent on foodstuffs or tobacco; it was a medium of immediate exchange, not a store of value.

⌊Not only had the Tikopia separated off the kinds of *transactions* in which money enters; they had also separated off to a considerable extent the money-using *role.*⌉Young men who had been abroad to work were, by 1952, usually familiar with the use and the values of money and some of them had a very clear knowledge of currency and prices. But many men, including most of the elder men, and nearly all women, were still ignorant of even the rudiments of monetary knowledge and had to rely on a helper or on the trader to pick out for them the appropriate notes or coins in exchange. In other words, it was in 1952 still possible for a large section of the Tikopia community to exclude the money-using function and to allocate it to other people in the community. Despite the fact that most people had handled money in one way or another, there was still much bewilderment as to the relative values of different kinds of notes and coins. As Spillius recorded, many people did not know how many shillings made up a pound or that twenty shillings were equivalent to two ten-shilling notes. Terms for money were '*foi siling*' a shilling, '*foi mane pepa*' a paper money. These terms used English words with the Tikopia particle of specification. This is in contrast to the term for buying with money, which is *tauvi*, the ordinary Tikopia word for a barter exchange or a payment at a fixed rate. To some extent *siling* and *foi mane pepa* were regarded not merely as separate types of monetary medium, but as separate scales of value, the equivalence between which was unknown. One term on which there was general agreement in 1953 was *foi mane fuangafuru* (ten monies) which always meant ten shillings in amount. But a term in common use, *foi mane sokotasi* (one money), was obscure. To some it might denote a shilling, to others a pound, and to others again it simply implied a single monetary unit of uncertain value.

This vagueness about exact values and equivalences of European money may be best illustrated by the following incident recorded by Spillius. The eldest son of the Ariki Taumako came to his father in their house one day and asked for some money because he wanted to buy a few things on the visiting ship. His father indicated the box where the money was kept. (There were three or four pound notes, two ten shilling notes and some silver.) 'Take some and leave some for me,' he said. The boy plunged in his hand and brought it out with a pound note, a ten shilling note and some silver. It is obvious that neither he nor his father had any idea how much was taken or left—it was just 'some money'. Again in March 1952, just before the vessel which landed us sailed again, a man stopped me. Holding up thirty shillings in notes he said 'I want some tobacco, friend.' As I had to do some business on the vessel before she sailed I said 'No' and went on in a hurry. I was struck by the fact that the man had money and was prepared to use it as an exchange medium, a phenomenon unknown to me a generation before. But I noted that he made no attempt to specify any amount of tobacco or to ask its price. He simply offered me his money and expected me to provide what I thought was the correct equivalent. A similar situation arose when Pa Fenuatara and his son went with me to purchase shot-gun cartridges from a vessel. They had with them a bag of money containing several pounds in notes and silver, and I understood from them that they were prepared to hand this over and let the trader pick out whatever he should demand for a box of cartridges.

These attitudes were very different from that of a Western person who goes into a shop to buy an article and waits for the shopkeeper to tell him the price. He is aware of the relations of the monetary units he holds and he usually has some idea of whether the price stated is in accord with general market rates or not. The situation for most Tikopia is unlike this. They are aware that money is a medium of exchange, but they are unaware of general prices in the open market and they do not even know clearly what are the relations of the various units of money they possess. Consequently, money is to them not a standard of value—it is a medium of exchange but is a unit of account only to a most limited degree and in a very vague way.

These limitations of monetary knowledge by a large number of Tikopia allow for a greater exercise of monetary skills by those who have acquired them. Such diversity opens up a new potentiality of development in Tikopia life. Traditionally there has been almost no scope in the Tikopia economic system for taking advantage of margins of exchange—still less for cheating in a transaction. Nor has there been opportunity for developing anything in the nature of export/import trade. As yet, no Tikopia middlemen have arisen, buying European goods abroad and re-selling them to Tikopia at home at a profit. Nor, although some men have helped to sell local goods to ships, have they taken a proportion of the price. The social system has inhibited this. But in the long run, if fragmentation of social units and of the kinship system occurs, with weakening of obligations to make gifts and loans, it may well happen that such middlemen will arise and gain a premium for their monetary facility.

The reasons for the rapid acceptance of money when previously a century or so of trade had not made it acceptable were three-fold: the recruitment of labour from Tikopia with payment of wages largely in money had accustomed many Tikopia to the facility of its use. Secondly, the acute shortage of food and tobacco had brought home to the Tikopia that if they had money these things would not be refused them, whereas if they had only mats and other Tikopia items to offer, the things they desired might not be given in exchange. Thirdly, the increased contact with the outer world had developed interest in a range of other Western goods which could be purchased only by money.

Despite vagueness regarding monetary units, the Tikopia did attempt to solve in some directions the problem of the equivalence of money to European goods and food. They tried to establish some article of relatively standard quality, in particular trade tobacco, as a reference point. Using the terms of exchange of this article for money, they then set this article against other European items; but such attempts were not very successful because the prices quoted by Europeans fluctuated according to the circumstances of the time and with the trader. Moreover, in the case of trade tobacco, the Tikopia themselves in their barter with one another during an acute period of tobacco shortage inflated its value and so rendered it useless as a standard from which to calculate other transactions.

The pandanus mat tended to emerge as the nearest reference point of their own from which many other calculations could be made. For many years a usual exchange for such a mat was either a bush knife or a fathom of calico, though tobacco or fishhooks were also accepted by some people. But by 1952/3, new values had begun to be attached to the mat, primarily those of money. In discussions about relief shipments of rice to alleviate the famine, for instance, the Government while realizing that the Tikopia could not pay for the rice, nevertheless suggested that a gesture of gratitude in Tikopia terms would be appreciated. The obvious gift by the Tikopia, and one suggested by themselves, was pandanus mats. This raised the question of how many mats, i.e. their value? Their equation with money was discussed at length by a meeting of chiefs and executive officials. It was generally realized that a mat was not equivalent in monetary value to a bag of rice, and that in any case the shipment of mats would be *sorimori* (gift) and not *tauvi* (exchange or trade). But it was thought by the Tikopia that their gift was a substantial contribution.

Yet the value of the mat was difficult to calculate. In 1952/3 the frequent calls of vessels led to trade on an unprecedented scale and gave rise to some markedly irregular local exchange rates. For a pandanus mat £12 was asked in one case, while in another a small mat of the value of ten shillings at ordinary rates was traded for a wood pipe value 3s 6d. But the Melanesian crews of both Government vessels and of the *Southern Cross* customarily paid £2 to £3 for a Tikopia pandanus mat—this was the same price as they paid when buying from Tikopia labourers in Honiara—and a recruiter-trader said that Tikopia 'usually charged' £2 for a mat. As time went on the standard price asked from casual visitors to Tikopia finally became 'two pieces of paper' (£2) for a mat. One immediate effect of this monetary equivalence of a mat was that the former one-to-one unit barter became no longer acceptable. Whereas formerly one bush knife or one fathom of calico was regarded as the correct equivalent, it was now realized that £2 should buy a bush knife and something more. Hence, in barter, two items for a mat tended to be demanded from Melanesian visitors—a knife and a fathom of calico, or two fathoms of calico and a tin of talcum powder. Some Melanesians paid in this way. But in general Europeans were asked for money.

One effect not anticipated by the Tikopia in this new situation was their subjection to the laws of supply and demand operating in a relatively open market. Their export of several hundred mats as a gift to the Government to mark their appreciation of the relief supplies of rice saturated the Solomon Islands market for such commodities. Although the mats were in demand by both Melanesians and Europeans because of their durable quality, the demand was in fact a very limited one. Much to the chagrin and dismay of the Tikopia labourers in Honiara, they later saw these mats being sold at 10s 0d or £1 apiece instead of the figure of £2 or so which they had expected.

Even at Tikopia, these considerations had their effect with buyers who knew the market. In mid-June 1952, one recruiter-trader said that £2 for a mat was too dear; in his house in the Solomons he had about 100 mats still unsold to Europeans from a previous trip. Consequently, he reduced his price to about £1, with variation for quality. Tikopia sellers had to conform to this. One man who asked £2 sold his mat for twenty-six sticks of tobacco —equal to about half his demand. Another man got thirty-five sticks of tobacco for a very fine mat, and a third got 25s 0d. The Tikopia, thus faced by the law of supply and demand, had to be given explanation. The trader's Tikopia agent translated into this terms of taking advantage of their economic plight: 'Now that the land is in a bad state the price of mats is lowered—you know the mind of the white man.' (This may have been honest misunderstanding. The trader had actually said that while the mats he had bought before at a high price had proved unsaleable, since the land was in a bad state he would be prepared to take some more, though not at inflated values.)

A question of interest is the stocks of money held in Tikopia. Most of this has come from workers who have been abroad. Nearly all labour recruits returned in 1952/3 with some money, ranging from 5s 0d to £2. Small sums in addition were often sent by men to their families. All the chiefs had in their possession varying amounts which they had received from immediate kin, the highest amount being about £10 held by the Ariki Tafua. Until very recently the wealthiest man on the island was the Melanesian priest who received £27 annually in salary and a few small sums sporadically from Tikopia, who were making confession or doing penance. Eight salaried Tikopia Mission teachers on the island each received 30s 0d per annum. An estimate for 1952/3 would be that about £150 to £200 was held in European currency on the island, hidden in the boxes of the various households. Some idea of immediate money stock can be gained from trading turnover. One recruiter-trader said that in June 1949 he had taken £200 in cash from Tikopia, and he understood that another trader in October 1948 had taken £400. In June 1952 he took £30 from the Tikopia—nearly all spent on food. About the same time the master of the Vanikoro Timber Company recruiting launch sold calico, knives, tobacco and cosmetics to the amount of £46, and he said he would probably have doubled his takings if his stock of tobacco had not given out. Later, Spillius was approached by the priest to send a radio message for a case of tobacco. He explained that such a case would cost £29, but was assured that it would be sold in one morning.[1]

By the immediate kin of the returning labourer his money was looked upon in the same terms as calico, beads, kerosene, etc., that he brought back—for the benefit of his family and other kin—to be distributed among them. As time went on, however, it developed that the returned labourers did not always share this view. While they did not voice much public opposition to this attitude, they freely expressed resentment privately over it. Two such young men, for instance, complained to Spillius at length that they had nothing to show for the years of labour away from Tikopia. All that remained for them

[1] He did not test this and grant the request because the radio telephone was reserved for messages of more importance, and fulfilling this one might have stimulated similar requests.

to do in this hungry land was to go abroad again, earn money and bring it back; this indeed was what seemed to be expected of them. An indication that money was slowly coming to be regarded as belonging exclusively to the person who had earned it was the fact that no money was included in the chiefs' gift boxes made up by the Tikopia labourers (p. 123). Explanations for this omission were: (*a*) money is not something to be put in the chief's box; it is inappropriate; (*b*) it is the job of the immediate members of a chief's household to present money to the chief; (*c*) the chiefs all have sons who can go abroad and earn money for them. In other words, there was an unmistakeable impression that money was rather different from other goods and should be treated as more personal property, even although it was not being so treated by the kinsfolk at home.

Money in 1952 had practically no internal use in Tikopia. The only instances I recorded were payments by a Tikopia hospital dresser (whose income at the time of £90 per annum was much greater than that of any other Tikopia). He gave in separate transactions to different men: £6 and a box for a drag-net of three sections; £6 and an axe for a net of Anutan type; £3, a knife and beads for another drag-net of three sections.

In cases recorded by Spillius money was given freely to a bond-friend (*soa*). The amount was usually between 5s 0d and £1 and in two instances this gift was reciprocated at a later date. It must be remembered that it is easier to part with one's money to a member of one's own age group since the prospects of the bond-friend himself earning money in the future are good. Between sweethearts, money was not sought or given. The reason for this quite plausibly was that such a gift could not be worn or otherwise displayed easily among age mates, and if found by the family could not be explained away as e.g. an ornament, as if it belonged to a friend. Tikopia love affairs were, in general, *sub rosa* as far as the community as a whole is concerned, although they were usually well-known in the peer group. Among the unmarried girls there was keen competition in displaying ornaments, including those of new Western style, at an evening dance. But money they did not regard as something which could be flashed and made attractive.

The use of money in ceremonies on Tikopia was recorded only twice, on both occasions at funerals. As a substitute for large fishhooks 2s 0d in cash was given in each case, and it was explained that *mane* was itself a valuable (*koroa*) and the *mane e rua* 'two monies' were equivalent to two fishhooks.

Although in Santa Cruz and other islands of the Solomons money is used extensively nowadays by the natives in transactions among themselves—in bride price and purchase of food, pigs or canoes—in Tikopia at this stage in 1952 money was used almost entirely in the dealings which the people had with the outside world. It had not been effectively equated with Tikopia food, goods, land and services among the Tikopia themselves. It was not then a *general* medium of exchange. It was a medium in a limited economic sphere. The Tikopia were not yet using money as the bridge in translating the relative worth of goods and services from the Western economy into terms of goods and services in their own internal economy, and, in particular, in evaluating these latter among themselves. In other words, the mere presence of money does not in itself mean that it will be employed as a medium of exchange. The internalization of it into the economy is dependent upon a recognition of its appropriateness as a social instrument.

In 1952, the possession of money in Tikopia was not regarded as a significant sign of wealth. Wealth lay in the possession of goods and the ability to summon goods (believed to be inherent in every European). The role of money in this was not fully appreciated. Though it was understood that no Tikopia could import goods except through the use of money, no Tikopia was singled out for remark by his command of money. Money was something which belonged or accrued in a rather mysterious way primarily to Europeans. Yet the beginnings of a new understanding of conceiving wealth and social status by reference to money as well as to goods could be seen in 1952. This is illustrated by a song composed to the anthropologists by the Ariki Fangarere. It was as follows:

Tafito:	*Kua kake ki runga*
	Tou uru mane kua matea
	Ko Fosi e tufunga o te tusi
Kupu:	*Soa e soa ma*
	Remeni e Jamesi ra
	Ea taufenua
	Fakamaseke toru fare moriporipo
	Your reputation has ascended
	Your money is immense
	O Firth the expert of writing.
	My friends my friends
	O Raymond O James
	My word! You are rich
	Magnificent is your house gloriously shining.

This song, a *lau*, was specifically said to be in praise of our money, which was indeed vast (by Tikopia standards). The 'gloriously shining' appearance of our house referred not to its walls, but to the many gleaming tins and bottles inside which aroused the admiration of the Tikopia.

The easy acceptance by the Tikopia of the use of money as a medium of exchange with the outside world rests in part on their traditional operation of certain of the functions of money. These functions were performed variously by different kinds of objects in their economy, and the objects were not mutually convertible. Their media of exchange were very specific; operating for only a few types of goods and services in very narrowly delineated circuits. They had standards of value in the sense that there was a comparative rating of objects and services in a broad way, but no general standard existed. They had the concept of a stock of purchasing power fairly clearly defined in their accumulations of mats, and bark-cloth, with disbursement for capital works and payment for various kinds of service. But their economic idiom did not aggregate these functions. The notion of a general medium and general standard of value is a function of situations where there is a wide range of goods and transactions among a dispersed population. What the Tikopia have shown is that it is not difficult to introduce a new medium of exchange and give it a wide range, and that the impediments to its generality throughout the entire economy are social rather than economic in character.

It is probable that money will, before long, become a fairly general exchange medium in Tikopia. One problem of interest then would be the extent to which this would affect the symbolic quality which now exists in much Tikopia exchange. The traditional Tikopia goods might then be forced into the background as reciprocity for ordinary goods and services, with money taking their place, while their reservation for ceremonial transactions might enhance their symbolic character. On the other hand, it is feasible that money might come to be used symbolically or at least ceremonially in transactions with a strong social component in a way quite alien to its use in Western countries. Such assimilation of money to traditional goods in, for example, marriage payments, would endow it with an additional function to its normal economic one and so produce an added factor in determining its value.

* * *

We have seen how change in the occupational patterns of many male Tikopia took place in the five years or so between about 1948 and 1953, primarily in response to the opening up of a new market for their labour. This circumstance was outside the control of the Tikopia and the reasons for it were beyond their ken. But while arbitrary and unexpected, this implied to them much more than a simple discontinuity in their employment; it seemed to presage some radical changes in their social structure. The possible implications are examined in Chapter XI. Meanwhile these changes did not occur at once; the effects were cumulative. In Tikopia in 1952 the chiefs were still getting 'windfall gains' from the sudden opening up of the external labour market; members of the lineage and other kin were still receiving much of the income of the labourers in food, clothing, lighting, etc.; and the structure of the recruitment situation, and of potential migration was still governed largely by the existing social forms.

In succeeding chapters the character of these social forms in 1952 and their differences from 1929 are further examined.

CHAPTER VI

Changes in Rights over Land

Since agriculture in 1929 was basic to the Tikopia economy an important question in 1952 was to find out what changes, if any, had taken place in the interim, not only in agricultural practices but in particular as regards control over land. It was not easy to disentangle the general changes that had taken place in agriculture, including land holding, over a generation, from the special influences of hurricane and drought in 1952. But some differences were fairly clearly due, not to the immediate crisis, but to more long-term influences, which hurricane and drought had merely exacerbated.

General Situation

In 1952 the interest in land as a source of food and as an index of status was maintained at least at the same level as a generation before. This keen, almost anxious, interest was linked with the recognition of the growing pressure of the population upon subsistence.

It was not easy to get any direct proof of the extent to which such pressure had mounted over a generation. Population had increased by more than 30 per cent. But comparative quantitative data on productivity were lacking. It was possible, however, to draw some inferences from indirect or qualitative information. It was evident that during the interim hardly any new agricultural resources had been tapped, no radical improvements had been made in technology, and the structure of agricultural production had remained basically unaltered.

The island resources in land were extremely limited and incapable of any significant expansion. No additional fertile areas of any size, previously uncultivated, were available in Tikopia itself. There were no ancillary unused lands, as, for instance, on small islands off the coast. There were no idle stands of coconut palms or timber which could be converted into products to meet a new market, as by the manufacture of copra or other saleable article abroad. Even the possibility of resort to marginal lands, hitherto regarded as too poor for cultivation, was extremely small. The few untilled areas of sand and coral boulders lying near the sea edge were tiny and infertile. Even the swamps were fairly heavily planted with giant taro, and simple reclamation measures on the borders of the lake had been able to give only very little more cultivated land. There remained the possibility of the introduction of new higher yielding crops. But while the Tikopia were keen to try out new plants they had discovered none which added substantially to their production.

Between 1929 and 1952 there had been some slight improvement in agricultural technology. Iron crowbars had become more common as digging implements; they were more efficient than wooden sticks and had been sought after. But there had been no radical technological change, nor would any such have been possible without great capital expenditure and a complete economic reorganization of the use of time as well as the use of land.[1] After a generation I found the system of economic co-operation in agriculture to be of the same order as before—with qualifications about limitation of land rights, as discussed later.

Attempts to meet the rising pressure technologically were, therefore, limited as far as the land as a whole was concerned to pushing out the margins of cultivation on the border land, reducing the fallow period of the garden lands and intensifying cultivation by planting short-term crops among the trees in the orchards. There was also a tendency to substitute easier growing and quicker maturing crops such as manioc and sweet potato for those demanding more care and maturing more slowly, such as taro. As far as I gathered, such measures did increase productivity to some extent. In the long run, however, some of them were threatening to be deleterious. Shortening of the fallow period tended to exhaust the fertility of the soil. Manioc, while it supplies abundant carbohydrates and some vitamins, is very low indeed in protein. Therefore an increase in productivity by planting more manioc tended to alter the economic balance in the community—either by affecting the labour power nutritionally, or by demanding compensation through additional production of other body-building food supplies.

The experience and opinion of the Tikopia themselves supported this view of the seriousness of their problem. They were not aware of its purely nutritional aspects. But their more responsible members were fully alive to the economic dangers—which to them were in part an exemplification of their traditional fears.

In a discussion in mid-1952 the Ariki Kafika said in a general way, not in reference to the famine, that the land had been swept clear of food (metaphorically), yet marriage had increased greatly. In many families all male siblings had married—every one. 'As their children are born, what are their children to be fed on? As they look and look (for food), they go and steal, they and their children. Formerly only the eldest married, but now recently they have all married throughout.' The old chief gave examples from the lineages of Maniva, Paoari and others which, at the time of my former residence, had few married members and small numbers, but had now

---

[1] For example, Tikopia water supplies, which are basic to agriculture, are very limited. Any systematic water control either by draining or irrigation would almost certainly necessitate dams and piping, requiring quite a different level of capital and technical skill than now obtains. Chemical fertilizers are in practice out of the question because of the cost. Deep sea fishing on any scale would demand heavy capital expenditure, with alteration of techniques and a new system of education for technical training. There are no mineral resources on the island. In 1953, Spillius noted a rumour that Europeans were coming to Tikopia from Vanikoro to mine the land and give riches to all. This, like many Tikopia rumours, was a wish fulfilment. Cf. Raymond Firth, 'Rumor in A Primitive Society', *Journal of Abnormal and Social Psychology*, vol. 53, pp. 122–32. 1956.

increased greatly, though having as before few lands. In 1952, as in 1929, it was said by the pagan chief that the abolition of the *fono* (public assembly) in Uta had led to improvident behaviour.[1] People were no longer enjoined with ritual publicity to remain celibate, practice continence and conserve food supplies. It was said that people were driven by sex; that now men went straight to marry and not to take mistresses as before, or that they carelessly made women pregnant and then had to marry them. Such gloomy expressions of opinion were of the same general order as in 1929,[2] but they seemed more acute. In 1952 the situation was said to be worse than in 1929. An additional reason of sociological interest was also given—that there was now often some jealousy of the eldest son by his siblings, who all wanted to marry and have issue. 'Why should he alone have children to inherit the land?' From the point of view of the elders in 1952 this was a loosening of the sense of responsibility, which in 1929 had seemed still strong enough to keep many junior men bachelors.

To many Tikopia, especially chiefs and elders, the problem was viewed primarily in community terms—how to cope with the overall pressure. Hence in 1952 there was talk of migration and, in particular, a sense of urgency about the need to export labour. But the problem was inevitably envisaged also in sectional terms. It revived ideas of expulsion of part of the population —which it was expected would be from the people of commoner status.[3] Again, even at the beginning of the famine the increase of thefts of food and the frequent occurrence of disputes over planting rights and crops led the more responsible Tikopia to forecast disruption of the social order whenever more unfavourable climatic conditions should suddenly contract the food supply further.

Hence, in a situation of such gravity, one might expect some reaction to be seen in changes in rights over land.

Major Pattern of Land Rights

The general system of control over land in Tikopia in 1952 was essentially the same as in 1929. The surface of the island was divided up into orchards (*tofi*), gardens (*vao*) and house sites (*turanga paito*), as before, and to ordinary observation the divisions were practically identical with those which obtained a generation earlier. As I moved about the island I found that the same place names were in use, applied to the same areas as before, and with slight modifications the boundaries of the land units were the same. The plan which I drew in 1929 of the names and distribution of orchards in Uta was valid also in 1952. The only modification was in houses, which in a few cases had disappeared or altered slightly in site. For example, the major temple in the orchard of Vaisakiri had been allowed to fall into decay when the Ariki

[1] *Primitive Polynesian Economy*, 1939, pp. 44–5; *Work of the Gods in Tikopia*, 1940, pp. 189–215.

[2] See *Primitive Polynesian Economy*, Chap. II, esp. pp. 45–50.

[3] For rumour of expulsion of commoners in 1928/1929, see *Primitive Polynesian Economy*, p. 47, 'Rumour in a Primitive Society', *loc. cit.* Cf. *supra*, p. 93.

Fangarere became Christian; it had been rebuilt on a nearby site by his son who assumed the mantle of the pagan chieftainship. Shortly before I arrived in Tikopia the temple in Rarovi had been burned down because some children were careless and allowed the oven fire to run up the thatch wall. The same general pattern of distribution of rights over land in terms of clan interest, rights of chief, lineage rights and use rights by elementary families and individuals obtained. Apart from this major frame of land tenure, the ancillary rights of a generation earlier were still recognized in principle, but had suffered some modification as I shall describe later.

In terms of general clan interest a plan of Tikopia land holdings presented in 1952 the same picture as in 1929. But just as a generation earlier, the clan interest in land was of a very general character. It consisted essentially of a rather vaguely defined obligation on clan members to defend the interest of any one of their body if threatened from outside, and a reversionary interest exercised at the discretion of the chief if all members of a lineage exercising more immediate rights died out. In this respect then no significant reallocation of land in clan terms had taken place.

The situation with regard to the distribution of land in lineage terms was also practically the same over the generation. In Tikopia there has been no mechanism for sale of land. Transfer of rights between lineages (and *a fortiori* between clans) can be made only in one of three ways: by gift, as for example as dowry on the marriage of a daughter or sister; by reallocation of land by the chief when a lineage has died out; or as the result of some social drama, when an offender is expelled from land by his chief who assumes the rights, or when the chief grants traditional or new land rights again to an offender who has purged his offence.

In 1952 I was told of a few cases in which land had been granted as dowry, but these had occurred before 1929 and were still kept in memory as cases of special interest. As far as I know, no such dowry grants had occurred in the generation between my visits. There were a few cases in which the death of all members of a lineage had resulted in a transfer of land rights. One case which I noted particularly was that of the lineage of Nunga.[1]

There was one case of transfer of land rights in dramatic circumstances. Some time before 1952 the Ariki Taumako divided off a section of land controlled by him in the Rakisu taro field to be used by Pa Mapai of the lineage of Morava and his descendants in perpetuity. Since the land was given by the chief it could in theory be resumed by him. But instead of annual resumption as with most of the land planted in the sacred taro field, he did not expect to interfere in its use or to require Pa Mapai to seek his permission periodically to cultivate there. What was the occasion of this? Some time after 1929 Pa Mapai, as an unmarried man, had had relations with a girl termed in Tikopia his 'true sister', the daughter of his maternal uncle, the former Ariki Taumako. After grave scandal, since this was incest to the Tikopia, he and his immediate paternal kin were banished from the district and expelled from much of their land, which was resumed by the chief. After a period, when the former chief

---

[1] Cf. *We, The Tikopia*, pp. 395–9, and *infra*, p. 232.

had died, Pa Mapai came and in humble obeisance to the new chief—his cross-cousin and brother of the woman with whom he had sinned—begged for a patch of taro land. The chief thereupon returned to him that section of the field which had been cultivated formerly by his lineage—the area of No. 86 in Plan 3B.

It will be seen already that the general overright of a Tikopia chief in regard to the lands of members of his clan obtained in 1952 as in 1929. But these rights now tended to be implemented in a somewhat different way. On the one hand there were cases in which a chief tended to sharpen the exercise of his rights over land which ordinarily he and his family did not cultivate. On the other hand, with the change in the religious allegiance of a large number of Tikopia, there had been some tendency to whittle down the chief's rights to first fruits and other ritual yield from the lands. Each of these all will be discussed in relation to the more general problem of change in the character of land rights.

Reduction of Rights over Land

In 1929 it was the convention that periodically certain rights of culling at random from orchards a limited amount of produce for specific ceremonies could be exercised. These levies were known as *aru*. They were sanctioned by traditional usage and beliefs in spirit control. One of the most notable was the *aru* of coconut and bananas gathered from the cultivations of Rotoaia and Rakisu for the rites of Takarito.[1] By 1952, however, this ritual levy had been abandoned. The Ariki Kafika, under whose jurisdiction it lay, had found that the people in general, and in particular the Christians of Faea, objected to it and so he gave orders for its discontinuance. Again, the offering of first fruits known as *muakai* had been largely discontinued owing to the advance of Christianity, and in these and other ways, the rights of the chiefs to a proportion of the produce from cultivations of members of their clan had been much attenuated.

Another type of right which had suffered great reduction was that of freedom to cultivate in the vacant land of others. In 1929 it was generally recognized that even without asking permission a person was entitled to go and clear land and plant thereon, provided that when the crop was ready he made acknowledgment to the land owner by presentation of a small amount of produce. During the famine in 1952/3 there was a great reduction of such planting rights in fallow land. According to Spillius, it became mandatory during the famine to ask permission before planting in someone else's land, and such permission was rarely given. According to later information this rule was being continued even three years after the famine had come to an end.[2] There had also been a similar reduction in the right of collecting wild produce such as aerial yams or hibiscus from the land of others.

Reduction of rights also occurred in respect of married women. An unmarried woman exercised her land rights within the lineage territory of her

---

[1] *Primitive Polynesian Economy*, pp. 260–1; *Work of the Gods*, p. 293.
[2] Personal communication from Mr James Tedder, May 25, 1956.

father. When she married she was generally conceded the right to plant in and to take food from these lineage lands. This right, which continued during her lifetime, could also be extended, with the consent of her male kin and of the chief, to her children. This affinal tie was often very important to her husband, affording him additional support if he himself controlled few land resources. But a problem was always latent here and sometimes became acute. While the lands of a set of married brothers remained undivided, it was recognized as proper for their sisters to use the joint holdings also. When, however, the brothers partitioned their holdings (see later, p. 162), then came the question of the definition of sisters' claims. Should they be allowed to resort to all their brothers' lands or to only some? This could give rise to friction. Perhaps partly due to this as well as directly to the growing pressure of subsistence, there had arisen over the generation a tendency to supervise more closely the interests of married women in their lineage lands. Such consideration was especially noticeable where, as had happened in a few cases, a woman had actually been handed over the control of certain lineage lands for her use and that of her children while she was alive. Such transfer apparently was tending to be abrogated even before the famine.

Traditionally there has been considerable freedom of land use in Tikopia. Planting in the land of another without permission, granting a parcel of land to a woman who married, recognizing her right and that of her children to use the land of her brothers, are all traditional practices. Settling semi-permanently to live on land of others has also been a fairly free practice. All such rights were reported in 1952 as being appropriate. As one man said to me 'This land (community) does not quibble. As where a man will dwell on kin ground which has been allotted to him by the man who owns the ground. If a man has had trouble with his patrilineal kin he will go and live with his mother's brother. If that family dies out then he will continue to live there. People say "He dwells in the place of his mother's brother". He himself will say "I live on my mother's brother's lands". But should he say "My lands", then in course of time his mother's brother's clan will come to him and will chase him away because he called the lands his. But so long as he acknowledges their ownership they will allow him to stay.' This was the traditional position. Practical use was allowed so long as the title was conceded to the true owners. But in this case, as in the others, increasing pressure upon resources seemed likely to modify the custom. In part the mother's kin might want the lands themselves immediately; in part they might fear that, as the land situation tightened, it might be more difficult to evict their nephew should they wish to do so.

Differentiation of Rights within the Lineage

As regards control of land by lineages, it appeared that there was a rather closer definition of rights among the constituent parts of the lineage than a generation before. This was specifically stated to be due to processes of natural increase and high marriage rate. In 1929 it was usual for members of an extended family to control the rights over a number of orchards and pieces

Old and new in Tikopia ideology. The man is tattooed, wears his hair long, and has as a neck ornament a tooth of a kinsman as a token of affection. He also is wearing a calico kilt over his bark-cloth girdle, has a ring on his finger, and a Cross on his breast

7   Emerging from mourning. The wife of the Ariki Taumako, with a mourning garment slung round her neck, but with festive flowers in her ear-lobes. Her tattooing is clearly visible

8 Chiefs in conference. Ariki Kafika and Ariki Tafua in discussion with Government representative, 1952

of garden land as against other extended families within the major lineage. Such rights were often exercised in common without differentiation among elementary families. By 1952, it appeared that there-had been a somewhat closer definition of land rights and a tendency to divide the extended family in land-holding terms at an earlier stage. While some brothers with families of children still held their lands in common, it seemed to me that this practice was less widespread than in 1929.

Division of the land of a sub-lineage may follow either or both of two procedures. In one procedure lands are apportioned as separate parcels among the various parties concerned without any alteration of boundaries; each party gets one or more separate orchards, garden plots, etc. On the other hand, the land in one or more of the parcels may be subdivided and new boundaries set up, thus decreasing the size of the units concerned. This latter procedure is known by the Tikopia as 'splitting' (*fai*), whereas the former is termed 'separation' (*mavae*). The procedure adopted depends upon the number, size and quality of the orchard or garden lands concerned. Both of these procedures had been in use in Tikopia over the generation between 1929 and 1952, but on the whole my impression was that 'splitting' had become more common with increasing demographic pressure.

When an orchard is either reallocated or 'split', the man to whom it is assigned has the sole right of access—this right extending, of course, to his wife and children. But he may grant subsidiary rights at his discretion. For example, in 1952 Pa Rarotoa had two large orchards, one in Rotoaia and the other up in the mountains. He kept the latter for himself but he allowed his close patrilineal kin access to the other—but only for the cultivation of manioc, not for the collection of food in general.

As an example of the process of division and redistribution of rights, take the orchards of Pa Teauika (known in 1929 as Pa Taitai),[1] of Raroakau sub-lineage. In 1929, he had five orchards in which his brother Noel, then a Mission teacher in Anuta, had also an undivided interest. By 1952, Noel had married and was known as Pa Fasi, with two male and four female children. Pa Teauika himself had the same number of orchards as before. But three of them, Aroaro in Rakisu, Paukarei in Rotoaia, and Fongararo, had been 'split' and divided with Pa Fasi. A fourth orchard, Angina in Tumuaki, had been 'split' with Pa Rongomatini of an allied sub-lineage. The fifth orchard, Matori, Pa Teauika retained for himself undivided. In addition, one orchard to which he had not resorted earlier, Te Takia in Tufenua, was divided in 1952 between him and Pa Fasi, and another orchard, Fasi in Tai, was divided between his eldest son and Pa Fasi. Pa Fasi, in addition to the shares divided from the five orchards mentioned above, went alone to a cultivation in the swamp area.

Thus, there had been partition and reallocation between two brothers of Raroakau; there had also been some reallocation between them and the allied sub-lineages of Variari and Rongomatini, with which they made up the major lineage of Fasi.

[1] Cf. *We, The Tikopia*, pp. 91–4.

L

The situation was explained by Pa Fasi as follows: 'Formerly our cultivating fields stood and Paito i Rangirikoi (Variari), Paito i Rongomatini and we all used to resort to them. We went while we had something firmly to obey, a fixed origin, and we went all of us because we were a single body of kin. Today we have divided, we have divided in two, we have split up the land. Paito i Variari and Paito i Rongomatini go on their side and we two (he and his brother) go to our side. (Moreover) he and I split up recently because Pa Teauika was married and I married. Formerly we used to go jointly.' Pa Fasi added that the area available to each, formerly large, now was much less. (He said that the orchards were divided by using as boundaries stones in the swamp areas and trees in the hillside.) By contrast with this, the Rongomatini group, consisting of Pa Maungakena, Pa Rongamatini and their immediate patrilineal kin, continued the traditional practice; they used their orchards jointly. They said 'Our family (group) we go jointly as one'. By 1952 this had become almost an old-fashioned attitude.

Pa Fasi pointed out that the divided sections of orchards are aggregated again when branches or sub-lineages of a lineage die out without direct heirs. 'Whomsoever of another *paito* is alive will aggregate it to himself. But if there is no man at all, if they have died out altogether, then it goes to the chief.' He added that some lineages have in fact aggregated lands, but that by far the greater number have divided theirs.

The only lineage land which I knew to have been aggregated since 1929 was in the case of Rangimarepe, a sub-lineage of the major lineage of Rengaru. This had happened because the only son of the dead Pa Rangimarepe died abroad, having been lost on a sea voyage about 1944, leaving women alone representing that branch of the lineage. To live with this female kin came the son of Pa Rengaru, as a young man of about twenty-two. He married and assumed the name of Pa Rangimarepe in turn from the house in which he lived. In the olden days six orchards which had belonged originally to the lineage of Rengaru had been divided, two going to the main Rengaru sub-lineage, two to the Rangimarepe sub-lineage and the other two being split up between them, each being halved. This had been the situation in 1929.[1] Later, all six holdings had been joined again under the control of Pa Rengaru, but while retaining general over-rights he had handed over one half to his son, Pa Rangimarepe, for his own use.

As I pointed out in 1929, the general Tikopia principle is to divide up the lands of an extended family after the death of the father. While two married brothers will divide up their lands, a father does not normally separate his lands from those of his married son. This is based upon recognition of a structural difference.[2] There is not thought to be a competitive relation

[1] Cf. *We, The Tikopia*, pp. 393–4, where the son of the former Pa Rangimarepe controlled the orchards of Saupe and Fakaete, with use-rights in Fongataku.

[2] Cf. the Chinese principle of 'division of family' described by H. T. Fei, *Peasant Life in China*, 1939, pp. 66–7, 195; Lin Yueh-Hwa, *The Golden Wing*, 1947, pp. xiii, 123–4, 128; Francis L. K. Hsu, *Under the Ancestors' Shadow*, 1948, pp. 114–5. Hsu mentions how in the Tali area, if there is only one son in the house, the family may not divide when he marries, but if there are several sons and one or more have children, the family will definitely divide.

between father and son, since only the son is creating a new family. Thus, Pa Rengaru said that he had divided his lands from his brother, Pa Rongo-taono, but not from his son Pa Rangimarepe—'because we two eat from the one orchard'. Even the pressure of famine did not divide the holdings of father and son, between whom there is expected to be a moral bond trans-cending economic individualism.

What at first sight resembles such a division, however, is when an elderly father divides his holdings not between himself and his son, but among his sons as a set of brothers. In this case he will himself resort either to all the lands or to those of that one of his sons with whom he lives.

In 1929 the orchards of the Kafika family had not been divided, and Pa Fenuatara then expected his father to leave them as a single inheritance for him to administer in the common interest. He thought that only in the next generation might the lands be divided. But by 1952 the aged Ariki Kafika had, in fact, made an apportionment of the lands. His eldest son, Pa Fenu-atara, controlled two large orchards and had a share in three others; in addition, he had access to two of the orchards controlled by his second brother and one controlled by his next brother. The chief's second son, Pa Taramoa, controlled, alone, three orchards of fair size and had a share in three others; the next son, Pa Fenuafuri, had a similar endowment. This division had taken place during the lifetime of the chief because, owing to his great age, his sons' sons had begun to marry and were producing children of their own. The active use of the lands was, therefore, tending to be very much in the hands of the chief's grandsons, so that there was no real discrepancy between what had happened and what Pa Fenuatara had envisaged a generation before.[1]

Moreover, the special status of a chief meant insistence on an over-right by the head of the lineage unnecessary even when the lands had been divided. It was pointed out to me that the Ariki Kafika himself had the right to access to all these orchards, though since he was old and no longer really mobile Pa Fenuatara, as his acknowledged heir, went in his place to cultivate. Pa Taramoa told me that when the Ariki would die and Pa Fenuatara would become Ariki, he would have access to all the orchards since all the house sites (in effect, temple sites) therein were his.

It was impossible in the time available for us to make any systematic large survey of Tikopia lands. But in 1952, from seventeen haphazard examples of sets of married brothers, four sets still held their lands jointly, whereas thirteen sets had divided up their holdings. This process is sometimes called 'individualization'. But it is rather to be described as a closer definition of land rights in elementary family terms instead of in extended family or sub-lineage terms. If, however, there were a system of record and registration of title in Tikopia, the tendency would undoubtedly be to put the title in the name of the male head of the family; in this specific sense then the title would be 'individualized', with consequent narrowing of legal rights.

The reason for this separation of land rights among brothers is given by

[1] Cf. *We, The Tikopia*, pp. 390–1.

the Tikopia in two ways. One is that with growth of families comes a separation of activities and interests. One man said, 'We have split our orchards, each going to plant food in his own orchard. Its basis is that each has his own oven. Because otherwise one goes and lays hands on the food of another—it is good that each goes to his own orchard and that each lays hands on food of his own.' In other words, a correlation has come to be more sharply established between labour and the right to its fruits. But apart from this assertion of principle, there is also a recognition of its implication, that if divisions are not set up, strife is likely. Another man said that he and his brother divided their lands, each going to his own food, because 'if not, we were likely to fight. Thereupon we divided and he and I do not fight. The two of us do not behave evilly.' In this case, as in most others, the partition was done by agreement, not arbitrarily by the senior brother, who is normally the group representative and principal administrator. (If lands are divided among brothers by a father, then he is responsible for the partition.)

It should be noted that the effects of pressure are different in land ownership from what they are in canoe ownership. A canoe cannot be divided. The rights to it must be shared, or some other arrangement made. But if some co-owners are to be expropriated they must be compensated, and in turn must lay out capital to build a new canoe or lose canoe rights altogether. This normally has not happened in Tikopia; there has been no convention of 'buying-out' other canoe co-owners. If a family has more than one canoe, the craft may be apportioned among married brothers. But many brothers who have separated their land interests will, for want of capital resources if for no other reason, continue to share a canoe. Hence the physical nature of capital may dictate the degree of definition of individual rights, i.e. the form of ownership.

By 1952, such partition, coupled with inequalities in numbers of male siblings in a family, had resulted it seemed in perpetuating, if not accentuating, the disparity between amounts of land held by individuals as family heads in Tikopia. The increasing pressure of population upon subsistence had not tended to produce any levelling of resources, but on the contrary had sharpened up interest in them. This disparity can be gauged to some extent from a review of orchards controlled by different men. These orchards varied considerably in size, a few of the largest being upwards of ten acres and some of the smallest only half an acre. But in a general way the number controlled by a person was a good index to his economic position. The norm of wealth in land was about five orchards of assorted sizes. In a sample of thirty cases comprising one chief, seven other men of chiefly houses and twenty-two commoners, all these men owned, in sum, 135 orchards, giving an average of slightly less than five apiece. At one end of the scale were two men with one orchard apiece. At the other end two men had nine orchards apiece and one man had eleven.

One of the most wealthy men in Tikopia was the Ariki Taumako, who controlled nine orchards as well as two large taro areas in Matatori and Matamata and several other garden plots elsewhere. As one of his cousins said to me, 'His cultivable plots are many; of the chiefs, those of the Ariki Taumako are foremost.' The brother next to him in age controlled four orchards of fair size, two of them being sections from originally very large orchards owned by the Taumako chief in Maunga and Reani. In addition, he had two garden areas. The other brothers of the chief had lesser holdings. The Ariki Tafua also was, like his grandfather in 1929, a wealthy controller of land.

Commoners with control over considerable areas of land included Pa Raroifi, Pa Rengaru, Pa Rarovi, Pa Nukumata (of Sao), Pa Raropuka—nearly all the senior representatives of lineages which formerly had ritual elders. Among men of medium holdings could be reckoned members of the sub-lineage of Niukapu, an offshoot of Taumako. The heads of the three main branches of the sub-lineage respectively had four orchards, five orchards (two being sections of large holdings) and one orchard (a very large one) under their control. Similarly, the head of Vainunu sub-lineage, of Tongarutu (see Gen. 2), whose grandfather had been a chief of Kafika, had control of five orchards (or large sections of orchards); in addition, he and his brother resorted jointly to an area of swamp land in which they cultivated giant taro. Again, in the sub-lineage of Rangipaea of Tafua, two brothers used the several orchards of the sub-lineage in Namo, while their father's brother, living in Faea, used the four orchards there. In addition, there was a large orchard in Tufenua to which most of the sub-lineage members went, each to his own section. To be contrasted with this was the position of such a man as Pa Nukuraro of Nukuraro lineage who had only two orchards which he and his own family used, and two others divided in half and shared with other members of the lineage. All these he described as 'baby-orchards, not large'. Again, the head of the lineage of Morava, a distant offshoot from Taumako, had two orchards only, and Pa Nukuro of Tongarutu (see Gen. 2) had five orchards, but all extremely small. This and other information of real poverty in land, obtained by Spillius, bears out what the Ariki Kafika said to me much earlier about the straitened position of some lineages.

To a considerable extent differences in wealth in land were the product of differences in ancestral lineage endowment, and in the size of the male sibling group which married in each generation. But there was a further complicating factor which seemed to have intensified in the last generation since 1929. That was the tendency of eldest brothers to try and secure for themselves the lion's share of family lands on the plea of necessity to secure the future of their own children. Up to a point this could be regarded as a reassertion in more modern terms of the old thesis that only senior males should perpetuate the family and that younger males should remain celibate to preserve the food supplies. Since by 1952 they commonly did not remain celibate, 'the devil take the hindmost' would be a colloquial rendering of what seemed to be the attitude of eldest brothers. Since an elder brother often had a family of young children by the time his younger brother married, his immediate case for preferential treatment was strong, and the situation, once established, was difficult to alter.

The structural advantage in land rights obtained by the eldest brother was not always exercised to the full. Pa Nukutapu, son of Pa Tarikitonga, formerly the premier *maru* in Tikopia, controlled seven orchards as well as sections of two other large orchards which he divided with his second cousin, the Ariki Taumako, and one other which he divided with that chief's younger brother. Formerly, Pa Nukutapu also used land on Reani. But he said to me 'Now I have announced this to my brother (in reality his father's brother's son) Pa Pike, that he may go to it—I was disinclined because it was too far.' This reallocation was possible because Pa Nukutapu had ample land for his own use. But his attitude in general was an accommodating one. He had not divided the lands between himself and his younger brother, Pa Toa, but allowed the latter free access to all. He recognized in practice the fraternal tie. 'So Pa Toa and I go to the same orchards, because I do not want to eat from them alone.'[1]

On the other hand, there were at least half a dozen cases in which elder brothers exercised their jurisdiction apparently to the detriment of their younger brothers. Two cases will illustrate this. In the Rengaru family, in 1929, Pa Rengaru and Pa Rongotaono operated a single oven and joint orchards; by 1952 they had separated. The younger complained that the elder in the division of lands left him with only two orchards, taking four himself, apart from those over which he had acquired control from the Rangimarepe family (*v.* p. 162). Pa Rongotaono said of his elder brother's attitude 'It is bad; he wants to eat largely from the soil. I object, but he is strong and so is his wife, so I object but I remain with bowed head; I do not speak.' He said that he was resentful partly because he had many male children while his elder brother had only one male child. He alleged that while he was away as a Mission teacher in Anuta, his brother had looked after the joint orchards and so came to regard them as his own. As far as I could see, while this was true, Pa Rengaru had additional responsibilities. He cared also for two boys and their widowed mother, the family of his eldest son who had died. According to him, his younger brother had three orchards which he, Pa Rengaru, had 'split' and he himself had the other halves of these three as well as two orchards undivided; in addition, each had a section of an area of garden land. As regards the lands acquired from the Rangimarepe sub-lineage, he had handed over half of one orchard to his own remaining son for his sole use and the other half to Pa Rongotaono. While Pa Rengaru represented the position rather differently then, it was still clear that he had by far the larger resources.

The second case was that of Pa Maneve. In 1929 he was unmarried and shared with his brothers, then married, the lands of Maneve sub-lineage which had separated from the allied sub-lineage of Resiake. By 1952, the lands of Maneve sub-lineage had been divided. Pa Maneve's eldest brother had two orchards, one in Tufenua and one, Osiri, which had been divided

---

[1] Pa Nukutapu took his name from a large orchard in Ravenga. This was known of old as Te Roma, but an Uvea man Patita (see Rivers' *History of Melanesian Society*, vol. I, p. 300) introduced the name Nukutapu from his own kin group in Uvea.

earlier with Paito i Pangisi. The brother next in order, Pa Fenuafou, had three orchards, and in addition two areas in Uta with valuable swamp land, and two areas of swamp land in Ravenga, making seven pieces of land in all. Pa Maneve had only one orchard, which was also shared by his eldest brother's family. In addition, he had a section of swamp land near his house in Tai and a share in some manioc land on the hill of Tumuaki which his eldest brother also used. The manioc in this dry land had perished in the drought of 1952. Pa Maneve had a wife and three children. He asked me bitterly 'How can a man who eats from only a single orchard live?' (cf. p. 265). He went to Pa Fenuafou and explained his plight—which was indeed very grave. He asked if his brother had any giant taro left in his swamp land. The reply was 'No.' Pa Maneve said to me 'He lied. Affection is lacking!' I asked why he did not apply to his chief for help, but he said he was ashamed. He explained the essence of his position like this: (*a*) He spent time after the cyclone not in planting food but in building his brother's canoe. His wife and son were lazy and did not plant. Then his foot became inflamed, and so his planting was quite recent and he had no food well advanced when the famine became severe. (*b*) He and his brother, Pa Fenuafou, were in bad relations. He said his brother had 'a bad gullet' and wanted to keep all the orchards for himself. He himself had only the one 'origin', i.e. source of food. His portion of swamp had been invaded by the sea waters and spoilt. So he had only a few giant taro around the margin. (*c*) Long ago he was a Mission teacher but had resigned from illness. Though the priest and teachers called upon him now and again, they didn't relieve his situation. 'They talk in the words of the Gospel—that to him who hungers shall be given, that he shall be assisted. I give them the lie—they come here and look upon me who am hungry and do not speak. Yet great is the wealth of the priest.' (*d*) As mentioned above, he had had no help from his brother or chief. (*e*) Therefore, the only remedy he proposed was to ask for help from the next recruiting vessel in migrating to another land with his young children. He was not fit for hard work, he said, so he wished to be dumped in another land and to take what fate sent him.[1]

Pa Maneve's story was confirmed by the grandson of his eldest brother and also by Pa Fenuatara. The latter said that the division was unequal, but that some brothers were like that. A man would insist on some pretext that he have many orchards and that his brother have only a single one. But he then added that the orchards of Maneve were apportioned by the Ariki Taumako, and he gave much to Fenuafou because he helped in many (pagan) ceremonies which the Ariki performed, while Pa Maneve (a Christian) did not. From other evidence this seemed to be quite correct. Thus the factor

---

[1] The sequel to this was that Pa Maneve did recruit on the next vessel, though alone. He spent most of his time, apparently very happy, languidly cutting minute quantities of grass on the lawn of the Manager of Lever Bros. plantation, much to the Manager's commingled exasperation and amusement. Yet he was really quite a clever craftsman in wood. His bitter statements to me in 1952 about his chief contrasted with his views in 1929, when he stressed to me how generous was a chief in giving food to his people.

of the clan chief's religious and political views may enter the situation and lead to unequal distribution. This is particularly the case with those lineages which, like Maneve, have sprung from chiefly stock. In theory, and to some extent in practice, especially in times of crisis the lands of such lineages are held to be put at the disposal of the chief from whose ancestry they originally came. It will be remembered that this over-right of the chief existed to an equal extent in 1929, but it seemed to me that it was stressed more in 1952.

Yet where it seemed clear that there had been an unequal allocation of rights over land among brothers, for the most part the situation was overtly accepted. The younger brother whose interests had been damaged was resentful, but made no public challenge to his senior sibling. Why should this be so? One reason was the Tikopia tradition that the distribution of land was the right of the senior sibling. He had a moral obligation to deal justly by his brothers, but this lay at his own discretion. In the absence of any Tikopia courts of law he had to justify himself only morally—and as we have seen the senior brother usually could put up some kind of a case. Another factor was the attitude of the clan chief. He was in one sense a substitute for a developed law. An injured party could go to him and protest, seeking redress. Normally he would not expect to interfere in a land distribution, but he could, if justice seemed to be too much outraged, bring pressure to bear upon the offending brother. Hence, if the chief was not moved to bring such pressure, then a younger brother who felt himself outraged would have no other source of redress.

One question of economic importance is whether reduction of holding, either by fragmentation or by allocation had been so great in some cases as to render it difficult for the owner to gain a living. This certainly appeared so with some of the cases mentioned. At a guess the holdings of men at the lower end of the scale were not much above one acre each. For themselves and families, this did not provide adequate food unless they also had some access to other lands or supplementary help, through kin gifts or neighbourly charity. In time of acute food shortage generally, such help was least likely to be given, especially since reciprocity in the future was doubtful.

Some supplementation of food supplies could be obtained by craft-work, by the production of paddles, bowls, dance bats, etc., commissioned by fellow Tikopia, and reciprocated in kind, or made as a speculation and bartered with strangers on visiting vessels (pp. 139, 146). But such supplementary resources could not act as a substitute for land completely, since the demand was too precarious. There was then little incentive for land-poor families to develop as craft-specialists in any regular way.

Disputes about Land

Another sociological index to the mounting pressure on land was the frequency of disputes about it. It will have been noted that in most cases brothers accepted what they regarded as inequitable distribution. So sometimes did other people. Pa Nukurotoi of Ratia lineage told me of an orchard of his which he said had been taken over completely by Pa Nukutapu of Avakofe. He said 'It has been completely eaten out by the house of Nukutapu. They are consumers of orchards, they and the house of Rangifau. It was our orchard from of old; they were ignorant of this.' He did not contest their appropriation, and there was no strife. But sometimes claimants fought. Pa Rarovi of Kafika clan told me of a boundary stone to his orchard that Pa Taramoa, son of the Ariki Kafika, had shifted to his own advantage. This was challenged by one of Pa Rarovi's sons. They wrestled and Pa Taramoa was thrown, cutting his face. On hearing this, Pa Rarovi at once ceded the orchard, 'because the blood of a child of chiefs had flowed'.

Many disputes did not produce physical struggle but engendered resentment, covert or overt. One related to the ownership of a piece of land in Rakisu. Pa Fenuakimoana of Tafua from Namo and his wife were clearing manioc in that area (No. 5 of Plan 3B) when I talked with them. He was an angry man. He said that the land was his, but that sa Terara had planted taro in it and then manioc. He told them to take out the manioc but they left it and he had taken it over. Paito i Kamota had also planted taro in one portion. He told them to pull it out and go elsewhere.

Disputes over land took on a particularly sensitive character when one of the parties was a chief. In 1929 there were cases of entry by a chief on the lands of commoners, and this was resented, although no formal protest was made.[1] The main offender here was the old Ariki Tafua. In 1952 a somewhat similar situation occurred with his sons and the grandson who had then become chief.

When I was discussing with Pa Fenuakimoana the ownership of land in Rakisu I said of an adjacent area (No. 8) 'Wasn't that the land of Pa Te Urungamori, son of the old Ariki Tafua?' The woman said in a whisper, 'They have appropriated it.' The husband said that the basis of the whole land lay in sa Fusi (of Tafua clan) from ancient days—from the time of the expulsion of Nga Faea, he alleged. He said that the patch in the angle in the south-east (the area of No. 1 on Plan 3) belonged to Taumako because the mother of the late Ariki Taumako came from sa Fusi and it was given with her. Pa Fenuanefu, to whom the land belonged, had confirmed this. He had said much more recently that since a daughter of the Ariki Tafua had now married the present Ariki Taumako and a son had been born to them, the land should stay in Taumako possession. In fact, a *tapu* sign of coconut had been put up there a few days before by one of the elder Taumako men. At the western end of the area, the land of Fangarere (in No. 16 on the Plan) also came from sa Fusi through a woman marrying from there into the Fangarere chiefly family. But all the rest of the area was indubitably the property of sa Fusi. The land taken by Pa Te Urungamori had been recently that of Paito i Samoa, a branch of sa Fusi. My informant said that his ancestor, a former chief of Tafua, had not approved of such appropriations. He said 'Certainly the land "obeys" the chief, but its "obeying" is different (from the right to work it).' He meant that the chief was indeed the overlord but that

[1] *We, The Tikopia*, p. 383.

did not entitle him to take the land over; the real basis of ownership lay with sa Fusi. He added that the father of Pa Te Urungamori, the old Ariki Tafua, whom I knew in 1929, had been a land-grabber too, but that his successor, my friend Pa Rangifuri, on the contrary, had behaved well in such matters. Once he died, however, his brothers had behaved like their father. He added that the present Ariki Tafua followed his father—but this statement may have been tact. (Popular opinion as the famine developed gave the Ariki Tafua the reputation of a land-grabber like his grandfather.) In these attitudes of Pa Fenuakimoana there was probably some degree of resentment arising from quite another issue. His grandfather had been a chief, but he himself was now well away from the line of succession. He may, therefore, have been jealously critical, as one who had lost the rights of chieftainship against those who had retained them. But what he said did coincide with common views.

The issue when a chief is a party to a dispute is complicated by his status rights. Descendants from the chiefly house must acknowledge his over-right. I asked Pa Maneve about the Taumako land cited above: whether it belonged to sa Maniva or sa Avakofe, both of whom seemed to have an interest. He answered 'We do not talk like that, the land belongs to the Ariki.' Again I asked Pa Raropuka, an elder of Kafika with no vested interest there, about the entrenching on the land of sa Fusi by the Paito i Tafua. First he denied this, saying it was the land of the Ariki anyway; but then he admitted that all that area was actually the property of sa Fusi.

Friction between members of other chiefly families and their clansmen had occurred in other cases too. Pa Raropuka observed that a man who 'ate' orchards was Pa Taramoa. He had driven off the people of Porima and had appropriated part of an orchard of Pa Rarosingaro, who had only four orchards. He said that Pa Fenuatara on the other hand was a fine man—the one person who caused land trouble in Paito i Kafika was Pa Taramoa (cf. p. 169).

But with chiefs as with others, land-grabbing usually had some basis of claim. An example of this, noted by Spillius in 1953, was the seizure of part of the large orchard of Marinoa by the Ariki Tafua. He had resorted to the orchard, which was the traditional property of Marinoa lineage, on the grounds that his father had done the same before him. Then in order to clarify the situation, he insisted on a boundary line being drawn down the middle of the orchard—he taking half and the original owner, Pa Raroifi, the other half. Pa Raroifi protested that he and the Ariki had amicably used the orchard together and there was no need to differentiate their holdings. The chief gained his point after all; as Pa Raroifi said, 'He was the chief'. At first sight this may seem outrageous conduct. However, it is significant that the mother of Pa Raroifi himself was of Tafua chiefly stock,[1] and the chief's father's mother was a woman from Marinoa. As such, her son would expect to use the cultivation during her lifetime and, since Pa Raroifi was a generous man, the extension of this right to the woman's grandson might be claimed.

[1] *We, The Tikopia*, p. 393.

Here was a concession of which the new chief took advantage. If the orchard had remained undivided and he simply had right of access to it, the title to the soil of it all would have been with Pa Raroifi. By partition of spheres of interest, however, he secured a definite separable title to a part of the ground.

One of the features of the sharpening of land interests seemed to be a tendency for a chief to take a somewhat more active part in questions of land ownership and decisions thereon. This emerged in the actions of the pagan Ariki Taumako in using land control directly as an instrument of religious and political policy (i.e. as a threat). It also emerged, in questions about the tenure of lands which had been transferred with women on marriage. As with rights of collecting and planting, such parcels of land should revert at the death of a woman unless permission to continue to hold them had been accorded to her descendants in each generation by the lineage concerned. The exception to this is an outright, permanent transfer to the woman and her descendants—as when a chief traditionally gave over lands to his daughter who married an immigrant. An instance of this in 1952 was the lands occupied by Pa Pangisi and his children. These lands came through his wife, a daughter of Pa Resiake (who left no male heirs) and were allocated to her and her husband on marriage by the then Ariki Taumako. Since then Paito i Pangisi had treated these lands not as those of which they had the usufruct, but as lands to which they had title on an equal footing with other lineages who had title to their own lands. Now, by 1952, with the pressure on land and some animus on the part of the later Ariki Taumako, a question of interpretation had arisen. There were three possibilities: (*a*) that the lands had been transferred outright and belonged exclusively to the Paito i Pangisi, i.e. to all the descendants of Nau Pangisi; (*b*) that while the lands were transferred with normal title, Paito i Pangisi, as descended from Pa Reisake and thus an offshoot from the Taumako chiefly house, held their lands ultimately at the chief's discretion and could be evicted should he wish; (*c*) that the lands were held simply by the life interest of Nau Pangisi and should automatically revert either (i) to the allied lineage of Maneve (her father's father's brother's son's sons) or (ii) to the Ariki Taumako. The issue became overt when Spillius was still on the island in 1953. He recorded that Paito i Pangisi tended to take view (*a*), whereas some close kin and supporters of the Ariki Taumako took view (*c*) i or ii. The view of the Ariki Taumako was (*c*) ii— that the lands should revert to him when in the course of time Nau Pangisi would die. But views (*b*) and (*c*) were not exclusive. Indeed the Ariki Taumako, irritated by interference in political as well as religious matters, threatened to exercise the rights he claimed under (*b*) and take their lands forthwith.[1]

---

[1] Spillius recorded that the chief, when questioned by the District Commissioner why he didn't 'pull' the lands away from Paito i Pangisi, replied that if he did the priest would counter by making formal humble obeisance to him (pressing nose to the chief's knee) and begging their return. By Tikopia custom, the chief would have to accede to this. (Cf. my *Authority and Public Opinion in Tikopia*, p. 170).

There is no doubt that in the state of Tikopia society at the time, while all Tikopia might not have agreed that (*c*) was the correct interpretation in this case, they would unhesitatingly have endorsed (*b*). But here is the germ of an extremely important problem, namely the balance of right between title holder and regular user and occupier of lands. Tikopia society in 1952 uniformly acceded to the view that the title holder, especially if a chief, had final claim. But in the recent history of peasant proprietorship in many parts of the world, the tendency has been for the rights of users to receive recognition against inactive title holders. It is true that in Tikopia the chiefs' title to land has not been simply based on mystical conceptions, but is politically well integrated with the present structure of the society. But as Western concepts and presumably Western administrative forms are more firmly established in Tikopia, it would not be surprising to find that the overriding powers of chiefs as regards their claim to lands tend to be acknowledged in theory but never exercised in practice, and ultimately become disregarded completely.

Specific Changes in Use of Garden Land
So far I have talked about land in general and much of the material has referred to orchards in which standing trees of coconut, breadfruit, paper mulberry and areca tended to form the most important economic resource and ground crops were often secondary. Here on the whole by 1952 there had been no radical change in the type of utilization of land. In the fields specifically utilized for ground crops by large numbers of people together, however, some changes in land use over the generation were seen to be quite marked. This is illustrated by a comparative study of a garden area of approximately ten acres in Rakisu. In 1929, I plotted the distribution of ownership and planting in detail for this area. In 1952, this area was replotted with almost identical boundaries by the same methods by Spillius, and some of the results, as well as the general pattern of cultivation, were checked by myself. The attached diagrams (Plans 3a and b on pp. 174 and 175) illustrate the change over the generation.

In analysing the position the first point to be made is the general similarity of the major pattern—both of field division into plots, and of cultivation— as between 1952 and 1929. The Rakisu garden when I visited it after twenty-three years looked as if cultivation had gone steadily on in the same way ever since I left. The main paths still traversed the field, as before—only a few bends ran a little differently. Stones of traditional and symbolic value still stood on the same sites. Pandanus trees, patches of cordyline and other shrubs marked off other significant points as before. Initial enquiries soon showed that the patterns of control and use still operated in former style. In particular, there was a clear-cut separation between the owner of the soil and the owner of the crop—though as before as in any one case, a man might cultivate his own land and be both at once.

But differences were apparent. Some major ones are indicated by reference to Table V.

TABLE V

COMPARISON OF CULTIVATION IN MAJOR FIELD
FOR ROOT CROPS—1929–1952

(Based on pace survey and sketch plans)

	1929		1952 (a)		1952 (b)	
	No. of plots cropped	Sq. yds.	No. of plots cropped in 1929 area	Sq. yds.	No. of plots cropped in extra area	Sq. yds.
Total area used for cultivating	55*	40,000	187	40,000	14	2,000
Land remaining fallow as main crop approached maturity	—	20,000	—	2,500	—	—
Area under taro	55*	20,000	29	3,000	3	200
Area under sweet potato	—	nil	40	3,500	2	200
Area under manioc	—	nil	118	31,000	9	1,600

* A portion of ground containing six plots of taro (Nos. 1-5, 13) in the 1929 survey was omitted from the 1952 survey. But some taro in Muripera and Matamata, not plotted in detail in 1929 (see map), if included in this table would have raised the 1929 proportion of taro still higher relative to the 1952 crop.

The first noticeable difference was a considerable *extension of cultivation*. This was due primarily to a heavy reduction in land under fallow. In 1952, only about one-eighth as much land was lying fallow when the main crop approached maturity in the same area (*a*) as in 1929. In addition, a significant area of about half an acre—(*b*) in Table—had been taken into cultivation from the surrounding land which, in 1929, had been left untouched in orchard (e.g. in Nos. 18, 19, 21, 23, 25, 27, 29, 64, 65, 68, 70). The reduction of fallow land and increase of cultivated area were obvious responses to pressure upon subsistence.

Another marked change was in *crop distribution*. In 1929 the Rakisu field was for crop purposes entirely taro-growing. It served no other purpose and the fallowing was specifically meant to restore fertility for future taro cropping. By 1941, when Sir Harry Luke walked through the area, there was a considerable admixture of manioc among the taro (p. 42). By 1952, the total area under taro had fallen from about five acres to about three-quarters of an acre, while it occupied only about one-sixth of the plots cropped. Conversely, its place had been taken, to some extent, by sweet potato which took up rather more area; and especially by manioc which occupied four

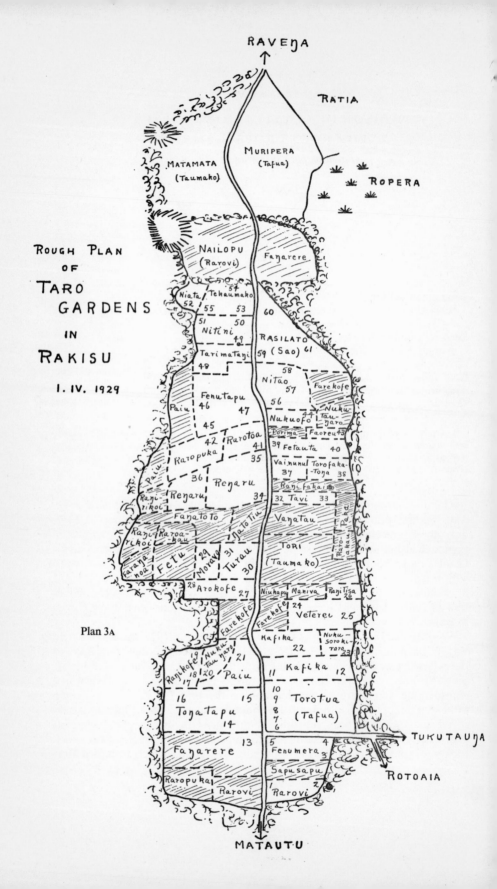

RAVEŊA

RATIA

MURIPERA
(Tafua)

ROPERA

MATAMATA
(Taumako)

ROUGH PLAN
OF
TARO
GARDENS
IN
RAKISU

1. IV. 1929

NAILOPU
(Rarovi)

Faŋarere

Niata Tehaumako 57
52 55 53 60
51 50
Nitini 49
Tarimataŋi 59 RASILATO 61
(Sao)

48 58
Fenutapu NiTao
46 47 57 Farekofe
45 56 Nuku-
Nukuofo 44 tauŋaro
Porima Faoreu 43
42 Rarotōa 41 39 Fetauta 40
Raropuka 35 Vainunui Torofaka-
36 37 Tona 38
Reŋaru Ranifakai
Reŋaru 34 32 Tavi 33
Fanatoto Vaŋatau
Raroa- Nato Tiu
Raŋi bau Tori
rikoi 29 31 Turau (Taumako)
Farana Moraŋa 30
noa Fetu 28 Arokofe 27 Niukapu Maniva Raŋitisa
26
Farekofe 24
Veterei 25
Kafika Nuku-
22 soroki-
tara 23
Raŋikofe Nuku 21
18 20 Paiu 11 Kafika 12
17 19 tauŋaro
16 15 10 Torotua
9 (Tafua)
Toŋatapu 8
14 6
13 5 Fanarere Fenumera 3
Sapusapu
Raropuka Rarovi Rarovi 2

Plan 3A

TUKUTAUŊA

ROTOAIA

MATAUTU

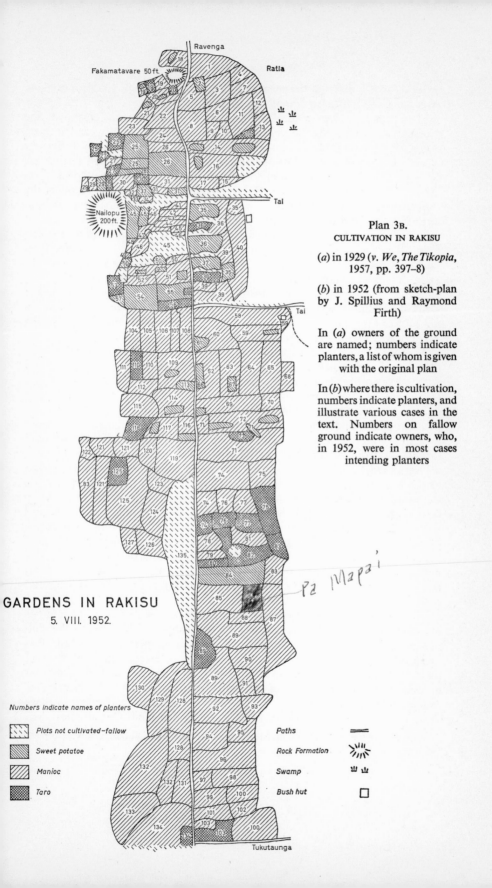

Ravenga

Ratia

Fakamatavare 50 ft.

Tai

Nailopu 200 ft.

Tai

Plan 3B.

CULTIVATION IN RAKISU

(*a*) in 1929 (*v. We, The Tikopia,* 1957, pp. 397–8)

(*b*) in 1952 (from sketch-plan by J. Spillius and Raymond Firth)

In (*a*) owners of the ground are named; numbers indicate planters, a list of whom is given with the original plan

In (*b*) where there is cultivation, numbers indicate planters, and illustrate various cases in the text. Numbers on fallow ground indicate owners, who, in 1952, were in most cases intending planters

Pa Mapai

GARDENS IN RAKISU

5. VIII. 1952.

Numbers indicate names of planters

▨	Plots not cultivated – fallow
▨	Sweet potatoe
▨	Manioc
▨	Taro

Paths

Rock Formation

Swamp

Bush hut

Tukutaunga

times as many plots as the taro and forty times as much space—i.e. many large plots were planted completely in manioc.

There were several reasons for this, most of them associated with the pressure upon land. At the first sight of so much manioc in what had been exclusively a taro field, my thought was a comparison with parts of Eastern Nigeria—where manioc, through progressive exhaustion of soil fertility, is the only crop which will grow effectively and is regarded thus as the last crop index before fallowing is due. But in Rakisu, according to Tikopia, the substitution seemed not to have been due so much to exhaustion of soil fertility as to the drought-resisting qualities of the manioc tap-root as against the taro corm. But it was planted for other reasons also. Firstly, manioc matured in such a way that it could be used for food at an earlier stage than most taro; secondly, when mature it did not need to be dug almost immediately, but might stay in the ground and be dug in small quantities when required. Thirdly, this quality meant that it served as a crop-guard against would-be planters seeking vacant land in which to put their crops. Sweet potato had also these qualities but to much less extent; its main virtue to the Tikopia was that it gave a relatively quick yield.

Another change in the situation as compared in 1929 was the *subdivision* of many of the earlier plots into much smaller units. There seemed to be a very considerable fragmentation of plots, to judge from the much smaller crop areas into which many of the original plots had been divided. But care must be taken here and the interpretation must be guided strictly by a proper ethnographical understanding. The fragmentation was in terms of land use by cultivators, not land owners. The number of actual *planter units* had increased—from 55 in 1929 to 100 in 1952.[1] (By a 'planter unit' is meant an individual man or woman, a married couple or other combination of persons who plant or service one or more pieces of land and jointly use the product.) There is no doubt that this increase was a direct response to land shortage. More people had pressed in to take advantage of any vacant piece of land in this desirable area, and the result had been that many of the plots of crop had become much smaller. Those of any one planter unit sometimes were dispersed. This had some economic effects. Dispersion helped a person to spread his risk from pests; yet, even with such a simple technology it was apt to involve loss of time in working a number of scattered plots.

But while the number of planter units had increased so much, the number of *owner units*, i.e. individuals or sets of individuals with rights to the soil, had increased in this area very little. What had happened mainly was that more people with rights to the soil had decided to exercise these rights, and plant in their lineage or sub-lineage lands, though they had not found it necessary actually to divide up the land. In all, less than a dozen cases of change or partition of ownership of ground were noted. Only a few of these involved permanent division of hitherto undivided land. One of these was

[1] I.e. in the same area—excluding Muripara and Matamata and the portion with plots nos. 1–5 and 13 of 1929.

the case of the sons of Pa Vainunu. Pa Marakei had defined his plot (at No. 35) distinctly against that of his brother, Pa Nukurua (at No. 39), and Pa Nukurua in turn had made a definition of land against his own son, Pa Rangimarere (at No. 40). (This last was very unusual and was stated to be somewhat improper by other Tikopia.)

This relative lack of 'splitting' garden holdings among the owners is in contrast with 'splitting' of orchards. The primary reason for the difference would seem to be in the different type of cultivation in each. In the orchard, the standing crops are perpetually open to use, whereas in the garden the whole of the crop tends to mature at a specific time. Hence, even if the land of the garden is undivided, it is much easier for a planter-owner to identify and secure for himself the results of his labour than it would be with orchard land. Moreover, maintenance of his continued interest in the land for cropping is helped by the new crop, manioc. This can be drawn upon in small amounts as required, and the empty land replanted immediately without need to fallow (or so the Tikopia think), so not leaving the land open for use by someone else. Thus, in effect, manioc as a crop is a substitute for a boundary stone.

There is of course one obvious difference between fragmentation of user's plots and of owner's plots. With the latter, the land ultimately reverts to fallow and the tenure situation is as before.

But if there had not been fragmentation of land holdings in this area, there had been *sharper definition of land interests.* Formerly, planting of crops in someone else's unoccupied land was quite common.[1] A 'rent' (in Tikopia view, more in the nature of acknowledgment of land ownership) was paid in the form of a small proportion of the crop. By 1952, there was a definite hardening of attitude by owners, due primarily to the famine (cf. p. 71). The 'rent' paid was still of the customary type—a basket or so of the produce; there was no attempt to force up this rate. Formerly permission to plant was not obligatory. Now a request for permission to plant was normally expected in advance, and planting in unoccupied land without first getting such permission was apt to be resented. For instance, Pa Nukumanaia cleared a small, unattractive patch of stony ground in a corner of a Rarovi holding (near No. 41) in order to plant yams there, but was 'chased away' almost immediately by the eldest son of Pa Rarovi in order, he said, to preserve the land fallow. Not only was permission required in advance; the request was often refused, or granted only as a special case. Pa Ngarumea, brother of the Ariki Taumako, went to the chief and asked his permission to plant manioc and sweet potato in the *vao tapu*, the chief's sacred taro ground. The Ariki agreed —hence No. 84 of Plan. But later in conversation he said to me that if it had not been for the famine he would not have allowed the ground to be so used. Linked with this strictness about grant of planting rights was a distinct tendency for owners of the ground to plant it all up themselves.

In 1929 I examined the land use of Rakisu from the point of view of the degree to which people cultivated in the land of their own or of another clan,

[1] *We, The Tikopia*, pp. 400–4; *Primitive Polynesian Economy*, p. 261.

M

and in their own or another district.[1] Calculations in the same way from the 1952 materials (*v.* Plan 3b) compared with that of 1929 and Plan 3 (*a*) gave the following table:

TABLE VI

LAND UTILIZATION[2]

Cultivation using land of people belonging to:

	Same District				Other Districts				Total	
	Same Clan		Other Clan		Same Clan		Other Clan			
	1929	*1952*	*1929*	*1952*	*1929*	*1952*	*1929*	*1952*	*1929*	*1952*
Faea	19	50	8	5	7	4	6	1	40	60
Ravenga and Namo	15	58	5	13	0	3	1	1	21	75
Totals	34	108	13	18	7	7	7	2	61	135

From this it can be easily seen that over a generation there has been a big swing towards the cultivation of the land of people with whom one is most closely connected by clan tie or by residence in the same district. The planters of extra-clan land used in 1929 were almost one half as many as those of intra-clan land, whereas in 1952 they were less than one-fifth as many. The planters of extra-district land in 1929 were more than one-quarter of the number of those on intra-district land, whereas in 1952 they were much less than one-tenth as many. In 1929 less than 60 per cent of the plots cultivated were on lands of people belonging to one's own clan in one's own district. In 1952, the proportion had risen to 80 per cent. Where, in 1952, there was resort to land outside one's own clan, it tended to be to that of people within the same district. (Moreover, though I have not shown it in a table, a fairly high proportion, rather more than 40 per cent of the total plots cultivated in 1952, were actually in the land held by the lineage or sub-lineage, i.e. on what people ordinarily called their own ground. This is a much higher proportion than in 1929.)

Examination of cases of planting in lands other than those of people of one's own clan, or own district, show some interesting features. In clan terms Kafika and Taumako used such exterior lands fairly freely in 1952, but Tafua much more sparingly. In every case but one of the forty-five instances of Tafua planting in Rakisu they had resort to lands of their own clan. In only one case (No. 27) was there planting on the lands of someone not of the same clan. I found no special reason for this single case, though

---

[1] See *Primitive Polynesian Economy*, p. 262.

[2] To preserve comparison, the figures of the 1929 Plan and Table have been used here, though the coincidence of the land boundaries with 1952 is not quite exact. Re-calculation for precisely the same area of land in each case, either in terms of planter units or of individual plots, gives almost the same proportions.

the planter, Pa Te Urungamori, was a land-grabber (see earlier). The intra-clan solidarity in this particular agricultural field may have been coincidental, since Rakisu was only one of a number of planting areas. But it was in accord with a similar trend in marriage behaviour (cf. Table XIV). With the other clans it was intra-district solidarity that seemed of more importance. Of the twenty cases in 1952 in which extra-clan lands were used, I was able to trace an immediate kin tie in seven cases. One of these (No. 109) was through a sister's son relation and six were through affinal ties. Three of these (Nos. 18, 41, 98) were dependent upon a wife's right to cultivate in her lineage land, and three (Nos. 43, 47, 52) upon a tie with a sister's husband. Some other cases probably depended upon recognition of specific land rights within a more general designation of owners, and upon neighbourliness. But there must have been well over a dozen cases with no such basis. These were dependent, as in 1929, upon the general principle that an intending cultivator may use any fallow land not protected by a taboo sign. What was clearly evident, however, was that the exercise of these principles was much less wide than a generation before. Hence the 'ideal' of relatively free access to land (i.e. a free relation of men to the soil for purposes of temporary produc-tion) was constrained and limited by the practical exigencies of growing land shortage.

Despite the sharpening of land interests by 1952, one feature of land production had altered significantly—the meaning of taboo signs. In 1929 sections of coconut frond were frequently set up on fallow land to indicate that the owner wished to reserve it for his use. Analogous signs were set up in orchards to preserve coconuts and other fruit. Some of these signs were intended to protect as well as to warn. That is why they were fitted with 'teeth' by means of ritual formulae which were intended to induce tutelary spirit powers to harm persons who might steal.[1] By 1952, the situation had changed. Signs to protect fallow land and crops were still set up. But such signs were used as much to advertise thefts as to protect against them. 'A *tapu* sign is an indication of a theft that has taken place—that the news may spread abroad.' Moreover, from all reports the practice of equipping them with such 'magical' power had definitely ceased. The Ariki Taumako indeed told me that the use of such magical media was a custom of the Melanesian south, not of the Tikopia. I reminded him that such magic protection used to be widely alleged by the Tikopia of a generation before. He then said it was true, it formerly applied to the coconut and the areca. Then he nodded rather wryly and said 'Not a *tapu* sign is worth tying at the present time. Coconuts are lacking and betel materials.' But he also said that formerly a man who stole from a chief would be pierced by a garfish at sea or bitten by a shark—and that this still happened. The reason for the general disarming of these taboo signs is probably three-fold: dislike by Christians of the use of such pagan spirit powers; distaste for the moral attitudes implied in wishing to harm others; and a growing disbelief in the efficacy of the claims made.

[1] See Raymond Firth 'Sociology of "Magic" in Tikopia', *Sociologus*, vol. IV, New Series 1954, pp. 97–116.

In summary, one may say that Tikopia agriculture in 1952 was in a condition of economic pressure. Though intensified by famine, the pressure did not originate in this. The results included a division of land holdings by married brothers, a tendency to restrict the interests of married women in their lineage land, and a sharper definition of personal rights in land as against rights of other lineage and clan members, and community members. Such developments could have been anticipated. In fact, in speculation before my return to Tikopia, I thought that increasing land pressure might mean a tendency not for the lineage as a land-holding group to become more solidly united against others, but for quarrels within lineages to occur and for brothers to tend to split up. But it will be noted that in Tikopia land pressure has not destroyed the unilateral system in favour of an ambilateral one. Tikopia unilaterality has been reinforced by pressure.

Another point of general interest arises, in reference to what has usually been called 'individualization'. As the result of studies of social change in the last generation or so, it has often been pointed out that individualization, including individual rights in land, tends to be a concomitant of increasing Westernization. There are good reasons for this. But Tikopia is a case of a society where Westernization has not as yet penetrated far into the institutional field. It is true that some of the most important sanctions for marriage and for social control have been modified, or have received new force from Western authorities. But the basic forms of the institutions are in the traditional Tikopia mould. On the other hand, internal pressure on subsistence has tended to operate in a parallel way to the forces of Westernization. In the sphere of land use the pressure of population has tended to promote a definition of personal interests and rights such as has occurred, for example, in other communities faced by a new cash crop market. One would say then that the impetus to 'individualization' can come from internal as much as from external pressures. It is a question of relation between goals and the means of achieving them. Where the gap between these widens, there is stimulus to individualization as one of the possible ways of maintaining or increasing personal satisfactions.

CHAPTER VII

Indices of Social Movement: Patterns of Residence and of Marriage

The concept of social change may refer to two kinds of phenomena—alteration in the structure of the society, or alteration in persons and relations within the structure, while still leaving the general structural principles as before. This latter process may be termed *social movement*. The importance of studies of social movement has come to be realized more clearly in recent years. In particular, analysis has been made of the degree of spatial mobility in a society expressed, for example, in the relation between kinship and residence, exhibited in the developmental cycle of family or domestic group life. But such studies have, as a rule, been made on a synchronic basis. By using quantitative data of distribution of households of various composition and reported data of a genealogical and other attributed order, inferences have been drawn about the way in which members of a family arrange their domestic affairs over time. Such inferences are very plausible, but they are essentially an interpretation of process over time by comparison of phenomena at one period of time. To give such inferences more validity it is advisable to examine material at two different periods of time. This enables one to see how far the distribution at the later period represents an actual and not merely an imputed social movement. The analysis in this chapter has this aim.

While little structural change had taken place in Tikopia society by 1952 as compared with 1929, there had been a great deal of social movement. In this chapter I examine two phenomena, residence and marriage. Here the patterns of social relationship in any society are often not expressed in any abstract rules by the participants, and the structural features are of a 'covert' or 'latent' kind. Information on such patterns is desirable not only to complete the ethnographic picture, but to allow comparison of magnitudes—for example, to see how far changes in the economic or religious system of the Tikopia were matched by corresponding changes in the patterns of their dwelling and marrying.

Local Grouping

In Tikopia local grouping in 1929 there were three main types of unit: district, village and household.

Districts were two only, Faea and Ravenga. Namo was a sub-district of the latter, having for some social purposes, for example dance organization, a distinct entity of its own. Of varying degree of specificity also were the large population units of Rofaea and Fare, constituting Faea; and the very small population units of Uta and Tai, addenda to Ravenga.

In 1952, the situation was similar in all major respects. After the generation interval there was still the similar relation of part co-operation and part hostility between the two major districts. But there were minor differences. The position of Faea and Ravenga, traditional and deep-rooted, by 1929 had become in effect one expression of the conflict between Christianity and paganism. By 1952, the balance of this religious division had been much altered, though much of the traditional opposition still continued. Again, the area of Tai, formerly hardly to be ranked as a sub-district was, by 1952, claiming at times to be recognized as such, though the people admitted that they had no separate dance organization and that they danced with sa Ravenga.

In 1929, villages in Tikopia numbered twenty-one, apart from a few scattered houses. No village had a regular plan; the dwellings were highly concentrated and it was often difficult to see any clear-cut division between one village and another. For the most part, the villages had no specific traditions of founding. The first settlers could be identified by tradition in a few cases, but no particular value was given to such traditions of village origin, and the descendants of the original settlers were given no formal recognition. There was no concept of a 'village founder' as in some African communities. Similarly, there was no conception of a village head. Any man of rank living in a village exercised influenced there, but not specifically or formally as headman. Yet social unity of the village was considerable. Only one village, Matautu, was recognized as divided into sections, each with its name and local owners of the ground.

In 1952, the same system of settlement patterns obtained with the same general location and names as in 1929. No new villages had been constructed; there had been no village fission or migration. There was one difference in name emphasis. By 1952 Matautu was known more commonly as Potu i Motuangi—a shift from name A to name C on Plan 4—probably because of an alteration in the local balance of forces, which gave growing influence to the Kafika people living in that section. This was a revival of a name used for the village two generations before, but rarely heard in 1929.[1]

Households in 1952 were of the same style as in 1929. Dwellings were of timber and thatch, with coconut sinnet ties, no nails at all being used in construction. The floor was of sandy earth covered with coconut leaf mats. A fire on an internal hearth at one side of the dwelling gave some light and warmth; it was used to provide brands for smoking, and for roasting yams and fish. A cookhouse nearby with large earth-sunk oven using hot stones was used to prepare most of the household food. Another adjunct to the household was commonly a canoe shed, usually standing near the beach. A medium-sized house in which half-a-dozen people lived had, as before, an average floor space of about forty square feet and a capacity of about two hundred cubic feet per person.[2]

---

[1] See 'Potimatuang' from Durrad (1910) in Rivers, *op. cit.* I, p. 334 and map p. 335; also *We, The Tikopia*, p. 61. (The inclusion of Rotoaia in Table XII, as a residential area not in occupation in 1929, is not a case of the founding of a new village, but of temporary occupation on old house sites to cope with immediate food shortage.)

[2] The Tikopia house taken over by the expedition, and which had formerly housed six persons, measured 20 ft. 9 in. by 12 ft. 9 in. It was 8 ft. to the ridgepole, but lowered to 2 ft. 9 in. at the eaves.

Residential Patterns

In seeking indices to the history of a society one finds that residence is one fairly simple but significant indicator. After an interval of a generation it is reasonable to expect some change in the locus of action, some spatial mobility among the people. But change of dwelling place is not simply a material change. It reflects structural considerations, and personal choices. It may be related to principles of descent and inheritance; it may mean change in size or constitution of residential kin groups; it may have repercussions on relations with neighbours. In short, physical movement may relate to the concept of what makes up a proper social unit. It may also mean a change in the availability of resources. Even in Tikopia, where any cultivation is accessible by a walk of less than an hour, if a man changes his dwelling he may alter his accessibility to some of his lands. If, as is common, these are dispersed over the island, he has to decide whether or not it is worthwhile continuing to cultivate a particular garden; sometimes he leaves it to be used by a kinsman living nearer.

If in Europe a person has never moved more than two miles from his village, it is regarded as a sign of a stable, even stagnant, existence. In 1952 there were nearly 1,500 Tikopia in this position. But their social life, though it might show only micro-movement in spatial terms, was not stagnant. Their small-scale residential changes had social importance.

In a society that is increasing by natural process only very slowly, there is no *prima facie* case for change in residence—save by one spouse in each pair that marries. As families grow, more people can be got into a house. Hypothetically, despite even a very great increase in population, one might have found the Tikopia continuing to occupy the same houses as a generation before. If, for example, they had been Alpine peasants, one might have expected to find larger families in each house—no increase in the number of houses but more people per dwelling, which had been originally built to accommodate them or later enlarged. Polynesians often do display elasticity in housing accommodation since the paraphernalia of their domestic existence are small—a sleeping mat for each person and a few utensils for the household. If necessary, at a pinch, whole extra families can be accommodated. Over the generation 1929 to 1952 then, one might have postulated a small alteration in residence with the new generation in part succeeding to the sleeping and living places of the old, and only in extreme cases having built fresh housing. Yet although the small size of the island gave building land a definite value, the situation was more complex. In technical terms, marriage in Tikopia was mainly viri-patrilocal, in 1952 as in 1929.

Residential patterns of the Tikopia have three elements in combination, each representing a social relationship. These are: (i) a name of a dwelling; (ii) a site; (iii) a unit of personnel. I discuss first name and site, and their relations.

Name of Dwelling and of Occupier

In 1929 every dwelling in Tikopia had a personal name, and this name tended to adhere to the site. Names of dwellings and of sites in long occupation were structurally important since they were also used as lineage names. These names tended to have a symbolic or mystical quality, especially through their association with revered ancestors, who in pagan times were buried under the house-floor. Other names commemorated experiences of Tikopia abroad.[1] The system of house names also gave social identification to persons. The head of the household, if a married man, was commonly known by the same name as the house, with the appellation 'Pa', equivalent to Mr; his wife similarly bore the same name with the appellation 'Nau'. Such designations ordinarily lasted throughout life. But if a person regarded his house name as unlucky he might change it by his own volition. Again, he might resign it and take another when one of his sons married; the son then commonly continued to live in his father's house, bearing its name, while his father removed to another house near by, and changed his name accordingly. Here change of house name marked change of social personality with transfer of responsibilities over a generation. Such customs in general tended to preserve continuity of relationship between house site and householder, and to facilitate social description, in the absence of a system of surnames.

In thinking of possible changes that such a naming system may have undergone, there are several alternatives. In the most extreme case the Tikopia, after a generation of more intensive Western contact, might have abandoned altogether their system of naming house sites and dwellings. (Many other Oceanic peoples do without personal names for houses altogether; why should not the Tikopia have adopted the same practice?) Again, they might have continued to assign names to houses, but not in fact to use them as aids to social description. (The names could be purely ornamental, as when in large Western cities, they are disregarded by the postal authorities, and numbers insisted on for address.) Or again, the Tikopia might have continued the system of naming, but discarded their ancient names wholesale, as being old-fashioned, and adopted a new set of names more in conformity with their modern ambitions.

All these are theoretically possible, but by 1952 none of them had occurred. The Tikopia had retained the character of their residential naming system. As a rule householder and house site were still associated by name, and the processes of adaptation mentioned earlier were still in vogue. For example, a man whom I knew in 1929 as Pa Paiu had changed his name to that of his dwelling (no. 7 on Plan 4) by 1952 and was known as Pa Te Urangamori; he thought the former name had brought him illness. The man I knew in 1929 as Pa Koroatu, who lived in a house of the same name, had by 1952 become Pa Raveiti; his eldest son was now married but had continued to live in Koroatu and had assumed his father's former house name. Some new foreign names had been introduced, but comparison of imported names borne by houses and by married couples in 1929 and 1952 showed that there had been no significant change in style.[2] This general conservative adherence to traditional

[1] See *We, The Tikopia*, pp. 81–7.

[2] Married men's names in 1952 included: Pa Otara—from my house of 1929, which in itself had been named from the district where I lived in New Zealand; Pa Niuaus—'new house'; Pa Mosbei—from Moss Bay in the Solomons, where some Tikopia labourers had worked; Pa Uistin—from the Western District where some men had been. It was also likely that there would be soon a Pa Kanada—from Canada, the homeland of Spillius.

names was surprising; one might have expected that growing Tikopia interest in novelties from the outside world would have led to much greater incorporation of foreign names into their scheme.

Use of Alternative Residences

In 1929 there was no 'housing problem' in Tikopia in the Western sense of shortage of accommodation. But Tikopia housing was not just a matter of finding a place to dwell in. A house site was normally an object of ownership in kin terms, including lineage and clan terms, and there was great attachemnt to this patrilineal title. New sites could be opened up, but most of the old ones—even though left vacant—were not really deserted or abandoned from the point of view of social interest. Commonly a man built only on a site of his mother's kin. A 'squatter' was very rare and usually intruded only when a title was disputed. No person might build upon the vacant site belonging to some other family or lineage without first obtaining permission. Such permission was usually accorded and a slight acknowledgment made by gift. There was no sale of sites and nothing in the way of regular economic rent for them.

This was related to the Tikopia custom of spare sites on which alternative residences might be built. The number of house sites in Tikopia was not fixed. Many of them were said to have been traditionally in occupation for many generations and as such were regarded as devoted to dwelling purposes. But there was nothing to prevent a person from setting up house anywhere else on land which he controlled. Later the site might be abandoned for residence and allowed to grow up into brush or it might be taken into cultivation again. This possibility of expansion or contraction of house sites was one of the elements in the social structure facilitating mobility and segmentation in lineages.

This use of alternative or spare house sites depended on a number of reasons. The dictates of seasonal cultivation made it convenient to live in different orchards at different times. In periods of food shortage kin might concentrate in a common household to use their resources in a single oven, to the best advantage; or they might disperse among their orchards to protect the growing food supplies there. But economic reasons were not solely responsible. Family sentiment might make a man keep in repair and use occasionally an ancestral house which was less convenient for him than a newer one on another site. There were also ritual considerations. A natural succession in housing terms was not simply a matter of replacing dwellings and occupying them; there was the problem of the dead, who did not merely vanish, but had to be disposed of. The old Tikopia pagan custom of burying the dead under the house-floor embodied sentimental and moral ideas of sheltering the grave from sun and rain and ritual ideas of averting the wrath of an unprotected ancestral ghost.[1] But proximity to the dead was dangerous—not for hygienic reasons, but from fear of the spirit if the bodily resting-place should be defiled. Hence, when an ancient house site had become too 'loaded' with dead for peace of mind, another house was built near by.

Apart from such ideas there were considerations of personal comfort, in-

[1] Cf. Raymond Firth, *The Fate of the Soul in Tikopia*, 1955.

cluding a notion that change was good in itself. Some people moved from
dwelling to cookhouse and back, for freedom of floor space, or convenience.
Some had in addition to their usual dwelling, a 'refreshing house', literally a
house into which the breeze could blow (*paito angiangi*) near the beach, where
it was cooler at night, with fewer mosquitoes. Some young men built
'bachelors' houses'—also usually near the beach—which they used as refuges
from their family, and places of assignation. When a young man married, he
might turn this house into a permanent dwelling and migrate there with his
wife, using his old home as an occasional resort. For all these reasons, many
Tikopia men had alternative dwellings—a house in the town and a house in
the country, so to speak.

By 1952, one might have expected to find that, with increase of population
and pressure on land, there would have been a decrease in the number of
alternative residences. There might even have been a reduction in the total
number of dwellings—a tendency for cultivation to encroach on house sites.
This was not the case, even despite a temporary shortage of accommodation
immediately after the hurricane owing to lack of leaf thatch. I shall deal with
totals later. But as regards alternative residences there was, if anything, evidence of an *increase*. This increase was partly to keep other people off the
sites. If a man already had a house on a site and occupied it periodically, there
was less opportunity for someone else to ask permission to build (which it
might be difficult to refuse, but which might later on be used in making a claim
to the land). But other reasons also operated. Pa Nukumata, only son of my
old friend Pae Sao, who had died by 1952, had two houses, only ten yards
apart—Notoa, where his father had lived, and Nukumata, his own house—
which he occupied alternatively, just as he felt inclined. His mother, Nau Sao,
had gone with a daughter to live permanently in another ancestral house in
Uta. Pa Resiake, youngest son of the late Ariki Taumako, was living in 1952
with his family of young children not in his main dwelling but in the adjoining
oven house. He said 'Here it is much easier—we can make a mess here'. In the
oven house less formality was necessary, especially as the children did not
have to be kept off the ancestral grave mats, which occupied some space in the
main dwelling.

In this use of alternative dwellings and shifting from one site to another,
one is struck by the social significance of even small movements. Even a
minimal shift of location may have considerable social import. There is no
doubt that socially, physical scale, or magnitude of territory, is important.
Facility of communication, time taken for public meetings to assemble, speed
of organization, for instance, depend upon it. Yet for intensity of social relations, for attitudes about integration and severance, physical distance may not
be particularly relevant. In Tikopia, micro-movement may be enough to
create social distance. This can be seen in cases of temporary banishment,
where it may be sufficient for a person to go out of his village and sub-
district, to put him at an effective distance from punitive action: if he goes out
of his district this will cater for quite severe offences. Traditionally, in
Tikopia, when it is said of a man of Ravenga that 'he has gone to live in

Faea', it is equivalent to saying that he has gone to quite another part of the country, partially cut off from his usual village and kin life. If it is said that 'he has gone to live in Tufenua' it is equivalent to saying he is at Land's End— living an isolated and desolate life. Yet all this is within a couple of miles!

In 1952 the same general principles were in vogue as in 1929. I recorded three cases of such banishment as having taken place in the interval—one for food theft, one for general bad relations, and a third because of an intrigue with his chief's daughter, a cross-cousin (see p. 158). In all three cases about half a mile seemed to be the limit of appropriate removal. In any correlation between physical distance and social distance, then, a society seems able to make its own rules. For Tikopia the observer needs a magnifying glass as an aid to interpretation.

Continuity and Change in a Village

It must be clear at the outset that the basic system of Tikopia residence was unaltered by 1952. This included continuity in the number and the irregular structural plan of settlements; in the interior plan of dwellings; in the conceptual isolation of dwellings and of house sites as social entities, especially by the assignment of names.

The first point that struck me in 1952 was the continuity of many dwellings; apart from minor repairs, many of them obviously had gone on unaltered from 1929. But there had been changes—some old sites stood vacant, or had disappeared under a rearranged set of houses; and there was a crop of new dwellings. There had also been some changes of house name. For comparison, I had my own census of 1929 and some village plans, and similar data for 1952. But I could also enquire of the people themselves. Here the system of name-retention raised not only a problem of memory, but also of social identification. It was possible for me to test the knowledge and memory of people by getting their identification of sites of houses standing in 1929 and disappeared by 1952. It soon became apparent that even among the older men there were differences of opinion as to the location of the vanished houses, and the degree to which present buildings were a continuation of them or new social entities. Not only memory was at stake, but also the question of what constituted an entity—'the same house'. The maintenance of continuity of a house as a social unit in itself could become a matter of contention. On the whole, as one might expect, ignorance and denial of continuity or break tended to be greater with people more remote in residence or kinship from the case at issue.[1]

Since residential movement or change has so much social significance for the Tikopia, conceptualized in structural and organizational terms, the degree to which it has taken place over a generation is relevant to the wider problem of changes in the nature of the society as a whole.

To understand the processes at work, an example from a single village, for which there are comparative plans in 1929 and 1952, will suffice (see Plan 4).

The Tikopia housing pattern had great social stability. Although the hurri-

[1] Pa Maneve, living in Tai, said he could not identify the site of a vanished house in Namo—'because I am of another land (*fenua*)'—less than a mile away!

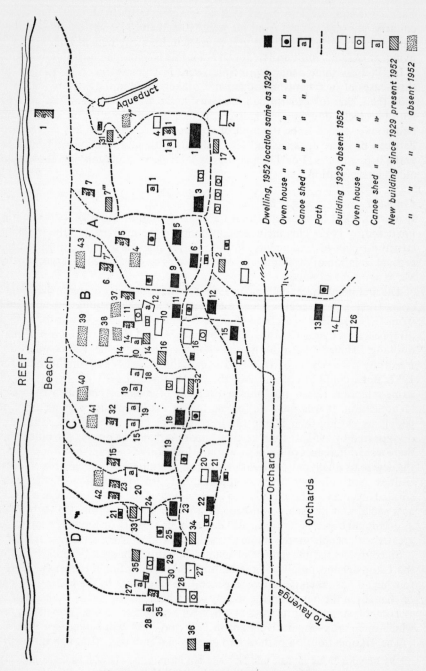

Plan 4. VILLAGE OF MATAUTU IN 1929 AND 1952

Section A, Matautu proper, is the land of the Tafua chiefly lineage; B is of Raropuka lineage; C (Potu i Motuangi) is of Marinoa; and D of Fasi (Rangirikoi). Numbers 1 to 30 refer to buildings of 1929; later numbers indicate more recent buildings cane of January 1952 swept the island and did so much damage, the basic patterns of residence survived as regards occupancy of site and kin group rights in it. Disaster shook the people but did not lead them to abandon their domestic habits. This may be regarded as conservatism, but on the other hand it can be looked on as capacity for adaptation and resilience in the face of catastrophe. Yet there was movement.

In the village of Matautu in 1929 there were thirty dwellings. Excluding the house of the anthropologist (no. 30 on Plan 4), one house abandoned (Marinoa) and three vacant (Saumarei, Feneitai and Matautu)—nos. 26, 20, 23 and 4 on Plan 4—there were 25 dwellings in actual occupation by Tikopia at that time. In 1952, when a re-survey was made there were 27 dwellings, of which 26 were inhabited,[1] the vacant one being Motuapi (see later). The village of Matautu was suffering more than most from a shortage of building materials after the hurricane. This was illustrated not only by the lack of any spare housing, but also by a reduction of oven houses from 22 in 1929 to 19 in 1952, and of canoe houses from 13 in 1929 to 10 in 1952. The number of inhabitants of the village in 1929 was 122, and in 1952 it was 170, giving a rise in average household membership approximately from 5.0 members to 6.5 members. Though the number of dwellings had hardly increased, changes had occurred in the use of sites and naming of dwellings. The general position was as follows:

TABLE VII

DWELLINGS IN MATAUTU, 1929 AND 1952

In 1929, dwellings in occupation		25	
vacant		3	
	Total	**28**	
In 1952, the position was:			
Dwellings of 1929			
(a) persisting on site with same name		16	
(b) persisting in name but shifted to another site[2]		5	
		21	
(c) Disappeared			7
New dwellings after 1929			
(d) built, but disappeared by 1952			10
(e) built and standing by 1952		6	
	Net total in 1952	**27**	(lost **17**)

[1] My original plan of 1929 has been followed—cf. *We, The Tikopia*, Plan I. A re-survey was made by me in April 1952, and repeated in more detail later in the year by Spillius, who also collected details of the building history of the village over the previous generation.

It may be noted that the figures given ehre differ slightly from those given for Matautu in Table XII; this is because the Plans do not include a small area to the south known as Nukutureki, which is included with Matautu in the Table.

[2] In this village no house persisted on the same site with a changed name.

The reasons for the changes were as follows:

(*a*) The hurricane wiped out most of the houses near the beach. Among these were houses built in the interim period,[1] including seven houses of bachelors, which tended to be more lightly built than the rest. Early in 1952 some people had already announced their intention to replace a number of these houses when materials were available.

(*b*) There had been some movement towards the beach to allow extension of cultivation so as to grow bananas, papaya and manioc in what was formerly orchard land. The forty per cent local increase of population had meant some increase of pressure on their lands.

(*c*) There was lack of male issue in some cases and sometimes the elementary family had died out as an economic unit. For example, Pa Nukuomanu died without issue and his house (no. 10) was abandoned. So also Feneitai and Farereu (nos. 20 and 24) were abandoned as their owners died. Moreover, the Pa Mukava of 1952 was the brother's son of the man of that name in 1929, having moved in (to no. 2) to fill the place of the dead man who had died without offspring.

(*d*) With marriage came need for space for the growing family. Hence, there was a tendency for a man who had lived as a bachelor in the home of his married brother to build a new house on marriage or as his children increased. Alternatively, he took over a house abandoned by the death of a kinsman.

(*e*) A change of house name occurred because of a change of social status. The house Rangifuri (no. 17) was inhabited in 1929 by Pa Rangifuri and next door to him in Motuangi (no. 18) lived his father's sister's son, Pa Motuangi, a widower. Later this man joined his cousin. When Pa Rangifuri became chief on the death of his father, the Ariki Tafua, he moved to the chief's ancestral residence—Motuapi (no. 1). Pa Motuangi stayed on, remarried, assigned his former house and name to his married son, took that of Pa Raroifi ('under the chestnut tree') and changed the name of the house Rangifuri to correspond.[2] He also shifted it to a more landward site—no. 32.

(*f*) Fear of ancestral spirits of the dead buried under the floor motivated some shifts of residence. In 1929 the house Tarakifiri (no. 16) had two burials in it—father and grandfather of the then owner, who was a bachelor. He later became a Mission teacher, married and had children. He wished to get away from such pagan practices as burials under the house floor. He also had dreams that his father and grandfather came to him and asked if he was not ashamed to leave things lying on their grave mats; they also objected to the children playing above their heads. The atmosphere was unpleasant for him, so he dismantled the house and moved it a few yards towards the beach. In 1952 the old house burial site was kept as a family graveyard. Similarly, Pa Taitai,[3] who had renamed himself Pa Teauika, told me that he moved his dwelling

[1] Included here are Matautu, Nukuraro and Te Urungamori, each rebuilt for a time on a different site from the earlier house of that name. (See nos. 4, 14 and 7 on Plan 4.)

[2] *We, The Tikopia*, Plate VIII, pp. 61–2. Pa Raroifi took the house-name of his father's father's brother, who with his wife committed suicide (before 1910) leaving no descendants. (Cf. Rivers, *op. cit.* pp. 347, 359.)

[3] *We, The Tikopia*, p. 124 *et passim*.

(from no. 28 to no. 36) because of the interference of Feke, the octopus god, with members of his family. His brother, Pa Fasi, did the same.

(g) Some house sites were changed for more general convenience. The Ariki Tafua said that he built the house now named 'St Peter' (no. 31) for a variety of reasons. He wanted a house near the beach to get the breeze, and to be near the fish-drive when mackerel shoals appeared. He wanted an extra dwelling to serve as an overflow house to accommodate his affinal kin when they visited him from the other side of the island. He also wanted a house that would be more convenient for European visitors in having a much larger doorway than had his ancestral home. Moreover, Europeans tended to stand in his presence, which was taboo according to Tikopia custom; he minded this breach of etiquette less in a new secular dwelling than in the chief's ancestral dwelling. This house, Motuapi (no. 1), which was 'heavy' with ancestral graves and the presence of spirits, was accordingly used only on Tikopia ceremonial occasions. Finally, as an ardent Christian and leader of Christians, the chief wanted to give his house a Christian name and have it blessed by the priest. But he did not dare to change the ancestral name of Motuapi since this might possibly offend the resident spirits. So he built a new house which could serve as a Christian centre.

Indices of Residential Continuity and Change
To give more precision to this concept of internal mobility I looked for more general indices. In 1929, the total number of houses listed as in regular habitation in Tikopia as a whole was 228.[1] By 1952, the total number of houses regularly occupied had risen to 298. I compared then:

(a) the number of houses in 1952 which were identical in name and site with those of 1929;

(b) those existing in 1952 on the same site but with another name;

(c) those existing in 1952 on another site but with the same name;

(d) those existing in 1929 of which the site had been absorbed by 1952;

(e) those existing in 1952, with name and site new as regards 1929.

The proportion of houses in (a) relative to the 1929 total gives an *Index of Identity*, while the proportion in (b) and in (c) gives an *Index of Partial Change*. Together these two give an *Index of Continuity*, that is, the degree to which the house as a social locus persisted over the generation. Apart from this, houses which had disappeared by 1952, i.e. which were not represented either by a site in occupation or by name, could be regarded as representing a social loss. But in effect they had been replaced by a proportion of the new building since 1929, hence they may be indicated by an *Index of Replacement*. In addition, since by 1952 the total number of houses was greater than in 1929, even making allowance for the replacement of those of which the site and name had disappeared, one can speak then of an *Index of Accretion* (over and above 1929) for the Tikopia community as a whole.

[1] This figure includes seven permanent houses vacant at the time but used as spare residences. Most survived and were in use in 1952. For the importance of house-name as a basis of social continuity in Tikopia see *We, The Tikopia*, p. 86.

The position may be represented in tabular form as follows:

TABLE VIII

TIKOPIA DWELLINGS IN 1952

by comparison with 1929

Condition	No.		Index		Per cent
Identical in 1952 with 1929	151		Identity	(a)	66
Same site, new name	27		Partial change	(b)	12
Same name, new site	12		Partial change	(c)	5
Total remaining from 1929	190		Continuity		83
Sites absorbed/abandoned (dwelling disappeared by 1952)		38	Replacement	(d)	17
Total dwellings in 1929		228			100
Completely new by 1952	108	(70)	(Accretion		30)
Total by 1952	**298**	**(298)**	Compared with 1929		**130**

Before going on to discuss the reasons for the various changes that occurred in Tikopia housing between 1929 and 1952, it is pertinent to inquire, who occupied these houses? Was there occupation by the same people over the generation, or was there much movement around? How far could one speak of continuity not only in the material frame of Tikopia society, but also in the social units inhabiting that frame? Did the pattern of domesticity correspond in any way to the regularities of the housing situation?

To answer these questions I have not thought it necessary to go through the laborious work of plotting the whereabouts in 1952 of all Tikopia who were alive in 1929. Two types of inquiry suffice. The first is to examine a set of sample households to see how significant the changes may have been in the personnel of specific Tikopia domestic units. The second is to see how far control of all such domestic units may have passed to other hands.

As far as personnel of domestic units is concerned, a simple method is to re-examine households already analysed earlier. In 1929 I set out in detail the membership of four households which seemed fairly representative.[1] The membership of the same households (i.e. domestic units occupying the same or substitute dwelling) in 1952 was as follows:

Taramoa. This unit of Kafika was described as a multiple family household in 1929, shared by two married brothers. This had rather the character of an augmented family household a generation later. The personnel had altered considerably, but there was much continuity. Pa Fenuatara, former head of the house, had gone with his wife to live in Uta. But four of his sons and one of his daughters still lived in the house, and another son, a member of the

[1] *We, The Tikopia,* pp. 121–5.

Solomon Islands Protectorate police force living on Guadalcanal, stayed in the house when he was on leave. Only the eldest of the sons (Rakeivave of 1929) was married; his wife and their three sons lived with him. In addition, the old Ariki Kafika lived in the house. His wife was dead, and he was now making his home with his grandson, though he also spent much time in Teve, his former home, with his son Pa Taramoa. The old chief's third son, Pa Fenuafuri, who formerly lived with his family in Taramoa also, had gone to live close to his brother Pa Taramoa, in a new house named Fenuafuri, also occupied by his married son and family. A former 'adhering child' Savatau, who used to live in Taramoa with his adoptive father Pa Fenuatara, had married (taking the name of Pa Mapusanga, that of his lineage) and had gone to live with his own father in Faea. Thus, after a generation, instead of two married brothers and their families, plus an adopted child, this dwelling housed the eldest married son of the elder of them, with his unmarried brothers and sister, his own family and his aged grandfather.

Notoa. This unit of Tafua was described as an augmented family household in 1929. By 1952, my old friend Pae Sao, who had once been known as Pa Notoa, was dead, as also his bachelor brother and two of his sons, who had all lived in the house with him. Three of his four daughters had married and were living not far away, while the widow and the fourth daughter, still unmarried, had gone to live near the ancestral temple in the Sao orchard in Uta. The house Notoa was occupied in 1952 periodically by Pae Sao's only remaining son, married and with seven children. Known as Pa Nukumata, this man lived for most of the time with his family in Nukumata, a house next door, and used Notoa as an alternative residence.

Raroakau. In 1929 this house of Taumako was occupied by an augmented family—by Pa Taitai, his wife and two children, his widowed mother, his bachelor elder brother, and his two unmarried sisters. By 1952, this unit had dispersed. The widow and her two daughters were dead, as was likewise the firstborn child of Pa Taitai. His brother had married and built a house nearby for himself and family. Pa Taitai himself had now three more daughters and two more sons, none yet married. With his wife, they all lived together in the same house, now shifted from its original site, and renamed Teauika. Pa Taitai himself was now called Pa Teauika in accordance with the new dwelling name.

Rangifuri. In this house of Tafua in 1929 lived an elementary family—Pa Rangifuri, his wife, his one remaining son, and three unmarried daughters. Another daughter, also unmarried, lived near by with a kinsman. By 1952 Pa Rangifuri, after succeeding to the chieftainship of Tafua, was dead, as also was his wife. His son had succeeded as chief in turn and gone to live in his own house in the chief's domain. Three of the four daughters had married and gone away, two to Ravenga and one to Anuta. The dwelling itself had been shifted. The only occupant remaining from a generation before was the unmarried daughter. She shared the dwelling with her father's widow—a woman who he had taken as second wife after 1929—and a miscellaneous collection of boys—two sons of her brother, a son of one of her sisters, and a kinsman from Anuta. This was a composite or mixed household in kinship terms.

After a generation, then, each of the four households had undergone considerable change. Yet in each there was some continuity of membership—at least one person in each had been living there a generation before. The essential structure of the domestic units was the same. But the processes of death, marriage and procreation had become manifest through replacement of personnel. One unit had altered its character from multiple family household to augmented family household, and two had become simple or elementary family households; one had changed from a simple family household (diminished by one member) to a composite household.

A more general comparison would show similar movement throughout the whole community. But the shifts of personnel would not reveal any fundamental change in the nature of the domestic grouping, nor in the continuity between those who occupied the dwellings in 1929 and those who occupied them a generation later.

Now I turn to the question of continuity as exemplified in recognition of control of household affairs.

There were no formal heads of households in Tikopia, but each household had a male senior representative. It is sufficient to consider who was in effect the head of the house at these two periods. I have accordingly classified the households of those dwellings which remained from 1929 (identical, or with partial change) in terms of the relation of the head of 1952 to him of 1929. The results are as follows (the head of the house was male in every case but two):

TABLE IX

CONTINUITY IN OCCUPATION OF DWELLINGS IN 1952
COMPARED WITH 1929

			Cases
(a) House identical:			
Head	(i)	same man as in 1929	64
	(ii)	patrilineal descendant	58
	(iii)	sibling	7
	(iv)	other agnatic kin	13
	(v)	other kin	4
House vacant			5
		Total	**151**
(b) and (c)—site/name of house as before:			
Head	(i)	same man as in 1929	17
	(ii)	patrilineal descendant	19
	(iii)	sibling	0
	(iv)	other agnatic kin	3
	(v)	other kin	0
		Total	**39**

These figures show the high degree of continuity of social units in Tikopia residence. Of the 190 cases of preservation of residence over the generation, 81, or 43 per cent of the households were still headed by the same men who occupied that position in 1929. Of the remainder, 77, or 40 per cent, were headed by patrilineal descendants of the earlier heads; in 72 cases these were sons, in one case a daughter, and in four cases, sons' sons. (In two other cases, sister's sons inherited.)

What do the figures tell us of the succession by the sons? Where the sons were sole male child in each family, the succession was obvious—there were seven such cases. But what about succession by senior or junior sibling? In a strongly patrilineal community such as Tikopia, with relatively small-scale households, and an emphasis on the status of an eldest son, one might expect that as an eldest son married and begat children he would move out of the parental dwelling and set up house for himself. In such case the majority of houses occupied a generation later by sons of the original heads would have younger sons as their heads. The data do not show such movement. Of the sixty-five cases where senior and junior brothers were concerned in succession to residence-headship over the generation, the result was:

		Cases
Eldest son	(married)	36
	(bachelor)	5
Younger son	(married)	21
	(bachelor)	3
	Total	**65**

In some of these cases the eldest son may have moved back into the family residence after his father's death; but these were few. It is obvious that in Tikopia there was no clear-cut rule for household succession by senior or junior son; if anything the bias was in favour of the eldest son taking over the headship of the residence. In the twenty-four cases where a younger was in possession of the father's home, the elder son was dead in thirteen cases and was living as a bachelor with his younger brother in two cases; in only ten cases was his elder brother, married, living elsewhere. In general, relations between male siblings in Tikopia manifested a fair degree of amity. Where the elder brother was the head of the father's house, in more than a third of the cases he had a bachelor younger brother living with him, and in nearly a third of the cases a younger brother, married, was the head of a house near by, with the two households in close economic and social relationship.

Having examined the degree of continuity of Tikopia residence and some aspects of the change, I now consider the reason for change.

Reasons for Change of Dwelling
Details from the village of Matautu have illustrated most of the reasons for Tikopia residential movement. As far as the general picture for the whole

community was concerned, I was not able to find out just what the specific reason was in all cases of change. But, with the help of Spillius, I was able to obtain reasons in rather more than half of all the cases where name or site of dwelling were changed or site abandoned, and in practically all cases of new building. The reasons, in summary form, for all these changes were:

natural disaster, rather more than five per cent;
expansion or contraction of kin units, rather more than forty per cent;
economic motives, about fifteen per cent;
change of social status, rather more than ten per cent;
esoteric reasons, rather less than five per cent;
reasons of personal comfort or whim, twenty-five per cent.

As might be expected, practically all the cases of disappearance of houses which were in existence in 1929 were due to natural disaster, or to lack of issue or immediate heirs. In contrast to this, growth of family and personal comfort (such as having a dwelling near the beach to catch sea breezes) were responsible for four-fifths of the cases of new building, although new houses in significant number were put up that people might open up new cultivations or guard an existing cultivation against theft.

Although the number of houses where there was partial change (that is, either in site or in name) was fewer, the reasons for the alterations were perhaps the most interesting. The most important reason for changing the house name while retaining the site was change in social status. The assumption of new responsibility by a man on his marriage meant alteration in his status relative to others in the household. The general tendency was for him to assume either a traditional but temporarily unused family name and for that to be assigned also to the house, or to take a quite new name of his own devising and for the house likewise to bear it. Sometimes, however, the house name changed because there was a new occupier not in the ordinary line of succession. This occurred when people of the lineage of Morava were exiled from the village of the Ariki Taumako (cf. p. 158). Their houses were occupied by members of the chief's own lineage. Though kin to the exiled men, they renamed the houses from ancestors of their own. Another reason for change of house name was to alter bad luck. In the case of Atavi, for example, it was said the name was changed because of *mara*, i.e. the lack of fertility and fortune, which came from the spirits. My informant described how two brothers of the lineage owning the house fought, which was improper. So the son of one of them, previously living in the same house, built his own house separately. Later, the two men died (supposedly because of their sin) and other owners of the land resumed the site, rebuilding the house and giving it a name of their own, Te Aravaka. But the site had been desecrated because of the *mara*—so 'their children were lost completely'. Hence the timbers of the building were taken inland and the house rebuilt there, with another name. The expression for change of site in such cases is 'the standing place of the house is abandoned because of misfortune'.

Misfortune was often attributed in 1952 to burial of forebears under the house floor. 'In Tikopia a person is buried in the centre of the house. Evil comes to us from him. The white man is correct in burying outside. Hence, nowadays the corpse is laid down in another place, is carried and buried apart, is buried in the white man's fashion.' The propriety of the modern custom was confirmed by some Tikopia by referring to the traditional practice in regard to chiefs. It was pointed out that chiefs in Tikopia in recent times had never been buried within their own dwelling houses. They had been buried in places which they themselves indicated, either outside the living house or in a temple in Uta. If buried in their own house or if buried away from other chiefs, it was believed that they would wreak spiritual ill upon their descendants. 'The clan will be completely lost. They will bring misfortune.' Views of this nature were cited more frequently in 1952 than in 1929 to explain site changes. One reason for this difference of stress was probably the virtual disappearance of the domestic kava cult of pagan ritual elders, and of other procedures by which offerings were made to the ancestral dead buried in the house. The modern Christian of 1952 lacked the former means of control of ancestral spirits, and hence felt that he and his family were especially vulnerable to them, if they continued to share the same residence. As mentioned earlier in such site changes (p. 190), the shift of location need only be very slight. It is enough to rebuild the house a few yards away, to remove it from over the graves and so block the malign influence of the dead ancestor.

Some of the complications which occur in the relation between house-site and house-name in Tikopia as independent variables can be shown by two further examples.

Of olden times the house Matangirere stood in the village of Faretapu on a house site owned by Fatumaru lineage, but no house of that name existed in 1929. After 1929, a man of Porima went to live there with his sister's children of Fatumaru. Then he married and went back to his 'basis' in Potu sa Kafika to live. He took with him the name of the house he had formerly dwelt in and applied it to his new house. The old one meanwhile fell into disuse. But later, one of the members of the Fatumaru group rebuilt the old house and lived in it, still keeping its old name. So while in 1929 there was no house bearing the Matangirere name, in 1952 there were two houses of the same name (a most unusual circumstance).

The other case concerned two houses of the Maniva group. Many years ago an Anuta man was married to a Tikopia woman and took the name of Pa Tavarei. He lived in the house Motuomanu in Ratia. Then the house name was applied to a young man of the group of Rangimatere and he was called Pa Motuomanu. The house itself was destroyed in a great storm about 1930 which took away part of the coastline. But the name was transferred to another house in Potu sa Taumako occupied by the name-bearer. Meanwhile, one of the sons of Pa Maniva had married and taken the name of Pa Tavarei from the Anutan connection. A house called Tavarei was built for him in the village of Sukumarae where some others of his family lived, the timbers from it being supplied from Nukutaukara, a house standing (in 1929) in Ratia, in which Pa Tavarei had spent his youth. Later still, when a member of the Taumako chiefly family became a missionary, a house was built for him by his

kinsfolk on the spot formerly occupied by Nukutaukara, and called Tanu-
kofe. I was told that about fifty years before a house of another name still,
Sauoro, stood there and was inhabited by a member of the Fusi group.

Hence, while in Tikopia the general structure of the residential system
remains the same, there has tended to be a continual flux in terms of houses,
house names, sites, people who live on them, and the names that these people
bear. The residential history of the community over a generation throws much
light on the realities of social process.

Residence and Kin Alignment

The residential position of social units in 1952 must now be compared with
that in 1929. There are two main aspects to this: the internal constitution of
household units in their kin relations; and the external significance of household units in kin group terms in regard to wider issues of political pressure.

As regards the internal constitution of the household, a primary question
concerns the elementary family.

The building and occupation of new houses has meant the creation of new
residential units and some reshuffle has taken place within the households
occupying the same sites continuously. It might be put forward as a hypothesis
that, with the advance of Westernization in Tikopia, with the extension of
Christianity and the consequent weakening of ritual obligations, there might
be a tendency for more households to be composed of elementary families
alone. It might be expected that fewer Tikopia children would be found in
households other than those of their parents, and that there would be more
denuded family households with widows and orphans not living with their
kin. Households in general might be thought to be of smaller size. Putting the
matter from another point of view, if there are more houses in 1952, who have
gone into them? Is it the elementary families who have moved out or is it the
attached kin who have moved out to make way for the new elementary families
as they form? Let us examine the figures.

The net increase in the number of dwellings between 1929 and 1952, it will
be remembered, was about thirty per cent: this was roughly parallel to the
increase in population (about thirty-five per cent). The rise in population,
then, had been met not by any serious overcrowding but by keeping approximately the same ratio of dwellings to people. In 1929, the average size of
household was slightly less than 5.9 persons, and in 1952 it was slightly more
than this, a difference of no practical significance—especially when the effects
of the hurricane are taken into consideration. But while there can be said to be
a Tikopia norm of domesticity, this is a matter of statistical expression rather
than of overt recognition. There was a wide range of variation, with some redistribution over a generation.

The comparative distribution of households in terms of the number of
persons in the household unit is shown in Table X.

Though households of persons living alone increased considerably, the most
significant increase in the number of households was in the medium range
(five to eight persons). Households of three to four persons actually decreased

in number, while those of ten to eleven persons increased much more than in general proportion.

TABLE X

HOUSEHOLD COMPOSITION BY NUMBER OF PERSONS

Year	1	2	3	4	5	6	7	8	9	10	11	12	13	14	15–17	Total
1929	11	17	20	27	33	28	28	24	15	7	3	5	0	2	1	221
1952	21	23	16	24	44	47	34	36	23	16	8	4	0	1	1	298

But who occupied these households? Distribution of households in terms of kinship components is as follows:

TABLE XI

HOUSEHOLD COMPOSITION BY KIN COMPONENTS

Type	No. of households 1929	No. of households 1952	Variation approx. per cent
Solitary male	9	10	80
Solitary female	2	11	
Married couple only	5	4	
Elementary family only	94	105	20
Polygynous family	3	4	
Denuded family only (widowed spouse & ch.)	10	19	
Elementary family *plus* sibling	27	22	
Elementary family *plus* parent/& sibling	23	36	50
Elementary family *plus* any other kin	21	39	
Denuded family *plus* other kin	8	19	
Mixed household containing siblings	13	14	50
Mixed household, other	6	15	
Total households	**221**	**298**	**+35**

The figures indicate that the general patterning of Tikopia households in kin terms remained much the same over the generation. There were few households without a nucleus of close kin. But the distribution of kin had altered in some respects. The increase of solitary females, and of denuded family households (i.e. with only one parent) is attributable primarily to losses of husbands at sea. Over the generation, the elementary family, alone or in combination, remained the core of household life in the great majority of cases (nearly 75 per cent in 1929 and nearly 70 per cent in 1952). But it was proportionately somewhat less of a *separate* household unit than before. The tendency had been for elementary families to be combined with parents and/or other kin, thus giving a higher proportion of households in the medium range of size. Any suggestion by 1952 of closer definition of elementary family rights in movable property was not paralleled by any closer definition of elementary family as an autonomous household unit. But this may have been only a temporary phenomenon, since it occurred mainly in one district. In Faea, where housing was most difficult in 1952 owing to the hurricane, the number of elementary families living alone or with siblings had *decreased* considerably in 1952 by comparison with 1929, and the total number of households with an elementary family as primary component was almost precisely the same after the generation interval. This implied that, owing to housing and possibly food stringency, members of elementary families had dispersed to some extent.

In summary, there were proportionately fewer households in 1952 than in 1929 containing the elementary family as a component; there were only 23 per cent more households containing elementary families in 1952 compared with a rise in population and a rise in the total number of households of about 35 per cent. But as regards our earlier question of who had moved into the newer houses, one can say that this had tended to be immediate family offshoots—married sons founding families of their own; younger married brothers splitting off from older married brothers when both had children; unmarried brothers wishing freedom and starting new households through the mechanism of the bachelor dwellings.

In general terms then, Tikopia group-living concepts were still just as important to them in 1952 as a generation earlier. Christianity and other Western influences had not physically disturbed their residential patterns. They had responded to demographic changes and to economic pressures rather than to the tendency to individualize for its own sake. They had retained as ordinary components of their household system the various associated kin, either ancillary or dependent. They did not develop the isolated elementary family. Putting this another way, the social attitude of the Tikopia in relating the family to the wider kin unit was still maintained in residential terms. There was, as yet, no residential contraction of the kin unit. A man owning a house gave shelter, oven facilities and domesticity to essentially the same range of kin in 1952 as in 1929. Even when times were hard there had been no perceptible tendency to drive out the dependent kinsfolk.

So far I have talked mainly of gross changes in population and social relations. But how had this affected specific named social units? Had it affected them differentially? Later, I show how these effects were expressed in social and political terms. But here I wish to indicate how one aspect of Tikopia social change was expressed in the residential distribution of he major social units. Take first the four clans. In 1929 and in 1952 I classified the households of Tikopia according to the clan of the leading male member. In a few cases house sites were in occupation by members of another clan (e.g. one man had settled on his mother's brother's house site), but usually the head of the household coincided in his clan affiliations with those of the recognized owner of the site. Conversely, residence on a site was apt to be regarded publicly as a tacit claim to its ownership or at least to the exercise of *de facto* influence in the neighbourhood. Hence, any redistribution of clan members among house sites could be significant in terms of claims to land or demonstration of power over land.

By 1952, each clan had enlarged the total number of its *households* as against 1929. Theoretically, it would have been possible for each to have increased its households proportionately and (granted the advance of population) to have remained static *vis-à-vis* the others. But, as against an increase of about 35 per cent in the population and nearly the same in the number of households in the whole community, the household increase in clan terms had differed significantly. Table XII on p. 202 illustrates this.[1]

This means that—

Clan Tafua   (2nd in the rank of its chief) had increased by 7 per cent
Clan Kafika   (1st in the rank of its chief) had increased by 26 per cent
Clan Fangarere (4th in the rank of its chief) had increased by 47 per cent
Clan Taumako (3rd in the rank of its chief) had increased by 72 per cent

In terms of total numbers of households, Taumako clan had risen from third place to first place in a generation.

All clans had expanded as regards the number of *villages* in which they were represented. Here again Tafua had expanded least, but Fangarere showed most relative movement and Kafika most absolute movement. By mid-1952 Kafika was found in all but four settlements of the island and Taumako in all but six settlements.

What allowed these clans to move outwards into fresh settlements and what did this expansion mean? It was possible for two reasons. The dispersed nature of much land-holding often gave a man of one clan an available house site in or near a village occupied by members of other clans. Again, kin ties outside the patrilineage provided the basis for seeking permission to dwell on a site not on the lands of one's own clan. Such expansion, establishing a household in a village not previously occupied by members of this clan, indicated some weakening of local exclusiveness. From the outsider's point of view it might mean a more positive extension of his descent group's interest in disputed or marginal lands in territory dominated by another clan.

This process of clan dispersion fits fairly well with the Tikopia traditional stories. These state that after an original confinement of the major clans to one district, that of Uta on the inner shore of the lake, they broke out and carved up the rest of the land among themselves. The modern dispersion then may be interpreted as a continuation of a yet unfinished process whereby, in the long run, all the Tikopia will be thoroughly distributed residentially through the whole island.

But there is also another and more self-conscious aspect of this matter. This dispersion may be related to attempts at local domination through control of land. My friend, Pa Fenuatara, and other leading men expressed their fear of Taumako expansion of this kind, having in mind the assertive political

[1] This Table follows the same form as Table I in *We, The Tikopia*, p. 66. The figure of total households in 1929 now appears as 221, not 218 as in the original Table. This is because on reconsideration it has seemed more appropriate to list as separate households three sets of people who as marginal cases were formerly treated as living with kin whose alternate residences they were using; the figures for Potu sa Taumako and for Matautu have been altered accordingly. One reallocation has been made (in Tukutaunga), owing to an incorrect clan attribution in the original Table.

TABLE XII NUMBER OF HOUSEHOLDS OF CLAN IN VILLAGES

VILLAGE CLAN	Year	Total No. of villages and residential areas in which clan members found	Tai	Ratia	Sukumarae	Potu sa Taumako	Faretapu	Potu sa Kafika	Potu sa Fangarere	Potu i Fara	Asanga	Nuku	Ravenga	Uta	RAVENGA Total	Potu i Akitunu	Potu i te Ava	Nuaraki	To Roro	NAMO Total	Rotoaia	Sapei	Potu i Siku	Tukitaunga	Matafanga	Matautu	Potu i Korokoro	Potu i Fangatafea	Potu i Rofaea	Potimua	FAEA Total	TIKOPIA Total
Kafika:	1929	18	2	1	3	2	2	17	0	0	2	4	0	0	31	1	0	0	1	2	0	3	4	1	1	14	2	3	15	1	44	77
	1952	23	3	0	3	2	3	22	3	0	3	5	2	2	46	1	0	1	2	4	2	2	5	2	2	14	1	2	16	1	47	97
Tafua:	1929	14	0	1	0	3	0	0	0	0	0	0	0	0	4	3	6	5	2	16	0	1	0	6	4	8	8	4	3	3	47	67
	1952	15	0	0	0	2	0	0	0	0	0	0	0	2	5	3	11	7	2	23	1	0	6	6	5	8	18	2	2	2	44	72
Taumako:	1929	16	4	4	2	13	3	0	0	4	5	2	2	1	40	6	0	0	0	6	0	0	3	2	6	4	1	0	0	0	16	62
	1952	20	8	4	4	19	6	0	0	5	14	2	0	3	65	6	1	1	2	10	0	2	8	1	10	8	2	0	0	0	32	107
Fangarere:	1929	4	0	0	0	0	0	0	10	0	0	0	0	0	10	3	0	0	0	3	0	1	1	0	0	0	0	0	0	0	2	15
	1952	7	0	0	0	0	0	0	12	0	2	0	1	0	15	3	0	0	2	6	1	0	0	0	0	0	0	0	0	0	1	22
TOTAL	1929	25	6	6	5	16	5	17	10	4	7	6	2	1	85	13	6	5	3	27	0	5	8	9	11	26	21	7	18	4	109	221
	1952	26	11	5	7	23	9	22	15	5	17	9	8	8	131	13	12	10	8	43	5	4	13	9	17	30	21	4	18	3	124	298

role of members of this clan in the recent past. This dispersion of clans in the generation 1929–52 into what were formerly alien settlements had been assisted by Christianity. The settlement of a Taumako man of rank, a Mission teacher, in Namo in what was earlier a Tafua stronghold was facilitated through the advance of Christianity. I was told that such an intrusion would not have occurred in earlier days.

One can say then that while the general form of Tikopia residence was maintained during the generation 1929–52, there had been redistribution among the various units. This redistribution on the whole was part of the 'normal' process of social living, whereby the successors of the older generation re-ordered their affairs in conformity with their specific individual and group interests. But some of this re-ordering seemed likely to lead to more basic changes in the control of lands and of village affairs. In the long run, this may result in overt structural changes in Tikopia society.

PATTERNS OF MARRIAGE

Considering the changes that had taken place in Tikopia society generally between 1929 and 1952, one might have expected some change in the patterns of marriage. Some temporary alterations in marriage rates did seem to have occurred. The export of labour involved the absence of a considerable number of young men and presumably delayed a number of marriages that would otherwise have taken place. To some extent reinforcing this, the famine following the hurricane of 1952 undoubtedly caused certain marriages to be postponed for lack of the food supplies deemed socially essential to the celebration of a wedding.

Change and Persistence in Marriage Practice
What about more long-range changes? In particular, one might have expected that, with the advent of Christianity and its interest in sex *mores* of young people, there might have been a rise in the marriage rate greater than the rise in general population, owing to pressure put on young people to marry instead of remaining single and having sex intrigues.

This hypothesis, however, is not borne out by the facts. In 1929, my census count gave 189 simple unions, i.e. married pairs; in 1952 there were 234 simple unions. If we add the unions in which widows, widowers and poly-gynous wives had been concerned, there were in 1929, 252 unions and by 1952, 335 unions. This meant an increase of only 21 per cent in married pairs, or of only 33 per cent in spouses of all kinds. Since the increase in population was rather more than 35 per cent, it is clear that there had been no significant development in the marital situation. This was backed up by general evidence about the sex intrigues of the young unmarried, which appeared to have gone on in 1952–53 in much the same way as in 1929, among Christian and pagan alike. Despite the injunctions of the Mission priest and some of his teachers, the influence of Christianity in the field of sex *mores* had not been marked. There had been no change in the social and moral responsibilities of marriage and the subsequent kinship involvements. There seems, however, to have been a progressive modification in the Tikopia marriage ceremony, by cutting down the number of formal acts.

Some traditional food exchanges had been abbreviated. The initial feast prepared by the kin of the bridegroom was no longer reciprocated. This was said to have been done at the instance of a chief of Tafua, who stated that when a man married, since he had taken a woman from another group it was right for him to make a feast in compensation—but it was not then necessary for the woman's kin to reciprocate this in turn again. The scale of food resources needed for marriage had also been reduced by omitting the large presentations of food made to the Ariki Kafika at Somosomo by any man who married a Kafika woman.[1] These reductions were done not only in Christian marriages; pagans had followed suit, perhaps being only too glad to be relieved of an onerous burden. But all other presentations in the marriage series were still made and reciprocated in the traditional way. Moreover, so important were ample food supplies for the proper celebration of a marriage in Tikopia, that the rigours of famine were allowed to affect seriously the timing rather than the standards of wedding feasting and display. Even among Christian Tikopia, marriages were postponed—up to a year—until a 'proper' amount of food could be assembled. Here Tikopia customary ceremony was regarded as essential; a simple Christian church marriage would have been regarded as indecent. On the other hand, there had been a marked reduction in the violence of the antagonistic relations between the groups of kin of groom and bride concerned in a marriage. In particular, the practice of ritual capture of the bride, which was formerly general with families of rank, seemed by 1952 to have been finally abandoned, and formal protest by her kin at her leaving them seemed also to have been dropped.[2] I have no direct evidence on this myself owing to lack of marriages during my stay, but in neither of two marriages recorded by Spillius during the latter part of his stay did such formalities appear to have occurred.

It might seem that the influence of Christianity would have appeared particularly in marriage preferences. Since in other societies it is common in Christian circles for objection to be made to the marriage of Christian with pagan, one might have expected this in Tikopia. No doubt the Mission hierarchy had views on this matter. But in practice the Tikopia did not seem to pay great attention to this point. In general, the religion of a wife tended to agree with that of her husband. There was no case known to me of a husband who was a practising Christian having a wife who had remained unbaptized and a practising pagan. But there were in the 1952 census ten cases of a husband who was a pagan having married a Christian wife, who then in effect abandoned her cult in order to follow his. Of these, most notable was the case of the wife of the Ariki Taumako. She was a Christian girl, a daughter of the late Christian chief of Tafua in Faea. Alleged to have been one of the mis-

---

[1] An account of earlier procedures is given in *We, The Tikopia*, ch. XV, and *Primitive Polynesian Economy*, p. 323; v. also *Work of the Gods*, pp. 311–15.

[2] Cf. *We, The Tikopia*, pp. 538, 544 *et seq.*

tresses of the Ariki Taumako, she was said to have risen in the night from her home and come over, in Tikopia style, to the other side of the island to marry her lover. It was alleged also that she was instigated to this action by her father for political reasons. Yet her husband, the chief, was stalwart in his paganism in 1952 and she participated fully in the traditional religious affairs of Uta. Here again, Christianity in Tikopia was not yet strong enough—or deep enough—to overcome the exercise of personal choice in spouses. For a few women it could not wholly control even ritual procedure, in outward conformity to the rules of the accepted faith. But for the most part, by 1952 Christianity was so widespread in Tikopia that religious difference in marriage was not of great statistical weight.

As part of the rule of Christian marriage, Tikopia in 1952 had an overt marriage proscription of polygyny. The entire abolition of polygyny would have had little effect in Tikopia because its incidence in recent generations seems to have been always low. But as in Muslim countries, the right to have more than one wife has been regarded by Tikopia as reasonable even by those who did not take advantage of it. The practice of polygyny was, in effect, regarded as more respectable than that of regular extra-marital intercourse though the impediments to it in the way of female jealousy were probably held to be greater. It was interesting, then, to note that while the number of polygynous unions in 1929 was very small—only three effective unions[1]—in 1952 there were also three cases. Two of these were unions in which all three spouses in each case were Christian, and in the other case one of the polygynous wives was a Christian. (These polygynists had, of course, been excluded from attendance at church until they should remedy their state and repent.)

In 1929 rules about choice of marriage partners in Tikopia were simple, though not very clearly defined. There was no rule of clan or lineage exogamy. There was a prohibition on sex relations and on marriage between kin described as *maori*, i.e. 'close', 'true'. The prohibition applied not only to parents and children, and to siblings, but also to any kin of the first degree, including parallel and cross-cousins. It was in regard to the union of siblings or first-cousins that the Tikopia were most articulate; they regarded it as improper, incestuous, and liable to result in lack of issue or illness or death of offspring, and dying out of the family—through intervention of the ancestors. Breaches of the rule were sometimes tolerated, subject to a supernatural sanction.[2]

In 1952 a similar situation obtained. Intra-clan and intra-lineage marriage were permissible and occurred. The union of 'close' kin was reprobated as before, though it was permitted in some cases. The son of Pa Orokofe made pregnant his father's brother's daughter. She gave birth to a child, and after much heated discussion their elders in disgust and helplessness let them marry. But marriage might be blocked on other grounds than close kinship. In one case two young people of Kafika clan, not very closely related, were

[1] *We, The Tikopia*, p. 565.
[2] *We, The Tikopia*, pp. 329–36; 'Marriage and the Classificatory System of Relationship', *J.R.A.I.*, vol. LX, 1930, pp. 235–68.

stopped from marrying by the parents of the young man who disliked the alliance. The result was that since the woman had already conceived by her lover, she bore a bastard child, which was adopted by her mother's brother's wife and that woman's father.

It should be noted that few of the intra-clan marriages were actually intra-lineage unions. Thus in 1952, of all fifty-five intra-clan marriages only ten, or less than one-fifth of the total, took place with members of closely affiliated sub-lineages, i.e. with people having recognized proximal ancestors. By far the larger number of such intra-clan marriages were with members of different lineages, or where common origin was regarded as of distant ancestral separation—e.g. Avakofe and Aneve, whose common ancestor was about eight generations back.

The offence of Pa Mapai of intrigue with his chief's daughter was intensified and given a touch of horror by the fact that she was his *kave maori* (cf p. 158); that she was of another lineage was irrelevant. In another case, where the couple had been allowed to marry, it was pointed out that they had different fathers and mothers, but a single grandparent. 'It is bad. It is like the body of a single person. When the people of old used to behave in this way, as time went on their offspring disappeared. The *mara* appeared on the bodies of the males and of the females.' The term *mara* is in general the opposite of *manu*, or *mana*,[1] and means infertility or lack of prosperity; in this case it refers to ulcerations produced by supernatural causes. An extension of the same attitude is seen in the following case. A man had married the daughter of his elder brother's wife's brother. Though the woman was not a close consanguine of her husband, she was his brother's 'daughter', and the elder brother's wife regarded the marriage with disapproval. She pointed out that the married pair had no children—the wife had had a miscarriage—and she thought that this was perhaps because the ancestors were angry with them. But at a practical level her resentment took a more overt sociological form. She said 'Aunt and niece address a husband by the same term!', and I concluded that her personal disapprobation of this equation of herself with her niece was more responsible for her moral attitude than her objections to their union as a case of a breach of the rule about close kin generally. Although the Church presumably expects the Table of Consanguinity and Affinity to apply in Tikopia, in practice it seemed in 1952 still to be the traditional Tikopia rules which obtained. The Motlav Mission priest himself did not seem to be quite clear how far he would be prepared to disregard Tikopia custom in sanctioning a marriage.

Class Preferences in Marriage

In 1929 there was an opinion, though not a formal rule, that members of chiefly houses, especially women, should not marry commoners. The reasons for this endogamous attitude, it was held, were to ensure that each chief of the clan would be descended from a chiefly woman, and to allow members of

[1] Raymond Firth, 'The Empirical Study of Mana', *Journal Polynesian Society*, vol. 49, 1940, pp. 483–510.

chiefly houses to expel the commoners without complication of kinship ties if famine should eventuate. But it was recognized that this was only nominal, that in practice this attitude had not been followed at all rigorously, and that the then Ariki Tafua and Ariki Taumako were 'commoners sitting in the seats of chiefs'.

The old Ariki Tafua stressed that such intermarriage of members of chiefly houses with commoners was of relatively recent occurrence. But such inter-marriage was in no way the result of European influence. It began before that influence was perceptible, and there was no external motive to cause it—the Tikopia themselves gave personal attraction as the sole reason for its occur-rence. On the other hand, in the fictional class endogamy of chiefs and their offspring there was no hint of eugenic purpose; their preference was for per-petuating social differences, not a particular physical stock.

But examination of their genealogies shows that the endogamy of chiefly families was by no means always practised, even in early Tikopia history. As much as eight generations ago, e.g. according to tradition, a chief of Taumako married a woman of Sao and his grandson married a woman of Raropuka. Both of these latter were important lineages but of commoner stock. The theory of chiefly endogamy represents then an ideal. But its existence does give a standard by reference to which free intermixture with commoners could be checked. On the whole, the men who have become chiefs in Tikopia seem to have married women of chiefly lineage or of lineages which have sprung fairly recently from the chiefly houses. Even by 1929, when unions between chiefly and commoner houses had become frequent, the code could be invoked to render them difficult. Depending on the personalities involved, at least a protest might be made when a commoner man and a woman of a chiefly house wished to marry, and the outcome in any given case might be uncertain —the man and his kin might be too terrified to proceed.

Now let us compare 1929 and 1952. By the latter date, the views about preferential marriage among chiefly houses seemed to have largely died away, though they might have come to expression if the question of the marriage of a putative heir to chieftainship had arisen. It is interesting here to examine the figures of married pairs comparatively from this point of view. Details are as in Table XIII on p. 208.

From the decrease in the proportion of commoner-commoner marriages over the generation, it might look at first sight as if there had been indeed a change, a liberalizing of the class attitude, and a greater commingling of commoners with members of chiefly houses as spouses. But the situation has not been such in reality; the impression is due to a relative increase in members of chiefly houses generally. Let us assume a norm of monogamous marriage, and also that any young people of chiefly house who did not marry had not been prevented from marrying in their own class. Then, in 1929, of twenty-six possible marriages of chiefly pairs (dictated by the maximum number of chiefly women available), only eight were made (31 per cent); while in 1952 of forty-six possible marriages, fifteen were made (33 per cent). This very slight increase of unions between chiefly pairs does not indicate any significant loosening of a prescription of intra-class chiefly marriage, over the generation. Rather it indicates that in effect people were following their personal choice—that even in 1929 the stated preference was simply an ideal; that it was not necessarily a dead letter, but the objections to union between members of chiefly house and commoners were not sufficient, save perhaps in exceptional cases, to inhibit ordinary choice. This is borne out if we look at the marriages of chiefly women—about whom there was said to be most sensitivity—from another point of view. In 1929, their marriages had been just about one-third with members of their own class and two-thirds with commoners; in 1952 this proportion was maintained.

TABLE XIII

SOCIAL CLASS AND PREFERENTIAL MARRIAGES

	By 1929 No.	By 1929 %	By 1952 No.	By 1952 %
Marriage of chiefly males with chiefly females	8	4	15	6
chiefly males with commoner females	32	16	38	16
commoner males with chiefly females	18	9	31	13
commoner males with commoner females	131	70	153	64
Total marriages[1]	**189**		**237**	

This is the position for Tikopia as a whole. But there is a fairly marked difference between the behaviour of Kafika and Taumako folk on the one hand, and Tafua on the other. Intra-chiefly class marriage in both Kafika and Taumako rose from three cases to six cases in the generation 1929 to 1952. In these groups, marriages of members of the chiefly class with commoners rose in the case of Kafika from eight cases to fifteen cases and in Taumako from twelve to fifteen. But with much the same proportion of eligible members, Tafua had only one intra-chiefly union in 1929 and only two in 1952, while unions of members of the chiefly class with commoners rose from nineteen to twenty-four cases. That is, the proportion of intra-chiefly class unions was far lower, and of chiefly-commoner unions far higher with Tafua than with Kafika or Taumako. To see any reason why this should be so we must turn to the geographical or residential distribution of the chiefly groups in Tikopia.

Clan and Locality Marriage Patterns
In 1929 kinship was traceable, in theory at least, between all people in Tikopia who were likely to marry. Though the descent principle was patrilineal, there was no barrier to the marriage of agnatic kin as such. The incest proscription on close kin applied equally to cognatic as to agnatic kin. Marriage within the

---

[1] In Tables XIII, XIV and XV, the figures are those of married women. For the 189 simple unions of 1929, data for three wives are lacking, but data of three polygynous wives have been added, making a total of 189 women considered. For 1952, to the wives in 234 simple unions, data of three polygynous wives have been added, giving a total of 237 wives considered.

clan and within the lineage was allowed providing the incest prohibitions were not transgressed.

In 1952, as I have shown earlier, the rules were the same as in 1929. But what about the general practice in terms of positive patterns? How far in an unformulated way had there been maintenance or change in the type of marriage choice? Among the possibilities two suggested themselves as plausible. Firstly, because of the pressure of population there might have been movement in marriage to take advantage of differential landowning and wider land rights. For example, there could have been a tendency to more marrying out in order to get advantage of the wife's usufruct from her own land rights in another lineage; this would have benefited a group containing many male members. Or again, polygyny might have increased, to give a wider range of land use. But of such movements there was no sign. By 1952, as in 1929, there was no indication that men were marrying for fortune, or even to help make a living. (The limitation of a woman's right to life interest would perhaps seem to have been an important factor here.) Polygyny again was rare; being apt to be with sisters, it gave no land advantage.

A more plausible effect might have been that because of Christianity there might have been a tendency to widen the clan range and local range of unions —for Christianity, as it were, to free the marriage market by reduction of old animosities. The following tables throw some light on this. The first classifies marriages in clan terms:

TABLE XIV

MARRIAGES BY CLANS

CLAN OF MAN	CLAN OF WOMAN											
	Kafika '29	Kafika '52	Tafua '29	Tafua '52	Taumako '29	Taumako '52	Fangerere '29	Fangerere '52	Other (Anuta) '29	Other (Anuta) '52	Total '29	Total '52
Kafika	18*	17*	18	22*	19*	28	8	10	3	2	66	79
Tafua	18	23	22	24	10	9	2	4	1	0	53	60
Taumako	23	34*	11	22	15*	13	2	8	1	2	52	79
Fangarere	10	11	3	4	1	2	2	1	1	0	17	18
Other (Motlav)	—	—	—	—	1	1	—	—	—	—	1	1
Total 1929 / 1952	69	85	54	72	46	53	14	23	6	4	189	237

* Includes one polygynous wife each case.

When the figures of 1952 are compared with those of 1929, account being taken of the rise in the volume of marriages over the generation, there is seen to be very little change in the over-all pattern.

O

It is clear that there were some *clan preferences* in marriage patterns in 1929 as in 1952. Kafika and Taumako showed a considerable affinity, about a third of Kafika marriages, both men and women, being with Taumako, and nearly one-half of Taumako with Kafika. Fangarere showed a marked preference for Kafika, over half of its spouses being drawn from that clan. By contrast, the lack of marital relation between Taumako and Tafua was very noticeable, though rectified to some extent by marriage of Taumako men with Tafua women by 1952. As regards intra-clan marriages, there was a slight relative decrease with all clans by 1952, but not of significant proportions. But here too, a difference among the clans was to be seen. Whereas only one-fifth of the marriages of the men and women of Kafika and of Taumako, and only one-twentieth of those of Fangarere, were within their own clans, one-third of the marriages of Tafua were intra-clan. Bearing in mind the relatively low proportion of Tafua intra-chiefly-class marriages, one may say that Tafua, in 1952 as in 1929, was relatively 'endogamous', in part by marriages between its chiefly group and its commoners.

Are there any correlates for this situation, which to me was somewhat unexpected? The alignment of Fangarere with Kafika in marriage might be put down to its great ritual and social dependence upon Kafika, and to a traditional friendship. But the attraction between Taumako and Kafika could hardly be put down to any 'special relation' between them, such as the common defence of paganism by their chiefs. And no parallel reason could operate for Tafua. As a clan they had no special isolation by Christianity, since there have been a large number of Kafika Christians from the first. One factor which was certainly included in Tikopia views was the feud which had developed between Tafua and Taumako two generations before my first visit to Tikopia, because of the killing of Kaitu, heir to the chieftainship of Tafua, by Pa Resiake and his brother, of the chiefly house of Taumako. The general effects of this had hardly died away even by 1952, and this may well have helped to account for the low proportion of marriages between Tafua men and Taumako women. But this killing was symptom as much as cause of the traditional feud, and in itself was hardly enough to account for the pattern as a whole.

I looked, therefore, at the locality patterns for some clue. When Tikopia marriages were classified in terms of the local relationship of bride and groom before marriage, as well as by clan of the husband, the results gave the table opposite (XV).

Summarizing these figures in overall terms, one can see there has been a high degree of preference shown by men for taking their spouses from fairly close at hand. Both in 1929 and 1952, marriages between people of the same village were about one-sixth, and between those of adjacent villages about one-third, of all unions. In other words, in an island with the most remote potential marriage partners not much more than a mile away, there was a sharp falling-off in choice of spouses beyond adjacent villages. Marriage of a man to 'a girl next door', or 'a girl in the next village', comprised half of all marriages, whereas marriage to a girl on the other side of the island was only an eighth or a seventh of the whole. This high degree of local conservatism or parochialism is in line with the general conception of Tikopia society as compressed in its relations, operating its social ties with full intensity, but on a miniature geographical scale. In terms of all clans, the overall pattern had not changed much by 1952 as compared with a generation before.

The preference for choosing spouses in marriage from close at hand did not seem to have been affected by the advance in religious conversion over a generation. So far from Christianity having significantly widened the range of marriage choice by any spirit of increasing general amity, it seemed by 1952, to have had no effect, or almost none. District solidarity and factionalism were as high as ever.

TABLE XV

PROXIMITY OF WOMEN SELECTED IN MARRIAGE

Wife taken from Village

lan of sband	Same		Adjacent		Other in same district		Other in allied sub-dist.		In opposite district		Foreign		Total	
	'29	'52	'29	'52	'29	'52	'29	'52	'29	'52	'29	'52	'29	'52
ika	15		17		13		11		7		3		66	
		11		25		21		8		12		2		79
ua	6		28		3		9		6		1		33	
		16		19			6		9		10		0		60
mako	10		10		18		7		6		1		52	
		10		28		17		11		11		2		79
garere	1		10		0		0		5		1		17	
		1		8		5		2		2		0		18
eign	—		—		—		—		1		—		1	
		—		—		—		—		1		—		1
al 1929	32		65		34		27		25		6		189	
1952		38		80		49		30		36		4		237

As regards the separate clans, some changes were perceptible. Taumako and Tafua men, in particular, showed a tendency to *contract* the range of their choice of partners, Taumako from any village on its own side of the island to adjacent villages, and Tafua from adjacent villages to the village where the husband resided. But though the 'inbred' tendency of Tafua was still more marked than with the other clans, it could be seen to share a parochialism with the other clans in terms of marriages on a district basis. The apparent anomaly of Tafua intra-clan marriages was, then a function of their much greater residential concentration in Faea.

Summary
Finally, if we compare these effects with the general expansive tendency of clans as far as settlement was concerned (Table XII), it would seem that

Tikopia men were more adventurous in economic affairs than in marital choice. Marriage was generally viripatrilocal at the start. But unwilling, initially, to risk taking a woman out of her own district as a wife, a man was willing enough to go with her elsewhere than in his natal village once he had begun to establish a family.

We have here the converse of the common situation of localized clans which are exogamous and hence extraverted in marriage. In Tikopia there is a group of dispersed clans with a tendency to still wider spatial dispersion, but with a strong predilection to localized choice in marriage. This high degree of local solidarity has been tested by the experience of a generation between 1929 and 1952, with the advent of a new universalistic type of religion. The question is can this be correlated with the isolation of the small size of the island, permitting an intensification of the activities of the component parts of the social organism? Here would seem to be a case for comparative study.

By 1952, we had in Tikopia the following marriage situation. Marriage choice was not completely random, since it was restricted by incest prohibitions and class attitudes. But these in themselves did not inhibit marriage with someone of a non-adjacent locality. Opportunity for courting also was common through dance and free movement of young people at night. Hence, Tikopia unions could be in theory distributed fairly evenly all over the island. Such distribution was, *prima facie*, assisted by the general social expression that it was good to marry into another lineage so that the marriage gifts might 'go out'. In contrast with this, in fact Tikopia marriage choice was locally orientated to a significant degree. Group values of association in the everyday events of life with people with whom one shared neighbourhood relations were among the primary elements in the constitution of Tikopia society.

The results of this quantitative analysis showed no startling changes over a generation. But while structurally such major elements as social alignment in residence and patterns of marriage had altered little, careful documentation shows how, despite this absence of structural change, there had been much social *movement* of a kind to be regarded as part of the social organization.

CHAPTER VIII

Changes in Descent Groups

In 1929 it was clear that the unilineal descent group structure of the Tikopia was a cardinal feature in their whole social life. One of the most important questions then on my return was the degree to which there had been any alteration in this system. Consideration of the descent group system after a generation, however, posed a problem of presentation. The theory of descent groups has developed more than any other branch of social anthropology during the last two decades, and there has been much elaboration of concepts and terminology. Though the terms used have by no means always been defined in the same way, and some issues have been unduly magnified, the modern analyses since the material from my first visit was presented have undoubtedly given much more sensitivity to studies in this field of kinship. It is necessary then, before I consider the situation in 1952, to re-examine briefly the situation in 1929 in the light of theoretical developments since that time.

GENERAL CONSIDERATIONS: TERMINOLOGY

In Tikopia in 1929 the descent group system in its basic principle was firmly unilineal, taking the form of named, non-exogamous patrilineal descent groups. These were of two orders: segmentary units (termed by the Tikopia *paito,* and referred to by me as 'houses' or *ramages*); and aggregative units (termed by the Tikopia *kainanga,* and referred to by me as *clans*).[1]

The Tikopia term *paito* in 1929 had several referents. It meant a house, in the sense of a physical dwelling, the actual building. It also meant the small kin unit, elementary or enlarged family, living in the house and performing domestic services in relation thereto. By extension, it might also refer loosely to the whole household personnel. But apart from this, the term was also used to describe the agnatic descent groups which were basic to the whole social structure. Each of these groups was a named collectivity, defined in terms of patrilineal descent from a common ancestor. The *paito* was not demarcated by exogamous prescription. Its members lived residentially dispersed, and though ownership of lands was corporate, these lands also were spatially dispersed.

I applied the term *ramage* to these groups because the term could refer to their process of formation by branching, which has generally come now to be termed segmentation or fission.[2] I thought they should not be termed lineages,

[1] A useful summary of the system of Tikopia descent groups is given in George C. Homans, *The Human Group*, pp. 226–9, New York, 1950.

[2] *We, The Tikopia*, pp. 345–70. Cf. *Primitive Economics of the New Zealand Maori*, p. 99.

because they were not exogamous, unlike 'lineages' as then understood. I now think it preferable to speak of the *paito* as lineages, in view of their strictly unilineal character, and to reserve the term *ramage* for 'ambilateral' descent groups, in which membership allows some choice between male and female sides.[1] Such choice often involves property or status criteria.

From the structural point of view the Tikopia *paito* was a descent group envisaged with clarity by the people themselves as genealogically determined, unilineal and agnatic. But from the organizational point of view they were not such purists; they used the term to refer to a family or household unit in which affinal kin, particularly wives, and cognatic kin such as daughters' children, might be included. This usage was specifically operational in reference to the preparation of food and social affairs involving economic activity.

In this range of Tikopia usage an important theoretical point is involved. Part of the essential character of a unilineal descent group is its exercise of certain kinds of rights, for example, those over land. Claim to and exercise of such rights may occur without necessarily any physical intervention by the parties concerned. For the performance of services, however, some physical action is required and practical co-operation may well involve, for convenience, others than members of the unilineal descent group. Conceptually then, it was simple for the Tikopia to treat the *paito* in the form of a right-holding agnatic descent group as a structural unit in quite a clear way, while continuing to use the same term for a unit of more mixed composition, involved in the performance of many services.

But members of unilineal descent groups must live somewhere. Many kinds of rights can continue to be exercised effectively only when the owners of them are living close to the scene where the rights are claimed. Hence in societies of large scale there tends to be one or other of the following situations: (*a*) The rights which a unilineal descent group claims and exercises are of a non-spatial kind, not requiring any particular location for their exercise, e.g. rights to such immaterial property as songs and dances, or to badges and emblems; members of such a group may live dispersed. (*b*) The rights have a spatial referent, especially when they relate to land. Here, the members of a unilineal descent group may all live fairly close together so that they can exercise their rights in common as occasion arises. The very fact of their living close together means that they are almost certain to have with them spouses from other descent groups, and this in turn involves joint activities conducted under the name of one descent group, but actually involving members of others. (*c*) A third possibility is when the rights have a spatial referent but when the members of a unilineal descent group live dis-

---

[1] See my article 'Note on Descent Groups in Polynesia', *Man*, 1957, No. 2. But compare Ward H. Goodenough, *Property, Kin and Community on Truk*, 1951, pp. 87 *et seq.*; Morton H. Fried, 'The Classification of Corporate Unilineal Descent Groups', *J.R.A.I*, vol. 87, 1957, pp. 6, 11; Marshall D. Sahlins, 'Differentiation by Adaptation in Polynesian Societies', *Journal Polynesian Society*, 1957, pp. 291 *et seq.*; *idem*, *Social Stratification in Polynesia*, 1958, *passim*. In these works different criteria have at times been adopted.

persed. By a system of delegation the spatially fixed rights may be exercised by those members who reside in the vicinity, or distant members may exercise their rights only rarely or may waive them. With the Tikopia, the need for such alternatives has hardly arisen. The island is so small that a member of a descent group can exercise his rights personally, including his land rights, in any part of the island should he wish, while having his residence in any other part. A few cases of delegation of rights have occurred, but in general the problem of residence as a complicating factor to the exercise of functions as a member of a unilineal descent group has had minimal effects.

An extension of the *paito* concept in 1929 was the *kano a paito*, literally 'collectivity of houses'. This was an ego-oriented group of kin and affines, functioning particularly at birth, sickness, death, etc. It changed in composition from one person and occasion to another, but structurally was definable in terms of a small aggregate of descent groups, primarily: father's paternal group; mother's paternal group; wife's brother's group; sister's husband's group. Operationally, it usually consisted of a nucleus of representatives of descent groups with affinal relatives, mainly wives and sisters' husbands or wives' brothers, who came to lend their services in accordance with customary kinship ties.

In terms of function, then, one could distinguish in the Tikopia situation of 1929 three different types of kin group based upon agnatic descent group. One, the structural unit of the 'pure' unilineal descent group, possessed, claimed and exercised rights as, for example, rights over land. The second type was a group of more amorphous character, with a nucleus of agnatic kin of one descent group, but involving also other kin for the performance of practical day to day tasks. A third type of group was the ego-oriented collectivity of kin, defined in terms of several descent groups related to ego and ordinarily referred to in such terms, but operationally involving affines as well. This group had as its most significant functions the performance of major social services for specified persons. Such a threefold functional typology is probably widespread in societies with unilineal descent groups.

A significant feature of descent groups is whether they may be said to have a corporate character or not. The criteria of what constitutes a corporate group have not, however, been clearly agreed. Maine, in speaking of corporations, laid the emphasis upon continuity, but linked it with the exercise of rights. Max Weber emphasized the exclusive character of corporate groups and their regulation by administrative authority. Radcliffe-Brown was more eclectic, including not only the control of collective property and the existence of authoritative representation, but also even occasional assembly of the members of the group as entitling it to be termed corporate.[1]

Some of these criteria are not very satisfactory. If occasional assembly

[1] H. S. Maine, *Ancient Law*, 1874. Pp. 187–8. Max Weber, *The Theory of Social and Economic Organization* (Trans. by A. R. Henderson and Talcott Parsons), 1947, p. 133 *et seq.* A. R. Radcliffe-Brown, Introduction to *African Systems of Kinship and Marriage*, 1950, p. 41. Useful discussions of the concept have also been given, e.g. by M. G. Smith in 'Segmentary Lineage Systems', *J.R.A.I.*, vol. 86, 1956, pp. 39–80, and Morton H. Fried, 'The Classification of Corporate Unilineal Descent Groups', *J.R.A.I.*, vol. 87, 1957, pp. 1–29.

alone of members of a group is to entitle them to be termed a corporate group, then the term seems to be equivalent simply to a body of people and could indeed be a synonym for 'group' itself. Despite the weighty arguments of Max Weber, it would seem that the existence of administrative authority is not so much a separable criterion of a corporate group as a concomitant of the exercise of rights by that group. Continuity beyond the personal existence of any member of the group would seem to be implied. But there is a difficulty since one can imagine some types of corporate group—e.g. a commercial corporation—formed for specific purposes and being dissolved once those purposes have been achieved, without lasting even as long as the lifespan of any individual member. I would prefer to argue that although continuity beyond personal lifespan is normally a criterion of corporate groups, the prime criterion for definition of a group as corporate is that its members collectively exercise a set of rights and may be subject collectively to a set of duties. In a corporate group any member cannot be involved individually *de jure* in the exercise of the rights or performance of the duties *vis-à-vis* any external person or group—though *de facto* he may act individually in such matters. *De facto* also, when we are speaking of descent groups as corporate, they normally have continuity, but this I think is secondary to the exercise of their functions, although their functions may be exercised with this continuity as assumed.

From this point of view the Tikopia *paito*, i.e. the structural units of agnatic descent group type which I propose from now on to call lineages, were in 1929 clearly corporate groups. The body of agnatic kin collectively exercised rights over definite portions of land, and these rights had apparently been held in most cases for generations. These lineages acted also as major units of social action or social reference in many spheres, ranging from crisis of personal life to the provision of ritual offerings to ancestors and gods.

Now for the *kainanga*. In 1929 the *kainanga* were each an aggregate of a set of *paito*. In each *kainanga* some of these *paito* were connected by descent from common ancestry; according to tradition they had been formed by fission from the chiefly stock which bore the *kainanga* name. But others of them were said to belong to the clan by accretion, as the result of some special event long ago (usually by marriage of their ancestor with a woman of the chiefly stock). A few others again, and these of high status, did not necessarily claim any common ancestry with members of the chiefly body, but were traditionally linked with the chiefly lineage by some mythological association. In 1929 membership in the *kainanga* was rigorously unilineal—a person belonged to it through his father in accordance with the traditional principle. But since not all its members claimed common patrilineal ancestry it could only be described as a 'descent group' and not a 'common descent group'. The title to membership was by unilineal descent, but not every member shared the same ultimate patrilineal ancestor.

In my earlier presentation of this material[1] I applied the term 'clan' to the

[1] *We, The Tikopia*, pp. 361-71.

kainanga, knowing that this was anomalous from the point of view of the usage current at the time, which normally saw exogamous regulations as a feature of clan structure. I think that my usage has been justified. As time has passed, the criterion of exogamy has been seen to be less significant as a critical feature of the structural demarcation of such large kin-based groups.

Since I wrote, however, further questions about the applicability of the term 'clan' have arisen. In particular, G. P. Murdock[1] has introduced a revised terminology with three criteria for recognition of clan, which is described as a 'compromise kin group'. These are (1) unilineality, (2) residential unity, and (3) 'actual social integration'. All are important features.

I have shown that membership in the *kainanga* was by unilineal rule of descent, although not every member of the *kainanga* claimed common ancestry by this unilineal principle. Marriage and consequent bilateral kin ties meant that *de facto* all *kainanga* members could trace common ancestry through *some* line. The *kainanga* again could be said to have actual social integration: there was positive sentiment of unity shown by use of the name, and by acknowledgment of common tie to the *kainanga* chief; moreover, there were many occasions of *kainanga* assembly with performance of ceremonial functions. But Murdock has complicated the situation by his insistence upon 'residential unity' as a criterion of clanship. Some localization of descent group members is a common feature in many societies. But unless marriage is completely endogamous, some people must move when they marry. Some close association with members of other descent groups and some loss of clan members on marriage must therefore occur. Residential unity must therefore be only relative, limited as a criterion mainly to men or to women members (see above, p. 214). To prescribe 'residential unity' as a necessary criterion of clanship introduces a difficulty for the conventional recognition of the many large-scale African or Melanesian unilineal descent groups, which have been called clans but the members of which are dispersed through the society in different villages.

In immediate reference to Tikopia, what is meant by 'residential unity'? Murdock speaks of 'the residential rule', the 'normal rule of residence'. In Tikopia terms does this mean the *principle*, which was that of virilocality (with some close neo-local variation)? Or does it mean the actual *location* of *kainanga* members? In Tikopia the situation in 1929 was mixed. Members of all *kainanga* were to some extent spatially dispersed in various villages,[2] but three of these villages (*Potu sa Kafika, Potu sa Fangarere, Potu sa Taumako*) bore names of *kainanga*. The first two of these consisted of *kainanga* members only—apart from in-marrying spouses. On the other hand, the *kainanga* of Tafua had no village bearing its name, and no village in which the major population consisted of Tafua members. Are we then, in Murdock's terms, to regard Kafika and Fangarere as 'clans' and Taumako and Tafua as 'sibs'? This would not be very helpful because in all other respects than this village

---

[1] *Social Structure*, pp. 67–9.
[2] *We, The Tikopia*, p. 66.

residence the *kainanga* were of the same order, and were treated as such in
the social structure by the Tikopia. The 'residential rule' as a principle and
the actual spatial location of kin group members are very important as
determinants or correlates of many kinds of social action. But to attempt to
combine both the exclusive principle of unilineality and the exclusive principle
of residential unity to describe a kin group means, as Murdock has seen,
that the group must be a compound, 'composite' in membership, from the
descent point of view. What in fact Murdock has done has been to mingle
structural and operational or organizational criteria in defining such a group.
While some may find it appropriate to use 'clan' for this purpose, I am,
therefore, continuing to employ the term 'clan' to describe the Tikopia
kainanga, implying by this its unilineality of descent principle, without
reference to the residential distribution of its members.

How far was the *kainanga* in Tikopia in 1929 a corporate group? It had a
common name. Its members regarded themselves as a single body with
certain privileges and claims against members of other clans; it had some
general rights over land; it had important functions in ceremonial and (apart
from certain denudations as a result of Christianity) in ritual. The *kainanga*
was also a unit of major importance from the point of view of social reference,
many activities and relationships being described in *kainanga* terms. In many
respects the *kainanga* acted in virtue of its leader, the hereditary chief en-
dowed with sacred powers. From this point of view the *kainanga* was a
political unit, since the maintenance of social order in the Tikopia community
rested to a very large degree with the chiefs, each exercising his authority
largely (though by no means exclusively) through his *kainanga* headship.
From all this, and in particular from their exercise of common rights, it is
proper to term the *kainanga* a corporate group.[1] The Tikopia clans in 1929
were also ranked, their order being indicated by the rule of precedence of
their chiefs on ritual occasions.

Aspects of Change in Descent Group System
The possibility of change in the Tikopia descent group system over the
generation 1929 to 1952 can be looked at from several aspects—the *general
principles* of the system, its specific *component units*, and the *operations* or
activities in which the units engaged. Broadly speaking, these aspects involve
attention to both the form and the content of the system or, from another
point of view, to both the structure of the system and its organization. For
convenience, then, I deal with the operations in the context of the discussion
on components.

Principles of the System
In Tikopia in 1929 the general principles of the descent group system were a

---

[1] Fried seems to have regarded my views on this point as uncertain, and I would accept
his statements as a clarification—though I would regard the exercise of authority by the
clan chief as not being the essential part of the definition of a corporate group. (Fried, *op.
cit.*, pp. 24–5.)

rigorous unilineality, and a constitution of two orders of descent groups—
a segmentary lineage order and an aggregative clan order. There was no rule
of exogamy and the descent groups were dispersed in residence. The groups
of each order were of corporate type, though the functions of the lineage in
this respect were more elaborate. Each order of group had a central authority,
a hereditary head, by reference to whose traditional ritual functions the
group was graded for some corporate purposes. With the adoption of
Christianity by half the community, the ritual functions of one chief, the
Ariki Tafua, and of some lineage heads (including some not in his clan) had
been theoretically abolished and in practice very much reduced. But all these
leaders in 1929 had themselves earlier practised pagan rites and still received
respect as the repositories of esoteric knowledge, while in the other half of
the island the elaborate series of pagan rituals continued without much
alteration. Although for the community as a whole the ritual sanctions for
lineage and clan action had in some cases been abandoned, and ritual ties
had therefore been curtailed, the memory of such ritual sanctions and ties
still persisted and they were regarded as being latent or in abeyance, rather
than non-existent. The social and political principles involved in clan operations were still active.

In Tikopia in 1929 not only were clans ranked in certain ritual contexts,
but there was also ranking of lineages, though with rather less completeness
and precision. This ranking was in a ritual context and referred rather to the
functions and privileges of the lineage head than to the status of all members
of the lineage. From this point of view these ritual elders were of major
importance. Commonly, pride of place was claimed by more than one ritual
elder. If two at the top of the hierarchy were thus in dispute, by the community in general neither might be given superiority, although both could be
acknowledged as superior to all other elders in their clan. In other words the
order of precedence was imprecise, although any elder had his place recognized in general terms as being towards the top or the bottom of the scale.
Below the ritual elders came the heads of lineages who had no ritual functions
in the community at large. But this ranking of offices did not imply social
stratification of descent groups. There was, however, social stratification in
the general separation of all members of chiefly lineages from members of
lineages not classed in the chiefly category. All members of *paito ariki*
belonged to a superior social class than did members of *paito fakaarofa*,
commoner lineages, although there was some intermarriage between them
and the line was not very sharply defined.[1] This hereditary class principle cut
through the clan structure.

In 1952 these principles, the cardinal frame of the descent group system,
were almost as in 1929. The orders of clans and lineages, the patrilineal title
to membership in them, their naming, their ranking, and the social class
alignment of chiefs and commoners in lineage terms, were still recognized as
an integral part of the primary constitution of Tikopia society, valued and

[1] *We, The Tikopia*, pp. 358–60.

unquestioned.[1] Qualification, however, must be put in respect of ritual sanctions and ritual ties. These had been still further diminished in action by the defection of more lineage heads to Christianity. Though this had not impaired the principle of clan leadership, it had tended to put a question mark against the future of the ritual relations of clans and lineages in the Tikopia community as a whole. But socially and politically, the principles of clan and lineage structure operated in general as before.

Components—Clans

As component units of the descent group system, empirically in 1929 the clans numbered four, each with its chief, their ranking order accordingly being Kafika, Tafua, Taumako, Fangarere. (The first three were roughly of equal size, the fourth was very much smaller.) The principal lineage in each clan was that of the chief, and bore the clan name. (In historical reconstruction this order of attribution could be reversed; the clan probably received its name from that of the chiefly lineage.)

In 1952 this scheme was still in vogue. The number and names of the clans were precisely as they had been a generation before. In general attribution of land rights and in social and political affairs as a whole also, the clan divisions were as meaningful as a generation earlier. In the ritual field the content had altered a little. In the Work of the Gods, the general division of functions by clans was still clearly marked. But with the advance of Christianity the final remnants of Tafua participation had fallen away, and the rituals were now completely an affair of the other three clans only. The name of Tafua had completely disappeared in this context.

While the clan alignment in general was still quite clear-cut, there was a hint that its internal structure might not continue to be so rigorous. It seemed to me that there was a tendency, of which I have no record in 1929, to lump Fangarere together with Kafika as a single clan. On several occasions they were spoken of as if they were one. The tendency to align Fangarere with Kafika was probably stimulated in part by the disappearance of Tafua from the ritual sphere and the consequent tendency to envisage the ritual arrangements in balanced reciprocal terms of two clans, Kafika and Taumako, rather than three. One of my Taumako informants confirmed this identification by an unusual argument. He said 'As the talk goes, the village of sa Fangarere adheres to sa Kafika, and they are termed the one clan. They are divided simply because there are four chiefs (in Tikopia), but they are termed one clan.' There were, in fact, very many occasions on which Kafika and Fangarere were cited separately, but this statement exemplified a certain tendency to consider the chieftainship as not necessarily co-terminous with complete clan jurisdiction. It would be possible speculatively on this view to consider Tikopia with a Fangarere chief but no Fangarere clan—or rather, with a Fangarere chief who might have followers from Kafika assigned to

---

[1] I asked one of our servants, who knew his patrilineal genealogy well, what was his mother's lineage. He told me, but had no idea what was his mother's mother's lineage, i.e. who was his mother's mother's brother.

him and bearing his clan name for a time in order that certain social requirements should be fulfilled. This, I must emphasize, is an implication from my
friend's statement, not my own original speculation. Normally, one would
consider chiefs as dependent on the existence of clans, not clans upon chiefs.
This point of view suggests an interesting alternative evaluation.

The idea of lack of coincidence between chief and clan was supported by
what to me was a most dramatic discovery—the split that had occurred in
the chieftainship of Fangarere in the intervening generation (see pp. 280–3
for details). This had given a pagan chief and a Christian chief to the clan,
each with some separate functions and each for some social purposes the
leader of the clan, though in general the pagan chief was regarded as of
higher status. This anomalous situation had not split the clan completely
into two separate sections; there had been no structural segmentation.
Fangarere still continued to operate as a single large-scale unit on major
social occasions which were neutral from the religious point of view, yet the
one clan had two chiefs. But since on pagan ritual occasions the clan was
weakened, this may well have stimulated a public tendency to align it with
Kafika.

The other modification in clan alignment which I observed in 1952 was
some lack of clarity in the attribution in clan terms of one major lineage.
This was Sao, a group which in 1929 had been led by a pagan ritual elder of
very high status, but who by 1952 had died and was succeeded by his son, a
Christian. The principal branch of the lineage of Sao had lived for generations
with their primary home in Ravenga, in immediate association with the
Ariki Taumako and under his protection. This special relationship was
validated by a traditional tale which was told to me in 1952 in the same form
as in 1929. In 1929 the lineage of Sao was recognized by all, old and young,
as belonging to clan Tafua by ancestral assignment and mythological ties.
But the ritual elder of Sao, since his own chief, the Ariki Tafua in Faea, had
become a Christian, had transferred his religious co-operation to the Ariki
Taumako and had supported the latter's rites. Yet the elder of Sao himself
was quite definite in his statements that he owed his general ritual and social
allegiance to the Ariki Tafua, and made this clear by various personal and
ceremonial acknowledgments.

One might have thought, by 1952, when the head of the Sao lineage was a
Christian, his ancestral ties with the chief of Tafua, also a Christian, might
have been re-emphasized and those with the Ariki Taumako, still a pagan,
might have been severed or attenuated. But this was not the case. He continued to live in Potu sa Taumako, close to the Ariki Taumako. There were
close kinship ties between them and a great deal of economic co-operation.
Now some young people were attributing Sao lineage to Taumako clan. One
young man of Taumako living in the village just mentioned, when I asked him
about the clanship of a certain man of Sao lineage, said 'Formerly of the clan
of Tafua, nowadays of the clan of Taumako.' Another man of Taumako of
middle age, in reply to a question of mine about this new attribution, said
'You are right. They dwell there, sa Tafua, sa Taumako; they are divided

into two. Look here, father' (addressing me direct by kinship term), 'its origin is that they were chased away by Pu Tafua from Uta and so they were left to the Ariki Taumako to dwell with him. They were left to dwell on shore, otherwise they would have been driven off to sea. When anything of the Ariki Taumako is performed they are not absent. They are called "the chips of Taumako", compared to the chips of the oven' (wood used to light the fire). 'When the Ariki Taumako dies a man of Sao will die and is buried with the Ariki.' I commented that when I was in Tikopia before, the people of Sao were still called Tafua without question. The man replied 'The origin is in the abandonment of the kava by Pu Tafua, while the Ariki Taumako was still performing his rites. So they resorted to those. Whatever the Ariki Taumako was doing, they were not absent, they went continually.' This puts clearly from the Tikopia point of view the close ancestral and ritual association of Sao lineage with the chiefly lineage of Taumako, and more generally, the ritual criterion of descent group affiliation.

The reference to death is interesting. I had heard earlier that by some mystic association the death of a chief of Taumako would be followed by the death of the elder of Sao. Apparently this is, in fact, what did happen during an epidemic in 1942. My old friends the Ariki Taumako and Pae Sao died almost at the same time.

The modern tendency was then to allocate those members of Sao lineage who lived in Faea to Tafua clan and those who lived in Ravenga to Taumako clan. A contributory reason here too was that in the new religious system the Christian Ariki Tafua could not appoint the head of Sao as a religious elder, and so the traditional ritual ties between them—ties which Pae Sao had, in fact, maintained out of loyalty, though in reduced form—had not been renewed. Now only social ties remained. At this level, proximity, together with kin relations to the Ariki Taumako tended to align the head of the Sao lineage with the latter in clan terms.

In 1952, the social situation had not been completely clarified. The parent temple of Sao lineage still stood in Uta and was used as a dwelling, while the major dwelling of the head of Sao stood in Potu sa Taumako. When the time came for recarpeting the ancestral temples, many Christian households in Ravenga renewed their floor mats, and some who occupied dwellings formerly used for kava rites prepared a basket of food (*fonakava*) for their chief. In mid-1952 Pa Nukumata, son and successor to Pae Sao, was understood to be making a conventional food gift from his own dwelling of Notoa to the Ariki Taumako as his father had done. But about the temple of Sao there was some uncertainty. If he had recarpeted it formally and then had prepared *fonakava*, this would have been carried over to the Ariki Tafua in Faea, in accordance with tradition. But the pagan associations of the temple of Sao were so strong that its celebrations were most likely to be discontinued by the Christian head of Sao. (I was ill at the time and had no record of what was done, but I am practically certain there was no such celebration.) Hence, though in general the Ariki Tafua and the head of Sao now shared again a common religious system, there were no specific ritual ties in this new system to unite them; residential, social and economic ties, therefore, had full play.

This can be looked at as an illustration of the tendency for operational local ties to replace structural descent group ties. It indicates how rights are correlated with duties. If the duties are not performed, the rights—in this case of clan name—may tend to lapse if there are not other opportunities for social action available. But it must be noted that this was not a matter of questioning the principle of clan alignment as such, but only of questioning what should be the classification of a component unit in terms of the principle. There was no question of change in the unilineal character of the clan structure, as by suggesting that alignment should be in terms of descent through a female. But though overtly the unilineal principle was not questioned, in fact the tendency to put residential propinquity above traditional affiliation did offer a threat to the integrity of the clan as a descent group. In broad terms this is reminiscent of Maine's antithesis between blood tie and territorial tie—and the tendency, as social experience and inter-relationships widen, for the one to give place to the other. From this point of view, then, the single case noted may be a significant step towards the gradual blurring of the clear-cut lines of the Tikopia clan system.

Components—Lineages

In Tikopia the lineage system in 1929 had a segmentary form, but the conventional picture of 'equal and opposite' segments, defined by genealogical grades, did not have much significance.

Operationally, the size of membership was of very considerable importance (see later, p. 234), and might be crucial if a contest occurred over land claims. But structurally the position was more complicated. Since the patrilineal descent principle was paramount, it was the number of male members which was of structural relevance; the number of female members had no importance from this point of view. But there was a further qualification—the structural implications of the number of the male members were related to the degree to which these might marry and produce further male children. (The Tikopia principle in the past, observed partially at least, that junior male siblings should remain celibate meant that tendencies to segmentation of lineages were reduced.)

In estimating the relative position of lineages from a structural point of view, I think it is primarily a matter of the collective rights they are acknowledged to possess, the collective obligations they acknowledge that they owe, and the jurisdiction extended by the members collectively in regard to the actions of any one of them. The genealogical position in itself does not define the position of a lineage in the social structure; this depends upon the whole social content of lineage recognition in which the relevance of genealogical position is weighed against the relevance of other social factors.

(In Tikopia, priority in the genealogical record was certainly one significant criterion in estimating the relative position of a lineage in the social structure. Other things being equal, a lineage sprung from a senior ancestor exercised wider and more inclusive rights than a lineage sprung from a junior ancestor.)

But other things were often not equal. While priority in the genealogical record might give the basis for some pride and assertion of status superiority, it was a separable claim from other claims to lineage rights and status. Genealogical priority in itself did not give inclusive control of the rights exercised by other lineages of more recent genealogical antecedents derived from the same original ancestor. Traditional events such as incurable illness of an ancestor or his death before accession to office were cited to account for the fact that genealogical seniority and social seniority of a lineage did not always coincide. Hence, a genealogically senior lineage such as Tavi or Mapusanga (Gen. 2), might have much more circumscribed rights and be less in social status than their genealogically junior agnates of the Kafika chiefly house itself. Structurally, as far as the social framework of status rights and obligations is concerned, the Tikopia lineage system recognized a grading not in terms of simple genealogical order but in terms of differentiated status, etc., irrespective of the precise genealogical position of the units concerned. This was so in 1952 as in 1929.

A special feature in the genealogical sphere was the claim to autocthonous descent, to have sprung from the soil (*afu kere*).[1] In 1929, claims to such 'earth-sprung' descent were made by several main lineages, including that of Rarovi. But the only lineage which was generally acknowledged to be entitled to such a claim was that of Raropuka, whose ancestral god was generally acknowledged as the original male deity of the land. It was alleged by many people that all other autocthonous lineages had died out at various times and been replaced in their ancestry by later immigrants. It will be noted that the ritual elder of Raropuka in the days of full paganism shared with the ritual elder of Rarovi the highest status in Kafika clan next to the chief. In 1952, the elder of Rarovi seemed to have abandoned his claim to autocthonous origin; he told me his ancestor was an immigrant. This may have been related to his abandonment of ritual performances, of which the associated status had formerly demanded 'earthborn' assertion.

In structural relations *vis-à-vis* one another and the clan chief the ritual attributes of status attached to the office of ritual elder are of prime importance. It has been held that in a segmentary lineage system the actual genealogies have been modified in many cases to fit the social frame—that social fictions have been created in order to support the existing social structure. It is sometimes implied that such manipulation of genealogies is an essential feature of such a lineage system. This need not necessarily be the case. Tikopia genealogical relations may well have been modified as memory has lapsed and social functions have altered, and the claims to autocthonous origin were certainly fabricated. But the genealogies have not necessarily been modified at all levels in order to bolster up social claims to status. For the last six to eight generations the Tikopia have seemed quite content to accept the assignment of status on other bases, without feeling it necessary to fiddle about with their genealogies to justify this. In other words, they have not regarded genealogical order as in itself the prime validating principle.

[1] See *We, The Tikopia*, pp. 231–2.

Genealogical seniority has been recognized as subordinate to title to office established by virtue of specific status components or prescriptive rights. They have accepted inconsistency between genealogical chart and current distribution of status as a normal part of the social process. So, in Tikopia, lineage segments of the same genealogical level are often structurally not equal, and if structurally equal they are often not genealogically opposite. Genealogical level is only one of the factors involved in the order of lineage ranking.

In 1929 the major lineages of Tikopia numbered about thirty—including the four chiefly lineages identified with the names of the clans. Each lineage had its personal name and its acknowledged head, and each was a component part of a specific clan under the authority of the clan chief. There was considerable variation in the genealogical depth of these main lineages. That of Fangarere was only eight generations from Fakaarofatia, the founding ancestor and chief of the clan, or nine generations to Volotu, his father and chief of Nga Ravenga, to whom the founding ancestor succeeded. On the other hand, the lineage of Kafika had nineteen generations from the chief to the ultimate originating ancestor of the group. Some main lineages had genealogies of ten, eleven or twelve generations from the oldest living members, but other main lineages had as few as seven generations to their founding ancestors.[1]

What gave these major lineages their position as basic social units was not their genealogical separateness. Some had independent ancestors; others were offshoots from chiefly lineages. Their significance was in the last resort an operational recognition—a public acknowledgment both in speech and in action that these units were autonomous, whether separately developed or major segments from traditional stocks. But there was for most of them a more concrete test, that of ritual privilege and obligation in structural relations with the chief of their clan. As already mentioned, this was made manifest specifically through the office of ritual elder (*matapure*, or *pure matua*, or for short, *pure*). This office was held by the senior representative of the lineage, but only after nomination and formal investiture by the chief. In 1929, all the main lineages whose senior men had their homes in Ravenga were so headed by ritual elders (or as in the case of Fatumaru, such appointment was soon expected). Of those whose senior men lived in Faea, nearly all had had ritual elders within recent memory, during the last decade, and most of the original incumbents were still living. The ritual elders themselves were graded in status in a broad way, in particular as they had the right to perform their own kava or not. Here is a list of the major lineages entitled to ritual elders in 1929, by clans. The list is headed by the chiefly lineage in each case:

[1] The genealogies of the chiefly houses given in *We, The Tikopia*, pp. 347 *et seq.*, were not given in full since they were intended to demonstrate only some principles of lineage relationship. To that of Kafika (thirteen generations) six names in the earliest period should be added, making nineteen generations in all. Likewise to Tafua (eleven generations) three names should be added. At the same time it must be recognized that these earliest names are cited by the Tikopia in a line without the genealogical expansion characteristic of the later names.

P

TABLE XVI

MAJOR LINEAGES IN 1929 ENTITLED TO RITUAL ELDERS

Kafika	Tafua	Taumako	Fangarere
Kafika	Tafua c.	Taumako	Fangarere
Rarovi	Fusi	Niumano	Rangimakini
Porima	Sao	Fatumaru v.	
Raropuka c.	Korokoro c.	Farekofe	
Marinoa c.	Notau c.	Ngatotiu	
Tavi	Samoa	Maniva	
Torokinga		Siku c.	
		Fasi v.c.	

c. The ritual elder or chief, a Christian, not practising full rites.
v. Office of ritual elder vacant.

The total of these major lineages with ritual status was twenty-three. In addition, there were about half a dozen other lineages of comparable importance which did not have the privilege of ritual elders at their head, but which could claim considerable seniority in their genealogical record, and in particular which operated as autonomous major units in social affairs generally, and had the responsibility of furnishing a ritual presentation of food at the recarpeting of a temple associated with their lineage. Mapusanga and Tongarutu (Paoari) in Kafika; Akitunu and sa Rarupe in Tafua; sa Sanga and Rangitisa in Taumako—all of chiefly stock—were the primary examples here. But they were not clearly differentiated from other lineages which were also offshoots from chiefly houses such as Rotuma or Fenutapu in Tafua, or Oliki or Aneve or Turau in Taumako, or Totiare in Kafika. These last were best described as intermediate lineages because of their lesser social importance, though they too were autonomous in many affairs and had direct ritual relations of varying kinds with their clan chief in each case. In other words, since the Tikopia term *paito* could apply to the lineage and its component core at any level, from the major social unit to the man and children bearing the lineage house name, once the definite criterion of ritual office attached to a lineage head was left behind, there was no firm indicator by which lineage order in Tikopia could be specified.

In 1952 these general conditions still obtained. There had been no alteration in either the number of main lineages or in their names. As primary units in a structural scheme of Tikopia society, Rarovi, Sao and the rest still served as major points of reference over a wide range of social situations.

An Example of Lineage Operations

A good example of lineage operations was a ceremonial anointing of the Ariki Taumako and presentation of bark-cloth and food to him at a feast he gave in March 1952 after his return from Anuta. According to custom, in celebration of his 'settling in' at home once again, female representatives from each of the major lineages of mothers of former Taumako chiefs and of his own mother came in line, knelt behind the chief and in turn presented him with a brand-new bark-cloth garment. As each piece of bark-cloth was given to him, at his right side, the chief took it up and laid it on a coconut frond mat in front of him. This was an offering to the chiefly ancestor concerned. At the same time each woman in turn smeared the back, belly and arms of the chief with turmeric pigment as a mark of distinction. This was *te fakamailonga o te ariki*, the distinguishing of the chief. Baskets of food were also presented, and a kava rite completed the proceedings.

As I watched the ceremony, I noted the order of anointing and presentation as follows:

(1) In the name of the founding ancestor of Taumako clan, Pu Ariki, by a woman of Kafika.

(2) Matakai and Vaisaro by women from Siku and Ratia.

(3) Rimarenga by a woman of Sao.

(4) Matakai (II) by a woman of Fangarere.

(5) Tavake by a woman of Rarovi.

(6) The late Ariki Taumako by a woman of Fusi.

(7) The present Ariki Taumako by a woman of Niumano.

The presentations were of plain undyed bark-cloth, except the first and the fourth, which were orange-dyed bark-cloth. This was not in celebration of the special status of the two chiefs but of that of their mothers' principal god; in each case the bark-cloth was a symbol of the supreme deity of the mother's lineage. Each woman, I was told, represented not only her lineage but also the god of that lineage.

This rite of presentation was essentially the same as one of which I was given an account in 1929,[1] but which I did not personally observe, connected with the installation of a new chief. As in 1929, in 1952 the pieces of bark-cloth were described by the Tikopia as *noforanga*—'seating-places', the interpretation being that they served as resting-places for the spirits of the dead chiefs. On the religious plane, they were thus a symbolic means of reintegrating the new or travelled chief with his predecessors and the maternal gods of his predecessors. (His paternal gods could be deemed to be in direct communication with him already.) But since the maternal gods of these predecessors were in fact the major gods of the lineages from which their mothers came, on the social and political plane the rite served as a formal re-integration of the chief with a set of major lineages both within and outside his clan, of prime importance to him.

Lineages and the Genealogical Record

These presentations were very interesting from other points of view. From page 356 of *We, The Tikopia*, I reproduce part of the genealogy of the chiefs of Taumako (Gen. 1).

From this it may be seen how each presentation of bark-cloth mirrors a marriage and mother/son relationship indicated in the Taumako genealogy. Reversing the order of the genealogy and beginning from the most recent

[1] Briefly described in *Primitive Polynesian Economy*, 1939, pp. 225–6; and cited by William J. Goode, *Religion among the Primitives*, 1951, pp. 167–8.

GENEALOGY 1
Chiefs of Taumako

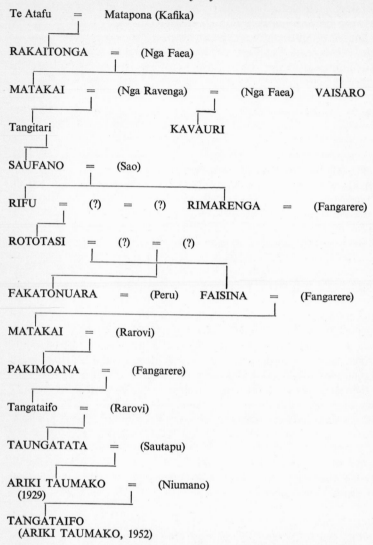

Te Atafu   =   Matapona (Kafika)

RAKAITONGA   =   (Nga Faea)

MATAKAI   =   (Nga Ravenga)   =   (Nga Faea)   VAISARO

Tangitari   KAVAURI

SAUFANO   =   (Sao)

RIFU   =   (?)   =   (?)   RIMARENGA   =   (Fangarere)

ROTOTASI   =   (?)   =   (?)

FAKATONUARA   =   (Peru)   FAISINA   =   (Fangarere)

MATAKAI   =   (Rarovi)

PAKIMOANA   =   (Fangarere)

Tangataifo   =   (Rarovi)

TAUNGATATA   =   (Sautapu)

ARIKI TAUMAKO   =   (Niumano)
(1929)

TANGATAIFO
(ARIKI TAUMAKO, 1952)

generation, one sees that the mother of the present Taumako chief came from Niumano, and his father's mother came from Sautapu, which is a sublineage of Fusi. The mother of his father's father came from Rarovi (the chief Tavake is, I think, an alternative name for Taungatata in the genealogy). At the fifth generation Matakai (II) sprang from a mother of Fangarere; at the eighth generation Rimarenga from a mother of Sao; and at the twelfth generation Matakai and Vaisaro, the hero brothers who repelled the Tongans, sprang from a mother of Nga Faea. In this case, since there were two chiefs to be celebrated, each had a bark-cloth and the honour of furnishing it was divided between the sub-lineages of Siku and Ratia, which together formed the major lineage of Siku and were one of the modern representatives of the ancient chiefly lineage of Nga Faea. In the first bark-cloth offering, Pu Ariki was the Rakaitonga (Pu Lasi) of the genealogy, his mother being from the chiefly lineage of Kafika.

My record of this rite in 1952 was relevant in several ways. Firstly, it gave a confirmation of the correctness of my genealogy recorded a generation before. Secondly, it was even more significant as an indication of the persistence of genealogical memory in social action. Thirdly, the rite gave to the onlookers a conspectus of the traditional history of the Taumako chiefly line. Fourthly, the celebration was an example of the principle of what I have called 'representative status'[1] (or, as it has been described for the African field, of 'perpetual kinship') whereby lineages through selected members maintained a constant relationship to a line of chiefs by virtue of traditional ties with their ancestors.

The rite showed some interesting organizational points. Comparison of the procedure of 1952 with the Taumako genealogy shows that lineage representation in the rite was compressed and several generations of chiefs went unrepresented. This was partly because of certain gaps in the genealogical record—it can be seen from Gen. 1 that the lineages of the mothers of Rototasi, Fakatonuara and Faisina have not been kept in the record. Shortage of food may have affected the procedure. Again, this feast was held in the inland district of Uta, and was not regarded as important as if it had been held in the beach district of Ravenga. I was told that the roll of lineage was not complete, that when a full feast takes place as many as a score of *noforanga* might be offered. Furthermore, this was a pagan rite, and adherence to Christianity inhibited the attendance of many lineage members. The selection of Rimarenga rather than his elder brother Rifu for celebration was probably due to the wish to give recognition to the assembled lineages of sa Sanga and Rangitisa, whose pagan members, descended from Rimarenga, formed an important section of the audience and providers of the feast. But Christian allegiance had not prevented demonstration of lineage loyalty to chief completely. Although Pa Rarovi had abandoned his kava by 1952, he still provided the *noforanga* for this pagan ritual—an indication of the strong attachment of the Tikopia to traditional social bonds.

This example has shown how genealogical validation for social action was still maintained by the Tikopia in 1952 as in 1929. But in many cases the lineage head of the generation before had died by the time of my second visit, and had been succeeded by a younger man. In such case the genealogical record had had one, or it might be two, generations added to it. I made no complete re-recording of lineage genealogies comparable with my records of 1929—mainly because of lack of time. But from the genealogical material

[1] *We, The Tikopia*, pp. 268–70.

given me in many contexts in 1952 it appeared that there had been no particular tendency to maintain the genealogical frame constant by dropping out any generation from an earlier period. Variations from 1929 could be attributed to changes mainly in the religious situation, which gave less point to maintaining genealogies for ritual use. In other words, the period of twenty-three years interval had brought about a lengthening of genealogies, an addition to the social content of the lineage validation, while retaining constancy in the basic principle. In general terms, genealogies in Tikopia are not simply instruments in the maintenance of an existing social structure; they are given a certain factual autonomy as regards near-contemporary events.

Sub-Lineage Growth

While the number and names of the major lineages had remained constant, there had been over the generation some changes in the sub-lineage field. Normal processes of growth and differentiation had produced a new crop of small sub-lineages, some having revived traditional names and some having adopted new names.

An example haphazardly selected is the lineage of sa Sanga of Taumako. In 1929 the membership of this lineage was thirty-two males and twelve resident females. In 1952, the corresponding membership was thirty-seven and thirty-three. In 1929 this lineage consisted of four sub-lineages, Kamota, Rarokofe, Mataioa and Kavasa. The first three traced their ancestry back for five generations to Pu Kamota, eldest son of the Ariki Taumako Rimarenga, and the last to the chief's youngest son Pu Kavasa. (An intermediate son, Pu Rangitisa, was the ancestor of the lineage of Rangitisa.) Another sub-lineage directly descended from Pu Kamota, Pireni, was said to have died out some three generations before. The last bearer of the sub-lineage name, Pu Pireni, lived in the early nineteenth century and went abroad in a Tikopia canoe. In 1929, this sub-lineage was represented by the family of Pa Panapa, descended from one of the other sa Sanga sub-lineages, but now constituting in effect a fifth sub-lineage. With the exception of one household living in the ancestral dwelling Kamota in Uta, all members of the lineage were living in the two villages of Potu i Fara and Asanga, in Ravenga. The sub-lineage of Kavasa had been reduced to a single representative, an elderly widower, who occupied no house of his own but lived with a 'brother' of Kamota.

In 1952, the lineage was described thus by one of its members: 'collectively a single *paito*, sa Sanga; divided, Mataioa, Kamota, with Rarokofe and Pireni—and Kavasa which has died out.' The single representative of Kavasa sub-lineage, now dead, had left no descendants, and the name had not as yet been revived. Comparison of the sub-lineages in household context, over the generation interval may be seen from Table XVII.

Over the generation, the number of households occupied by sa Sanga had increased from eight to sixteen, and the number of married males in the lineage from nine to thirteen. While no new sub-lineage had arisen, that of

Kavasa was extinct and that of Pireni firmly re-established. At the lowest level there were additional dwellings and additional family units, some with new names, to serve as points of further sub-lineage departure when desired. Such differentiation would seem most likely within the sub-lineages Kamota and Mataioa.

It will be noted how conveniently the Tikopia system of naming dwellings

TABLE XVII

LINEAGE SA SANGA, 1929 AND 1952

Occupants

(Personal names indicate married men. Reference numbers in brackets apply to married men of 1929. Other numbers indicate sons, daughters, etc.)

House name	1929	1952
Sub-lineage Kamota:		
Tarorotai	Pa Kamota (1); w; s; 2d	Pa Nukurere (2); w; b; 2s; Pa Kamota—s of (2); w; adopted s
Rangiora	Pa Nukurere (2); w; 2s; d; fb; 'b' from Kavasa	Pa Rangiora (3); 2s; 3d
Kamota	Pa Rangiora (3); 2s; 3d	—
Nukurere	—	s of (1); d of (1)
Navero	—	s of (3)
Sub-lineage Mataioa:		
Mataioa (old house)	Pa Manono (4); w; 3s; d; fbs; Pa Mataioa (5)—yb of (4); w.	s of (4)
Nukutau	Pa Nukutau (6)—yb of (4); w; 2s; d	2s of (6); w of (6); 2d of (6)
Rangiferoikofe	Pa Rangiferoikofe (7)—eb of (4); w; 2s	Pa Rangiferoikofe (7); Pa Toriki—s of (7); w; 2d
Mataioa (new house)	—	Pa Mataioa—fbs of (5); s; 4d; widow of (5)
Manono	—	Pa Manono—s of (4); w; m; sis; adopted s
Nukurangi	—	Pa Nukurangi—s of (7); w; 2s; d
Sub-lineage Rarokofe:		
Nukufuti	Pa Nukufuti (8); w; 4s; 2d; sis	Pa Rarokofe—e.s of (8); w; s; 4d; b; adopted d
Nukutoto	—	Pa Nukufuti (8); w; 2s
Nukukakeake	—	Pa Nukukakeake—s of (8); w; b; w.m. sis
Sub-lineage Pireni:		
Pireni	Pa Panapa (9); w; 4s; d	Pa Pireni—s of (9); w; 3s; d; 2 yb; sis
Mauke	—	s of (9)
Panapa	—	Pa Panapa (9); w

and married couples lends itself to the easy differentiation of new descent groups at an early stage.

Lineage Grafting and Lineage Increment
Important in the structure of the lineage system in 1929 was the method of reconstitution. By name alternation, as one branch died out or was substantially reduced by the loss of all married males, another took on its role in an alternate house name (cf. pp. 184, 190). Again, a junior branch could simulate a senior or assimilate to it, by taking over the name. This process may be termed *lineage grafting*. A new lineage shoot is grafted on to an old lineage stock. In 1952, this process was still current.

A case of lineage grafting occurred in the *paito* of Marinoa, of Kafika clan. In 1929 I had been told of the sub-lineage of Saumarei, 'It is lost; only one woman now.' But by 1952 it had begun to be reconstituted by a young man of Marinoa who had taken that house name on his marriage.

A more interesting example of such social replacement occurred in Taumako clan. I was surprised in 1952 to find a flourishing family of Nunga, since in 1929 I had understood the lineage to have been last represented by a couple of old women and to have died out. But in 1952 it was explained to me by a member of Nunga that he was a member of an allied lineage (Fetu) who had taken the name and succeeded to the lands of his kinswomen. When I raised the matter with the Ariki Taumako he said, 'The house of Nunga disappeared, but the house of Fenuatai (Fetu), the one house, succeeded to it.' The chief confirmed that there had been two old women as the last survivors of the house of Nunga, though he himself had not seen them. One, he said, had married Pa Turau and became the mother of a male and a female child who were still alive in 1952. This statement agreed with my genealogical records of 1929. It is interesting to note that in 1929 there had been contest between the house of Fetu and the affinal kinsfolk of Turau over some Nunga land; when I left the issue had been undecided.[1] But by 1952 resolution had occurred in favour of Fetu. It is significant that this was a distant link on the male side and not a closer one on the female side, which furnished the sub-lineage taking over the succession.

In 1952 then a traditional principle of lineage maintenance was still in operation: the social personality of a lineage segment could still be revived by name-grafting, although the lineage in the physical personality of its male members had died out. So long as the unilineal principle was preserved, the precise genealogical relation of the grafted branch was not relevant.

Another feature of interest by 1952 was an example of *lineage increment*. This occurred through the rise of the Melanesian priest's family to nascent lineage status. Originating from Motlav in the Banks Islands, he was known with his wife as sa Pangisi, Mr and Mrs Banks. In 1929 this term referred primarily to the spouses since the children were too young to constitute a social unit larger than an elementary family. By 1952, with two sons married

[1] *We, The Tikopia*, pp. 395–6. If the chief has resumed the lineage lands in the meantime, the lineage will be reconstituted only if he grants the lands back.

and with offspring, and with another son very active in public affairs, the group was known collectively as *paito i Pangisi* (house of Banks).

The clan affiliation of this lineage illustrated in contemporary Tikopia society a principle which was said to have been traditionally in vogue, i.e. the classification of a lineage matrilaterally (or uxorilaterally) through the founder's wife when the founder was an emigrant. Pa Vangatau described this to me. He said 'the *paito* of Pangisi was a lineage of Taumako. Its father came and fastened on to us. Its father came and became a son to Pa Pike, Pae Avakofe. He was a man from Motulava. He dwelt and he married also into our chiefly house, a body of chiefs. Thereupon some lineages objected to it. The father of Pa Fenuafou made a fighting demonstration, objecting to Pa Pangisi and saying that he should be killed. He objected to his daughter's marriage (the woman was actually his father's brother's son's daughter). But because the man obeyed my grandfather the union was adjudged correct. My ancestor, Pa Pike, said 'It is proper for an emigrant (literally a "bird", i.e. meaning a stranger, a protected person) to marry. It is their wish, the woman and the man.' So they dwelt together and sa Reisake (the males of the woman's lineage) died out altogether, whereupon the married pair came and lived in Tuarangi, her ancestral home and cleaved to the lineage of the woman. When they united, the priest said that their name should be sa Pangisi, that of the father's homeland.'

The house of Pangisi may be termed a nascent lineage because of its lack of genealogical depth. But it cannot be described as a sub-lineage because there is no parent major lineage to which it was attached. The process of its development has been in accord with that described by the Tikopia in the formation of some of the major lineages such as Sao, Ngatotiu and Marinoa. Significantly, while the clan affiliation was taken from the wife, the lineage name was given by the husband in reference to his own origin, and descent was henceforward patrilineal.

In 1952 then Tikopia society in lineage terms was continuing to reproduce itself by the well recognized techniques.

Expansion of Descent Group Units

Having discussed changes in a number of descent group components as social units, we must now consider the question of changes in their strength, that is in the numbers of persons composing them.

One notable difference in Tikopia in 1952 as compared with 1929 was, as already shown, the expansion that lineages and clans had undergone. This had various implications, particularly since the expansion had not been uniform.

As regards the clans, the alteration in their relative magnitude was not apparent at first sight. But calculation from my census showed that after a generation Taumako had moved to first position in clan strength, while the other three clans had maintained their relative order. This greater rate of expansion by Taumako and their emergence as the numerically largest clan had apparently not been realized by the Tikopia elders in 1952. They were conscious of the increasing pressures involved, but not of their relative magnitude in specific terms. They saw attempts to acquire control of land, but they did not simply count heads.

Such expansion had dual aspects. On the one hand the size of the clan was a source of strength politically in giving wider support in cases of friction between clans and a basis for boasting or for self-depreciation. On the other hand, economically it was a weakness. Land resources being virtually in-elastic, the pressures upon subsistence which were always before the eyes of the elders were felt to some degree in intra-clan terms. An increase of clan size did not mean a flat reduction of land available per head. It did not operate in clan terms immediately. But ultimately it tended to have its reper-cussions on the clan as a whole through the segmental system in which families and lineages were bound together in clan membership under the charge of their chief. He could to a considerable extent reallocate some lands or favour the access of some members to land. Hence, pressures felt in some sections of a clan were apt to extend throughout the whole group. This was so particularly because some more powerful lineages, i.e. primarily those of chiefly descent, tended—or were thought to threaten—to move in where they could on to lands of their weaker kin or clansfolk.

Hence one must consider not only clan expansion but also the relative expansion of lineages within the clan. From this point of view, changes in the magnitude of the chiefly lineages (*paito ariki*) are most significant. It is interesting here to give a retrospective glance at the table and analysis of my material in 1929.[1] From this I pointed out that while Tafua and Taumako were relatively the two largest chiefly lineages in land control, the pressure on Tafua was likely to have been greater during the ensuing generation (i.e. that which has just passed) and that on Taumako during the present genera-tion. This prediction would seem to have been borne out. A glance at the comparative table below will show how great had been the growth in the chiefly lineage of Taumako and its immediately associated lineages. This occurred through the marriage of many of the males who were unmarried in 1929. Whereas the male membership of the other three chiefly groups had increased on the average by less than 50 per cent by 1952, that of Taumako had nearly doubled. In particular, the lineage of Avakofe had grown from twenty males and eight females in 1929 to forty males and twenty-six females in 1952. The implications of this growth were very clear by 1952 to members of the lineage. By then, although they were still relatively wealthy in land, some of their young men had begun to feel the impending land shortage as a hindrance to their marriage.

The difficulties, however, were felt far more widely than in Taumako alone. It is significant that the membership of the whole set of chiefly groups of Tikopia had risen from being 19 per cent of the total population in 1929 to 23 per cent of the total population in 1952. In other words, they had not merely shared in the general increase, they had outstripped the commoner groups in the pressure of their personnel on their land. The relatively minor

[1] *Primitive Polynesian Economy*, pp. 53–7.

TABLE XVIII

GROWTH IN MEMBERS OF CHIEFLY LINEAGES 1929–1952

| | 1929 | | | | 1952 | | |
	Males	*Females*	*Total*		*Males*	*Females*	*Total*
Kafika	31	26	57		46	26	72
Tafua	43	39	82		57	50	107
Taumako	44	24	68		87	64	151
Fangarere	23	16	39		36	34	70
	141	**105**	**246**		**226**	**174**	**400**

expansion of many of these commoner groups had still left them wondering where the next generation of their members would find enough land to culti-vate. Even in the chiefly house of Tafua, by 1952 the problem was regarded as very urgent. The Ariki Tafua, as an only surviving son of the former chief, himself controlled relatively large areas of good land. But in 1952 he had four young sons and was considering their future. For this reason he argued overtly that he was entitled to make every use of his land claims on territory cultivated by others—even though this was interpreted by such people as a definite encroachment on their land (see earlier, pp. 170–1).

Indices of Sub-Lineage Differentiation
I want now to examine the way in which expansion in numbers of people is related to lineage structure in terms of sub-lineage differentiation or, as it is generally known, lineage segmentation.[1] How does such differentiation occur? Has increase in lineage strength resulted in definitive segmentation? If any segmentation has occurred, has it been as between equal and opposite units or has it taken place in units of different grades?

First it is necessary to consider the indices of descent group differentiation in Tikopia. In 1952, as in 1929, there were four such main indices:

(*a*) *Separation of Ovens.* Oven cooking in Tikopia was an activity lending itself to group participation because of the labour and time involved in heating the stones, preparing and extricating the food. (Simple grilling could be an individual matter.) Agnatic kin, especially brothers, frequently had only one oven in operation among them, particularly if they lived close to one another. This co-operation could be symbolic of their membership of the same undifferentiated descent group. In 1952 a man said to me 'When you were here before, my brother and I had the same oven; today each has his own oven.' By this he meant not simply that they now cooked food separately, but that they regarded themselves now as independent units at the domestic level.

[1] See Raymond Firth, 'A Note on Descent Groups in Polynesia', *Man*, 2, 1957. So long as the process is one of internal specialization of functions and differential use of resources by sub-groups among themselves, I prefer to speak of *differentiation*. When this differentiation affects other groups significantly, as by giving rise to public recognition of a new unit or other structural modification, then the term *segmentation* seems appropriate.

(*b*) *Separation of Land Interests.* When two brothers lived with their families in separate villages, they might have separate cooking places but still use orchards and gardens in common. Separate oven facilities, however, were often linked with separate agricultural facilities. The division of rights to land was a more definitive index of social separation than division of oven work, which could be reversed at a few hours' notice and involved much less possibility of dispute. Depending on their numbers, size and allocation, orchards and gardens could be apportioned separately or 'split' (cf. pp. 160–8). Such an apportionment or splitting meant that the parties concerned could run their dual economic activities without reference to one another and so gave a basis for differentiation in the social field as well.

(*c*) *Separation of Canoe Interests.* Brothers or wider agnates whose land interests had been divided, might still share a canoe as a sub-lineage property, since canoes were relatively much fewer in numbers than orchards. In 1952 especially, trees suitable for building canoes were very scarce. But even when the sub-lineage had more than one vessel, the several craft might still be used as common property. Separation of canoe interests, however, might occur and indicate a further differentiation within the sub-lineage.

(*d*) *Separation of Ceremonial and Ritual Contributions.* The various services and presentations of food involved in fulfilment of social and ritual obligations tended to be provided collectively not only by the elementary family and household units, but also according to occasion, by sub-lineages of various degree and sometimes even by major lineages or their representatives. The practice of *fiuri*, contribution of raw food to an oven, though not confined to lineage participation, was a very common measure of effective lineage membership. He who regarded himself as an effective sub-lineage member took care to provide his *fiuri* for the more important food preparations of the group. Hence, consistent abstention from provision of *fiuri* to the lineage representative, or provision of a separate contribution of cooked food direct to the recipient group in ceremonial, stamped a person as regarding himself as belonging to a socially autonomous unit in such contexts. In 1952 this was done by the sub-lineage of Niukapu, for instance. Said Pa Raveiti (in 1929 known as Pa Koroatu) 'We who live here are many-branched; the houses are called separately. One man marries, divides off, he is called by his own name, and his own orchard is given him. If the chief holds a feast, the house of Niukapu, Koroatu and Nukutao (Rutu)—each prepares its contribution of food from its own orchard.' In this sub-lineage, moreover, each branch had a separate canoe. In the more highly symbolic ritual field, with political overtones, when the clan chief is the recipient, the same process operated. At the recarpeting of a sub-lineage temple or the resacralizing of a sacred canoe, the assumption of personal responsibility for these food gifts marked the emergence of a new lineage segment. Usually the senior man of such a segment took it upon himself to initiate such action and to deal direct with his chief instead of assisting as before in the food presentations by a more senior man.

Variation in Sub-Lineage Behaviour

(Some general points may be made here about these indices of differentiation.[1] In 1952 as in 1929 this differentiation did not operate automatically; there was variation according to personal circumstances. Group differentiation frequently began between brothers, and the idea of division of their resources was to avoid friction; once they had begun to quarrel, land division was almost automatic. It was commonly done by a father when his sons had married and begotten children. But some brothers continued to draw jointly on the family lands and to pool their food preparation and contributions to public affairs if they felt they could do so without friction)

The position of the Ariki Taumako and his brothers in 1952 may be contrasted with that of his close kinsmen of Tarikitonga. The former operated their orchards separately. 'The orchard of one man, another man does not go to it because they have been separated from of old.' In other words, they had been traditionally regarded as different properties and so their allocation to the separate owners had been easy. Without implication of family strife, the members now operated them separately, though in itself the division was probably made to avoid family friction. But in Tarikitonga, as noted earlier (p. 166), the elder brother shared with his junior—yet both were married, with children.

[Although my records are very incomplete, such comparison as I can make between 1929 and 1952 indicates that at the earlier date there were proportionately fewer divisions of land between brothers. In the intervening generation many orchards had been 'split'. In part this had been due to the growth of population and the maturing interests of the people who were unmarried before. But in part it was due to the greater feeling of pressure on land and the desire of men to safeguard and define the interests of their children, even against their own brothers.]

Mere augmentation of members or mere maturity of a family of children did not mean division. According to the principles of male control of land resources and of patrilineal inheritance, a household of female siblings tended to remain as part of a unit headed by their father's brother or male orthocousin. According to the principle of seeking separation of interests only as among peers, sons usually did not wish to separate while their father was alive unless he himself promoted this to avoid quarrels after his death. According to the principle that even for males, marriage and the founding of a family were normally prerequisite to separation of interests, bachelors usually remained in a unit headed by a married brother.

An example from the lineage of Fusi will illustrate possible variation. In 1929, four brothers in the Tereata branch of this lineage were dispersed in residence. Pa Orovaru and his wife lived with two small daughters in Potu i Korokoro in Faea, while an elder brother, Pa Rangivae, lived with his wife and three sons in Potimua, half a mile away. They had separate ovens, but

[1] J. Spillius has suggested to me that the distribution of European property may also be considered as an index of lineage differentiation. This would relate especially to conditions post–1952.

shared their lands and their major property. Pa Tereata, the eldest brother
of the four, was living in Ravenga on the lake shore in a house occupied also
by his wife, two unmarried daughters, an unmarried son and the fourth
brother, married, with his wife. By 1952, Pa Orovaru and his wife were dead,
leaving four daughters all unmarried though most were full-grown. Pa
Rangivae and his wife, both still living, now had three sons and a daughter.
His brother's daughters had come to live next door to him in Potimua. I
asked him if he had adopted them as 'adhering children'.[1] He replied 'There
is no adopted child among them, they are simply children of my brother
living with me. They are completely looked after by me.' In fact, the oven as
well as the lands of all these people was now in common. In 1952, the former
Pa Tereata still lived with his wife in the same house, though they had changed
their name to sa Farekarae and they now spent part of their time in a house
on the coast. Their young son of 1929 had now married and was bearing his
father's former house name of Tereata. He was living with his wife and five
young children in a newly built house on the coast at Namo. The fourth
married brother, Pa Nukutumau, who used to live with them, was now living
separately but also in Namo not far away, with his wife and four children,
two sons and two daughters. These three households used their orchards as
a single unit and also shared a single canoe which, said one of the men, 'is of
our *paito*'. Hence, two original households in Faea and one in Ravenga had
become, over a generation, one household in Faea and three in Ravenga, the
lineage members increasing from seven to nine in the first case and five to
twelve in the second. Through aggregation in the first and despite dispersion
in the second, their ovens, lands and canoes were held in common as far as
each group was concerned.

From a comparative point of view it may be noted that unlike the position
in many African communities, in Tikopia spatial or residential separation in
itself is not necessarily an index of lineage segmentation or internal differentiation for all purposes. For the Tikopia, economic activity as manifested in the
control of resources is the significant element. The contrast, however, is not
fundamental since in an African community it is in most cases the ability
to utilize new land by migration that gives the spatial mobility its importance
for social segmentation.

Differentiation of sub-groups within the lineage in Tikopia can occur at
different levels in respect of the same index. But normally separation of oven
interests is a differentiation at the domestic level and operates between
married brothers with children. It is primarily a definition of interests among
the maturing members of an elementary family which has expanded. Separation of land interests, while it may ultimately be the first step towards the
definition of a new lineage segment, is much of the same order. But separation
of canoe-using interests, which rarely occurs among brothers, even if married
and with children, does mark a more clear-cut internal differentiation within
the lineage and commonly takes place between agnatic kin of wider span.
Separation of ceremonial or ritual contributions may not occur even if the

[1] *We, The Tikopia*, pp. 203–6.

other separations have taken place, and it rarely occurs if they have not. This is the index of differentiation of highest order in ordinary social affairs, and tends to mark the emergence of a new sub-lineage. Separation of ovens or canoe or land interests is primarily an internal matter for the group concerned; it does not necessarily demand any specific recognition by the lineage as a whole. But separation in transactions concerning food or valuables with other groups calls for external cognisance. Apart from questions of responsibility for resources and prestige in taking initiative, the reciprocity in such transactions involves the question of who is to be the recipient—the sub-lineage head or the head of the particular branch. Hence, some onus is laid upon other parties to the transaction in recognizing the degree to which intra-lineage differentiation has become a *public matter*, i.e. segmentation in the full sense has occurred. The direct and separate line of ritual relationship with the clan chief, established by furnishing with him *fonakava* and *monotanga*, is also of prime importance. The lineage is not solely a political group—it has significant social and ritual functions of a non-political order. But individual relations with the clan head are the clearest expression of the emergence of a new sub-lineage.

Further light is thrown on the process of differentiation by the custom of variance in ritual presentation, known as *saeakinga*.

The essence of this is a departure from normally accepted procedure. Pa Fenuatara explained the situation in this way. 'The idea is like this. A man sits and thinks, thinks about himself. The clan is assembled for the recarpeting of the one temple, their minds having gone like that along a single path. Then the man says "Oh, I am going to make a variant for myself—to prepare a canoe acknowledgment by myself for the chief, to do it differently." ' Then Pa Fenuatara continued with a gesture. He said 'There is the path, there' (pointing one way), 'whereas *saeakinga* turns aside like that' (pointing his hand another way). The meaning of this was that a ritual elder, having been newly appointed by his chief, decides to express his individuality by varying the day for sacralizing his temple or his sacred canoe. Such a variant procedure may not have any implications from the point of view of lineage segmentation, if, for example, the new elder is the eldest son of the late elder. Indeed, like Pa Ngatotiu, such an heir may decide not to make any variation. But if, like Pa Timoio of Tavi, the new elder has been selected from another branch of the lineage, then his variant procedure may be one way of expressing the fact that this branch is now to be considered as a major sub-lineage in its own right.

The concept of *saeakinga* may also operate outside the sphere of ritual elders. A man who is not such an office holder, but is the head of a branch of a lineage, may decide that the time has come for this branch to achieve separate recognition as a major sub-lineage. Pa Fenuatara explained the custom in regard to segmentation from chiefly lineages as follows: 'This is a custom of chiefly lineages. When they have separated, each dwells in his house. Now, the practice in Tikopia is like this. A man who has separated from the chief (i.e. segmented from the chief's lineage) has to prepare his food acknowledgment for the chief. If not from his house, he prepares it when he builds his canoe. If he builds his canoe, the acknowledgment is called *monotanga*. If he does not do it for his canoe, he recarpets his house and the acknowledgment to the chief is called *fonakava*.' Such food presentation was termed generally *te auariki*, the *auariki* of the chief. It was not reciprocated by the chief. Such a man had a choice of which day he would select for making such a food acknowledgment. He might choose a general day when most of the temples or canoes were celebrated, or he might decide to strike out on his own and pick another day to emphasize the individuality of his gift. It is the separation or variance in this procedure which is implied in the term *saeakinga*. The symbolic character of the physical separations of time and of food gifts involved were clearly understood by the Tikopia. Time and place separation symbolized social separation and the emergence of lineage segments, as semi-autonomous units *vis-à-vis* their chief and the social body generally.

One point about the separate preparation of such a food gift needs explanation. Separation of ovens for the preparation of food might occur at quite different genealogical levels, and in very different contexts. At the domestic level married brothers, for instance, might separate their ovens for the purpose of ordinary daily food preparation. This might be as much for practical convenience as for any other reason, and its symbolic significance was low. It was part of the regular process of re-definition of elementary family out of joint family situations. The separation of food contributions from different ovens was another matter when the context was of a ceremonial or ritual kind. Food for a ceremonial presentation in the name of a lineage might have been cooked by one elementary family or by more than one; in one oven or in several. This was immaterial, provided that the presentation was made in their joint name. But when such food presentations were made separately, in the names of the several parties, this was socially a significant difference. What was significant was not the physical separation of the ovens but the social fusion or social differentiation of their product under a single label or with different group labels. It will be borne in mind, of course, that social separation of food presentations by different branches of a lineage might occur in some contexts, while in other contexts the branches combined under a single head.

Degree of Differentiation

Having considered the indices, we may now ask what differentiation did in fact occur in Tikopia between 1929 and 1952, in what conditions and how was it viewed.

In general, it can be said that there was some segmentation—some public differentiation of a number of sub-lineages at a depth of two or three generations from the parent stock (reckoning depth normally to a fully adult active member of the group concerned). As example, following upon the discussion of ritual variants, we may examine the list of *saeakinga* given to me in June 1952 by Pa Fenuatara, when temples were being recarpeted. He said that in recent times the number of houses from which *fonakava* were presented to the Ariki Kafika had been added to by the following: Tongarutu, Siamano, Paoari, Nukutauo, Timoio, Motusio.

The first three represented differentiations from the chiefly lineage of Kafika, as may be seen from the genealogy (Gen. 2; cf. Genealogy 1 in *We, The Tikopia*, p. 347). (The inclusion of Tongarutu was not in fact new; it was already being celebrated in 1929,[1] but obviously Pa Fenuatara had not remembered exactly when it achieved separate status.) In 1929 Tongarutu represented a lineage segment of five generations depth, and signalized the recognition by Pa Vainunu and his agnatic kin on the one side and the Ariki Kafika on the other that the descendants of Mourongo constituted a separate sub-lineage for many purposes. As Pa Vainunu said to me 'I separated to the rear.' But by 1952 there had been further developments. Pa Vainunu and his younger brother, Pa Paoari, who used to operate ritually as one unit, were both dead. But the latter's son had begun to make acknowledgment to the chief from his own house, Paoari, recarpeting it separately from the parent house Tongarutu. Though he and his agnatic kinsfolk of Tongarutu were first cousins, and Paoari was their collective lineage name, people were already beginning to speak about *paito i Paoari* as a separate group from Tongarutu. It is significant that the descendants of Pa Nukuro had not made a similar definition of their interest, although they were the eldest branch. The reason for this doubtless was that for a number of years they had lived in poverty and with a somewhat depressed status, having been 'chased away' from two settlements—in one case allegedly for theft. By 1952 they were spoken of as *paito i Nukuro*, as a minor sub-lineage of the Kafika chiefly house, but they did not attain the dignity of a ritual separation and procedure of their own with either house or canoe.

The separate celebration of the temple of Pa Siamano was due to the interest of this man and his brother in commemorating the branch of the chiefly house associated with their father, Fakarakeianga. Since he had attained the dignity of chieftainship, it was regarded as fitting that as time went on and his sons became elderly, they and their descendants should take on some ritual autonomy. But it should be noted that Siamano and Tongarutu were at very different genealogical levels.

Nukutauo was a different type of case. The house concerned was the property of the major lineage of Raropuka, but it appears not to have been ceremonialized by them during the last generation at least. The food acknowledgment from its recarpeting was carried to the Ariki Kafika by 1952, because it represented 'the path of Nau Ariki'. This title, formerly given to the eldest daughter of each Ariki Kafika, and carrying with it ritual powers and privileges, was borne when I was in Tikopia in 1929 by Nau Raropuka, the wife of the former ritual elder of that name. Their eldest son was living in the house Nukutauo in Rotoaia and bore that house name. By 1952, his father and his mother were dead, and he himself alternated his dwelling with that in which his parents had lived in Potimua in Faea. But his married son

[1] *Work of the Gods*, vol. I, pp. 158–9.

Q

GENEALOGY 2

Sub-Lineage Differentiation in Kafika

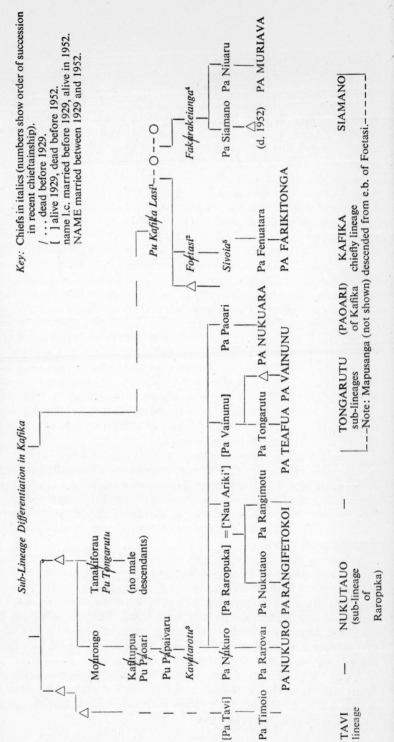

Sub-Lineage Differentiation in Kafika

Key: Chiefs in italics (numbers show order of succession in recent chieftainship).
/ . . . dead before 1929.
[ ] alive 1929, dead before 1952.
name l.c. married before 1929, alive in 1952.
NAME married between 1929 and 1952.

now lived in the house permanently and his brother's children lived nearby; they all combined to make the food gift in commemoration of their grandmother's relations with the Kafika chiefly house. They were coming to be known generally as *paito i Nukutauo*, being singled out from the parent lineage of Raropuka, and used this formal gift to the Ariki Kafika as a means of emphasizing their growing autonomy.

The celebration of the houses Timoio and Motusio signalized changes in the lineages of two ritual elders—Tavi in the first case and Porima in the second. Each represented the crystallization of a sub-lineage after three generations. (But the resacralization of Timoio temple was partly in replacement of a former usage since the main Tavi temple had been allowed to fall into decay after the death of the former elder.)

In all cases, of course, these sub-lineages were regarded as constituent parts of the main lineages in some contexts, e.g. overall rights to land.

In terms of social change there is an important point to be noted here—a change in the value of an index. By 1952 the ritual celebration of house or canoe was becoming a very imperfect index of sub-lineage differentiation. With the advance of Christianity and the consequent banning of the kava rites, sub-lineages which could signalize their differentiation in this way had become few and were likely to become fewer. In order to declare their individuality then, it had to be by their initiative in ceremonial transfers at funerals and other social occasions.

It is interesting to see at what point sub-lineage differentiation began to appear. It seems that it did not become an active process until a second generation from the traditional ancestor had come to maturity. In 1929, for instance, in the cases just discussed, Pa Paoari, Pa Siamano and Pa Nukutauo were all alive. But only towards 1952, when the first had died and the other two were aged, and their sons and brothers' sons had married and had children in turn, did the differentiation of the sub-lineage in ritual terms occur. In other words, there is a minimal generation depth socially necessary in Tikopia for sub-lineage recognition in the ritual context. It is from this point of view, speaking structurally, that the term minimal lineage—or more properly 'minimal sub-lineage'—would be appropriate.

Operational Considerations

But Tikopia recognitions are operational as well as structural. Moreover, the operational elements with which they are concerned are not simply institutional functions, e.g. land holding, marriage, ritual performance. They also include the very significant element of numbers of persons involved. From this point of view, what is necessary for the recognition of a differentiated sub-lineage in operational terms is a socially effective body of close agnatic kin. It is true that the structural differentiation is not overlooked. The Tikopia, in 1952 as in 1929, could speak of the *paito* of such-and-such as being, for instance, only one old woman. But for operational purposes this *paito* would be represented by the nearest agnatic kinsfolk—'nearest', usually genealogically, but sometimes varying according to special circumstances. Provided that a body of agnatic kin operates in the name of the sub-lineage, its genealogical depth is not of much relevance. Genealogical ties are significant when it is a question of establishing rights to land or attributing obligations for services. But in cases of dispute these are done in terms of the individuals concerned rather than of lineage groups; the precise genealogical depth may vary considerably among the individuals in the group, and is not important. Social impediments, as with Nukuro, may inhibit the differentiation of a particular genealogical unit as a lineage segment. On the other hand, sub-lineages of similar social magnitude, that is, operationally involved with one another in exchanges, etc., are often not equal and opposite in genealogical terms, but are genealogically of disparate orders.

There seems to have been no radical change in this position over the genera-tion between 1929 and 1952. This can be illustrated by a reference to the units participating in ritual exchanges during the sacred dances of the Work of the Gods. In 1929 there were certain exchanges of baskets of food which were traditional between chiefly houses, for example, Kafika and Taumako. Apart from this, social units, including members of chiefly houses, were free to contract food exchanges subject only to some readjustment in the interests of spreading the burden as equably as possible. It was notable that these food exchanges, although taking place in *paito* terms, were definitely not operating at constant generation level. For instance, the chiefly house of Kafika had a standing exchange with that of Taumako—in lineage terms between equal and opposite parties. At the same time, in 1929 the Kafika chiefly group had *ad hoc* exchanges with Notau, a main lineage with a ritual elder at its head, and with Kamota, a sub-lineage of sa Sanga (which ranked as a main lineage but not of major importance, having no ritual elder).[1] In December 1952, Spillius noted a similar set of ritual exchanges. Again, the chiefly house of Kafika exchanged with that of Taumako. Again, too, Kamota exchanged with the chiefly house of Kafika. Notau was no longer a participant since its members had become Christian in the interval, and therefore did not attend such pagan affairs. But Kafika chiefly house made two other exchanges with Ngatotiu and Rongoifo, the former being a Taumako major lineage with a ritual elder at its head, and the latter a sub-lineage of another Taumako major lineage, Niumano. Superficially then, the situation was similar to that of a generation earlier. But there was a significant difference. In 1929, the Ariki Kafika was still in active direction of affairs, and the food baskets were presented as from his household. In 1952, his sons were already elderly men and their sons in turn could assume mature responsibility. So in 1952 the exchanges were more specifically described as being between sa Fenuatara in Uta and sa Taumako, also in Uta; sa Ngatotiu and sa Nukuva—with Pa Fenuafuri (father of Pa Nukuva), from the house of Teve; sa Taramoa in Uta and sa Rongoifo in Namo; and finally sa Farikitonga from Taramoa and a bachelor representative of Kamota. In most of these cases, as in 1929, the principal parties had assistance from affinal kin or from friends. For instance, in the last case Spillius himself was called in as assistant to the

[1] *Work of the Gods*, vol. II, pp. 240–84. See also this chapter, *supra*, p. 231.

Kamota bachelor. But in 1952, as in 1929, the operational unit was essentially the household with its oven, the principal operators being the members of an elementary family. It was important that they represented a lineage or sub-lineage, but which particular lineage phase they represented was not important for matching purposes. A lineage phase of equal order did not have to be found.

Structurally then, the point of sub-lineage differentiation is significant for the exercise of certain kinds of rights, in particular, those to land. But for most operational purposes sub-lineage order in genealogical terms is not significant. For ordinary social purposes the sub-lineage of Avakofe was, by 1952, very important. As I have pointed out already, its male membership had doubled over the generation. It had become larger in membership than any other lineage of clan Taumako of any genealogical depth whatever, except the lineage of sa Sanga, which had four more members. Yet structurally, Avakofe was a very minor element in the genealogical and lineage field of Tikopia—of only four generations total depth—or one generation back to the founding ancestor, who was personally known to me in 1929. Organizationally, Avakofe played a major role in the clan and in Tikopia society as a whole. Some of its members took a most active part in clan decisions and community decisions (see p. 273), and the sub-lineage met on equal terms in marriage and funeral arrangements with traditional major lineages such as Rarovi or Porima. From this operational point of view, it would be absurd to describe such a unit as a 'minimal' sub-lineage.

Linked with this lack of Tikopia interest in the structural phase of lineage components was the use of the terms *paito* (house) and *sa* (collectivity) to describe social units of varying magnitude. The expression *paito i Kafika* could refer to the Ariki Kafika, his sons, and their children and grand-children, or it could include the wider agnatic kin comprised in the various sub-lineages indicated in Gen. 2 and already discussed. If the chief were a young man, his only descendants being his children, then the term could apply with even more restriction to that group alone. Similarly, the term *sa Kafika* could mean the Ariki Kafika and his wife; the chief and his descendants; the whole chiefly house, including the collateral sub-lineages, or the whole clan of Kafika. The context normally supplied the meaning, and if not, then further specification was given. (For operational purposes, too, wives were normally included in such collectivity when units of smaller magnitude were meant.) This freedom of use of the collective term was most noticeable when the head of the lineage bore the same house name as the lineage in general. In 1952 the ritual head of the lineage of Tavi was Pa Timoio. Sa Timoio or *paito i Timoio* had a restricted application, and could not apply to the whole lineage, whereas in 1929 the ritual head was Pa Tavi, and particular and general units could be covered by the same term, *sa Tavi* or *paito i Tavi*. This difference in the case of Tavi was not symptomatic of any general change. In 1952, most heads of lineages bore as house name the lineage name.

Linked with this system of names was the recognition of separable social units. This was illustrated by the behaviour of, for instance, the Ariki Taumako and the Ariki Fangarere when I discussed with them the lineage structure of their clans in 1952. Each of them was concerned to give a separate identity to quite small units which previously I had regarded as simply component parts of larger ones. The Ariki Fangarere, in particular, behaved as a 'splitter' rather than as a 'lumper', to use the old labels of taxonomy. He insisted on characterizing most units which lived separately as individual units, and to any question of mine, replied 'It is appropriate for them to stand separately'—(in my notebook). The upshot was that he listed fifteen *paito* as separate, i.e. sub-lineages proper to be differentiated, whereas in 1928 I had been told that there were nine Fangarere *paito*, including that of the chief.

Comparison of the two lists, with comments of the Ariki Fangarere, is as follows:

1928/9	1952	*Comment*
paito ariki	paito ariki	(Now led by two brothers, both chiefs.)
Nukurafia	Nukumanongi	'Closely associated.'
	Nukumasere	
Tekava	Tekava	'Closely associated.'
Matinimua	Matinimua	
	Vaisakiri	'paito i Nukutungasau has *saeaki*.'
	Nukutungasau	
Taferoa (Nopu)	Taferoa	'It is good that they should stand separately; the name of Nopu has been dropped—only women.'
	Tungatai	
Taraoro	Ngaruefu	'We don't know about Taraoro; it may be borne by the grandsons of Pa Taraoro, but his son is called Pa Ngaruefu.'
Nukufetau	Mea	'Their principal name is Mea.'
	Nukufetau	
	Maneru	
Fenumera	Fenumera	'It is good that they should stand separately.'
Rangimakini	Rangimakini	

All of these units were traced back to two chiefly ancestors who were brothers and who were placed in the genealogy five generations from the speaker in 1952. The whole Fangarere clan, with its component lineages, traced its membership to a single ancestor nine generations ago (see Gen. 3).

As the total membership of Fangarere clan in 1952 was only 142 persons, of whom twenty-four were in the chiefly lineage, this differentiation by the chief meant an average sub-lineage strength of less than nine persons. At this level, his sub-lineage reckoning became almost, although not quite, the reckoning of separate households. At the same time, the identity of their agnatic members in general lineage terms was not lost. The chief placed these sub-lineages as constituent elements in larger units. For example,

GENEALOGY 3

Segmentation in Fangarere Clan

Key:

△ male.
○ female.
Pu Mea dead before 1928/9.
[Pa Mea] alive 1929, died before 1952.
Pa Mea married before 1929, alive 1952.
PA MEA married between 1929 and 1952.

Pa Vaisakiri
PA VAISAKIRI

Pa Nukutungasau
Pa Nukumanongi   PA NUKUMASERE

Pa Nukurafia

Pa Tekava

Pa Matinimua
(or Pa Sapusapu)   PA MATINIMUA   PA TEKAVA

Pa Tatonga

[Ariki Fangarere]

Pa Nukumaro   Pa Rangiatatua   Ariki Fangarere
Ariki Fangarere

Pa Nukumaro   PA FENUATAFE

Pu Nopu

Pa Tafeˊoa   PA TAFEROA

[Pa Tungatai]

Pa Kirikirei   PA TUNGATAI

[Pa Nopu]

Pu Ngaruefu
Pa Raugoata   [Pa Taraoro]   PA NGARUEFU

Pu Mea

[Pa Nukufetau]   [Pa Maneru]

[Pa Mea]   [Pa Matofa]
PA MEA   PA NUKUFETAU

Pa Fangatau   [Pa Korofatu]   [Pa Fenumera]
PA FENUMERA

Pa Rangiˊakai   Pa Rangimakini

Pa Fofumera   [Pa Rangimakini]

though he said it was proper that Fenumera and Rangimakini should be listed separately, the sub-lineage names of Nukufetau, Maneru and Mea were collectively grouped by him under the principal name (*matua ingoa*) of Mea. While the component units had only two generations depth each, the collective unit was of four generations depth.

To people in general in 1952, as in 1929, Fangarere clan had only two major lineages, that of the chiefly house and that of Rangimakini, the lineage of the ritual elder of the Ariki Fangarere. In 1929, Mea sub-lineage provided the ritual elder (Pa Nukufetau), who was succeeded by his eldest son, Pa Mea. Soon after, he died, and by 1952 no ritual elder had been appointed after the death of this encumbent. Although by 1952 Rangimakini proper had died out as far as its male representatives were concerned—there being only one woman member living in the dwelling of a classificatory brother in another group—people still used the general title as the collective term for the lineage and often included under it Nopu and Mea as well.

A general guide to the significance of the lineage concept in Tikopia is given by the way in which units termed *paito* were referred to in different operational contexts. From my general records in 1929, and those of myself and Spillius in 1952, there are well over a thousand citations in which *paito* were mentioned by name. These references were of various kinds—in the form of *paito i Nea, tama i Nea, sa Nea*—'lineage of Such and such', 'child in Such and such', 'collectivity of Such and such', etc. Analysis of all this material shows that the term *paito* was used to refer to a lineage unit at any level of segmentation. Again, it was sometimes used with primary reference to a body of agnatic kin, but often by implication referred as well to the wives and other household members sharing the domestic units in which the agnatic lineage members lived.

In citing a person in terms of his lineage, there were many contexts in which the level of segmentation involved was indifferent. If one asked who are the mother's brothers responsible for the care of a person at a ceremony, the reply might be given in terms of the major lineage name. But it could equally have been given in terms of a minor sub-lineage name, that of the immediate ancestry of the men concerned. Use of the major lineage name did imply that ultimately all members of the major lineage had a responsibility to the person who was the centre of the ceremony. But so also did the use of the minor sub-lineage name, since any Tikopia would know that if the men of this special unit could not act, the responsibility would normally be assumed by a collateral agnatic kinsman in any branch of the major lineage.

From such linguistic usages it is again apparent that Tikopia lineage concepts had an organizational as well as a structural connotation, and that the Tikopia could use them flexibly, with more or less structural precision according as the context required. In general, the context of day to day economic and social activity tended to involve *paito* citation at a relatively low level of segmentation, whereas land rights and ceremonial and ritual obligations tended to involve citation at a major level. But this was by no means an invariable usage since Tikopia knowledge of the attendant circum-

stances and of the empirical lineage structure commonly allowed of translation from one level of meaning to another, where necessary.

On the whole, the spread of *paito* citations among units of different
genealogical depth was fairly even, and I found no significant difference
between the 1929 and 1952 usage in this respect or the others just discussed.

Trends of Change Summarized

I can now summarize and comment upon the main trends of change in the
Tikopia system of descent groups over the generation between my visits.
Structurally, the same general framework of descent group typology and
relationships operated in 1952 as in 1929. Empirically, the same major component groups identified by name were in existence, although, as could be
expected, there had been considerable replacement of their personnel from
natural causes. The principles of segmentation were active as before. The
general principle of patrilineality was unimpaired. The sole case of lineage
increment to a clan conformed to a traditional procedure in respect of a male
immigrant, and the several cases of sub-lineage grafting used agnatic stock,
and did not follow through female lines.

The genealogical material used as referent and validation for the descent
group system was of the same general character as before. Tests of genealogical knowledge which I applied in 1952 to the successors of men whom I
had known in 1929 showed that the main names and order in the genealogies
had been preserved. There were, however, some gaps in the ancillary material
—ignorance of some marriages at early periods, of the order of siblings in a
family and of the names of some people who had not produced descendants.
On the whole, my impression was that the genealogical evidence upon which
even lineage leaders relied for their picture of sub-lineage relationships had
become rather more attenuated than before; in a few cases it had become
almost skeletal. Even in 1929 this had been the case in some lineages, but it
seemed to me that the process had gone further by 1952. For the generation
or two before the speaker, the memory data were still fairly full—this was
the period for which the speaker could usually say he had *seen* the person
concerned—a very important index for the Tikopia. But beyond this, when
he had to say he had no personal knowledge, the conversion of history into
tradition became evident. From the point of view of the theory of lineage
validation, however, despite the blurring or cutting-off of ancillary material,
I did not notice any specific shortening of the genealogical depth of the
lineage—rather the reverse, since one or two generations had been added in
some cases because of deaths. Looked at from another angle, this implies
that the principle that lineage structure must have genealogical validation
was still regarded as normal in Tikopia by 1952.

But it is possible that the situation in this respect may change fairly rapidly.
With the conversion of the whole of Tikopia to Christianity in 1956, the
lineage system has lost a powerful support through the abandonment of the
pagan ritual. For the major lineages, of which sixteen were ritually involved
as pagan in 1929 and eight in 1952, this has involved abandonment of the

recital of the kava titles or analogous lists of ancestors at many points of the rites. This in turn has meant inevitable loss of a very important mnemonic for genealogical links. It seems likely then that, as the present generation of lineage heads who have participated in pagan ritual or been acquainted with it from their father dies out, knowledge of the genealogical material will weaken.

The religious changes may well affect the lineage system in other ways. With the abandonment of the ritual celebration of sacred canoes and the temples, two major food gifts to the clan chief in acknowledgment of his ritual interest in these sacred objects are likely to be given up. This, by doing away with opportunity for sub-lineage diversification (*saeakinga*) may decrease to some extent tendencies to lineage splitting. On the other hand, the abandonment of the food gifts will do away with important occasions of lineage assembly for collective action and remove an important type of symbolic tie with the clan chief, expressing the solidarity of the lineage towards him. A similar gap will have been left if there is abandonment of the *inaki* floor mat, specially plaited for the clan temple to cover the graves of the ancestor or god from whom the lineage has inherited its land. For a time, in 1952/3, one chief attempted to plug this growing gap by stressing the political rather than the ritual significance of this pious act. It will be interesting to see whether after 1956, and complete conversion to Christianity, such interpretation will still be valid and effective. Again, the virtual abandonment by 1952 of certain special lineage privilege ceremonies, as the *kura* of Marinoa, the *manongi* of Korokoro and the *ruku* of Sao, also did remove powerful inducements to demonstrate lineage solidarity and to maintain ancestral genealogical links.[1]

In general terms then, the traditional ritual associations of lineages in Tikopia have meant that the victory of the new ideology of Christianity has offered a serious threat to certain sanctions for lineage assembly and action, and therefore may have affected the integrity of the lineage system.

But has the lineage system any other supports which may still allow it to function, even although the traditional ritual buttresses are removed? One important feature in the lineage structure has been its identification with the system of land tenure. Subject to the other rights of the clan chief, the lineage in 1952, as in 1929, was the major title-holder to land in Tikopia. There seems little likelihood in the foreseeable future that there will be any move to alter this system. There seems little prospect of the introduction of documentary record of title, of any tendency to transfer land by process of sale, of any individualization of land title to the exclusion of the rights of the lineage as a whole. Such measures have been introduced in some other Polynesian communities. But in such cases the whole area has been much larger, much more accessible to the outside world, and in particular there has sometimes tended to be competition for land by Europeans. The isolated situation of Tikopia,

---

[1] See my 'Privilege Ceremonials in Tikopia', *Oceania*, vol. XXI, 1951, pp. 161–77, and further notes on same, *Oceania*, vol. XXVI, 1955, pp. 1–13. For re-interpretation of *inaki*, see Spillius, *op. cit.*, pp. 20–2.

and its poverty of resources, may well militate against such a change. As long as a system of land tenure is lineage-controlled, there would seem to be a very strong set of motivations for perpetuation of lineage form in general and recognition of genealogical ties among its members.

In the ceremonial field (i.e. a symbolic social action not involving appeals to ancestors and gods), as distinct from the ritual field, there also continues to be great scope for lineage operations in Tikopia. Some ceremonies focusing upon individuals have been discontinued or greatly diminished in scope. But ceremonies of birth, although diminished, were still substantial in 1952, and there seemed no indication that ceremonies of initiation of boys would be neglected once food supplies regained normal levels. Marriage and funerals —granted the exceptional reductions due to the famine—continued at a high level of assembly and transfer of goods. All of these were handled by social groups involving or implying lineage representation. In order that such a system can continue, the lineage structure must be operative.

But the new economic conditions coming into forceful operation by 1952 may affect the integrity of the lineage system. As migration plans for sections of the Tikopia population become fully effective, certain lineages must be denuded of some of their members or may disappear altogether as active elements in the society of Tikopia. Relations between the Tikopia abroad and the Tikopia at home may be maintained not in segmentary terms but rather on the model of relations between affiliated lineages of Anuta and Tikopia.[1] This will not necessarily affect the lineage principle itself. But it may well weaken the emphasis ordinarily laid upon the local Tikopia lineages as the most appropriate units for many social operations.

More serious may be the effect of the absence of younger men abroad as plantation and other workers. If such temporary migration continues, lineage stability may be affected by their increased command of resources through their earnings and a resulting change in the structure of authority in the economic affairs of the lineage. Should there be from them any widespread challenge to the authority of their elders, a series of lineage splits might take place, reducing the major lineages to a set of much smaller autonomous units. The lineage structure may be threatened in still another way by their absence, that is, through their land interests. The tradition of Tikopia has been that a person who goes abroad does not have his land interests imperilled. The land is worked by his brothers or other agnatic kinsmen and when he returns he takes up his individual rights again side by side with them. Until recently this has been a short-term situation for the most part. The exceptional individuals who have been away for years have been content with the same arrangement. Should working for wages abroad become a regular part of the Tikopia economy, then some solution must be found to the problem of exercise of absentee rights. This may be linked with the need for support by men at home of dependent relatives of the men abroad. Some system of compensation may be worked out. But failing this, there may be a

[1] See my 'Anuta and Tikopia: Symbiotic Elements in Social Organization', *Journal Polynesian Society*, vol. 63, 1954, pp. 87–131.

tendency for actual cultivation to be more closely linked with title to the land; or, in defence against this by absentees, the introduction of some system of more individual record of land title to preserve their interests.

One could speculate further, but I think I have said enough to show some of the possibilities in the situation likely to threaten the integrity of the lineage as a land-holding unit. Apart from this, the interest of wage-earners in keeping to themselves and their families wealth they have earned may lead to a closer definition of personal rights and property. The Tikopia have not worked out any traditional system of distribution of Western goods to the degree they have with their own cultural products. Hence the influx of new wealth may militate against overall lineage interest, especially when accumulation for ceremonial presentation takes place.

But an important feature in this whole situation is the position and role of the clan chief. Respect for authority in 1952, as in 1929, was a cardinal principle of the Tikopia social system. As will be shown in a later chapter, it has not seemed to have been impaired by changes in the religious system. In political terms, the Tikopia have been accustomed to handing over responsibility in the last resort to a single individual, a chief, who serves as the symbol and a rallying point for social order. So long as the Tikopia retain this respect for the chieftainship as an institution, they are likely to support that institution by social and by economic means. So long as these economic means are drawn primarily from the land held under general lineage title, there will be a direct relation between lineage and clan chief. In this sphere it would seem to be to the interest of the chief to have the lineage units maintained to their highest degree as affording him the most convenient means of unified political control over his clan. The abandonment of the system of ritual elders nominated by the chief has already meant the loss of a clearly demarcated leadership for many lineages. But Tikopia recognition of the general authority due to senior members of the lineage may well be sufficient to ensure adequate lineage representation without the ritual sanction.

As regards the relation of chief to lineage in the sphere of property derived from wage-earning, the issue is not so clear. If the chief is to continue as a focus for the accumulation and disbursement of resources, lineage units may well provide a very convenient framework for these operations. On the other hand, whereas the product of lands could be regarded as lineage property very simply, the product of personal labour abroad may not be so easily classified under this head. It may then suit the clan chief to maintain economic relations with the wage-earners among his clan members on an individual (or at least household) basis rather than a lineage basis. From this point of view, the system may operate more smoothly.

What has been said about lineages applies *a fortiore* to clans.

By 1952, the clans were still part of the traditional framework of the social structure. They had expanded differentially in households and in representation in number of settlements. But this geographical expansion had not given greater prestige to the units principally concerned, though it had given greater political thrust and was thought to offer some threat to land occupation. But in many social spheres clan alignment was recognized as very significant. Moreover, the position of the chief as clan head helped to preserve the role of the clan as a primary social unit.

The importance of the clan, however, had been very seriously impaired by the growing defection of lineages and individuals from the great ritual assemblies in the Work of the Gods. In 1929 some Tafua representatives still attended the pagan rituals and Fangarere was still fully pagan. By 1952 Tafua had no representation at all and Fangarere, though it still possessed a pagan chief, had the clan split through the defection of a large portion of it to Christianity, and the creation of a Christian chief. Increasingly, too, after the defection of the principal elders, the connotation of Kafika in the rites became lineage (*paito i Kafika*) rather than clan (*kainanga i Kafika*). Hence, the clans appeared at the pagan ritual not only very much under strength but also incompletely matched. This was an intermediate stage. After 1956, with the completion of conversion to Christianity, the clan temples to the traditional gods and ancestors will have been abandoned. With the transfer of religious worship to the churches, the (new) temples will have ceased to be clan centres and will have become local community centres completely. In worship in the village churches, members of different clans participate side by side. There are no religious occasions for clan assembly as formerly, no ritual obligations or privileges for clans as such. In the social sphere, assemblies such as competitive dance gatherings may become expressions of local solidarity rather than clan solidarity, as all pagan associations of dancing disappear. This is likely to be accentuated because of the Church festivals, which increasingly take responsibility for sponsoring dance festivals, but on a local Church basis, not a clan basis. It may be that in line with this, if respect for the institution of chieftainship is maintained by the Tikopia, that chiefs will tend to develop as leaders of their lineages and their local community, largely irrespective of their clan ties.

CHAPTER IX

Changes in the Political System

What is the meaning of 'political system' for a community such as Tikopia? In such a small-scale, technologically and economically under-developed community many of the forms and functions of what we ordinarily recognize as government must obviously be lacking. So also are the privileges and obligations of ordinary citizenship. For the British Solomon Islands, the rights of citizenship have been held to include: care in sickness and old age; assistance in time of famine and disaster; protection by the courts of life, land and property. The obligations of citizenship include: obedience to the law; payment of head tax; obedience to orders of headmen in conformity with the instructions of District Commissioner or High Commissioner; compliance with council resolutions; fulfilment of customary obligations.[1] By 1952, the British Solomon Islands Government had established some medical services on Tikopia, and had demonstrated their willingness to afford help in famine and disaster. But they had not established any form of local government on the island, and there were no courts, no head tax, no headman and no council. Internally, institutional care for public communications, health and education is rudimentary, if not alien, to the Tikopia society. Any system of levying private contributions of wealth for public purposes is so embryonic as not to constitute any regular form of indigenous taxation. Even the judicial and quasi-legislative functions of an African tribal council have not had any parallel in Tikopia. Yet the community has had a political as well as a cultural integration. From this community point of view the political system of Tikopia has related primarily to the preservation of its public order internally, and the maintenance of its cohesion *vis-à-vis* external bodies or forces. In this the prime agents have been the chiefs. But they have also performed another important function—they have served in a representative capacity. When questions of public policy have arisen it is they above all who have exercised as of right the role of speaking for the community as a whole and taking decisions which affected the well-being of all Tikopia. In the sense indicated by Schapera[2] 'the direction and control of public affairs by one or more specific persons whose regular function that is'—Tikopia has had a government, and not merely a political system.

But various questions now arise. Granted that the chiefs of Tikopia have been a major element in government, have their functions been restricted to this, or have they had other, perhaps equally important functions in other

[1] See Colin H. Allan, *Customary Land Tenure in the British Solomon Islands Protectorate*, Honiara: Western Pacific High Commission, 1957, para. 46.

[2] I. Schapera, *Government and Politics in Tribal Societies*, 1956, p. 39.

spheres? It will be clear from my previous analyses that the chiefs have been accustomed to do many other things than govern—and in their public, collective capacity, and not merely as private individuals. In addition to their economic roles as stimulators of production, and their social roles as ceremonial leaders, they were in effect in the traditional Tikopia system the lords spiritual as well as lords temporal. But in their performance and direction of major religious rites, they were often acting as much on behalf of the community as for themselves. They were regarded as having on the spiritual plane the main responsibility for the welfare and order of the community. In a sense then, their ritual functions were a projection on another plane of their political functions.

From the community point of view, the Tikopia chiefs have had responsibility for care of public order and representation of the body politic. But from the point of view of individuals or groups within the society, may not the Tikopia system of chieftainship have been simply a framework which gave some persons or sections, in particular the chiefs themselves, the opportunity to use their resources for the exercise of power? And may not this power have been employed primarily for private ends? It may be said at once that in the Tikopia society of 1929, though instances of abuse of public power for private ends by chiefs were recognized there was no tendency to attribute an exploiting role to chiefs in general; they were regarded as protectors and representatives of public interest. But this still leaves the question of how far may not such general exploitation of power by the chiefs have existed, but gone unrecognized? This is a more difficult question to answer, because of the lack of any generally agreed standard by which to evaluate effective contribution and equivalent reward. But in broad terms two points may be made. In the social field, chiefs and their immediate agnatic kin were immune from some of the consequences, including gross assault, of actions which in commoners would have been treated as offences. In the economic field, on the other hand, their personal benefits from community production did not appear to be out of line to any very significant degree from what they contributed to the economy. The reasons for this may have been partly technological—the lack of any very effective means for accumulation of personal capital on a large scale; and partly social—the conventions of disbursement and reciprocity which linked chieftainship with generosity. As in many other economic systems described by anthropologists, chiefs in Tikopia have been general channels for inflow and outflow of community income rather than specific siphoners-off of large amounts of it for their own use.

But while this was true of 1929, how far was it still true of 1952? In particular, how far had the distribution of political power changed after a generation? And again, seeing the modifications in the economic system, how far had there been alteration in Tikopia views of what such distribution ought to be?

The Tikopia Political System in 1929

The Tikopia system of government in 1929, as apparently for many generations before, may be briefly described as a loosely structured oligarchy. This 'government by the few' in Tikopia had as its core the institution of chieftainship. This had a characteristic form, the political system being independent of and somewhat different from that in any other Polynesian society. There were four chiefs, each termed *te Ariki*, and each bearing in his title the name of the clan over which he had jurisdiction and which he represented in all major public affairs.

Tikopia chiefs were not demagogues, but tended to remain somewhat aloof from their people and to rest their influence on their ritual qualities. In Aristotle's terms, they were an aristocratic oligarchy, a government by the few who ruled by their virtue rather than by their wealth—if virtue be interpreted as a quality of a mystical as well as of a moral order. But this special quality of chieftainship was not simply of a religious kind. To Tikopia, chieftainship in itself had an absolute value. Whereas I was inclined to think in 1929 that the ultimate sanction for chieftainship in Tikopia lay in the ritual field, the developments over the generation have made it clear that this did not continue to be so.

But how far was the government of Tikopia literally oligarchical, a 'rule by the few'? Each chief was autonomous as regards authority over his own clan. But there was no unified, central authority.[1] The Ariki Kafika, who had first precedence in the major religious rites, was in political affairs only *primus inter pares*. Each chief could bring influence to bear on every other chief, but this influence was only of what a lawyer might term 'persuasive effect'. There were definite mechanisms for bringing such influence to bear and they followed formally prescribed rules of etiquette. But it was always possible for one chief to refuse or ignore a suggestion made to him by another; there was no structure of command whereby one chief could impose his will upon another.

Hence there are two problems for us to analyse. One is that of definition—in what sense can the exercise of political powers by these chiefs in relative independence of one another be termed oligarchy? And, if each chief was autonomous in the final exercise of his powers, how was the government of Tikopia managed?

As far as definition goes, the term 'oligarchy' could clearly be properly applied to a set of chiefs who met together in council, discussed questions of

---

[1] Statements such as the following are accordingly liable to be misunderstood. 'The King wearing the mat, the sign of kingship, sits on his throne under the shade of a large tree'. (In 'A Visit to Tikopia' by [Archdeacon] H. C. V. R. [Reynolds], *Melanesian Mission Log*, vol. 51, pp. 54–5, Oct. 1945—Jan. 1946.) There are several misapprehensions here. The Tikopia have no office that can be properly called that of King. The 'mat'—evidently a *kie* mat of finely plaited pandanus leaf, decorated in red—is not a sign of chieftainship but may be worn by any man who can afford one. No chief has a state seat of 'throne' type; the coconut-grating stool or other seat he commonly uses is not taboo to other people. Similar remarks have been made at various times—cf. Captain Sinker in *Log*, vol. 10, p. 164, Dec. 1904.

For a much less excusable statement by Graebner that Tikopia at times exercised a kind of overlordship (*Oberherrschaft*) over Vanikoro, I have found no shred of evidence. (See p. 181 of F. Graebner, 'Völkerkundliches von den St Cruz Inseln', *Ethnologica*, vol. II, 2. pp. 153–213, Leipzig, 1916.)

public import and came to some agreed conclusions as to policy and action to be taken. There was no such formal mechanism, with regular meetings and procedure, in Tikopia. But the chiefs as a whole were ultimately held responsible for policy by the people. They strove for a common front on matters of general relevance and were keenly interested in the implementation of policy. Since, although they were autonomous, much of their policy was collective and forged in relation to one another's views, their government may be said to constitute an oligarchical rule. But because formal arrangements to this end were embryonic and irregular, one may speak of the oligarchy as loosely structured.

Yet authority and government in Tikopia were not simply dispersed among unrelated leaders. Although not unified, as the governmental system became in some of the larger Polynesian communities during the nineteenth century, the government of Tikopia may be termed *centralized and conjoint*. A chief could operate independently and often did so, but the more his operations affected matters of import to the whole community, the more his fellow-chiefs tended to become involved until they found it necessary to take action of some kind themselves. There were various mechanisms whereby one chief could ascertain the views of another and secure his acquiescence, and ultimately some collective activity could be promoted. A chief might visit another socially and take the opportunity to discuss public affairs with him. He might send a messenger of importance, bearing a specific request, or he might invite all the other chiefs to assemble with him for some common discussion. Apart from this, the chiefs tended to be cognisant of one another's views on current affairs through the frequent interchange of news and opinions with Tikopia paying calls of courtesy in the intervals of their daily occupations.

It was thus not difficult for chiefs to decide upon a common course of action if this were required. Moreover, apart from any overt exchanges of opinion, there was among the chiefs a tacit implied consensus on many matters of public policy, as could be expected from the general nature of their common economic and religious interests. Hence, the day to day administration of public affairs normally could be handled on a local basis, without necessarily any specific communication between the chiefs. Government, then, was maintained by a responsible direction of affairs by the chiefs. But they did not often intervene personally. They used as their instruments for action a set of men closely related to them agnatically and with considerable immediate authority of their own. Any legislative or judicial functions which a Tikopia chief may be said to have exercised were very amorphous, though he did occasionally make rules for public order and give judgment on whether someone had broken a rule or not. These rules and judgments related rather to matters of immediate administration than to matters of fundamental principles of order. Thus, the *maru*, the men who assisted the chief in implementing policy, tended to do so rather in terms of specific issues than with respect to abstract rules. For this reason, though it is convenient to call them 'officers' (*v.* later, *Maru*), they were as much officers for their chief as for the society at large.

R

[The powers exercised by a Tikopia chief were very wide.]They included ultimate control of the lands of his clan—a right with practical effect particularly for the lands of those lineages ultimately sprung from chiefly stock. [The chiefs' powers included also rights to certain first fruits.]Being regarded as taboo in his person, the chief received great respect and deference on ordinary occasions of seating, eating, or sleeping.[His powers were such that he might order off to sea as the extreme of banishment a man who offended him personally or broke a grave rule of conduct.]

Government of Tikopia through the conjoint powers of the chiefs raises the question of the jurisdiction which each of them exercised. The basis of the Tikopia political system lay in the chief as head and representative of his clan. Every person in Tikopia as a member of a clan acknowledged obedience to his own chief. But the jurisdiction of each chief was not simply restricted to a clan alignment. It also operated on a local basis, although this was less clearly defined. Each chief lived in a separate village and in that village exercised great authority. Moreover, his authority also extended throughout the whole district—or side of the island—in which he regularly lived. For social purposes the jurisdiction of the chiefs was closely related to this district division. In particular, the single authority of the Ariki Tafua in the district of Faea contrasted with the treble authority of the other chiefs who together held sway over the district of Ravenga and its subsidiary Namo. These political relations of the chiefs were very important in general district rivalry and intra-district co-operation.

But the jurisdiction of a Tikopia chief was not only in district terms any more than in purely clan terms. Every person in Tikopia acknowledged obedience to *any* chief in a situation with which both were immediately concerned. A chief could claim by general status much of which he was debarred from claiming by the lack of clan right.[In other words, there was a notion of a *general* order in Tikopia in which a chief, by virtue of his office, had jurisdiction in respect of the whole society.]This was linked with the ritual elements in the status of chiefs—the aura of taboo that surrounded them, the belief that each chief controlled powerful gods and spirits able to wreak vengeance on who who offended him. In 1929 the three chiefs who were still pagan were regarded by many Christian Tikopia as well as by pagans as having primary responsibility for the economic prosperity, health and welfare of the whole Tikopia community.

Although there was a ritual hierarchy of chiefs in Tikopia there was not a political hierarchy. In the major religious affairs of the Tikopia community when the society was completely pagan, the order of Kafika, Tafua, Taumako, Fangarere was represented in many ritual arrangements of operations by chiefs. Nevertheless, this did not mean that the clans as social entities were so graded, nor even that the chiefs had any similar differentiation in political power. While they maintained in the most formal seating arrangements at social affairs the same precedence as on ritual occasions, apart from this socially and politically they were equals. In stating that every chief had jurisdiction over Tikopia society as a whole, I am not implying that this jurisdiction must be regarded as of equal weight in all sectors of the society. Mass obedience was owed by people to their own clan chief. But by custom one chief deferred to another in matters which concerned the latter most closely. Many village matters affected primarily the chief living there, irrespective of the clan to which the person living in the village might belong. Hence, by implication there tended to be transfer or cession of authority to the resident chief by another chief who was the clan head of the person in question.

The notion of government implied in a definition in oligarchical terms must be clarified by reference to the position of the governed. How far can it be said that rule by the chiefs in Tikopia was autocratic or was it, as studies of analogous societies elsewhere have shown, ultimately by consent of the people? In one sense, Tikopia government by the chiefs had its basis in force —the chiefs had physical force at command in the persons of their immediate agnatic kin. But was this the ultimate basis of their power? Their prudent care for public opinion would indicate not. It is clear that in Tikopia the 'true' basis of government lay in a very sensitive adjustment between the interests and actions of the chiefs and those of the people. Moreover, the people concerned were not only the members of each chief's own clan.

There are three concepts indicated in Tikopia terms which are relative here. The first is *faoa*—the 'generality'. Tikopia chiefs and their immediate kin and officers have shown themselves very alert to the influence of 'people in general'. They paid great attention to public opinion, gossip and rumour, and were very quick to react against what they considered to be false imputation. They tried very carefully to ascertain public feeling before committing themselves in policy. But the term *faoa*, which can often be translated as 'the crowd', does not involve any particular notion of the community as a whole. The second term *te kano fenua*, or *fenua* for short, the 'collectivity of the land', or just 'the land', does convey an idea of the whole Tikopia community. This expression tends to be used in a broader context than the former, as when matters of public concern are in question. Neither of these expressions set off chiefs specifically from the body of the people. But a third expression, *nga fakaarofa*, used by chiefs and their agnatic kin, is of more definite political import. It means 'the commoners' in contradistinction to *paito ariki*, the 'lineages of chiefs' or *te kano ariki*, the 'collectivity of chiefs'. It is a very definite class-conscious expression and is correlated with the exercise of differential privilege and political authority.

Correlative to the notion of a general Tikopia social order in which the chiefs exercised a primary role, was the notion of a general responsibility falling primarily upon the chiefs. This was illustrated formally by the traditional announcement at the solemn religious occasion known as the *Fono* at Rarokoka in the Work of the Gods in which instructions were given ritually for the preservation of public order and for a population policy related thereto.[1] More generally, this concept of responsibility was illustrated by the informal statements of chiefs in regard to crop prospects, fishing results and health of the people. In particular, it was illustrated in the behaviour of the

[1] *Work of the Gods*, vol. II, chap. 7. *We, The Tikopia*, p. 491.

Ariki Kafika who, as the premier chief, conceived it to be his prime responsibility to care for the welfare of the island community as a whole.

Several questions come to mind here. How far was this responsibility collective; how far was it individualized; how far was it shared by other senior members of the community? How far was it dictated, not simply by a general concern for the common good, but also by a more personal self-interest of the principal parties?

The allocation of responsibility for public welfare was definitely regarded as collective and not merely individual. The actions of any chief affected first his own good name, but soon tended to involve that of the other chiefs. Under the pagan system of ritual most of the major rites performed by a chief had reference to a cycle of performances. Omission or delay affected the performance of his fellows, but were judged also in reference to the common weal. By the people, too, the acts of one chief were regarded as involving to some degree the views of the chiefs as a whole. The reason for this lay, however, in the concept of shared responsibility, being a correlate not only of community membership by the chiefs but also of their class membership. The chiefs were regarded as constituting 'a single body of kin'. Their combination on any public occasion calling for violent action was something to be feared throughout the community. When 'the wave of chiefs' should break, woe betide anyone who should be in its path. Any offender would be overwhelmed by the force which they could summon from their near agnatic kin. From this point of view the conceptions of responsibility held by the chiefs for the maintenance of public order were the direct expression of the need to maintain their own class interests. Yet to represent the exercise of responsibility by Tikopia chiefs as a simple assertion of class privilege would be to misrepresent the situation. Much of the appreciation of the requirements of the Tikopia situation, both economic and political, was shared by senior members of the community who were—e.g. as most ritual elders—not members of chiefly lineages. On occasions of crisis and disaster, while commoners might fear a combination of the chiefly lineages against them, chiefs on the other hand were apt to take measures in disregard of their own safety and interests in order to help the common people.

In brief, the political situation was one where the interest of a ruling elite seemed in many respects to be coincident with the interest of the body politic as a whole, and where the common people saw the situation in such terms. After the passage of a generation, how far had the strong influences that had come from outside changed this outlook?

External Political Relations by 1952

As regards external political relations, the community of Tikopia has been a part of the British Solomon Islands Protectorate since the end of the nineteenth century. In 1928/9 the Tikopia knowledge of this external government was vague, and they tended to assign to the administration a curious impersonal quality. There was general recognition that a remote European entity known as *kavemanu* held some kind of overriding authority over the

Tikopia. But its powers and functions were hardly understood at all. Its main role to the Tikopia was as a distant sanction against killing. It was firmly believed that if any person killed another on Tikopia, then the killer was liable to be ultimately taken away and put in 'calaboose'. But the remoteness of Government and the poverty of communication made it obvious that although Government might act suddenly and without warning it was unlikely to be cognisant of anything not reported specifically to it by the Tikopia themselves. Hence, during my first visit I heard only after some time and then in great secrecy, of an incident years before in which some Tikopia had clubbed to death the crew of a canoe which had fetched up there from some other distant island. Threats to report cases of theft or assault might be made by Melanesian Mission teachers, but these were not taken too seriously since no Tikopia had ever been charged by Government with such offences. Visits of Government representatives were few and perfunctory and, in effect, Tikopia was left to be primarily responsible for its own internal order.

Even by 1928/29, however, this order was not a Tikopia responsibility alone. The periodic calls of the Melanesian Mission yacht, and in particular the permanent presence on the island of the Melanesian Mission teacher, Ellison Tergatok, Pa Pangisi, meant the exercise of moral force of considerable strength upon Tikopia behaviour, as I have explained earlier.[1] The Mission also exercised considerable political influence, in many respects overshadowing that of the Government.

By 1952 the situation had significantly altered. The political influence of the Mission was still strong in the sense that it stood, as before, for the general maintenance of law and order and against lying, theft and violence. Moreover, the political divisions which the advance of Christianity had caused had gone even deeper into the Tikopia society. On the other hand, government of the Tikopia by the officials of the British Solomon Islands Protectorate had, by 1952, become much more overtly recognized and much more clearly defined than in 1929. Earlier, the power of the Government was regarded as distant, vague and operating largely in support of the Mission. Especially since the war, when the visits of Government officials had become much more frequent, and many Tikopia had had experience abroad, their separateness from the Mission had become patent. It was known now that Government took charge of offenders against the law and was responsible for their punishment, that Government operated quite distinct sets of establishments with employment of very diverse kinds—and sometimes at more attractive rates of pay—and that the recognition accorded generally to Government officials was in many cases greater than that accorded to missionaries. All of this made clear the concrete existence of an administrative authority of which the Tikopia had to take serious account. The continued concern of Government with the Tikopia was made manifest still further by such formal events as reading the proclamation of the death of King George VI and the accession of Queen Elizabeth. Though much of the detail of this

[1] *We, The Tikopia*, pp. 46–9.

was incomprehensible to the Tikopia, they understood the main drift, and were particularly interested in the succession of a woman to chiefly office.]

But Government interest in the Tikopia did not operate *in vacuo*, nor was it prompted simply by the wish to extend a sphere of influence. There were certain pressing issues which confronted the Government. One was what was to be done about the pressure of Tikopia population upon resources—a pressure which by the accounts of the Tikopia themselves was rapidly increasing? Again, what was to be the policy as regards the recruitment of Tikopia men for plantation work—a problem which was becoming more urgent as the demands of the plantations for labour grew? Linked with these two problems as an immediate expression of them, in part, was the question which arose especially between 1948 and 1950 of how to cope with the numbers of young Tikopia men who set off by canoe from the island on their own initiative to seek work and adventure abroad. Either they landed in the New Hebrides or the Solomons and had to be repatriated, or they were lost at sea, and the problem arose of how to prevent such waste of life. Linked still further with these questions was the suggestion that some section of the Tikopia population might emigrate to another island to allow room for local expansion. Above all, in 1952/53, the famine on the island involved the Government of necessity in much more active and direct intervention in Tikopia affairs than ever before (see pp. 58, 66–9). In the effort to solve these problems, both short term and long term, the Government tried to become more aware of the structure of Tikopia society and where the main power and responsibility lay. Moreover, an energetic effort was made to get fuller and more realistic discussion with the Tikopia than had been the case in earlier Governmental relations. In these efforts the Government was aided by the presence of the anthropologists on the island, serving as communicators and interpreters to both parties and, in particular, as catalysts to the Tikopia —roles which were fulfilled especially by Spillius in the year in which he was the only European on the island.[1]

For the Government the problem could be put in another way. What were the cardinal elements in the Tikopia political and administrative structure which could be used in carrying out Government policy? How could a representative Tikopia opinion be obtained to help in the formulation of Government policy and to gauge its success? Where could responsibility for Tikopia affairs be looked for most clearly and where could it be imposed most squarely when the administration of fresh resources had to be undertaken? When a decision on a matter of public import was required, from whom should that decision be sought?

It had been clear to Government officers for several decades that one important source of power in Tikopia lay in the chiefs—so much was obvious. But the Government was unaware of the degree to which the chiefs might exercise an autocratic rule following their own interests in despite of the opinions of the people, or how far they might be truly representative of public opinion in general. Moreover, the Government was unaware of how

[1] See Spillius, *op. cit.*

far opinions given by the chiefs could really be regarded as binding upon the Tikopia community as a whole. In other words, they had no idea of how the power of the chiefs was really exercised in the body politic. For a long while indeed they were ignorant even of the relative rank of the chiefs. In particular, they were not cognisant of the critical role of the *maru* in social control. It will be realized from my earlier account of Government contacts with the Tikopia (Ch. II) that their ignorance of the Tikopia political system was not the result of lack of interest but of lack of opportunity and trained techniques for observation of its working. Moreover, it should be said that while the anthropologists were well aware of the structure of the system, their own understanding of the details of the situation developed as time went on, and fuller implication of the interplay of structural and personal elements in the situation became evident to them also.

In the explanation of the changes that had taken place in the Tikopia political system over a generation, I explored first of all the internal aspect of chieftainship.

Position of the Chiefs after a Generation

As soon as we arrived in Tikopia in 1952 it was clear that the concept of chieftainship was of prime importance to the Tikopia, as it had been a generation before. The term *ariki* was in free use in a variety of situations, the notions of *mana* and *tapu* of chiefs still obtained, and strong attitudes of respect for all chiefs were evident, independent of the religious affiliations of the chiefs or people concerned. Three chiefs, those of Kafika, Taumako and Fangarere were pagan. One, the chief of Tafua, was Christian, as his grandfather had been a generation before—though there had been a surprising change in the religious alignment in the meantime (*v.* p. 280). The same type of selective system for chiefs was in vogue as appeared from the elections that had taken place since my first visit. The emphasis on primogeniture continued. It was assumed without question, for example, that Pa Fenuatara, eldest son of the Ariki Kafika, would succeed his father. The authority of chiefs was still regarded as supreme, and any issues of principle which might seem to put in question the authority of the chiefs, because of their relations with the Mission or with Government, were tacitly ignored by the general body of Tikopia. By 1952, the operations of sanctions in support of the authority of the chiefs had become more complex than in 1929. Yet to the Tikopia in general the limitations upon the power of the chiefs by the existence of external sanctions were not regarded as a restriction upon their authority. The chiefs were conceived as actively exercising their own authority in following out principles with which they themselves were thought to be in full and free agreement (see Ch. X). The essential unity of the chiefs and their immediate kin, in terms of the basic principles of the Tikopia structure, was indicated by their frequent exchanges of information, their general acceptance of their role in political and social affairs. At the same time the division which existed in 1929 between them in terms of paganism and Christianity had been deepened in the passage of a generation.

The maintenance of the prestige and authority of the Tikopia chiefs as a general phenomenon may be illustrated by two examples.

The first relates to their conduct in the hurricane of 1952. At the height of the storm, we were told later, people came from Tai to Uta seeking the three Ravenga chiefs who were assembled there. Groups of men from Faea, numbering between forty and fifty in all, also descended on Ravenga. These men came with their heads bound up as if for war, wearing their best garments and ornamented as for a ceremonial occasion and armed with a shotgun and with clubs and spears. They advanced down the beach of Ravenga, they shouted challenges and they fired shots into the air. Similarly, a crowd of men from Ravenga and Namo poured into Faea through the flat lands of Rakisu and over the gap in the hills of Te Rua, brandishing clubs, spears, bows and arrows. In each case the senior men leading the demonstration entered the house of the chief they had come to visit, pressed their noses to his knee in salutation and told him why they had come. The purpose of such visits while a storm is raging was to rally round the chiefs, not for protection but to see to their safety as the symbols of their clan and of the community.

At such time of heightened emotional tension because of the violence of nature, the traditional Tikopia response is a kind of mixture of bravado and anxiety. They put on their best clothes and dance ornaments. They simulate the actions of war as a kind of challenge to fate. They do unwonted things such as shouting and simulating violence in the vicinity of a chief's house, this being one of the few times when the rule of quietness around a chief's dwelling may be broken. In telling me of the incident the people said that if the men of one district had found a chief of the other dead through some accident in the hurricane, they would have regarded this as a sign that he had not been properly cared for by the people and they would have slaughtered the population of that clan in anger. This was an exaggeration, but if a chief had died there would undoubtedly have been violence. The test of the value of a chief—any chief—to the Tikopia community as their symbolic head is shown by the fact that the men of Faea who came to enquire after the safety of the Ravenga chiefs were all Christian, while the chiefs they came to visit were pagan. Similarly, both pagans and Christians from Ravenga went to enquire after the Christian Ariki Tafua in Faea. Spillius reported similar happenings when the second but milder hurricane came in 1953. Such visitations are part of the gestures which the Tikopia make on occasions of public stress to indicate their loyalty to the body of chiefs as a whole. In 1952, as a generation before, such mechanisms for emphasizing the integration of Tikopia society by reference to the chiefs were still in operation.

The second incident was much smaller in scale, but indicated the acceptance of a chief's authority irrespective of his clan jurisdiction. At a time when theft of foodstuffs from the growing cultivations was threatening the food supplies in Rotoaia, the Ariki Tafua ordered that area which was in effect part of Faea to be vacated by all residents. That afternoon I met Pa Marakei, a man of Kafika clan and then still a pagan. He had told me about two months before that he had built his house in Rotoaia after the hurricane in order to plant and watch over his manioc crop—he said taro would not grow in that sandy soil. When he had been expelled by order of the Ariki Tafua, I asked him if he and his companions had objected. He replied 'We don't object because the chief has said so.' Then he added 'What? Should we object to what the chief says? It is good.' This opinion was given in respect of an action of the chief not of his own clan nor of his own district nor of his own religion. Then I asked the opinion of a senior man of Taumako, who was a disinterested party —was the action of the chief right? He simply said 'It is all right, the chief gave the order.' The correlate to this acquiescence in the chief's action was in 1952, as in 1929, a confidence that a chief's public acts were designed in general for the public weal. There was trust in his decisions. Put in another way, this means that in matters of public concern the Tikopia were content even by 1952 to entrust responsibility to their chiefs. Neither the general issue of class interest nor the more partisan interest of religious division was regarded as fundamentally altering this situation.

On the other hand, there were signs that this blank granting of responsibility might not continue without question. There seemed to be a view among some Tikopia that the chiefs of modern times were not like the chiefs of old. One man of Taumako, Pa Maneve (cf. p. 167), expressed this opinion to me thus 'The proclamation from of old, from God, was that the chief was elected from the body of the people to look after the body of the people. If a man was hungry, he fed him. If a man was evil, the chief spoke to him (to mend his ways). If anything was wrong in the land and the chief spoke about it, the land became well. As a man dwelt and things went well with him, he prepared food and visited his chief.' I asked my friend why he did not go and request his chief for food to help him and his family. He replied 'I do not go and ask because the chiefs of nowadays do not behave like the chiefs who are dead. The chiefs who are dead used to feed the body of the people.' I asked 'What about your own chief?' He replied that he was ashamed to ask him for food. He said 'If a man enters his house and the food basket is hung from the ceiling, then he is given food. But the chief does not give a person green food.' In other words, at this time of shortage the chief gave food he had actually on hand; but he did not help people with gifts of raw food. This information ignored the fact that the Ariki Taumako could not have afforded much in the way of assistance with food at that time. Moreover, the speakers' position was made more difficult by the lack of religious sympathy between him and his chief. Such comparison of modern leaders unfavourably with those of former times must be common in many societies, but it is significant in its emphasis on the protective role of chiefs and their election specifically to fill that role. In this it differed from critical statements about chiefs which I heard in 1929 which referred rather to the lack of spiritual powers of the contemporary chiefs as compared with their forbears.[1]

Another indication of a qualification put to the people in the overall responsibility for Tikopia exercised by the chiefs was given me by the principal elder of the Ariki Kafika, Pa Rarovi. He was talking to me about the death

[1] 'The Analysis of Mana', *Journal Polynesian Society*, vol. 49, 1940, pp. 500–1.

of the Ariki Tafua, which had occurred about a year before our arrival. He implied that this was a punishment for sin. He said that the Ariki Tafua had made a proclamation to his fellow-chiefs in Uta saying *'Fenua ke ta'*—'Let the land be stricken', meaning that the commoners should be driven out to go and live in other lands. Pa Rarovi said this proclamation, which had been kept secret by the chiefs, was finally revealed in a dance song by one of the other chiefs. Pa Rarovi expressed strong disapproval of the alleged statement by the Ariki Tafua. All this was based on a misconception. But it was of course an example of a theme which has recurred periodically in Tikopia— the underlying uneasiness of the members of commoner lineages about their position when there is any question of acute pressure of population upon land resources.[1] The significance of this expression of view was that by 1952 the publicity given to such a theme might cause it to be interpreted not only as a recurrent expression of anxiety, but as the actual intention of the chiefs. So interpreted it could be taken by Government to indicate a lack of public confidence in their chiefs among the Tikopia and could make into an explicit breach what had previously been no more than a general underlying question. Be this as it may, there was on the part of Pa Rarovi no basic challenge to the authority of the chiefs, as was illustrated by his cession of a piece of land when a chief's son had been injured in a struggle for it (see p. 169).

Problems for the Government
The degree to which the Tikopia chiefs regarded themselves as exercising responsibility for the conduct of public affairs, and the degree to which they were so regarded by the people in general, was one of the primary problems which arose as Government action in 1952 became necessary to help the Tikopia in their difficulties. Government interest in the Tikopia system of administration was instituted for two reasons. One was that the distribution of relief supplies of food at a time of shortage and near-famine demanded some mechanism to ensure reasonable fairness in sharing out and (since the supplies were costly) that there was as little waste as possible. The flow had to be through some person or persons on Tikopia on whom the Government could rely for efficient service in this respect.[2] Another reason was that with the reintroduction of the practice of recruiting Tikopia men as labourers, there had to be some authority with whom agreement could be concluded about the conditions of recruiting and employment; there also had to be some agent who would assume responsibility for seeing that any payment made to the families of the labourers would be properly handed over. Furthermore, any long-term measures such as the introduction of medical care by the

---

[1] See my *Rumour in a Primitive Society*, pp. 130–1. The dance song referred to had been composed by the Ariki Taumako and, so I heard from another source, actually referred in a jeering way to a rumour apparently concocted by the people of Faea that the people of Ravanga were going to arm themselves to make war upon those of Faea.

[2] In the famine of 1952/53, the presence of the anthropologists on the island served the purposes of Government in this respect, as Spillius has clearly shown and illustrated. But this was fortuitous and in any future crisis it must be expected that the local administration will have to supply the control required.

stationing of a hospital dresser on the island involved proper control of supplies to him and proper arrangements for his housing and treatment. In all such important matters, the Government naturally tended to assume that the chiefs might be the most appropriate and effective instruments of administration.

By 1952, as concrete action was being demanded to deal with the administrative problems of the kind outlined, pressure began to be put by Government upon the Tikopia political system. This envisaged:

(a) *Meetings* of chiefs in assembly;

(b) a *common view* on matters of public significance;

(c) *decisions* from the chiefs on questions of labour, recruiting, etc.;

(d) *community action* under the chiefs' auspices, as in the provision of medical quarters or other facilities for the administration.

In 1952 the Tikopia, for the most part, had not seen the full implications of these matters. For example, the provision of quarters for the hospital dresser had been made initially, not by any decision or action on the part of the community as a whole, but by a device of customary style—by incorporating the stranger through bond-friendship into a section of the Tikopia kinship system. The dresser, a Melanesian from another island in the Solomons, was classified as a 'friend' of a Tikopia who had also been trained in the hospital. As such he was taken in and accommodated according to ordinary Tikopia custom by a branch of the Tikopia dresser's lineage. It is doubtful if most Tikopia—including the chiefs—understood that his services were for their benefit as a whole and that, therefore, his care should be a charge upon the whole community.

The problem of crystallization of the views and decisions of the Tikopia community, and their representatives the chiefs, to meet the requirements of the external Government is illustrated particularly by the initial history of the assembly of the chiefs for discussion on public affairs.

Assemblages of the Chiefs

The growing interest of Government in Tikopia affairs, and their wish to consolidate and use the chiefs, involved assembly of the chiefs. Traditionally, the Tikopia chiefs assembled formally as a complete group only in accordance with the ancient religious system at the *marae* of Rarokoka, in Marae in Uta, and at other points during the Work of the Gods. They also assembled at dance festivals, feasts and other gatherings, though not as a unit, for social rather than political purposes. After the defection of the Ariki Tafua from the pagan rites, about 1930, the religious assemblies of chiefs continued in a modified form, and the social assemblies took place as before. For political purposes the contacts between the chiefs were as before—informal, often indirect, and rarely as a full assembly. Government officers usually met them individually and attempts to secure a full meeting were not always successful. In 1952 they began to assemble fairly frequently, for purposes which were specifically political in nature. This was largely in response to Government request, but stimulated by the gravity of the situation and the suggestion of the anthropologists. In particular, the chiefs were asked to give a collective view on matters of general policy in regard to distribution of relief supplies, recruitment of labour, and migration of a section of Tikopia population elsewhere. What the Tikopia referred to as *te kau nga ariki*—the assembly of the chiefs—though not completely novel, became a fairly common feature of the political scene only at that time.

Such assembly involved several questions of importance—its publicity and its representative character; the degree to which its views could be influenced by pressure from outside its own body; and the degree to which its decisions were put into effect among the Tikopia community. Moreover, two specific features were very relevant—the position of the chiefs *vis-à-vis* one another in view of the fact that they were divided between paganism and Christianity; and the fact of differences in their personality, including the political implications of the great age of their senior member, the Ariki Kafika.

Traditionally there has been a very strong idea among the Tikopia chiefs, and supported by the people, that they should have a common mind on issues of public importance. The expression is *poi i te atamai sokotasi* or *me i te meranga sokotasi*—that they should 'go in one mind' or 'sleep on the one mat'. The latter, while usually a figurative expression, can be literal; when one chief goes to visit another, they may actually share a sleeping mat. This indicates confidence—in the olden days it would give a good opportunity for murder—but it also indicates the opportunity for the sharing of whispered secrets. With this ideology of a 'common mind', there is an opportunity for any strong-minded chief to alter the views of his colleagues on an issue if only he is prepared to stick firmly to his point. The others will then probably agree to fall in with him. Yet this is not invariable; moreover, the process of argument is often protracted, and a clear-cut decision is not always reached.

During my stay on Tikopia in 1952 there were six meetings of the chiefs and I was present at five. Comparison and contrast of their behaviour on these different occasions will illustrate the general principles of their common action.

(1) The first occasion was on March 15th. It was a meeting called by the District Commissioner who had accompanied us to the island. Its purpose was three-fold: to announce the death of King George VI and the succession of the Queen; to give certain presents to the chiefs from the Government; and to discuss some aspects of the food shortage. The address of the District Commissioner announcing the death of the King aroused no more than polite attention. Seedlings and other planting materials given by the people of Kirakira and Pawa, in the Solomons, to assist distressed areas in the outer islands, were presented with the explanation that these were a token of sympathy to the Tikopia. The old Ariki Kafika commented at this point, 'Oh, they will be distributed to all the people. Whoever wants can go and plant them in his orchard'—meaning that the chiefs would not keep them for themselves. Each chief was then presented with a spray-gun, with some liquid to help keep down insects. The interpreter explained 'You don't like flies and mosquitoes.' 'Tell him, no!' said one of the chiefs. But the great

object of attention was a shot-gun which was presented by the Government to the four chiefs, but which was later taken charge of by Pa Fenuatara.

This was essentially a meeting of the chiefs with the representative of Government. Although a crowd of people was present, most Tikopia were around the vessel at anchorage or at work. The meeting took place outside one of the sacred canoe sheds. The principal persons were seated on coconut grating stools. (The seating arrangements are shown in Plan 5.) Comparison

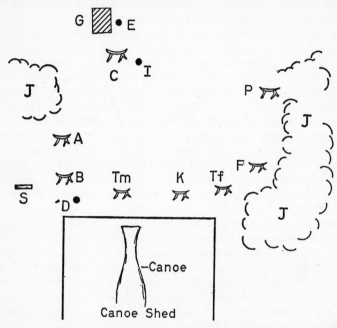

Plan 5. MEETING OF CHIEFS WITH GOVERNMENT OFFICER, MARCH 15, 1952
A, B, Anthropologists; C, District Commissioner; D, Hospital Dresser; E, Policeman distributing gifts; G, Gifts to chiefs; I, Interpreter; J, crowd of Tikopia; S, ritual stone; K, Ariki Kafika; Tf, Ariki Tafua; Tm, Ariki Taumako; F, Ariki Fangarere; P, Pa Fenuatara. Personages indicated were seated on coconut-grating stools

with other meetings showed how there was no invariable arrangement of the position of the chiefs. Their ritual precedence had some weight, but did not dictate relations in the political sphere. An anomalous position was that of Pa Fenuatara; although for the most part given precedence as the representative of the Ariki Kafika, he himself tended to yield precedence to the chiefs, since he was not by office one of them. Consequently, on some occasions he sat with them, particularly when the meetings were more private; on others, he sat apart and somewhat to the rear.

(2) The next meeting of chiefs took place about three weeks later (April 6th). It was in the anthropologists' house to discuss the food situation and suggest action. The principal organizer of it was one of the executive officers

(*maru*), Robinson Vakasaumore, who took an increasingly prominent part in public affairs as time went on (cf. pp. 272, 295). At this meeting the Melanesian priest, Ellison, was also present as well as the senior brother of the Ariki Taumako, as the most prominent executive officer. Also, uninvited, came the senior ritual elder of Kafika, Pa Rarovi. The Ariki Kafika was not present on this occasion, but was represented by Pa Fenuatara, sitting near the end of the line. Shortly before the meeting, I had asked for two major issues to be clarified: the problem of immediate relief—what was the severity of the food crisis; and the problem of recruitment—if there was willingness to recruit for the Solomons as well as the New Hebrides.

In reply to various questions which I put to the meeting several points emerged. The chiefs regarded the food situation at the moment as not too bad, but it would become desperate during the next two months, and after that would depend on the weather; some crops would take a long time to recover—taro about six months, coconut a year, and breadfruit longer. The chiefs desired a relief vessel immediately, but primarily for labour recruitment, though they had come to no very definite conclusion as to the number of men who should sign on. They thought that the men should serve for short periods, at their own wish—not on fixed long contract. They also suggested that payment for the labour might be made in advance to the kinsfolk or the chief of the labourer—in the latter case, for distribution to the kin. In all this discussion Spillius and I took but a minor part, our role being primarily to try and clarify the situation as between the Tikopia leaders and the Government, with whom we were in communication by radio.

General agreement was expressed among the chiefs on the proposition (put forward by Robinson as spokesman) that the opinion of the District Commissioner should be sought with a view to opening the route of recruitment to the New Hebrides and getting a vessel sent to take Tikopia labour. Payment for the labour was to be given in food, not money or other goods, and as far as possible should be made at once.

This meeting was remarkable for the forceful expression of their views by the chiefs and for their unanimity (making allowance for some rephrasing and contradiction of expression as they went over the points). At the same time there was a high degree of informality in the atmosphere. This was a clear indication that, given favourable conditions with freedom to be understood in their own language, the Tikopia chiefs could meet in a body and give effective joint opinion. It also showed how, in the Tikopia political system, publicity to some extent militated against freedom of expression between the chiefs; they were unwilling to appear to cross one another in public.

The meeting brought out again the absolute assumption by all present, the chiefs themselves and others, that they as a group held the key to public affairs. Politically, they were all-important. How far this political power was separate from the religious sanctions of chieftainship will be further discussed later.

(3) Three weeks later again (April 27th) another meeting of chiefs took place on the same subject. This was remarkable for the fact that it was a

meeting of the chiefs among themselves, in the house of the Ariki Taumako. Spillius and I had been present at all their earlier discussions and had been consulted by them extensively. On this occasion they wished to meet alone and crystallize their own views. The fact that their views were likely to be different from ours on the subject of recruiting to the New Hebrides probably gave an additional stimulus to their separate meeting.

This occasion showed the emergence in more crystallized form of what was in effect a committee of the chiefs, with a very few close executive officers, to discuss affairs of policy. This was a reaction to the need for closer relations with external authority, and to pressure of circumstances requiring decision —the threat of famine and the possible advent of a recruiting vessel. It appeared from this meeting that there was a tendency now for political authority in Tikopia to crystallize—to rest more directly on the chiefs than before, and for their view to emerge in more definite decisions. Mere opinion as such had tended to recede of necessity when confronted by the need for choice in action, especially in relation to an external authority that demanded an answer in fairly clear-cut terms. In other words, the pressure of external contacts was tending to firm up the Tikopia political system. Moreover, it was tending to reduce the religious aspect and enhance the political aspect of chieftainship. It may be noted that, although the Melanesian priest accompanied the Christian chief of Tafua across the island, he was not invited to the meeting. The Christian chief of Fangarere, however, did go.

(4) Abour a fortnight later, May 12th, the Government vessel came again, and the District Commissioner expected to have a meeting with the chiefs on these basic matters. I called for information on the Ariki Tafua, who said that the chiefs were meeting in Faea as had been arranged when they last met. If the vessel had come to Ravenga, he said, we would have met in Ravenga, but since it came to Faea we would meet there. But when I went over to the district of Ravenga at mid-day the Ariki Taumako and Pa Fenuatara were both sitting in their houses, from which they had not stirred. They held that they were waiting for the Government to send instructions to them. At last, in the late afternoon, a meeting was arranged in Pa Fenuatara's village, near the same canoe-yard site as before. Floor mats were set out on the ground and four stools, one for each of the three chiefs and one for Pa Fenuatara. There was also a stool for the District Commissioner and others for a few of the more prominent people. The chiefs, after some urging, took their seats to wait for the District Commissioner. Pa Fenuatara sat away in the background. At last his brother-in-law, Pa Motuata, one of the most respected men of Taumako, said to him, in peremptory tones 'Brother-in-law, go and join the group of chiefs.' He got up and very slowly made an impressive entrance, adorned as he was with ornaments for dancing. Slowly he took the stool set out for him at the head of the seating mat, withdrew it, and despite the protests from the Ariki Taumako, set it down on the ground in the rear. It was a beautifully studied gesture which indicated his humility yet marked the attention paid to him.[1]

[1] For further analysis of the political position of Pa Fenuatara, see my article 'Some

The District Commissioner then began his speech, having first asked the chiefs if he should open the discussion. He explained that this was his last tour, stressed his interest in Tikopia, and his sympathy with their plight, reported by our radio. He noted the overall rice shortage in countries around the Pacific. He expressed his regret at the pilfering of the sweet potatoes and coconuts which had been sent (v. later, p. 276). He also announced the coming of a recruiting vessel with half-wages in food for men who would recruit for plantations in the Solomons. He expressed his hope that the Tikopia would recruit and explained that the Government could not allow recruiting in the New Hebrides. He also tried to clarify the economic situation in that territory, and dispel some of the Tikopia misconceptions about the high wages they thought were being paid there at that time.

(5) Two days later (May 14th) another meeting of chiefs with the District Commissioner took place to discuss the recruiting situation, about which the Tikopia remained unconvinced. On the one side was the general opinion of the chiefs, in particular the Ariki Tafua and Ariki Taumako, in favour of recruiting to the New Hebrides. This was strongly supported and indeed, motivated, by the arguments of Robinson on the one hand and the family of the Mission priest on the other. The former had been in the New Hebrides at a time of high wages; so also had a son of the latter, and in addition his family had an interest in promoting relations with their father's natal land. On the other side, in particular, was Pa Fenuatara, who had weighed up the various elements in the situation acutely. In particular he saw that his own best interest, and that of the Tikopia, lay in conforming to the views of Government and maintaining the relation with them. At a private meeting with the District Commissioner (when, at his request, I acted as his interpreter) he explained his position. He said that his own allegiance was strong to the Solomon Islands Government; that the chiefs and the general body of the people had gone astray—they had listened to bad advice; that he had opposed this in one public meeting; and that the group of chiefs would wish him, as representative of the Ariki Kafika, to express their views at the next meeting with the District Commissioner. He would refuse to do this lest it should seem that their views were also his. He would sit silent by Government's permission when the meeting took place.

This meeting was of critical importance to the Tikopia. To them an issue of great significance was about to be decided. Yet only about 100 men with a few women and children attended. There were a number of people from Faea. But many of the familiar faces of the more senior people were absent. The gathering comprised mainly young men, as was natural, since for them the issue of recruitment was most important. They gave the impression to the outside observer of a bloc, following the lead of Robinson, with their minds made up. Pa Fenuatara was absent. The Ariki Kafika was there, however; he said no word at all, apart from one low question to the Ariki Taumako, who took the lead throughout. The Ariki Tafua was present

'Principles of Social Organization', *J.R.A.I.*, vol. 85, 1955, pp. 8–10; and 'A Polynesian Aristocrat' in *In the Image of Man*, ed. J. B. Casagrande, 1959.

and spoke; the Ariki Fangarere said nothing. No ritual elder had place in the gathering.

The meeting began with an explanation again by the District Commissioner about the situation in the New Hebrides, and the Government view that recruiting should take place for the Solomons. There was then a restatement by the chiefs of their allegiance to Government. Argument then began. One of the principal points made was that the Solomons was a bad place for illness. (A report had been spread abroad that there was no malaria in the New Hebrides.) At one point, Robinson turned to the crowd and said, 'Do you want to go to the New Hebrides?' 'Yes.' 'Are you afraid of the North?' 'Yes.' Then he turned to the District Commissioner and said, 'The people will die of hunger if they cannot go to the New Hebrides.' The Ariki Tafua then intervened and said 'The mind of the people is bad (i.e. set obstinately). The generation of our fathers is old and therefore they are afraid to go to the Solomons. It is good only for young men to go to the Solomons.' By this he meant that there were many elderly men, fathers of families, who also wished to recruit and that, if they were forced to go to the Solomons, the death-rate would be high. The chiefs also stated that they were thinking not of themselves in wanting the New Hebrides route open, but of the body of the people.

The Ariki Tafua and the Ariki Taumako bore very serious expressions, the latter in particular having a grim look. Robinson, who was acting as interpreter, was in an excited state, with his lips tightening and loosening, and swallowing drily with a tight smile. His power was, to some extent, at stake on this issue. 'What if the people go off to sea in canoes?' he asked. 'No, that is no good. They will die, or be brought back' said the District Commissioner. The Ariki Taumako reaffirmed his position—'We obey the Government. Tell him we are in his hands.' Occasionally one of the audience interrupted. 'When is the recruiting vessel coming? We want it to come and help us, to come and take men away and leave food.' Another commented 'He is blocking the road to the South.' Robinson said, at large, 'The island will break out in fighting.' The chiefs continued to express their opinions, the Ariki Tafua making the suggestion that there should be a division; those who wished to go to the Solomons doing so, and those who wished to go to the New Hebrides being also allowed to do so. Robinson then appealed to the chiefs for a decision on what should be done about the recruiting vessel which was then on its way from the Solomons, as to whether people should recruit on her, or should abstain in protest. The Ariki Taumako said 'It rests with the people.' Robinson replied 'Oh, give a lead!' The Ariki Taumako then turned to the crowd . . . 'Is it so, that you are afraid to go North?' Loud expressions of assent answered him—'We don't want to go to the Solomons.' The Ariki Taumako then said 'So, it is finished. Any man who has made up his mind to go (to the Solomons), let him go. The expression of the wish of the people is finished.' Then he turned to the interpreter, 'Tell him that the speech of the chiefs is concluded.' He meant by this that since the Government ruling had barred the New Hebrides, despite the opinion of chiefs and people, there was nothing more to be said.

S

This decisive statement ended that issue. The District Commissioner then raised the subject of people going on a visit in his vessel to Anuta, the neighbouring island, about eighty miles away. He explained that only a few people could go since the vessel was small. As he was doing so, he raised his voice in addressing the crowd, and the Ariki Taumako commented 'Tell him to talk to the chiefs. The chiefs are here to listen to him.'

After a final explanation by the District Commission on the Anuta voyage,[1] the meeting concluded.

Two points of particular interest arose in this meeting. The first was that, while the arguments of Government against the New Hebrides as a recruiting place were ignored, the fiat of Government was accepted. Therefore, the Tikopia implication was that responsibility in future would lie with the Government if men should go off in canoes in despair or if dire results should come from insufficient food supply. It was left to individuals interested to recruit for work in the Solomons. From the point of view of the mass of the people, they would go under protest. Such was the implication. In fact, recruiting was brisk, and the results were not deleterious.

The second point, sociologically, was the explicit consultation of the people. In Tikopia affairs one frequently got the impression that the chiefs were making decisions for the people. This time it was clear that they wished support from the people in their stand against the Government. On the other hand, the meeting was in no strict sense representative of Tikopia as a whole. The people consulted were only those present. Yet against this could be argued that only those present were the ones interested and, therefore, the only ones who had a right to be heard.

Later I received an interesting gloss on the meeting from the old Ariki Kafika. He said he agreed to the Government's decision. But he said the people were afraid of the Solomons—they thought they would die, perhaps. It was left by the chiefs to individual men to decide whether each would go or stay. The reason was, he said, 'lest it be thought that we are chasing people away'. This referred to the recurring theme of the anxiety of the commoners lest they be driven out by the chiefs, and to the counter-theme of the anxiety of the chiefs lest they be thought to be trying to drive out the commoners. The Ariki Kafika said that in fact plenty of men would go—and in this he was right.

(6) About three weeks later again (June 3rd) there was a discussion between us and the chiefs on a Government proposal to send ten tons of rice for distribution under our auspices. On this occasion the three senior chiefs were present as well as Pa Fenuatara, and a son of the Mission priest who was brought in by our express invitation. The Ariki Fangarere did not come. He was working in Uta as the aftermath of a dance festival which he had held the night before. (Pa Fenuatara said that such was the custom. When a chief has held a dance festival, he goes and puts in a day's work in the sacred district of Uta—he does not make kava, but his presence there is, so to speak, an acknowledgment to the gods.)

---

[1] See my article 'Anutu and Tikopia. Symbiotic Elements in Social Organization.' *Journal of the Polynesian Society*, vol. 63, 1954, pp. 87–131.

The chiefs accepted my main proposals for the distribution of supplies, but made certain observations thereon. They pointed out that the Government was furnishing the supplies and therefore it was for the Government to lay down the conditions for disposal. They said also that the land was 'the land of the chiefs', and that, therefore, anything done in their name was binding on all the people. Part of the proposal was that bags of rice should be allocated to settlements, with a senior person in each settlement to be responsible for distribution to a designated set of persons or householders. Later, Pa Fenuatara indicated that he would like to go over with me the list of responsible men and make some suggestions thereon. He also said that any surplus from the first distribution of food should be stored in the house of the Ariki Tafua who could move out to another dwelling inland to make room. Pa Fenuatara stressed that he did not want the food to be in charge of the priest. He said that anything from the Mission vessel, the *Southern Cross*, should be distributed by the priest; but anything given by the Government should be distributed by the chiefs. This was a separation of Church and State in clearer form than any observations I had previously heard.

A series of later meetings of chiefs when Spillius continued in residence on the island, gave still further crystallization to this situation. Intermittent for a time owing to friction with the Ariki Tafua, the meetings were resumed early in 1955 to discuss the affairs of the island. It is possible that the final unification of the community by Christianity, and the needs of Government, may regularise the assembly of chiefs as a politico-religious gathering.[1]

Difficulties in the Exercise of Collective Responsibilities

The need for the chiefs to collaborate in order to take advantage of Government assistance brought out a weakness in the Tikopia system of collective responsibilities.

On many occasions the chiefs assumed responsibility for public behaviour outside the affairs of their own lineage and clan. In May 1952 for instance, as Tikopia travellers to Anuta were preparing to go ashore, the Ariki Taumako addressed them all in stern tones, ordering them to behave properly and not to go raiding the cultivations, as their food shortage might tempt them to do. Although the party included members of three clans, they all obeyed his injunction. But it must be noted that he was the only chief present.

On the other hand, the Tikopia had a clear conception of separation of functions according to separation of status. There were many occasions when responsibility was deliberately evaded, or placed where it lay in theory rather than in practice by bringing up status considerations. An example here was provided by the conduct of Pa Fenuatara. In 1952 it was often difficult to see where responsibility for decisions lay in Kafika—with the chief or with his eldest son who took first place on so many public occasions. The people commonly spoke of 'father and son in Kafika' as if they had a single

[1] *V.* Spillius, *op. cit.* pp. 14–16 *et passim.* The Bishop of Melanesia noted that he had 'a conference with the assembled Chiefs over matters of importance' at the end of 1956, *Log,* Mar. 1957, p. 15.

opinion. But in ordinary secular affairs decisions were taken primarily by Pa Fenuatara, while in esoteric matters the old chief still exercised his powers of decision. In the yam rites, he simply announced to Pa Fenuatara that one day would elapse between the preparation of oven pads and the rite of the 'hot food', and this order was accepted with its implications for work by all concerned. In the ritual of Somosomo[1] both the Ariki Kafika and the Ariki Fangarere disliked the idea of abbreviating the proceedings because food was short, as the younger people wished. 'That will we finish today is good, and yet bad' said the elder chief. The other replied 'It is because our grandchildren object.' Then two of the old chief's grandchildren came in. The Ariki Kafika said to them 'Why did not your father tell you that we were to finish today?' They replied 'It is not for him to tell you. The pair of you chiefs discuss and decide. If you want to have a rite tomorrow, do so. The food baskets of both of you have been made ready.' The ultimate decision lay with the chiefs, particularly with the Ariki Kafika, but to be effective it demanded the acquiescence of the younger people whose job it was to do the work. Consequently, each party deferred to the other, though sometimes this was for appearance only.

This technique of leaving the decision to others—or making the gesture of doing so—was a recognized procedure in Tikopia and was very common in 1952 as in 1929. The expression of 'leaving' (*tuku*) it to another to decide implies a laying down of the decision, as if it were an object for the other person to pick up. This implied, of course, that the consequence would be laid at the door of the decision-taker. The way in which the Tikopia chiefs attributed responsibility to the Government in the dispute on recruiting is an example of this. Moreover, they put forward their own ideas as coming primarily from the people. Indeed, the Ariki Taumako secured public confirmation of his statement by his concluding words. In general, the Tikopia chiefs did not go directly against the view of the body of the people, or they would do so only if such view were not publicly expressed. They could act on their own responsibility and they usually did so, but on critical issues they tended to seek guidance by 'leaving it to the people'. This process, together with that of seeking 'a common mind' among the chiefs was of great importance in Tikopia decision-making.

Such a tendency for men of rank to assume a passive attitude and appear to be guided in their decisions and public actions by the general view had its dangers for public affairs. This was illustrated by the pillaging of foodstuffs brought in a Government vessel for distribution to the Tikopia in mid-May at the onset of the famine. The ship brought about four tons of sweet potatoes and about 500 coconuts. The instruction was given by the District Commissioner that he wished the food to be distributed by the chiefs among the people. Robinson Vakasaumore, as a principal executant, was told this and requested to notify the Ariki Taumako to get a message sent to the chiefs to 'nominate representatives' to arrange for the receipt of the food on shore. He went to the Ariki Taumako, but no effective arrangements were made for

[1] *Work of the Gods*, pp. 91–5, 303, *et seq.*

safeguarding the food. It was low tide when the food was brought ashore and it had to be carried from boats and canoes for some distance over the reef. Under pretext of assisting to carry the sweet potatoes, women and children walked off with them to their homes. The coconuts were to some extent preserved for the chiefs, but only through the efforts of a few men of influence. They asked me if that was what the Government intended, and then they shouted instructions to the people, but this was done on their own initiative and not as a result of any delegation of authority. Even then, many coconuts were thrown into canoes and taken off privately elsewhere. Robinson himself stood on the upper deck of the vessel and looked about him, taking no steps to interfere. When challenged, he said that the people were hungry and that that was why they took away the food.

This incident made for much bad feeling in the Tikopia community—not against Robinson, but between the two major districts and between chiefs and people. The people of the district of Faea were at a great advantage since the vessel was anchored off their villages and so they could slip the food away to their houses easily. The people of Ravenga could not carry the food across the island without attracting attention. They were very angry. They said that the people of Faea used to accuse those of Ravenga of murmuring about their need for food. Now, they argued, the tables were turned; it was the people of Faea who had proved themselves greedy. It was generally agreed that the coconuts should have been kept for the chiefs—not necessarily for their personal consumption but for them to distribute. That the people at large should pilfer sweet potatoes was not held to be very important—after all, it was argued, the food was meant for them. But the chiefs should have had the coconuts, the more choice food appropriate to their prestige. This was the chiefs' own view, but it was also held by many other people. There was much shifting of responsibility. Vakasaumore disclaimed authority and obligation; he simply put the onus on the general food craving. Another *maru* said to me in typical fashion, 'If I had been there I would have stopped the pilfering, but I was on the ship.' The chiefs in general placed the responsibility for the pilfering not on their own shoulders nor on those of their executive officers for failure to control the situation, nor on the Government for failure to safeguard what it had brought, but simply on the people for failing to listen to instructions. Control of the situation was made more difficult by the dispersed nature of the unloading of the food and the fact that it was not in large packages but in small units, even individual nuts and tubers. But in such crisis as these the Tikopia system of conjoint authority, which meant dispersed authority with a tendency to shift responsibility, was apt to be ineffective.

The Mission as a Political Factor

In the traditional Tikopia system, the jurisdiction of the religious and the civil power in Tikopia tended to coincide. They were not identical because the ritual elders had no specific political function, and the executive officers had no ritual function. But the chief embodied both and both stemmed from him. In the modern Tikopia situation, even by 1929 the alignment was very different and this was a cause of social strain. There was a division between the chiefs whose authority still was correlated with pagan religious sanctions, and the chief who buttressed his power by Christianity. There was also the division between the traditional chief as such and the new political power of the Mission leaders.[1]

It will be clear from what has been said already that by 1952 the Melanesian Mission had become an even more powerful political factor. The political changes were evident in several respects. Mission teachers, in particular the Melanesian leader, had attained a more important position in Tikopia public affairs. Ellison Tergatok, who was only a Deacon in 1929 had, by 1952, been a priest for nearly fifteen years. Whereas before he was known generally as Pa Pangisi (Mr Banks), he tended now to be known to all the Christian community as *Mama*, father, a term of respect applied only to senior church officers. The great respect he received from all Christian Tikopia lay partly in his personality and partly in the fact that the growth of Christianity in the island was almost entirely due to his initiative and organization. But he had also become wealthy in land given him by the Ariki Taumako at the time of his marriage. Through this marriage and his acquisition of land, and through his conformity in very large measure to most of the social usages of Tikopia, he had become absorbed to a high degree into the Tikopia secular society. His children were reckoned as ordinary Tikopia, belonging to the Taumako clan through their mother, and the group as a whole had begun to be known as *paito i Pangisi*, 'Banks lineage' (see pp. 232–3).

By 1952, Ellison had so increased and solidified his economic position that he was regarded in some respects as being almost equivalent to a chief. In terms of reciprocal presentation of food and other gifts, he had been such even in 1929. But by 1952 he was even at times actually referred to as a chief.[2] One of our Tikopia attendants when sent on a message to Faea, on being asked to repeat his message, said 'I must go to the two chiefs.' Since there was only one Tikopia chief living in Faea I asked 'What two chiefs?' He replied 'The Ariki Tafua and Mama Ellison.' At one period Ellison's unmarried son, also a Mission teacher, became a person of great influence in Tikopia politics, though this did not endure for long. All this created resentment among the chiefs. Both the Ariki Taumako and Pa Fenuatara were highly critical of the priest and his sons for what they regarded as interference in public affairs to which they had no right. The Ariki Tafua, as might be expected, was less critical of the priest, but there were occasions on which even this chief operated significantly as a separate entity in political affairs. It was noticeable that when the question of a house for us in Faea

---

[1] *We, The Tikopia*, pp. 46–9.

[2] The term *ariki* was sometimes used in an honorific sense in Tikopia affairs for someone not a chief in the full political sense. For instance in 1929, according to Pa Tarikitonga, then chief *maru* of Tikopia 'the elder of Rarovi is also a chief; great is his weight. He is executive elder of the chief; his is the Fire in the Work of the Gods.'

arose, the chief was anxious that it should be situated near him at his end of the village, and he did not acquiesce at all cheerfully in arrangements proposed by the priest which would have lodged us nearest to *him*.

Politically, influence was also exercised by Tikopia Mission teachers, largely due to the fact that a high proportion of them were *maru*, executive officers in the Tikopia political system. Hence, in much which they directed, it was not possible to distinguish clearly the different components of traditional authority and church authority. Moreover, in public affairs, the existence by 1952 of an overwhelmingly large and growing body of Church adherents meant that all decisions which affected the body of the people as a whole had to refer mainly to practising Christians, although they might be decisions taken by pagan chiefs. Hence, the political judgments of pagan chiefs had to make allowance for the probable behaviour of people who were in the large majority Christian. This position was summarized for me by Robinson Vakasaumore. Before I ever reached Tikopia he said 'The gospel, great is its *mana*. Formerly the great mass of people assembled round the chiefs and great was the *mana* of the things that were performed, of the "dark things" (i.e. pagan rites) of old. Nowadays it is not so; the gospel has become great.'

By elder Tikopia, reared in the traditions of their ancient faith, the position was apt to be seen somewhat differently. Even if Christian, they saw Tikopia society at the crossroads and regarded the political and religious deviations as deleterious, almost in some mystical way. But it does not seem to have been the religious division alone which caused disquiet, but the fact that the religious division had political effects and, in particular, marred the unity of the chiefs.

The political implications of the religious allegiance were indicated especially by two cases of succession to chieftainship in the generation between 1929 and 1952.

Religion of Chiefs as a Political Factor

The first case relates to the chieftainship of Tafua. The old Ariki Tafua, who had acceded in May 1910 and whom I had known, died in 1936.[1] His successor, as all had anticipated, was his eldest son Pa Rangifuri. This man, who had been converted to Christianity along with his father a decade or so before, and baptized under the name of Gabriel, was persuaded by the other chiefs after his election to revert to paganism. The unity of the chiefs as a body, as I have stressed already, was regarded as an important structural principle in Tikopia affairs. At the accession of the new Ariki, the pagan chiefs represented to him that now he had taken his father's place it was appropriate that the chiefs should be united once again and perform, as of old, their common pagan rites.[2] One may imagine the dismay of the Christian

[1] *Log*, Jan. 1937, p. 10. Rev. Stephen Talu reported towards the end of 1935 that the name of the chief of the Christians was 'Edward Tafua', i.e. the old chief (Mar. 1936, p. 10).

[2] That the chief still believed in the potency of his ancient rites is suggested by an incident noted by me in 1928. (*Work of the Gods*, vol. II, p. 222.)

Tikopia at being bereft of their only chief. To be chiefless must have been a severe blow not only to their integration but also to their prestige in their relations with their pagan opponents. This apostasy, by its reassertion of the unity of all the Tikopia chiefs, must also have given a severe check to the political power of the Melanesian priest.

On the other hand, the Ariki Tafua recognized a dual responsibility, to his fellow chiefs, and also to the Christian Church into which he had once been received. He was subject then to the conflicting sway of loyalties, arguments and emotional response to pressures. After two seasons of performance of the ancient rites, he was induced to return again to the Christian faith by the efforts of a band of evangelists imported from elsewhere in the Mission field. The return of the Ariki Tafua to Christianity after this temporary lapse must have given a great fillip to the political prestige of the Mission. This may be presumed because of events after his death in 1951. The succession involved no problems; it was conceded by all that his only surviving son was un-questionably the proper person to become chief. This young man had been a Christian from birth. Though he had been present in Uta with his father, and participated in the pagan rituals during the latter's apostasy, there seemed to have been no move by the pagan chiefs to persuade him to return to the ancient faith.

The alteration in the role of the Ariki Tafua from Christian political leader without ritual functions to pagan political leader with ritual functions, and then back again, did not of course affect himself alone. It involved the ancillary moves of some other men of high status, both in his clan and outside it. But by 1952 Christianity had recovered more than the lost ground.

This incident shows that a Tikopia chief unquestionably could function as a secular leader, quite apart from the religious functions which tradition assigned to him. At no time in the various changes made by the Ariki Tafua was there apparently any question of his not being accepted as a chief by all Tikopia. The decision as to whether he would be pagan or Christian was his, but whichever he was, he remained a chief. This view was reinforced by the election of his son, the first Tikopia chief ever to be *elected as a Christian*, that is, who had never conducted rites to the traditional gods. In all the turmoil of events accompanying the situation of famine, at a time when social relations between various parties in the society became strained, there was never any question of the right of the new Ariki Tafua to be chief. At times his judgment as a man was called in question, but there was never any derogation from his functions as *ariki*. In other words, the religious change in Tikopia has served to provide a test of the secular basis of a chief's authority.

Split in a Chiefly Office

A division between paganism and Christianity in Tikopia produced another type of resolution in the Fangarere clan. Here it was startling. In 1929 it would have been incredible to me that there could have been more than one chief in a Tikopia clan. Yet in 1952 I found that Fangarere had two chiefs. What made this all the more surprising was that this had continued to be by far the smallest clan in the community, and therefore the dual authority had no justification on grounds of increase of efficiency.

The reason had been an attempt by both religious parties to resolve a political struggle to their own advantage. The old Ariki Fangarere, whom I had known, had died about 1940. The situation at his death was complicated. He had been baptized a Christian some years before and his eldest son, Pa Nukumaro, had joined the Church at the same time. This man suffered severely from an impediment in his speech which made him stutter so greatly as to inhibit him from taking an ordinary social role in conversation. This difficulty would certainly have blocked him from the recital of the kava formulae, which were essential parts of the performance of Tikopia pagan ritual. (Interestingly enough, he was earlier a spirit medium, and as such spoke clearly and perfectly in his dissociated state.) For these reasons the eldest son, who otherwise would have been the normal successor, would not obviously have been the choice of the pagan chiefs. On the other hand, the Ariki Tafua as a Christian wished for another Christian chief to support himself. He even put this publicly, in structural terms. He argued that it was proper that there should be two Christian chiefs, Tafua and Fangarere, to match the two pagan chiefs of Kafika and Taumako. Adopting swift tactics he seized Pa Nukumaro immediately on the old chief's death and proclaimed him as chief to the crowd in the conventional style. Since his nominee was the eldest son and followed the faith which his father had adopted, there was a good *prima facie* case. But the pagan chiefs decided not to let the matter rest. In turn, they seized the younger brother, Pa Rangateatua, who had still remained a pagan, and elevated him as chief. The Fangarere clan therefore found itself with two chiefs, each properly elected by public process.

How was this situation resolved? It had no precedent. In olden days it was true that twice according to tradition there was dual ritual leadership, in two major lineages, sa Marinoa and sa Porima. But in each case after the death of one of the leaders the dual leadership was never revived. On another occasion in the history of Taumako, a self-elected chief had been spurned by a powerful group of electors who installed their own nominee in office, according to normal practice. But these cases were anomalous. For two contrasted parties each to elect a chief would in olden days almost certainly have resulted in fighting. On this occasion in the Fangarere clan nothing of the kind occurred. Both chiefs were accepted up to a point by the clan and by the whole Tikopia society—'they are both chiefs at the same time' (*e fetauariki katoa*).

The acceptance was not complete. The Christian chief of Fangarere was known as the 'Chief of the Gospel (*te Ariki o te Fekau*); the pagan chief was known as the 'Chief of the Chiefs' (*te Ariki o nga Ariki*). Both were sometimes still referred to by their 'house' names. The former functioned for church affairs and the latter for pagan affairs. When the Bishop and other Mission officers came to the island, they were met by the Ariki Tafua and the Fangarere 'Chief of the Gospel'. When any Church festivals or dance assemblies took place the Chief of the Gospel was present and was given the

status of a chief. On the other hand, when the pagan chiefs held religious
rites or sponsored a dance festival, the 'Chief of the Chiefs' in Fangarere
attended and was given the full honours of his rank. There was in fact a
division of jurisdictions, each chief having his own functions and roles and
the appropriate status.

But what about public affairs of a secular kind? And what about the clan?
In public affairs in 1952 on the whole it was the pagan chief who participated.
In the assembly of chiefs to meet a Government official the pagan chief
attended; he was the 'Chief of the Chiefs' and therefore took his rightful
place among them. To this the Ariki Tafua made no demur and used to sit
side by side with him. As regards the clan, the situation was more complex.
This was so partly because their relations to their chief had a strong economic
component; they had to support him by labour and by food. In this case one
would theoretically have expected to find segmentation, operational if not
genealogical. Separation of public functions and status of two brothers in
this way would have led, one might think, to a splitting of the clan. This had
not happened. In ritual matters, Christians followed the Christian chief to
Church, and pagans followed the pagan chief to the 'Work of the Gods'.
But in social and economic matters this separation was not clearly marked.
If the 'Chief of the Gospel' was involved in a feast or other economic event,
then representatives of the whole clan rallied to his support. This was so also
with the 'Chief of the Chiefs'. The reasons for this were twofold. The clan
was so small that splitting of it would have reduced effective manpower in
each case to a very low level. Again after all, to either Christians or pagans,
a brother of their own chief should be supported on kinship grounds, quite
apart from the religion which he professed.

There was, however, a distinction between the two chiefs in status as well
as in role. In general terms the 'Chief of the Chiefs' was of higher status than
the 'Chief of the Gospel'. Indeed, there were times when the latter was hardly
treated as a chief at all. It might be said that outside the sphere of specifically
Christian affairs the elder brother was a chief in name only. He was relatively
wealthy in land, but less so than his brother. He still stammered badly and
was mimicked by people in private conversation. At public meetings, including the assemblies (*fono*) in Faea, he had a position of prominence but
he did not occupy a stool side by side with the Ariki Tafua. For most of the
visits of the District Commissioners to Tikopia, he did not present himself
for introduction, coming on the scene only late in the series of such contacts.
On any public issue his counsel was never sought by the other chiefs or men
of influence. When Pa Fenuatara was discussing with me the reaction of
Christianity upon the position of a chief, he pointed to the 'Chief of the
Gospel' as an example of how the new religion could degrade a person to the
level of a commoner. On the other hand, any Tikopia seemed prepared to
state that the 'Chief of the Gospel' was really an *Ariki*. Moreover, in a food
distribution it seemed to be regarded as proper that he should have a portion
set out for him as with the other chiefs. On occasions when status was in
question he was assured by members of the public that he was in truth a chief

—though his need for this assurance in itself showed the weakness of his position and its lack of structural basis.

The semi-acceptance of the 'Chief of the Gospel' as an *Ariki* by the pagan leaders of Tikopia was an example of the principle of accommodation or expediency.[1] More especially it was an adaptation of the leadership structure in response to a change in external circumstances. This adaptation necessitated sacrifice—of time and energy by clanspeople and others in dealing with both chiefs at different levels; of symbolic unity in that the notion of two chiefs of one clan could not be regarded as normal and was, therefore, a strain upon ordinary concepts. The economic sacrifice was minimal, since on the whole pagan and Christian would have lent their support in social affairs to each brother, irrespective of who had been chief, but there was some economic drain. On the other hand, there was some compensation. Neither Christian nor pagan were faced by complete loss as one side or the other would have been had the issue been fought out in traditional style. Secondly, with the dual accession of the two brothers, the chiefly family of Fangarere was not split, and overt amiable relations continued between them, making it easier for social relations in general through the community. Thirdly, since the Christian chief had no children and was unlikely ever to have any, his election was only a postponement of the issue of an ultimate succession.

An important question was, who would succeed to either brother? His 'adhering child' was the eldest son of his younger brother, the pagan chief. But this 'adhering child', a young man in 1952, was already a Christian. It was expected that he would succeed his uncle, and if he also were to succeed his father the leadership would be united again. But as I guessed in 1952, with the advance of Christianity the pagans of Fangarere have become converted. It is probable that the two Christian Fangarere *ariki* will remain until one dies and ultimately the chiefly office be united again, in the person of the eldest son of the 'Chief of the Chiefs'.

Church and State in Tikopia

In discussing the relation of Church and State in Tikopia I have referred to the growing political power of the Melanesian Mission. But this process in 1952 received a check. Whereas at an early time, part of the political strength of the Mission lay in the fact that it represented the only effective Western power in the island, by 1952 its jurisdiction had become much more clearly differentiated from that of Government. This was due in part to some development of communications which allowed the Government to make more frequent calls than previously and to appear more often than the Mission. Again, with the general development of welfare concepts and their application to even the most remote colonial territories, Tikopia was conceived as a much more definite responsibility than before by the Solomon Islands Government, and administrative relations with the Tikopia were

[1] See Raymond Firth 'Some Principles of Social Organization', *J.R.A.I.*, vol. 85, 1955, p. 10.

made more obvious. But in particular, as the food crisis developed and as Government intervention intensified, the political and economic power of Government became evident. This necessitated a clarification of responsibilities and of the role of the Church in the political sphere. After some confusion owing to cross-currents of policy at certain stages, it was finally made clear by the Government that Church and State in the modern scheme were separate entities and that each should have jurisdiction in its own sphere. In other words, empirically, leaders of the Mission should not be expected to control public administration, which was intended by Government to be conducted under their aegis by the chiefs and their representatives.

Two features of interest are relevant here. The first is that in this way Tikopia, unlike some other Polynesian communities, did not develop a theocracy. The application of Government powers in some detail came before the religious conversion of the community allowed the full growth of a theocratic state. Although in many respects the history of Tikopia seems to be repeating that of other Polynesian communities brought into contact with Western civilization, in the political respect the Tikopia are unlikely to pass through any period of full Church control of their social order.

If the concept of Church and State be viewed more widely in terms of the general relation between religious and secular affairs, then a significant feature of Tikopia politics over the last generation has been the specific emergence of the chief as a symbol of secular power, if necessary divorced from religious power. It is true that in 1952 some of the ritual sanctions of the chieftainship still operated. The personal *tapu* of a chief was still regarded as strong. It was still sometimes stated in private that the Christian chief used sorcery to gain his ends. But all the main ritual sanctions linked with the performance of the kava had ceased to be effective. What still persisted was what may be termed the mystic aura of chieftainship, manifested in signs such as the stringency of the taboos against touching his head or body, the respect-behaviour in crouching in his presence, and in the generally acknowledged rules regulating the chief's own conduct. These last could be overborne on occasions. At one point in the receipt of relief supplies some men of rank were left alone with cases of goods. The Ariki Tafua, leading the way, lifted a case on to his shoulder and carried it to his house, despite the traditional rule that a chief should never carry anything on his shoulder like a common man. But there still persisted beliefs that in some way there was a relation between the personality of a chief and the success of his public enterprises and the general prosperity of the community. The special content of the term *te Ariki* for a Tikopia chief seemed to give it a different connotation, a more weighty significance, than when it was used for the captain of a vessel or some other foreign dignitary. The interest of Government in having recognized representatives in the Tikopia community, combined with the traditional respect for chiefs, and the chiefs' own economic power, will probably lead to their persistence as political figures irrespective of the changes in their religious affiliations.

The Role of Maru *in 1929*

I have referred earlier to the fact that even in 1952 Government officials were still apparently ignorant of the functions and perhaps even of the existence of the executive officers known to the Tikopia as *maru*.

In 1929 there were three main types of public office in Tikopia: chief, ritual elder and executive officer. The first, the chief (*ariki*), theoretically at least was elected by his peers or other men of rank, with the choice approved by the people. The second, the ritual elder (*matapure*), was nominated by the chief of the clan of which he was a lineage member, and inducted into office by him on his own responsibility. The third, the executive officer (*maru*), was neither elected nor nominated, but his office was ascribed to him by virtue of his hereditary position and his personal capacity. Whereas chiefs and ritual elders had specific periodic functions to perform correlated with their office, the functions of *maru* were much less specific and non-periodic, and a person who was classed as a *maru* might not, in fact, perform them. The number of chiefs and of ritual elders was quite precise and all the holders of these offices could be specified almost without thought by any responsible Tikopia. The number of *maru*, however, was not precise and though there was general agreement on the category of person who was a *maru* and upon all the more obvious persons recognized as *maru*, there was a kind of haze or penumbra about the marginal cases.

This lack of definition was to some degree due to the absence of any specific action by which the office was conferred upon the person, by comparison with the specific induction of chiefs and of ritual elders. But another reason lay in the structure of entitlement to consideration as a *maru*. I shall examine this a little later.

In previous work[1] I have spoken of *maru* as being essentially 'executive officials' of the chief. The lack of precision in their numbers and the lack of any specific action for assigning them to their functions has raised in my mind the question as to whether it is appropriate to use the terms 'office' and 'official' in this respect, or whether *maru* should be described simply as an executant fulfilling a given set of roles. Following Max Weber, however, one may consider an 'office' as a specifically legitimized status governed by rules which rest upon the impersonal order of the society and not upon the private interests of the individual concerned. In this sense, a Tikopia *maru* who fulfils his functions may be said to hold an office. His powers too are limited to a 'sphere of competence' under the authority of his chief—he may not, for example, occupy himself with ritual matters in which he has no competence whatsoever. It is appropriate then to speak of the *maru* as an executive officer, or simply, executant, provided that it be understood that the number of occupants of the office at any one time is not laid down in any clearly specified way.

There are several further points to be noted about the *maru*. They were not of equal rank; though there was no elaborate grading among them and though the relative status of many was never called in question, certain *maru*

[1] E.g., 'Authority and Public Opinion in Tikopia', p. 172, etc.

were definitely regarded as the leaders in their category. Secondly, the principle by which one became a *maru* was hereditary. On the one hand in Tikopia society this meant that the office could never overtly be resigned since the right to it inhered in a person's birth. He need not exercise his right, however, and in that sense became marginal in the *maru* field. Again, since the office was hereditary, it was sometimes difficult for a *maru* to detach the general interest from his personal interests or those of other members of his kin group.

It is necessary to elucidate these matters a little further because of the outstanding role played by some *maru*—but not others—in the Tikopia events of 1952 to 1953. In particular, it is necessary to see if any changes had taken place in the *maru* office by 1952 as compared with 1929.

The number of *maru* was undetermined in practical affairs, but it was not unlimited. The limitations were twofold. The basic one was that of kinship status. *Maru* were defined primarily in terms of their agnatic relationship to the chief of a clan. But while the number of persons who fell within the recognized field of agnatic relationship was quite large, in practice no such large number of executive officers was needed to give a lead in communal undertakings, preserve order and carry out the instructions of the chiefs. Hence, from among the wide range of passive *maru* only a few of the more active personalities tended to emerge as regular bearers of the major executive functions in the community. Moreover, a passive *maru* might step into the active role and out again on some specific occasion in which his personal status or the general interest was concerned. He performed then some functions but not others of his role. The *maru*, par excellence, were thus men who performed multiple functions and on many occasions.

The question of who were *maru* assumed a double form. In the one form it was—who were entitled to be *maru*, i.e. what were the limits of genealogical relation to the chief which allowed a person to reckon himself, or be reckoned as, a *maru*? Secondly, within the range of persons so entitled, who in fact performed the functions of executive officers and could be reckoned as *maru* from a practical point of view?

In 1929 I had many discussions with leading Tikopia on these points. Pa Fenuatara, as usual, was one of the clearest expositors. He began by saying that in Tikopia that only 'men of the land' (*tangata fenua*) were the *maru*—that the houses of the chiefs were different. He then went on to list the men or families of *maru* as follows:

In Kafika clan: (i) Pa Siamano.
                 (ii) Pa Niuaru.
                 (iii) Pa Vainunu.
                 (iv) Pa Paoari.
                 (v) Pa Tearairaki.

The first four he described as '*maru* and yet children of chiefs', the fifth as a *maru*, but his father was not a chief, only a seedling chief.

In Taumako: (i) Pa Avakofe and his sons.
               (ii) Pa Vangatau and his sons.
               (iii) Pa Nukurenga, Pa Fenuafou, Seremata, etc.
               (iv) Pa Morava and his sons—described as 'simply *maru*—
                    their ancestor was chief a long time ago'.
In Tafua: (i) Paito i Maevetau—a set of brothers whose father died
                    recently.
               (ii) Paito i Nukuariki.
               (iii) Paito i Matopo.
               (iv) Paito i Fenutapu.
In Fangarere: (i) Paito i Vaisakiri.
               (ii) Paito i Tekava.

Pa Fenuatara went on: 'The basis of a *maru* is a line of chiefs of old. A chief who has been elected of old, he dwells on and then he dies, and then his children who are alive will either succeed as chiefs or not—perhaps the chief who is elected is different—and so his sons live on, they then become *maru*. Thereupon they separate off to the rear and dwell there as a house of *maru*. But if they have not been chiefs from of old, then they are termed a site (i.e. potential source) of *maru* (*turanga maru*). Thus are dwelling the two brothers of Morava and the two brothers in Maneve—they are termed "sites of *maru*" (more literally, *maru* standing-places). The chiefly lineage and the *maru* lineage are the same.'

The essence of Pa Fenuatara's statement, backed up by the personalities and lineages he cited, was that the basis of the position of *maru* lay in their chiefly ancestry and not their lack of succession to the chieftainship itself. In effect, what the Tikopia had done was to convert a negative role into a positive one—to recognize the failure in succession as a positive entitlement to another status, that of supporting the person who succeeded. Clearly this was a tacit recognition of an important sociological mechanism—the assignment of moral obligation as a distraction from possible tension.

The functions exercised by a *maru* were then primarily derived from his relationship to his clan chief; his major role was to protect his chief. When Pa Maevetau, younger brother of the old Ariki Tafua, died in 1929, he received the honours due to a *maru*, including the firing of guns as soon as his death was announced. Pa Fenuatara told me that on such an occasion when a *maru* dies, the first man of importance—chief or 'man of the land'—to go to the house where the dead man lies, will enter, stop, look where the corpse is lying and call out to him 'Pa Maevetau! You have separated from your protecting of your chief. Let the chiefs be informed. Let pandanus mats be spread out for all orphaned children.' This formal address to the dead man is in acknowledgment of his past services and of his special role of safeguarding his chief. The term used is *reo ariki*, literally, 'voice of the chief'. If the chief, said Pa Fenuatara, was angry with a man, he called for his 'voice' and instructed him. The *maru* would go down to the beach and say 'Take his canoe and put it in the sea.' Then he would go to his house, grasp the offender by the wrist and order him 'Jump into your canoe and go to your land, the ocean. Who are you to compare yourself to my chief?' The offender would go, not daring to oppose the order because should he resist he would be killed where he stood. Such was the classic role of a *maru* of the chief. Less dramatically, and probably more commonly, the *maru* acted as the communicator of the chief's intentions to members of his clan on any matter of public order, as well as taking the initiative himself if occasion demanded.

But from another point of view the *maru* had a very important function as protector of the common people. As the communicator and executor of the will of the chief he acted to some extent as intermediary between him and the people. In consequence, he could act also as interpreter and ameliorator when the chief appeared to be over-harsh in his judgement. I have already described the operation of this function.[1] Moreover, not only could the *maru* mitigate the severity of action on behalf of the chief. He also acted very commonly as counsel to his chief. In this way, while serving as a very important buttress to the authority of the chief, he also was able to assist the ordinary people. From this point of view, the *maru* as executive officer was likened to the term *maru* meaning shade or shelter, 'The *maru* in this land is compared with the shade not stricken by the sun.' Or again, such a person was compared to the leaf of the umbrella palm used for protection either against sun or rain. A person could say in commemoration of a *maru* 'I who dwell here go under the protection of my umbrella leaf which is spread over my dwelling.' The power of a *maru* in Tikopia was considerable. It was generally agreed that if he was angered by a man he would snatch up anything handy and strike him on the forehead with it; that the man would not resent the blow but would efface himself. As a rule, however, a commoner would not run such a risk and any speech made to the *maru* would be conciliatory. In fact, during the year of my residence, I do not remember having seen a man so struck.

In Tikopia usage no formal difference existed in the status of different *maru*. All were in theory equal in rank. But practically there was a vast difference. This difference was due partly to relative closeness of agnatic relationship to the chief and partly to the personality of individual *maru*, some being more aggressive or responsible than others. But in 1929 there was a further factor which was in effect a special crystallization out of the other two. This was the premier position of Pa Tarikitonga. In my discussions with Pa Fenuatara he said 'The person to whom the land listens is Pa Tarikitonga. He is the premier *maru*. If any grave trouble arises, then every *maru* will go to him to discuss matters.' The position of this man did not rest simply upon his own capacities. It rested upon his father's reputation. His father, Pa Avakofe, was still alive as a very old man in 1929, and I visited him on several occasions. His position was unique in Tikopia. He was a younger brother of the father of the Ariki Taumako of 1929 and, while thus very close to the chief, was removed from the succession if the normal process continued. The awe which his name inspired was apparently due to his determination at a

[1] *Op. cit.* pp. 184–5.

much earlier date to enforce peace upon the land, and to his fearlessness and outspoken attitude in carrying through his intention. His unique position was generally accredited to him 'because it was he who blocked the evildoings in this land'. One of his outstanding achievements, by report, had been to prevent the killing of a crowd of castaways by chiefs and other men of rank many years before.[1] Hence, whenever the subject of *maru* was discussed, sooner or later someone would point out that the supreme *maru* in Tikopia was Pa Avakofe. There was another factor of traditional value. The clan of Taumako was noted particularly for the force and virility of its men. 'The clan of victory—because they are strong' is how they were described. The 'victory', which otherwise might be called the 'price of power', is the nearest translation of the Tikopia term *maro*, the acknowledgment of success in competitive achievement. The clan of Taumako—in particular the chiefly lineage—were recognized as the virile, strong clan of the land since it was their ancestors of old who fought against the Tongans and, through their steadfastness and craft in battle—according to the tradition—succeeded in beating off the invaders. According to the Tikopia, in 1929, these traditional events still had their effect. As I myself observed, most members of the Taumako chiefly house were, in fact, more vivid in personality, stronger in opinion and more gifted than others—though to what extent this was a reflection of the general prominence given them it was difficult to say. But from this point of view, Pa Avakofe owed his position in part to the fact that he was a member of a strong clan and lineage. He and his immediate agnatic kin were *toa*, the strong men of the land.

The real import of Pa Avakofe seems to have been that he was quite clear-sighted in his recognition of the nature of his role and of the need for peace in the Tikopia of his day. His eldest son, Pa Tarikitonga, told me himself of the advice which his father had given to him. 'Your brother, the eldest child, is dead, so it is for you to be the *maru* to the land. Do not trouble to remember formulae of the kava and other matters, leave that to the *Ariki* and the ritual elders. Your work is one only, to look after this land. If the overseas traveller comes, look after him; if the time comes when the chiefs and their people agree to go in anger against him, you protect him that he may not be killed or sent off to sea. That and that only is your work, to look upon the land that it may be well.' These wise words evidently epitomized Pa Avakofe's character and contribution. But by 1929 his advanced age had removed him almost completely from activity in public affairs. He still took an interest in what was happening. He was reported to have said 'I am now old and it was in another time that I had to go and help the land. It now falls on to the younger people.' Regarding one such younger *maru*, he said 'I am concerned about this our offspring. One day anger, another day anger. This is the man whom the house of the chiefs and *maru* must watch.' What he meant was that this man's frequent outbursts of rage might lead him to violence dangerous to the common weal. As a matter of fact, he was mistaken in his estimate or in what gossip had reported to him. But this was an instance of the conscious responsi-

[1] About 1885 *v*. Rivers, *op. cit*. I, pp. 340–1.

T

bility with which he—and other *maru*—regarded their duty to preserve peace
in the land. It was for them especially to keep an eye on turbulent characters
and to straighten out tangles and disputes between chiefs, and generally to
try and preserve the *status quo* and uphold the existing authority.

But since Pa Avakofe had become so old, the reliance of the land upon a
single power was not so clear. The Ariki Kafika said to me 'Now that Pa
Avakofe has become old and no longer goes about the country, it is I who
straighten out the matters of the chiefs.' This statement had some substance.
Pa Tarikitonga inherited his father's position, but he had not the same
personality. With a Tikopia chief concerned with ceremonial and ritual
functions, his personality did not necessarily obtrude itself and his status was
not so dependent upon it. But with a *maru* whose prime functions were the
preservation of order, personality obviously counted for a very great deal.
Pa Tarikitonga, though forceful, was much more limited in his grasp of
public affairs and took the lead as much from his hereditary position as from
any recognizable burning inner conviction. On the other hand, it was said
that even the chiefs did not bandy words (literally, 'barter speech'—*tauvi
taranga*) with Pa Tarikitonga. When he gave a definite view on a matter of
public order, the chiefs acquiesced.

Reference has been made to the possibility of confusion between the public
duties of a *maru* and his personal interests. This was recognized by the Tikopia
themselves. Pa Fenuatara pointed out to me how jealousy could arise between
maru, and how ambition could lead to trouble. 'A *maru* may desire that he
should dwell alone, that the land should listen to him and not listen to any
other person. Thereupon he may bewitch another *maru* so that he may die,
so that the land may give drink alone to the chiefs and to him.' Tikopia
tradition has many instances of such jealous rivalries, and I was told in 1929
of quite recent deaths attributed to such cause. Pa Maneve, father of my
friend Seremata, and Pa Veterei, eldest son of Pa Avakofe, were said to have
killed one another mutually by the use of black magic. The former died first,
but his rival soon followed. Their deaths were attributed to the internal
workings of their sorcery. By some people, however, the death of Pa Veterei
was attributed not to the machinations of an evil *maru* but to the black magic
of his own chief, to whom it had been reported that Pa Veterei was seeking
election to the chieftainship in due course to displace the chief's own son.
Whether these men of rank actually had engaged in any rituals to eliminate
their rivals is questionable. What these examples show, however, is that the
role of *maru* was not necessarily exercised solely for the public good.

Be that as it may, the more prominent *maru* regarded themselves as
custodians of public welfare and spoke with pride of their function and of
their own particular contribution towards it.

The Role of Maru in 1952

In the light of all this, it is interesting to see how far the principles and
personalities of a generation before were operative in 1952. Two questions—
did *maru* still exist on Tikopia, and who were they?—were answered quickly.

As we were going down to Tikopia from Honiara, I talked with Vakasaumore about the Tikopia political system. He made it clear that the *maru* still exercised their functions in Tikopia in much the same way as they had done a generation before. In answer to my question as to who were *maru*, he replied 'Nowadays I am a *maru*. I have succeeded to Pa Avakofe because he was my grandfather.' In this—and what he said turned out to be correct—he showed me that the principles of exercise of the *maru* function were still hereditary, by agnatic relation to the chief. He also showed how the reputation of Pa Avakofe had been preserved and gave succinctly the legitimization of his own claim by reference to this. He also stated who were the other principal *maru*. His list did not run counter to that of Pa Fenuatara a generation earlier, but it focused on a narrower field, as the close agnatic kin of the chiefs had become more numerous. In his own clan the principal was Pa Ngarumea, eldest of the chiefly brothers of the Ariki Taumako. It was he to whom the chief made known his views and he in turn communicated them to the grandsons of Pa Avakofe. In Tafua, the principal *maru* was Pa Matautu; he was the father's brother's son of the Ariki Tafua, the chief having no surviving brothers. In Kafika, the principal *maru* was stated to be Pa Fenuatara, though when his father, the chief, should die he would succeed and then the principal *maru* would be John Fararava and his elder brother; these two men were the representatives of the lineage of Mapusanga, which was an offshoot of the chiefly house of Kafika two generations before. Of Fangarere, Vakasaumore said 'Because both brothers had become chiefs together, there was lacking anyone who could become *maru*.'

In general, my informant said a *maru* must be a man of chiefly lineage on the one hand, and on the other an expert (*purotu*) in making pronouncements to the people. What he did not add was that he had also to be a man of personality, willing to take public action and possibly incur criticism for so doing. His stress upon the importance of being able to make pronouncements to the people was perhaps in part a reflection of the emphasis upon public speaking which he had had reinforced in his own contacts overseas. More strongly, it reflected his own conception of his own abilities and ambitions. He himself was a fluent public speaker and during the next year played an outstanding part in control of Tikopia public affairs, especially in imposing restraint upon theft and violence arising from the famine.

The significance of personality and ability in public speaking emerges in considering the succession to Pa Avakofe and Pa Tarikitonga, after a generation. The most senior man, Pa Nukutapu, eldest son of Pa Tarikitonga, had declined in status still further than had his father. Though a *maru*, and receiving considerable respect, he was not firm or able in public affairs and, by 1952, had slipped very much into the background. In contrast there was the prominence of Vakasaumore, who in effect had taken his grandfather's place. This brings out very clearly the difference between the almost automatic succession to the office of chief, and the highly selective operation of the active *maru* role. Vakasaumore was by no means the senior of the grandsons of Pa Avakofe; he was a younger son of a younger son.

Two obvious points which have emerged from the foregoing may be re-emphasized—that a *maru* must be male and that he need not be a married man. This latter criterion is interesting because, in a number of other Tikopia social contexts, a bachelor traditionally has not had the same weighty role as a married man. In 1929, the list provided by Pa Fenuatara included some names of bachelors. But by 1952, the possibility of a bachelor assuming a leading role as *maru* was assisted by the fact that his experience abroad, if he had been away working as a labourer, gave him a sophistication lacking to his seniors at home. This was one of the factors responsible for the leadership of Vakasaumore.

There are two further principles which bear upon the question of who were the most effective *maru*. The first principle is that on the whole the position of what may be termed operational *maru*, that is, the men who took the most part in public life, tended to fall to the younger rather than to the older representatives of a lineage. In 1952 this was demonstrated when, as in Tafua and Taumako, the chief himself was fairly young and naturally he tended to seek his confidants among men of his own generation. Even when this was not so, as in Kafika, there was a tendency for older *maru* to sit back, either not wishing to imperil their dignity or to disturb themselves by the energetic, even violent, action sometimes demanded of a *maru*. Hence, in Kafika, John Fararava and his brother were the *maru* who were most active and who first came to mind in considering the executives of this clan.

The second principle is one which differentiated the agnatic kin of the chief, the potential *maru*, into two categories. Pa Fenuatara explained this to me, particularly in 1952 when his own role was extremely important in Tikopia society and invited examination in relation to that of other *maru*. He said that the sons of a reigning chief in Tikopia (*tama te ariki*) are different from men of chiefly lineages who have separated off from the main stem. The latter are *maru* par excellence. Hence in Kafika, the lineage of Mapusanga and that of Vainunu were *maru*, the former being closer to the chief by virtue of their nearer relationship (see Gen. 2). In Taumako, the lineages of Avakofe and Vangatau were *maru*, the former being closer to the chief since their ancestor was the elder brother. In the Kafika clan, the sons of the chief, Pa Fenuatara and his brothers, were not executants 'of first instance' so to speak; so also in Taumako, the actual brothers of the chief were in the same category. When a public meeting was to take place, sons and brothers of a chief remained quiet at the beginning, they just sat. The procedure was for the lineages providing the primary executants (*paito e maru*) to decide among themselves who would speak. Then they said to one another 'Let us first go and sit down to listen to the speech which the chief will give us—as to what it may be—let us leave it to him.' Having found out what view the chief wished them to put forward, what the general policy should be, they then made their arrangements. As regards the entry of the *tama te ariki*, whether they spoke or not depended upon the *paito e maru*, who might ask one of the sons of the chief to speak or not. Unless he was asked, such a man would not put himself forward in the discussion. This, however, did not inhibit a son of the chief from calling a meeting on his own responsibility, but in so doing he ran the risk of not having the general support of the other *maru*.

With this difference in position was also associated a difference of function. On the whole the function of the sons of the chief in particular was to deliver comments on policy which represented the attitude of the chief, their father, in a way calculated not to emphasize differences between him and the people. The function of the *maru* who were not the immediate descendants of the chiefs, was to be prepared to take a stronger line and, if necessary, to criticize and berate the people in the interests of public order.

The first type of *maru* were said to deliver the *fono fakaariki* (the address according to the chiefs), the second to deliver, if necessary, the *fono pariki* (the address of evil significance). By the latter is meant the harsh instructions which require people to suffer restraint or even, by traditional Tikopia custom, enforcing a person to go off to sea.

This was a very ingenious mechanism. One effect of this division of function was clearly to remove from the chief the onus of particularly unpleasant decisions, and to put it upon the shoulders of people of rank who were not directly members of the chief's family. This applied particularly to any affairs in which differences of interest between chiefly groups and commoners might be brought to the surface. Hence this was one of the ways in which the symbolic head of the community was protected from the necessary consequences of his leadership.

There could be separation between the role of confidant to the chief and the role of principal executant in public affairs. I asked the Ariki Taumako in 1952 about his attitude towards his *maru*. He said he regarded as nearest to himself the brother nearest to him in age, Pa Ngarumea and the next brother in order, Pa Rangiuvea. If neither of these was available, then he would use one of the other brothers, and if one of them were not on hand then whomsoever of the other *maru* who might be. But he said that he used Vakasaumore as his major executive officer 'because he is strong in speech, therefore I as chief give my speech to him.' The other reason why he chose Vakasaumore was this man's knowledge of European ways.

During the period of our stay, Spillius and I had ample opportunity to observe the functioning of the *maru* system, and Spillius in particular studied it over a long period in connection with the control of social affairs during the famine. This was closely associated with the system of public meetings (*fono*).[1]

The status of *maru* was operative not only on formal public occasions, but also on informal occasions, even in private relations.[2] In 1952 I discussed

[1] See Chap. IV and, in particular, J. Spillius, *op. cit.* Spillius has in preparation an extensive study of the *fono* and the role of the *maru* therein.

[2] The term *maru* may be also used in an analogical sense. I was told by Pa Ngarumea on one occasion that I was for the Tikopia *te maru o nga ariki ki te tai*, 'the executant (or protector) of the chiefs towards the sea', that is, one whose function was to guard the chiefs in their external relations. This was an unusual explanation of the meaning of the term, and presumably had reference to the function of protection rather than executive power, since neither I nor Spillius assumed any direct executive role.

with Pa Motuata his participation in some pagan affairs of his chief, although he had been baptized as a Christian. I asked him did not the missionaries object. He expressed some surprise at this. He said 'They object, but it is all right.' Then he added 'Don't you know who I am? I am a *maru*. Nobody can object, because I am a *maru*. Did you not hear of *maru* before (in 1929)? What it is among Europeans is a policeman. I am just like him—a policeman. The Church which stands in my neighbourhood fears to oppose me.' This was boasting, but only partly so. As an elderly *maru* he was allowed great latitude. He did not participate as a rule in the public meetings, which tended to make him be looked upon by the people at large as of less weight than the younger *maru*. But in a crisis he could act with great effect. On one occasion he used his position to quell the beginnings of a fight, on another he used it to compel a ritual elder to return from setting out on an ocean voyage. Even in small matters he obtained respect. When he and another elderly man, a craftsman in wood, Pa Panapa, were with me one evening, we were looking at some photographs of headrests which I had collected on Tikopia in 1929. One of them was identified positively by Pa Motuata, who was leading the conversation, as the work of his companion, who did not deny this. The next day I saw Pa Panapa, and he said that in fact the headrest was not of his workmanship. He explained 'I did not speak because Pa Motuata spoke for me; because Pa Motuata is a *maru*, therefore I remained silent. No, I left it to him to make his statement. He had spoken.'

In 1952, as in 1929, the *maru* did not always act as a body of executive officers representing the views of the chiefs. To some extent they represented their own personal views in public affairs and, moreover, there were some factional deviations among them. Within the *maru* of a single clan public differences of view or conflict were not common. I asked Vakasaumore the question—what would happen if, say, the eldest son of a chief and the chief's younger brother spoke differently to the people? He answered that it did not happen thus; the chief would call them to meet beforehand and give directions on any matter on which they were likely to conflict. Basically this view seemed correct to me. When *maru* of the same clan stressed different aspects of a situation or took up different points in argument, it was to supplement one another, not in contradiction.

But there were more significant clashes between *maru* which were linked with structural cleavages in Tikopia society. While *maru* of different clans were usually at one in their views about basic policy for Tikopia, they were often by no means unanimous in their interpretation of how their policy was best to be carried out. For example, I heard from Spillius that when it was decided to block access for periods to a large section of Tikopia cultivations, one member of the chiefly house of Kafika vigorously protested against those measures which had been initiated by the *maru* of Taumako. He stalked off, declaring he would not conform. There were also other occasions on which *maru* publicly disagreed.

There was also another respect in which division of opinion tended to occur among *maru*, that is, because of the growth of Christianity. In 1929, the *maru* of Tafua were Christian, but only a few of those in the other clans were, and they were not the most powerful.

By 1952 there had been a most marked change in the balance of power. Most of the younger, more vigorous, *maru* were Christian. This led to a much more overt view than existed a generation before that there was a functional division in the society in matters of public policy. This was expressed in a variety of ways, only some of which had reference to the position and functions of *maru* (cf. pp. 80, 279). But as regards executants, a statement of Vakasaumore to me even before I saw Tikopia on the second occasion was symptomatic. He said 'Nowadays there are three *fono* which have gripped Tikopia—the *fono* of the chiefs, the *fono* of Government and the *fono* of the Church.' (Here the term *fono* is equivalent to jurisdiction.) He went on to say that formerly his grandfather, Pa Avakofe, had been very strong and the chiefs throughout the whole land valued his advice. Nowadays, he said, there was pulling in different ways. The land had become used to division. 'When a *maru* spoke formerly, the land valued him, there was only one *fono*. Nowadays the land has become different. Its basis is in us (pointing to himself), the chiefly house. I of the chiefly house of Taumako have gone out among the white men. From the chiefly house of Tafua, Mark Moana has gone out among the white men. From the chiefly house of Kafika, Remon (son of Pa Fenuatara named after me) has gone out among white men. I was the first of us to go.' He went on to say that after Pa Avakofe died his eldest son and the son of that man in turn did not have the same influence. People did not follow their advice. The land fell apart and *maru* lost their influence. There was a division into small spheres of influence (*viki fono*) with the traditional custom, Government and Christianity all affecting affairs. This argument he reinforced by citing the perennial theme—that formerly the chiefs had wished to kill off the commoners and keep the land for themselves when the population grew. He said that Pa Avakofe had put a stop to this. He was so powerful that if such an attempt had been made he would have objected and no chief would have opposed him. Even a chief (so Vakasaumore said) in such a case would have had to go off to sea! (This was an exaggeration.) Hence the land was kept in peace. His implication was that with this powerful personality no longer alive, and with the differences of policy manifest in each of the major spheres of influence, there was danger that as the population pressed once more against the means of subsistence, again the demand might arise among the chiefs to drive out the commoners. This time, he implied, it could not be resisted—although it would appear from his subsequent actions that he regarded himself as the natural successor to his grandfather and as the unifier of the land.

This view by Vakasaumore was forcibly expressed, and in some respects his fears were probably extreme. But the issues he saw in 1952 were very real. The Tikopia had been confronted for well over a generation by divergent sets of values and different sections had accepted different value schemes. For a small community of this kind, such differences spelt danger for integrated action in the face of acute economic and political problems.

This impression of inefficiency and danger in disunity was not shared to the same extent by all *maru*, even of Vakasaumore's own clan. On one occasion I listened to a discussion between the ritual elder, Pa Rarovi, and his son-in-law, Pa Ngarumea, the important *maru* of Taumako. Pa Rarovi was enveighing against the current theft and the inability of the *maru* to deal with it. He said that in former times that if a chief or another man of rank whooped in anger at a theft, the *maru* on all sides girded themselves, seized their weapons and sallied out to settle the trouble. Now it was not so. (This had been borne out by recent incidents when reports of thefts from chiefs produced no public reaction.) Talking in reference to Pa Ngarumea, Pa Rarovi said to me and others present that his son-in-law was the principal *maru* concerned with public affairs, but that he got no support from others. He said that his son-in-law was a *maru nga fakaarofa*, a shelterer of the commoners, that is, one who protected the common people from any exaction by chiefs and their families. But in the discussion ensuing, Pa Ngarumea himself made two interesting points. One was that if the *maru* of Tafua only lived nearer, he said, he would get support from them. This was in effect a dispassionate admission by him that district hostility and factionalism could be overcome in the interests of public policy. The *maru* of Tafua were of Faea and were Christian, whereas he was of Ravenga and was pagan, yet he regarded them as his allies for public order. His second point was that the work of *maru* was by this time (July 1952) rendered much more difficult because thefts were now being committed by some members of chiefly families and not only by commoners. The problem of punishing some of their own kind without exposing the *maru* as a whole to criticism inhibited the *maru* from taking very strong action in such cases.

SUMMARY AND PROSPECTS

To sum up, it may be said that Tikopia society had in operation in 1952 a political system of chiefs and executants of the same form as before, with the same general functions. The role of the executants as mouthpieces of the chiefs and with collective responsibility for law and order was as before. The respect given to them by the people at large was also of the same general kind. Some of them were new men, but some were the same as before. What had changed over the generation had been an intensification of the need for their function, and a realization among them that, while they shared a basic common policy, their sectional interests were more marked than before because of their different religious allegiances. Moreover, there was a growing requirement that these political functions should be exercised in relation to the overriding position of an external Government.

In 1929, the personal authority of the aged Pa Avakofe still threw a mantle over the preservation of order in Tikopia. He represented still a single influence to which all chiefs and other men of rank could appeal and to which they deferred. In that sense he represented *organizationally* for public order the principle of unified authority which *structurally* did not exist in the

Tikopia system. The relative lack of definition of status and functions of *maru* which, in 1929, had led to some clashes, by 1952, with a lack of unified authority, had been able to come to more overt expression. This was facilitated by the lack of any political hierarchy among the chiefs and the fact that their authority could be exercised in the land as a whole only in a conjoint way. For the most part, in 1952 the *maru* of the different parts of the island operated independently but in supplemental fashion, each keeping to his own sphere of jurisdiction but recognizing a common responsibility. It was an index of the strength of these responsibilities that at a time of such acute crisis as the famine there was so little challenge and clash among these executive officers, either on personal or on structural grounds.

Prediction in this field is difficult, but two factors make it probable that Tikopia once again may have a more unified system of authority. With the conversion of the whole population to Christianity in 1956, the deep gap in values on religious grounds will have been bridged and, to some extent, this should facilitate the co-operation of *maru* of different clans and different districts. Moreover, the increasing contacts with the external Government may well supply that ultimate judgment to which chiefs and *maru* can refer to secure an integrated approach to their problems.

How will the chiefs stand in future? In 1952 it appeared to be the Government view that until much closer administrative supervision from outside was possible. the Tikopia must be left to run their own day-to-day administration in terms of thier own authority system. This seemed to be sound policy. But as contact grows, the Government will need to use more intensively the services of agents of communication with the Tikopia. So long as they accept the Tikopia system of authority the power of the chiefs is likely to be increased by this. Here would seem to be the possibility of the emergence of a system of indirect rule in classic style as by a council of chiefs.

With the clearer emergence of the Tikopia chief as a secular authority, recognition of him as such by the Government is likely to consolidate his general status. This may seem to conflict with situations in the community— e.g. the tribute payments in which the decay of his ritual sanctions has meant also the decay of his political authority. But in one basic sphere the Tikopia chief is still in control, in that he is still regarded by others in the community as having an overright in clan lands. While this persists, while there is no system of record of title and registration on Tikopia, the public recognition that in the last resort a chief has a major control in land rights is a most powerful strengthening of his position.

The power of the chiefs is likely to increase relative to the commoners in another way, that is in contrast to the change in the role and status of ritual elders. Formerly, the more important ritual elders were men of great influence because of the general belief that they controlled most powerful gods. To some extent then in community affairs they acted as a counterpoise to the power of the chief, and they were important leaders of the commoners.

By 1952, while the conversion of one chief to Christianity had not radically threatened his authority, the authority of ritual elders was rapidly drawing to an end. Once the *raison d'être* of the office of ritual elder ceased with his conversion to Christianity, his political functions were likely to wither. Hence, the chiefs and their close agnates are likely for a time to obtain increased political power, while the commoners, represented in particular by the ritual elders, may have their political power diminished. Yet in the long run the external Government cannot remain indifferent to the attitudes of the ordinary people. Moreover, to some extent the Mission teachers can serve as an alternative channel of communication, particularly in reporting on whether the administration, through the chiefs, is effective and just. There are then some controls over the development of despotic powers by the chiefs and their close kin.

How will the *maru* stand in future? I would think that as executants for the chiefs they are likely to retain their importance. There are several alternatives here. In 1952 they were the only purely secular authority. Unrecognized by Government then, if a more formal system of public administration were instituted on Tikopia, they might now become an overt and important element in the official system of social control. They might, for example, operate as local headmen under the aegis of a council of chiefs. But even if unofficially operative, they may still be very significant. As executive requirements grow with the increasing importance of the relationship of the chiefs to the external Government, the role of the *maru* in issuing the chiefs' orders and in conducting public assemblies may be strengthened correspondingly—whether Government realizes this or not. But the overt recognition by the Tikopia that chiefs have a duty to the people and that *maru* should protect the people as well as the chiefs, may act as a brake upon the exercise of undue political power by the chiefs and some of their close agnates. The *maru* may even emerge to a more independent status as expressing the interests and will of the people against the chiefs if the latter prove too dominating. Again, perhaps in the long run more probably some *maru* may come to stand out as individual leaders, claiming their right to leadership by traditional status but in fact basing it upon their education, their sophistication in Western ways and their personal qualities. In this capacity, especially if Government takes an increasing responsibility for Tikopia communal welfare, the *maru* may virtually come to be the representatives not of community requirements and views but of sectional, even factional, interests.

In any event, much of the political future of Tikopia for a long time to come will depend upon the structural position of the persons whom the Tikopia will select and the Government will accept as local representatives.

CHAPTER X

Modifications in Social Control

Operational Concept of Social Control

The term 'social control' may have a wide range of meaning. It may refer to any ways in which the very fact of living in a society may influence the conduct of a member of that society. Usually, however, it refers more specifically to those ways in which a society maintains order among its members, keeps them from 'doing wrong', from anti-social behaviour, contrary to accepted standards. The very notion of control itself implies a direction, a command of action in reference to some conception of stability, a restraint of deviation from a norm. In Hoebel's words, 'The entire operating system of sanctioning norms is what constitutes a system of social control.'[1] Elaborating this, we may say that social control involves: a system of *values* of the society; a set of *categories* in which these values are expressed; *rules* for guidance about behaviour; *procedures* for establishing whether rules are kept or not and for taking action accordingly; and *sanctions*, positive and negative, whereby conformity to rules is promoted.

In anthropological analysis the automatic character of the forces of social control has been often exaggerated. All societies are faced by this problem of controlling actions of their members. But in this they are faced by the problem of deciding what actions are most *relevant* for control—in cases of infringement of norms, what are significant and what are merely trivial, what are primarily of public and what are of private concern? There are also questions of *efficiency*, of economy involved. When infringement occurs, what amount of resources is the society prepared to devote to the job of control, in view of the other calls on the time and energy of its members? There are also questions of *interrelationship* and *implications*. How far will application of sanctions in one direction, however desirable in itself, affect or interfere with action in other directions? So, when an offence is committed there may be a considerable area of uncertainty in which alternative interpretations, alternative courses of action, are possible. The result may be the imposition of sanctions or it may be only an apathy, a tolerant shrug, a resentful admission of weakness, a verbal criticism or other substitute for more positive action. The existence of these alternative possibilities is strengthened by the fact that 'the society' does not act en masse, but must be represented by individuals or groups of people among whom identity of interest and unanimity of opinion cannot always be secured.

I hold that this 'open-ended' character of social control is operative to

[1] E. Adamson Hoebel, *The Law of Primitive Man*, Cambridge, Mass., 1954, p. 15.

some degree even in a highly integrated society with developed governmental mechanisms. But this lack of automatic response of sanctions, this area of uncertainty in judgment and in action, is likely to be particularly evident when more than one system of norms is in operation, each being operated by separate mechanisms, not arranged in any hierarchy of control.

TRADITIONAL AND MODERN NORMS

This was so in Tikopia in 1929 and in 1952. At both periods a system of norms recognized by the Tikopia themselves as traditional was in operation side by side with another system of norms recognized by them as the result of the recent introduction of Christianity. Aligned with the Christian set of norms were others derived from the Solomon Islands Government, but in 1929 contact with this was so infrequent that in practice these norms were confused with those of Christianity and so interpreted by the Mission representative. By 1952, some differentiation between Government norms and Mission norms had begun to emerge and was clarified by administrative action (see p. 284). But in general the coincidence of these norms in the major fields of action was so great that for our purposes they may be considered together.

I now want to compare and contrast the traditional or pagan system and the modern or Christian system. To a considerable degree their respective effectiveness depended upon the extent to which they were congruent or non-congruent. Congruence between the two systems did broadly relate to certain major spheres of action. Both systems of norms reprobated personal violence on the one hand and unauthorized interference with property on the other. Both stigmatized lying, both placed a high value on respect-relations to certain categories of persons and things. But there were some marked exceptions from coincidence within these spheres and a marked difference of view about many of the kinds of persons and things to be respected. Congruent norms included disapproval of murder, assault, theft and lying, approval of respect to a father, a married woman and God. Non-congruent norms included a few which were strongly held by pagans and towards which Christian values were neutral—such as first-cousin marriage and many of the ceremonial exchanges at marriage, initiation and funerals. There were some strongly held by Christians, to which pagans were neutral or even benevolently inclined, such as not doing major work on the Sabbath and refraining from dancing in Lent. There were others which were regarded with approval by pagans but which were completely repugnant to Christianity—infanticide, abortion, polygyny, sex relations between the unmarried, and ritual acts of worship, offering, libation and even dancing oriented to the pagan gods. For the most part it was the norms of paganism which were repugnant to Christianity rather than the reverse—partly because to all Tikopia the norms of Christianity were held to represent to a very large degree those of the modern sophisticated Western world which they admired. Structurally, the system of social control with the dual set of norms had not changed greatly in Tikopia in the generation between 1929 and 1952. The external pressures were still much of the same general order. Internally there was almost the same division of responsibility for order between three pagan chiefs and one Christian chief (the Christian Ariki Fangarere being almost negligible from this point of view). The Melanesian priest still led the Christian faction as he had a generation earlier. Organizationally, however, there were some very significant changes. In particular, there had been a radical extension of the area of operation of Christian norms. From applying specifically to only half of the population in 1929, they now applied to nearly 90 per cent. This involved various consequential modifications, including a relative inability of the pagans to maintain some of their own norms among their own body. With it also was linked a much greater influence of the Mission teachers and a greater unification of social control under the general lead of the Melanesian priest.

I proceed now to examine Tikopia social control in more detail. Here I shall differentiate between Christian and pagan only where their norms are not congruent. In great areas of social behaviour it is possible to speak simply of Tikopia without religious specification. Since the main change between 1929 and 1952 was an enlargement of the body of personnel affected rather than in any major alteration in the systems of norms as such, I shall give the initial part of my analysis without any specific comparison of period.

VALUES AND CATEGORIES OF EXPRESSION

I have mentioned how many of the values of Christianity fitted closely into those which characterized traditional Tikopia society. Rules such as 'Honour thy father and thy mother', 'Thou shalt not kill', 'Thou shalt not steal', appealed to pagan Tikopia as reformulations under another aegis of values acknowledged by their own society. Where differences of opinion occurred was in two respects. Those circumstances in which the rule was held to be not applicable included for Christian Tikopia killing of an enemy in war, but excluded abortion and infanticide; these the pagan Tikopia regarded as allowable, having reference to the major object of restriction of population for conservation of food supply. Secondly, Christians argued but pagan Tikopia were only half-inclined to agree, that Tikopia society until quite recent times had been characterized by a great deal of killing in pursuit of private ambition, and that this was the nature of Tikopia society *per se*.

But in other fields the coincidence of value and of practice was close. Take, for example, the value expressed in the Tikopia general statement '*Te fafine avenga e tapu*' (a married woman is sacred). While expressed in the form of affirmation, this was in reality not a ritual statement but an injunction relating to social action. A married woman should be respected. Strictly speaking, from the Christian view man and woman united by traditional Tikopia custom might not be regarded as married. But I did not at any time hear either the Melanesian priest or any Christian Tikopia raise this issue. Christian and pagan alike accepted the traditional ceremony as constituting a woman as 'married' in the full social sense of the term, and entitled to all the respect which the traditional injunction laid down. The idea that a married woman was sacred implied to the Tikopia two things in particular: that no man should offer violence to her; and that she should not be available sexually to anyone but her husband. It was difficult to say how far the overt expression of these opinions did actually result in the appropriate behaviour in everyday life. But, from my observations in 1929, as in 1952, there was very close conformity of action to rule. By comparison with other types of behaviour in the same general range, striking a married woman was very rare, and so also was adultery with a married woman. Yet striking an un-married girl was by no means uncommon, and sex relations with unmarried women were very common. Neither of these latter types of behaviour aroused any particular public reaction of criticism, whereas in respect of a married woman very grave censure was likely to follow.[1] A similar differentiation between married and unmarried was not applied to the same degree to men. To strike a married man was not necessarily more open to reproof than to strike an unmarried man. It could be more dangerous because his power of personal retaliation and summoning assistance might be greater. A pro-hibition of some ritual force was in operation, that he should not be struck upon the head. In playing single-stick, for example, an unmarried man would be very careful if his opponent was a married man to touch him only in the ribs or arms and not to tap him on the head, as young men commonly did with one another. Adultery by a married man, though a matter of some talk and laughing criticism, was not taken to be a very serious affair unless he got the woman concerned with child.

The proposition about the sacred quality of a married woman might then be said to express an important congruent *value* of Tikopia paganism and Tikopia Christianity—the value of woman as wife and mother, as focus of domesticity, as symbol in some contexts of spiritual entities of great power. It was a value of demonstrable sociological significance. Parallel to it were many other propositions—about the sacredness of chiefs, the propriety of specific kinds of ceremonial exchanges, etc. But while such propositions were of basic importance as ultimate referents for action and were regarded as justified in themselves, they were for the most part too general to be effective guides to action. Nor could they provide a very direct approach to the subject of social control. They were supplemented by a wide range of more specific affirmations. These were of the order of 'A son must not take anything from above the head of his father'; 'If a man has gone off to sea without the per-mission of his chief and should be brought back, he should go to his chief with a ceremonial gift of atonement (*malai*)', and so on. There were many such formulations used by the Tikopia to point up the nature of right conduct and to pass judgment upon any particular item of behaviour. They referred to treatment of persons and property, and together they might be said to constitute the corpus of Tikopia rules of social behaviour. Collectively they formed a very important part of what might be called the 'customs' of Tikopia

[1] Cf. *We, The Tikopia*, pp. 132, 133–4, 394.

—a term for which the people themselves had the word '*tukutukunga*', which might be translated literally as 'things laid down'.

In such formulations, and in the judgment of actions, the Tikopia used two general categories of description, each with its antithesis. One was the category of correctness or rightness (*tonu*), with its antithesis of incorrectness or wrongness (*sise e tonu: sara*). The other was the category of goodness (*laui*), with its antithesis of badness (*sise e laui: pariki*). Such terms had a very wide range and might be applied in what we would classify as the aesthetic sphere as well as in the moral sphere. In application to the field of social control, they covered etiquette and manners as well as public order.[1]

These concepts on the positive and negative side respectively were very closely allied. Normally, that which was correct was good, that which was incorrect was bad. But they could be differentiated in some spheres. The test of correctness might be applied to accuracy of reproduction—for instance, to the copying of a design properly; to the repetition of a message accurately; or to the performance of a ritual set of actions in traditional order. Failure to perform these acts accurately might not necessarily be stigmatized as 'bad'. For example, to make an error in the accuracy of reproduction of a design could be termed *sara*, but would not necessarily be classed as *pariki*. But such a category slid over very easily into the field of moral judgment so that an action which was not an accurate reproduction easily became classified as one which was morally wrong. How far did such categories fit those of Christianity in Tikopia? In fact, the Tikopia expressions served for Christian categories of social control quite well, including moral categories. In particular, the term *sara*, used by the Tikopia to indicate an offence, particularly a ritual offence such as a breach of taboo, was adopted by Tikopia Christians as an equivalent for the term 'sin'.

But there was a difference between the traditional pagan attitude and the Christian attitude. To a Tikopia pagan, demarcation of actions which could be classified as *sara* was different from that adopted by Christian Tikopia. Both included under *sara* such acts as insults to a chief, or violence offered to a married woman. Both would probably include actions such as desertion of a wife or adultery by a married woman, though their judgment might be affected by specific circumstances. But they parted company in the ritual field. To a pagan Tikopia interference by unauthorized persons with objects classified as *tapu* would be *sara* and liable to be punished supernaturally by illness sent by gods or ancestors. To Christian Tikopia the degree to which this would be classified as *sara* depended upon their devotion to their faith. To the more zealous Christians such acts would be classified as righteous operations against 'dark things', but many Tikopia Christians as well as pagans would still look for illness or other misfortune to follow such inter-

---

[1] There were subsidiary terms to express various degrees of approbation or disapproval. For example, *taurekareka*, a term of praise, meaning when applied to a woman 'very handsome', or to weather 'very fine', meant in respect of actions, 'very appropriate' or 'highly approved'. On the other hand, *fakakinokino* meant 'very ugly', 'disgusting', 'at the depth of disapproval'.

ference.[1] To Christian Tikopia actions that were *sara* were then such as were indicated in the Ten Commandments, the punishment for which was withdrawal of God's favour. The second way in which *sara* differed between the two parties was that the imputation of *intention* was much more developed in the Christian attitude. Unwitting sin was very feasible for pagans; for Christians it presented a more difficult question. Of course for both Christian and pagan Tikopia there were human as well as superhuman sanctions involved when *sara* were committed.

Another Tikopia category closely allied with that of goodness but bearing a more substantival quality was that of *arofa*. This concept may be variously translated as sympathy, affection, love. In the traditional Tikopia scheme of social relations many actions were explained as being done from *arofa*. If they were explained as being done from *arofa* alone, this might imply that no specific kind of reciprocity was involved. But there were many degrees of interpretation possible here. This concept was applicable to great common areas of social relationship by Christian and by pagan Tikopia. By extension from the use of the concept in ordinary human affairs as between members of a family, it could also refer to relations between men and their ancestors or their gods. From descendant to ascendant *arofa* was shown by protection of the graves of the dead and by various memorial observances. By ascendant to descendant among pagan Tikopia *arofa* was shown, it was believed, by protection from danger at sea, by relief from poverty through promoting fertility of crops and fish and by protection from illness. But this *arofa* was manifest in practical affairs and material benefits, not in abstract, ideal, emotional relationship. One of the basic themes in Christianity is the love of God for man and the reciprocal obligation for man to love God. For this the Christian Tikopia used the term *arofa*. In Western views to interpret such love primarily in material services rendered by the other party would be to degrade the concept. In this sense very few Christian Tikopia indeed seemed to hold the general ideal interpretation. It was assimilated to the practical concept that love of God for man on Tikopia was manifest in abundant crops, freedom from disease and from disaster. Christian and pagan Tikopia seemed to share in 1952, as in 1929, the same category of *arofa* and to interpret it in almost the same way, although with reference to different religious entities. There was, however, one respect in which the Christian concept of *arofa* indirectly differed from the pagan aspect, and that was as regards ideals of peace in relations between man and man. Christians in Tikopia, like those elsewhere, by no means lived up to this ideal. But it was one of the achievements of the Mission and of the Melanesian priest in particular that the grosser forms of physical violence in Tikopia (including infanticide and occasional adult killing) had been practically eliminated. Tikopia leaders themselves played some part in this change, but there is no doubt that the Mission was the major influence.

In 1952 then, such general categories as I have mentioned and propositions regarding conduct in which they were embodied, were regarded by the Tikopia

[1] See *We, The Tikopia*, pp. 48–9.

as equally valid as in 1929. There were, however, in some fields of action differences in the degree to which these propositions were followed out.

The simplest way in which to approach our problem of modifications in Tikopia social control over a generation is to consider what actions were regarded by the Tikopia as relevant for public order. These became the subject of judgment by others in terms of categories, such as those just examined, and tended to involve consequential actions by other members of the society.

PROCEDURE IN CASES OF ACTIONS AGAINST THE PERSON

I consider first actions against the person directly. Assaults especially resulting in wounding or homicide were stigmatized in 1952, as in 1929, as being bad (*pariki*). They were not usually classified as incorrect in the sense of sinful (*sara*), although if a commoner were to assault a chief then this classification would almost certainly have been made.

But what constituted an offence here? Abortion and infanticide (by smothering) were 'causing the belly to flow', and 'turning down the face of the infant' respectively. They were in a different category from homicide by striking a person (*ta tangata*). Not all forms of assault were classified as bad. Some were given justification and approval by the traditional customs of the society. In 1929, in the traditional form of marriage, especially between people of rank, it was customary for the kinsmen of the groom to make formal apology and obeisance to the kinsmen of the bride, and even to be pummelled by the bride's kin. This pummelling was usually vigorous and sometimes violent, expressing some real resentment at the ravishment of the bride. Though sociologically it could be regarded as a cathartic as well as a hostility symbol, such an assault was not regarded as bad because it did not so much threaten social order as maintain it. According to custom, no resistance was made by the party making the apology.[1] But care was taken by responsible men to see that those of high rank among the visitors were to some extent protected from the blows, and they might be assisted to reach the side of the bride's chief, whereupon the pummelling ceased. By 1952 this custom was apparently obsolete. Such turbulence was not in keeping with the ideas of marriage promulgated by the Christians, and was regarded as out of keeping with the times, although judgment regarding it had not altered to the extent of classifying the violence as bad.

In the traditional Tikopia sphere of control, no public action necessarily followed in cases of assault, even if wounding or homicide resulted. Any subsequent action was at the incidence of the offended individual or his immediate kin. Organized or unorganized, this was unofficial. It was a sanction of retaliation rather than of punishment. In many cases, no overt action against the offender followed at all.

According to tradition, when Pu Atafu of Tafua was killed by Pa Resiake of Taumako and his brother, the Ariki Kafika of the day expressed great

[1] *We, The Tikopia*, pp. 544–5.

U

horror. But although the premier chief of Tikopia, he was said to have mobilized no forces to punish the killers, nor to have taken any action himself. The father of the man who was killed, though Ariki Tafua, took no vengeance. In his sorrow and anger he lifted off his neck a prized shell pendant and smashed it on a stone; that seems to have been his only expression of resentment and grief. But in understanding this situation, it should be noted that the man who was killed had been a bully and a bravo, and had made a habit of stalking through the land challenging all comers. It was argued by the Taumako folk that their ancestors finally took action because they could no longer endure his braggadacio. Mobilization against a killer might occur, but not be brought to a conclusion. When some time previously to 1928 Pa Teva, in a dispute over an orchard, shot Pa Raropupua with an arrow, perhaps accidentally, perhaps intending to wound, the man died and there was pursuit of the killer mobilized by the Ariki Tafua. But further action was then inhibited by the Ariki Kafika on the grounds that the people of Tafua had previously taken away the sister of Pa Teva to be married to one of their young men, and so he argued an equivalent had already been obtained.

In short, the characterization of actions as offences involved reference to several criteria: who committed them; against whom they were committed; the circumstances in which they were committed. Judgment of the act as bad might be followed by retaliation or punishment or not, according as those criteria varied. What in general was not called into question was the *intention* of the person who committed the action. Purposeful or accidental wounding of a person, or homicide, was judged by its results, not by its motivations.

Cases of violence against the person in 1952/3 were few—surprisingly rare considering the circumstances of strain over the famine, which tended to inflame tempers and which might be thought to have provoked much more widespread brawling and personal attack. The rarity of these cases of violence was an indication of the degree to which the Tikopia expressed their tensions verbally rather than by physical assault. The mode of reaction to offences against the person seemed to be of the same order as a generation before. Personal attack was stigmatized, but was judged in terms of its results rather than of its intention. The response to it was left as before to interested individuals and was not treated primarily as a matter of public policy.

There was one exception to this both in 1929 and a generation later. When a dispute reached the stage of physical violence, then a *maru* might step in to restore order. The function of the *maru*, as examined already, was primarily that of keeper of the peace. His role was not basically that of a judge. He was concerned with evaluation of the situation and advice on the outcome, primarily from the point of view of public order. Hence, he first quelled the disturbance, then enquired into it, and sent both parties away with injunctions to remain at peace.

Here is an example of the procedure as narrated by a *maru* himself. In April 1952, there was a fight in Namo over yams. Sa Torokinga of Kafika alleged that sa Rongoifo of Taumako had stolen yams from their orchard. Both sides battered the roofs of houses and the son of Pa Rongoifo struck one of his antagonists on the head. One of these men, in turn, stood with his bow and arrow ready to fire when a *maru*, Pa Motuata, appeared. As soon as he grasped the situation he entered a house, took down a club and strode out to the scene. Someone said 'Keep quiet, all of you. Don't you see a *maru* standing there?' The leader of the Torokinga faction then came and knelt down before him, pressing his nose to his knee in token of apology, and begging him to desist from his threatening attitude. So the fight ended. Then Pa Motuata went on his way, leaving a subdued village behind him. As he went, he saw a party from another hamlet coming along to take issue in the dispute, and quietened them too. So effective was his action that when, later that morning, we arrived in the village, it was absolutely quiet and no one at that time mentioned the recent affray to us. When Pa Motuata talked of it to us later, he said that the people would have been ashamed to tell us about it. I have no record of a challenge ever made to such exercise of authority by a *maru*.

This incident illustrates a type of offence in Tikopia which may be classified as *disturbance of the chief's peace*. In 1952, as in 1929, this included a range of anti-social actions, from making a loud noise by yelling or beating the roof of one's house in anger where a chief is sitting or sleeping, to direct contravention of a chief's orders. Included also were interference in a chief's sphere of interest as by carrying off a woman of his clan in marriage or going off to sea in a canoe without his permission—if one was his clansman or resident in his neighbourhood. All of these were actions within a chief's physical or social jurisdiction, and liable to cause him loss or unease. Action taken in regard to them was in two stages. One was the restoration of order as by imposing cessation of violence, seeking the return of the person lost, etc. The next stage was one of formal apology and of a symbolic restitution to the chief in the form of valuable property. This atoning gift, known as the *malai*,[1] normally consisted of a wooden bowl, a hank of sinnet cord and a bonito hook, accompanied by a presentation of cooked food. For disturbances of a minor character no *malai* was usually offered, though some formal apology was usually made to the chief's representative (as in the case just quoted); or to the chief himself.

There were in 1952 no assaults against men of chiefly lineages, although relations at times very strained and physical violence seemed near. But although no cases occurred, the principle which operated a generation before still seemed to have general agreement—namely that the judgment of the offence in a case of assault differed according to the relative social status of the persons involved. The general principle in Tikopia in 1952, as in 1929, appeared to be that members of the chiefly lineages could perform violent acts, especially against commoners, with little or no check, whereas conversely a commoner was likely to incur severe punishment if he committed violence against a person of chiefly lineage. To the outside observer this might appear

[1] *We, The Tikopia*, pp. 544–6; *Primitive Polynesian Economy*, p. 375.

unjust. By the Tikopia too when such actions were commented upon it was often implied that they were unjust; their judgment did not disregard the man-to-man relation. But in the field of overt action it was governed by respect to status differences. The implication here in 1952 as in 1929 was that in Tikopia society status difference in itself was a good thing—that it was part of the moral and quasi-legal fabric of the society.

It was in such circumstances that the Tikopia often uttered a kind of balanced judgment, which linguistically might seem contradictory. One such expression was, *E laui kae pariki*, 'It is good, yet bad' or as we should say 'Although in general it is a proper action, yet it has also its bad side.' Another expression, more cautious, was *E laui kae sise laui fakalaui*—'It's good, but not good properly.'

With this balanced judgment was also linked classifications of actions as offences according to the degree to which any particular individual or group was affected. Assault, for example, might be defended by one group as response against encroachment upon land boundary, but stigmatized by another group as being out of proportion to the original act of trespass. This showed again how it was the result, not the intention, which was primarily the object of judgment. It also demonstrated how there was no overall authority in Tikopia which summed up in terms either of intention or result, and which uttered final judgment representing the opinion of the community at large. In this sense then there was no 'law' in Tikopia in 1952 any more than in 1929.

In this chapter I have spoken of the sphere of social control and not that of law, partly in order to avoid controversy as to the nature of 'law', and partly because in Tikopia there was a great deal of social control which did not conform to any of the ordinary definitions of law. In particular, the conventional reference to the ultimate effectiveness of law through the exercise (or potential exercise) of force by a politically organized society did not fit the Tikopia situation too closely. Much of the controlling force exercised or threatened, took place *within* a politically organized society, but was not fully *representative* of that society. It sought public benefit by private gain. On the other hand, much of the control was obtained by suasion, not force; the appeal was to sympathy, not strength, although such an appeal might have almost binding quality.

Yet this situation in itself was relative to social conditions. As the famine developed, and as a more unified approach to problems of preservation of supplies of food became more urgent, some form of final judgment began to emerge through the agency of the public assembly, the *fono*.[1] Even here, however, there was no overall judgment for the Tikopia community as a whole. There were two *fono*, one on each side of the island, and for the most part they operated independently.

I have shown that Tikopia attitudes in regard to actions against the person maintained their character over a generation, and that reaction to offences tended to be either unorganized and personal, or if organized, to be unofficial.

[1] See J. Spillius, *op. cit* and Chap. IV of this book.

This is demonstrated similarly in reference to the supreme action against the self, suicide. In 1929, Tikopia reactions to suicide or attempted suicide were physically very much of the same order as found in a Western society. Members of a community tried to prevent a suicide attempt, sought vigorously for a person suspected of attempting to commit suicide, and so on. Yet while they might describe the attempt as stupid, ill-advised or unnecessary, they did not regard it primarily as an offence against the community. There was no moral stigma attached. Nor was there anything equivalent to punishment for a person who had failed in an attempt at suicide. There was to some extent a view that in committing suicide a person was depriving his lineage and his chief of a member and in that sense was committing wrong against them. But this point of view was never pushed. A person who tried to commit suicide and failed normally presented an offering of atonement and apology to his chief. But this was to meet the repairing of a canoe or the labour of the principal persons concerned in mobilizing and leading a searching fleet, or the disregard of the chief's authority in going off without his permission. It was not compensation for the attempt at suicide so much as for having caused such a great deal of public trouble.

In 1952 the same procedures obtained. Every attempt was made to prevent would-be suicides from accomplishing their purpose—often at the risk of the lives of those who sought for the missing person at sea. Some form of apology was commonly made to the chief of the clan of the person concerned. Material compensation was not necessarily offered; this, however, had its traditional analogue; I have from the pre-1929 era at least one case of lack of compensation of a similar type.

One might have expected some change in the treatment of would-be suicide with the much greater hold of Christianity upon the community. Since according to the Christian faith he who takes his own life imperils his soul, one might have thought then that religious sanctions might have been brought to bear against the persons who attempted to commit suicide and failed. Nothing of this kind had occurred by 1952. Mission teachers tried to dissuade would-be canoe-voyagers in the same way as any other people of rank in Tikopia did. But with Christian as with pagan, the reaction was the same; no attention was paid to any views of the Church as such in this matter, if indeed such views were expressed or understood. The religious sanction here had not been effectively integrated or internalized by the Tikopia Christians. One reason for this was that the borderline between intention of suicide and grave risk to life, with the intention to preserve it, was by no means clear-cut. With Tikopia men the grave risk of loss of their lives was undertaken in overseas voyages in which the prospect of death from drowning, starvation or exposure was very high indeed. In relation to offences committed, the suicide voyage was an escape from jurisdiction. A person who had committed some very grave offence or who had taken umbrage at some offence thought to have been committed against him, placed himself beyond reach of the community by evasion. If he was fortunate, this evasion would lead him to another land. If not, he perished at sea. But his canoe flight also served the purpose of expiation. If he was brought back by a searching party, or indeed if he returned of his own free will, his offence was not further brought up against him. He made his apology to his chief in particular, and by implication to the community at large, and was once more accepted as a fully functioning member of the society. Such was the traditional Tikopia attitude, and this was operative in 1952 as in 1929, among Christians as among pagans.

But by the latter date another kind of sanction had developed. As communications improved, the Government of the British Solomon Islands Protectorate became more aware of the frequency as well as of the implications of these risk-voyages. In general, the Government deplored canoe-voyaging where risk to life was so great that the voyager had probably much less than an even chance of survival. On the other hand, the Government ban on recruiting of labourers from Tikopia, which was in force until 1949, stimulated attempts at overseas voyaging. Young men took to their canoes and risked their lives to go abroad.[1] It was clear that so long as the existing Tikopia convention obtained that canoe voyaging was a legitimate solution of some difficulties, both communal and personal, the prevention of it by Government would have to be given effect by the provision of some alternatives—primarily avenues for gaining experience and income abroad by young men. With the opening up of recruiting again in 1949, the Government was once more in a position to take a strong line in prohibiting or at least discouraging such overseas canoe voyages by Tikopia. One can perhaps foresee the day when what to the Tikopia is flight from the results of an offence will become itself a new offence—when someone who takes his canoe out upon the ocean will be punished for disobeying a Government order. But by 1952 this day had not yet come.

Two further types of conduct which may be brought under the general head of interference with the person may be considered here—adultery, and mortuary behaviour.

Tikopia reactions to adultery appeared to be the same in 1952 as a generation before. No cases of adultery by a married woman were recorded in 1952,[2] and one of the two cases noted of adultery by a married man was strongly denied by the man in question. But from general reactions it seemed that the Tikopia viewed such a breach of sex relations as primarily a domestic matter. Although adultery by a woman was regarded as very grave, in contrast to that by a man, which was held to be only venial, in neither case was organized reaction on the part of other members of the community held to be appropriate. It was regarded as right for the other partner in the marriage to take action, assisted perhaps by his or her kin, but there was no general public move. It appeared that officials of the Church might be more ready than a generation before to take public action against an adulterer, but this was as part of their general reprobation of sex activities outside marriage, and not in specific reference to adultery.

[1] For heavy loss of life incurred, see W. D. Borrie, Raymond Firth and James Spillius, *op. cit.* p. 240.
[2] Cf. *We, The Tikopia*, p. 132.

There was some significant changes in mortuary behaviour affecting the person, in the generation between my observations. As in 1929, so in 1952, there was no particular respect shown to the corpse, no hushed voices or silence around the body as is common in Western Christian communities. Nor was the dead body taboo as among the Maori and some other Oceanic communities, and no purification rites had to be performed after contact with a corpse or funeral effects. But the actual burial practice had altered. Although the traditional practice of intra-dwelling inhumation was still followed in a few cases, most pagans as well as all Christians were now buried some distance away from the house—though not usually in a regular cemetery. This was primarily a change in custom due to Christian influence, expressing European views. The treatment of themselves by the mourners had also altered. In 1929 the death of a person was signalized by widespread hair-cutting on the part of the male kin. Chiefs and some other senior men alone did not shear their hair, but younger men, especially, did so. In 1952 nearly all the young men wore their hair short in any case, either because they had been abroad to work and had adopted the style current elsewhere, or because they had copied this fashion at home. A funeral, therefore, brought very little hair-cutting. Correspondingly, the wearing of circlets of hair of husbands or brothers by women was tending to decrease, though it was still quite common. In particular, the more violent, more 'savage' mortuary practices were falling into disuse. Among pagans, and to some degree among Christians, signs of grief such as branding the face with glowing twists of bark-cloth, or tearing at the cheeks with finger nails so that blood flowed, were still current. But they were done much less frequently, and with less intensity than before. In 1929 a frequent custom was for men to gash their foreheads with sharp knives at the death of someone closely akin. In 1952 many elderly men could still be seen with upright ridges on their foreheads, the result of such gashing in the past. But the actual practice had been completely abandoned by Christians, with a rationalization that their foreheads were taboo because it was there they had been baptized with the sign of the Cross. Pagans too appeared to have abandoned this custom. In the whole field of mortuary behaviour, then, the influence of the Church had been to push the Tikopia towards more conformity with Western usage.

Now what about interference with the personality, though not in a physical form? Here the Tikopia had several categories of social action. Slander (*fatufatu*) was feared and resented, and Tikopia frequently made enquiries as to who might have been slandering them. The discovery of the offender was a matter for recrimination and sometimes an exchange of blows. The offended person might go in protest to his lineage elder or to his chief in order to try and set himself right at the seat of power. But there was no provision for any public accusation of a slanderer or for his punishment. In this the situation was similar in 1952 to that of 1929.

As regards beliefs in sorcery (*tautuku*), the advance of Christianity between 1929 and 1952 did not seem to have effectively lessened the *belief* in the powers of evil magic among people of middle age, whether Christian or pagan.[1] In 1952 the power of sorcery was still attributed to Christians as well as to pagans but, as before, though private accusation and complaint was made, there were no public measures in the Tikopia system to deal with this phenomenon. Unlike the position in some African societies, Tikopia commoners could and did (privately) accuse chiefs and other men of rank of sorcery. Hence, beliefs in sorcery were not structured to support or reflect social order in this positive respect, though they might serve as a negative sanction. Since the Tikopia did not make any public accusation of sorcery, there was no need for any embarrassing public trial or other contretemps. So to a certain extent sorcery accusations could have a cathartic, safety-valve function since no community action was expected. Yet there were two areas of uncertainty of judgment here. One was whether in fact any overt act of sorcery had been committed. Accusations of this were as often denied as made. It was rarely admitted by a person that he had performed sorcery, although he might admit privately (e.g. to me or to his friends) that it was in his power to do so should he wish. Part of the difficulty in identification here was that much of the effect desired was thought to be obtained by the recital of appeals to spirits with only the minimum of ritual. Hence, it was very difficult for any one to check whether any particular spell had been laid on a person or not. The second difficulty was that all sorcery was regarded as evil, in that it was intended to be destructive of man or his property. (I have never heard any Tikopia say that sorcery in general or any specific act of sorcery was 'good'.) On the other hand, the degree to which sorcery could be regarded as an offence might vary. As in many other communities, powers of sorcery were regarded as being used for the punishment of thieves and other offenders against social order, as well as to put out of the way persons who stood in the road of one's ambitions. From the point of view of public order then, the performance of sorcery might be regarded as justified if it punished someone who had committed an offence.

But while belief in the efficacy of sorcery and in its contemporary performance may have still been about as widespread among middle-aged people in 1952 as in 1929, such belief was probably less prominent among the younger people. We did have evidence that young people still believed in sorcery. There was one prominent case in which a young woman who fell ill attributed this to sorcery by a man whose theft she had surprised. But though I have no very detailed evidence, it is my definite impression that young people on the whole paid less attention to such ideas. This, if true, would be due in part to the counter-influence and preoccupations of Christianity. But it may also have been due to the decreasing incidence of actual *performance* of sorcery and the socially accredited right and power to perform. The powers which enabled one to perform sorcery belonged above all to chiefs and lineage heads with ritual status, through their control of ancestral spirits and gods. As the numbers of persons with such ritual status in the pagan field

[1] See my 'Sociology of "Magic" in Tikopia', *Sociologus*, 1956. There I have discussed the appropriateness of the term 'magic' and the significance of the term 'sorcery' for Tikopia data, and have also drawn the contrast between 1929 and 1952.

declined over the generation with the advance of Christianity, there must have been an increasing public recognition that the sphere of sorcery was becoming more limited. The situation was not clear-cut because when a pagan elder became Christian he abandoned his *use* of his pagan gods rather than his *belief* in them and in his *control* over them. Similarly, the successor to a ritual elder, though without formal status and performing no overt rites, might still retain the spiritual armoury of his predecessor and use it if occasion required. But in general, cases of physical performance of acts of sorcery must certainly have lessed considerably.[1]

PROCEDURE IN CASES OF DISPUTES OVER PROPERTY

I now pass to consideration of a type of social action more liable to affect public order in Tikopia, that is dispute over property. I consider first property in land. In 1929 such disputes were traditionally of three kinds: inter-sibling disputes, especially between brothers; inter-lineage disputes, especially where consanguineal and affinal claims competed for a piece of land, the original owners of which had died out; and disputes between some members of a clan and their chief. Reference has been made in Chapter VI to disputes of each of these kinds in the generation since 1929. Sanctions have been shown to be of three main kinds—argument, force and the fiat of a chief. Argument and the pressure of personality were used commonly in the first two types of dispute. One sibling would maintain his claim on the grounds of a larger family, accessibility, inequality of the previous distribution, and so on. Lineages would argue fiercely with one another in terms of genealogical priority, earlier use, etc. One party might yield to the other, though with bad grace and maintaining that injustice had been done. If argument failed, physical force might be resorted to and in a struggle one party might be worsted. Usually, this did not go to extremes, but took the form of wrestling or threatening with weapons. The line between this and argument was not always easy to draw. A Tikopia might say he had been 'chased away' from cultivating a piece of land, meaning either that he had been simply ordered off by another claimant or that he had been threatened with physical violence. In cases where the two lineages concerned or their representatives were members of the same clan, and particularly when they both claimed descent originally from chiefly stock, disputes between them might be tempered by the fact that their chief might intervene. Either he might decide the issue in favour of one claimant or, if the issue was complex and neither party inclined to yield, he might decide to resume the land himself. Fear of this possibility was one sanction which tended to reduce disturbance in such cases. In 1952, as in 1929, it was freely acknowledged that though lands were held by lineages they were, in the last resort, the lands of the chief.

Very different was the situation when a land issue arose between a chief, or a member of a chief's family, and a commoner. There might be argument

[1] In 1952, sorcery (or witchcraft) was not a matter of interest to Government and there was, therefore, no administrative factor involved in any decrease.

between them and, rarely, some physical struggle—though never with a chief. But if the member of the chief's family pushed his claim, then the commoner would have to give way. If it were a chief, he might simply move in by planting on the land, and the commoner gave way without public protest. Privately he might resent bitterly the encroachment, and say so to his family and friends, but he made no public demonstration, and did not oppose the chief's action. In other words, in Tikopia in 1952 there had been no essential change over the generation in the system of control of land disputes. The parties concerned were free to use personal sanctions and did use them, subject only to control by the chief as the final guardian of public order. But since a chief was himself at times a party to a dispute, to this extent his interest could override those of other members of the community or at least those of his clan. In general, the structure of the community was of a character to deal effectively in 1952, as in 1929, with land disputes.

In another type of dispute over property the issues were of a different kind, and the influence of Christianity had been considerable over the generation. This concerned the use of property in ceremonial and ritual contexts. Here the dispute was not over actual ownership, but over the propriety of using resources for purposes, the validity of which was affirmed by tradition but denied by modernists. An example of this was the personal reintegration rite for a chief. When a chief returned after a trip abroad, by traditional Tikopia custom a large feast was prepared by his clansmen, and kava rites of worship to his gods were performed. These were naturally anathema to the Christians, and the feast itself tended to be brought under the ban. When in 1952 the Ariki Tafua and the Ariki Taumako returned from a visit to Anuta, the latter had his feast, but the former did not. It was said by his supporters 'The feast is simply for the chief who remains in darkness'—i.e. the pagan leader. In analogous way traditional practices of offering green food and bark-cloth to spirits, as part of mortuary rites, had been under attack by Christian leaders, as being compromising in religious terms and economically wasteful. They were in full use in 1929, by Christian and pagan, but had been abandoned by Christians by 1952. Here we see a form of social control by Christianity exercised through the concept of the use of private resources being a matter of public policy—a concept which pagan as well as Christian Tikopia traditionally accepted.

PROCEDURES AGAINST THEFT: INCIDENCE OF THEFT COMPARED

I now consider theft. Theft was only one type of abstraction of property without the owner's permission. In Tikopia in 1952, as in 1929, there were other types of abstraction such as culling coconuts from an orchard by a passer-by for drink, or taking an implement away for use with the general intention of returning it to the owner some time later. These actions, although without prior permission of the owner, might be deemed to have had his sanction in the sense that, though he might have grumbled at the taking of the coconuts or refused to allow the taking of the implement, he would regard both these actions as falling within the legitimate range of kin, neighbour or friend obligations. Such actions had their norms of behaviour. He who took coconuts for drink should stack the husk neatly under the tree and notify the owner later. He who borrowed the implement should notify the owner and, if it was an important piece of property, it was appropriate for him to accompany its return with a small gift of tobacco or betel. In 1952 these observations operated much as in 1929, save that the food stringency ruled out of account for most of the time the taking of items such as coconuts.

The line between legitimate abstraction and theft might lie to a significant degree in whether the abstractor revealed his own identity, and as soon as possible. Such a line was not always easy to draw. In 1952, on one occasion I missed a pair of small scissors which I had been using in public as I sat on a mat with some Tikopia watching a dance festival. Careful consideration and enquiry indicated that they were not lost, and narrowed down the responsibility in all probability to the Christian Ariki Fangarere. When taxed, he replied without embarrassment 'Oh, they went with me'—which left the situation delightfully vague—and restored them.

In all the types of action described so far, the classification was the same in 1952 as in 1929 and so, with the few exceptions noted, was the incidence. In one sphere, however, that of abstraction of food, the classification of the offence was sharpened and the incidence enormously increased. In 1929, I recorded only eleven cases of theft of food during the year in which I was there, whereas in 1952/3, over about seventeen months, about eighty cases of theft of food were recorded by Spillius and myself. Doubtless there were unrecorded cases at both periods. But they were likely to have been much more numerous in 1952/3, and the incidence of theft was probably at least five times as great in the latter period. In 1929 most of the thefts were towards the middle of the year, when food was short. In 1952/3, too, the thefts were not evenly distributed. They began about a month after our arrival and developed with increasing intensity as the food shortage grew more severe (see Ch. IV, pp. 65, 92). But whereas in 1929 most thefts were of semi-luxuries, coconuts, yams and areca nut, in 1952/3 a large number were of staple foods. In addition to thefts of food, there was also in 1929 some theft of other property, of torches, netcord and tobacco. So also in 1952/3, but in this case it was partly in order to gain food with it (e.g. theft of fishhooks for personal use, or of other objects to exchange against fishhooks) and partly in line with the general lessening of morale. I shall, therefore, treat the theft of various kinds of objects together.

In 1952, as in 1929, theft (*kaia*) was stigmatized. The term *kaia* was heard very widely and always in tones of complaint, reprobation, disgust. It was even suggested that thieves should not be given a share in the foodstuffs sent down by the Government to relieve the famine—but it was agreed that this was impracticable since it would hurt their families as well as themselves. The repetition of theft by some individuals gave rise to the view that such people had 'a thieving mind', and the expression *te vare kaia* was used of them, implying a kind of thieving frenzy thought to seize some people in the time of stress and to be akin to a kind of madness. Yet notable throughout the whole period was the way in which economic stress tended to widen the gap between ideal and practice. Everyone agreed that theft was morally bad. It was held also to be disruptive in practice because thieves took the crops before they were mature, and in fear of theft owners likewise took the immature crops before they could get full advantage from them. Yet, despite these moral sentiments and also increasingly rigorous action against thieves, stealing became widespread.

The pressure of famine made a breach in two of the Tikopia canons of behaviour. One ideal view was that theft was practised by commoners, but not by members of the families of chiefs—who should be the guardians of morality, not the breakers of it. But it was admitted that during the famine members of chiefly houses did steal food. The other canon was that ritual food supplies were safe from theft. Yet in 1952 the orchards of Uta were raided often even in those areas next to the sacred temples. Again, in July 1952 occurred an incident which horrified the people of Ravenga, and to which it appeared there was no previous parallel—the theft of a food basket destined for the canoe gods of a sacred canoe of the Ariki Taumako (*v.* p. 95). Even though the thief may have been a Christian, his interference with ritual food was an indication to the Tikopia of the moral breakdown which the famine had engendered.

Treatment of Theft

I now outline Tikopia behaviour at three stages: behaviour on the discovery of a theft; activity in following up the theft to attempt to identify the thief; and activity, both private and public, in the event that the thief had been identified or that no identification had been made.

In 1929, when a theft was discovered in Tikopia, the normal reaction of the owner of the property was anger and some kind of public interest. The common demonstration was to whoop '*Iefu!*' a number of times—the *forua* —while beating the thatch of one's house or a canoe with a stick.[1] If accompanied by violent cursing the demonstration was termed *fuatau*.

The same procedure took place on occasion in 1952. As I was passing down the beach near the village of Potu sa Kafika one night, I heard sounds of thatch being beaten. I went over and saw a crowd already collected and a man standing at the side of the house. He did not whoop, but he was saying over and over 'May his father eat filth. May his father eat filth. . . .' His wrists were being held by a woman, but from time to time he lashed out with his foot at the side of the house. After a while he subsided. Then Pa Rarovi, the premier ritual elder of Kafika, came on the scene. He addressed the crowd, saying 'Your doings are not good', etc., in the form of a general rebuke. Then he began an enquiry. It seemed that a pipe and some small fishhooks in a package had been stolen from the man's box. Someone must have got hold of the key and opened the box. Then one of the *maru* of Kafika came up. He spoke quietly, but the crowd listened to him with respect. He tried to

[1] *Primitive Polynesian Economy*, pp. 268 *et seq.*

find out who had been in residence that day and who had been seen around the house. Finally he said 'Someone of this house' (meaning of the local Motusio lineage) 'was responsible.' This was not contradicted by the crowd. Then Pa Rarovi said 'It would be good for the person who has taken these things to go and get ten fishhooks and give them to the man who has been robbed.' All of this took place in the moonlight and occupied only about a quarter of an hour. The crowd had collected with speed, and as soon as the facts had been generally established that it must have been an internal robbery, the people dispersed again. By this time the owner of the property had quietened down, and no further action of any public kind took place, nor did I ever hear that the thief had been identified or compensation made.

This incident paralleled in all essentials others of a generation before. A theft was discovered. The sufferer protested violently. This was in part catharsis for his feelings. He could vent some of his aggression at least on inanimate objects. In part also it was an advertisement of his loss which drew people to come to give him sympathy. Moreover, it also offered some possibility of identifying the offender and leading to redress. Neighbours assembled, listened to the complaint and discussed it, but did not actively do more. Finally, a man of rank took charge, restored order by quietening everyone down and conducted a preliminary enquiry. Some moral utterances then concluded the scene. The restoration of peace was a prime objective. Beyond this, there was no formal process: there was no tribunal, no formal taking of evidence, no institutionalized action against a suspected thief by representatives of the community at large. The theme of presentation of fishhooks to the man robbed embodied a notion of acknowledgment of ownership and some compensation rather than that of return of property or even full restitution. In a sense there was an idea that even a thief had grievances and rights—otherwise he would not have stolen.[1]

Another form of protest in 1952 might be subsequent to the *forua* or alternative to it. When food was stolen from cultivations, the owner might tie to a pole a set of young coconut fronds (*sakilo*). Traditionally, coconut frond bunches in cultivations have had two main functions in Tikopia. One, a simple spray of mature fronds, was an advertisement that the owner of a piece of fallow land or of a stand of coconut palm wished to reserve it, presumably for his own use. The second function, when the coconut frond was knotted, was to imply that in the knot was tied a spirit power which would injure anyone who interfered with the cultivation. Thus, the frond was not merely a 'Keep off' sign. It was also a taboo sign. This was also the case when immature coconut frond was used; it was set up with a protective formula. In 1929, the type of mature coconut frond notice was relatively common and that of the immature frond rare, though I noted cases. By 1952, the position had been reversed and immature fronds were more common. But the explanation of them had changed too. Now there was a notion that such an advertisement helped to shame the thief who saw it. 'That the thieving person may come and look at it and see that his theft has been

[1] Cf. *Primitive Polynesian Economy*, p. 320, pp. 206–9.

bound up.' This seemed to me a curious idea, partly because of the difficulty of getting any evidence that shame ever came to any thief in this way—though the Tikopia averred that it was possible. I took this to be an indication partly that Tikopia belief in the efficacy of spirit protection of their cultivations had considerably declined. This view was re-endorsed by the Tikopia declaration that hardly anybody then used such spirit-implemented warnings. Setting up a notice after a theft seemed like locking the stable door after the horse had been stolen. But it appeared to have several other functions. One was to warn relatively close kinsfolk that the owner objected to any taking of food supplies and that they should therefore refrain further from what might be otherwise normal abstraction. Secondly, it indicated in general that the owner was now on the lookout against thieves, and perhaps still it was hoped that it might convey a ritual threat. Thirdly, and probably the major function, was that of protest to the world at large by the owner, a relief to his feelings. All this would seem to be more relevant than the function of bringing moral conviction home to the thief.

But in 1952 protests of these main kinds were not always necessarily made. In May 1952, the Ariki Taumako began to suffer from theft and reported loss of pumpkins which he was keeping to ripen at the side of his house. He made no public protest. I have already noted (p. 92) how, in early June, his sweet potatoes had been raided and he made no public objection. All he did was to curse the children probably responsible and say that when a vessel called he would tell them to go in it; it would be a good thing for thieving children to go to some other land. He said further that their fathers must have put them up to this theft. But though very angry, he did not whoop formally or make any other demonstration. Apart from a couple of children who came up and one of his elders who strolled over later, no crowd assembled. The son of the Ariki Kafika, close by at the time and who must have heard what had occurred, continued to dig—perhaps because the land was in dispute between them. The lack of a crowd was probably due partly to some fear of what the chief might do, but largely to the growing incidence of theft, which made it an event of quite mundane character. Five days later the chief reported again that the night before he had seen the son of one of his neighbours, a boy about nine years old, digging up his sweet potatoes at the side of his dwelling. When noticed, the boy ran off but then stayed watching at a distance. Though angry, the chief did no more than mildly complain to me and others near. This time he said that the families of thieving men should be taken off when the Government vessel next called, and he asked me to tell the labour recruiter to take away those men who were lazy thieves. (I had to point out that this would not be the best credential to give them if he wanted them recruited.)

The chief did not make public protest on these occasions, largely because he was sharing the fate of nearly everyone else in the community. As others explained to me, he would have been ashamed to make a demonstration. His dignity required that he accepted his loss like everyone else. It will be noted that he did not pursue the thieves nor, although he thought he had identified them, did he go to the houses of their fathers and complain. Nor did he set up any coconut frond sign. Each theft at this time was treated on its merits as an isolated act—save for the identification of some persons as persistent thieves.

But a marked difference between 1929 and 1952 was that in the latter period the conventional *forua* was often omitted—theft had become so common that it was just not worth while yelling about it.

The follow-up procedure after a theft was, of course, primarily concerned with identification of the thief. If a person was surprised in the act of theft, people tried to catch him, but he usually escaped and in such case was not pursued far. On one occasion when sweet potatoes were stolen from the gardens by the side of a house in Potu sa Kafika, a man who was surprised on the spot was chased, but got away by swimming out to sea. It was not known who he was and it was said he could have returned to land in almost any part of the district. At times a more persistent attempt to discover the thief and the stolen property was made.

Sometimes this was not difficult. Not long after our arrival in 1952, we engaged in barter for ethnographic specimens and took in exchange for some fishhooks a large net-shuttle. A few days later, two men came and demanded to see this shuttle. They identified it, saying it had been stolen from the house of one of them by a noted thief, Pa Tekara. I said that our records showed that we had got it from the eldest son of the Ariki Taumako for nine fish-hooks. One man then reaffirmed that it had been stolen from him and said that it was the only one he had for his work. I told him to leave it with us for the time being and bring the other parties to me that I might be certain of the facts. Later the two men returned. They said that the accused man and the chief's son were waiting outside to return the fishhooks and—much to my surprise—they were. When asked, Pa Tekara admitted that he went secretly and stole the net-shuttle, announced to the chief's son that it was his and got him to act as intermediary in order to barter for it with us. The chief's son admitted that at the time when I had asked him if he had his father's per-mission to dispose of it, he had replied 'Yes', whereas in fact it had been given him by Pa Tekara. I handed the shuttle then to Pa Fenuatara, who hap-pened to be with me, to examine. He looked very serious and addressed Pa Tekara. 'What you have done, entering another man's house and stealing his shuttle, is bad. . . .' and much more to the same effect. Pa Tekara took it like a child, admitting his guilt and assenting to his condemnation. When he had gone, it turned out in discussion that he was well known as a thief; that he had been like that since a child; that he seemed to lack principle and not to be ashamed when caught. (It was significant in the light of this statement that he was a spirit medium.)

More often in 1952, as in 1929, the thief could not be pinned down or even identified at all. In May 1952, we had begun to suffer loss of food such as tinned meat and biscuit by thieves even bold enough to insert an arm through the thatch of the house while we were sleeping there and extract the food, or to enter through our small, low window. On one occasion a case containing two tins of biscuits disappeared. The reaction of the Tikopia was diverse. The Ariki Taumako and our two attendants happened to be present when the discovery was made. All broke out into violent curses against the unknown thieves. The chief at once gave instructions to our two attendants—who were his clansmen—to look out for digging at the sides of houses since the tins might have been buried there. Thinking also that they might have been taken into the woods, he suggested a rocky bluff near by as a possible place for search. Neighbours called in, to express condolence. They said that the theft was not good, that it was very disturbing, that 'it caused the sympathies to shake', that all Tikopia should be ashamed, since it was our food which had fed Tikopia. Several people asked where was the principal *maru* of the vicinity —why did he not instruct the people properly that they should not steal? The thief was lacking in sympathy for us, they said; and they, the commentators, were indeed very sorry that we had lost our food, and so on. . . . There was much discussion about the exact circumstances. When (not seriously, but to try and frighten off potential thieves by rumour) I suggested borrowing a gun and shooting anyone else who was discovered entering the house secretly at night, there was cordial agreement with me.

Another interesting development, of the possibility of which I had heard generally in 1929 but had no report of any case, was resort to spirit aid. It was suggested by one of our friends that we should have resort to 'the son of Sao'. This turned out to be not a living person but a familiar spirit, a still-born son of one of the local mediums, the wife of my old friend Pae Sao. This spirit, it appeared, was prepared to go and search for stolen goods. It was not known whether he went by day or by night—as a spirit he was not seen. It was stated that many people had asked his help in getting stolen goods located. When I asked for examples of his prowess, however, the only one cited was that of a length of tobacco which had been stolen and which was located by the spirit in the place where the thief had buried it. When I asked one of our attendants for more illustrations, he said that 'many of the crowd' had sought the help of the spirit, but that he had forgotten who they were.

Accordingly, we agreed that the help of the 'son of Sao' should be sought. Our two Tikopia servants then visited the spirit medium and presented her with three quids of tobacco and four areca nuts (in order that the presents should be 'weighty' one of our attendants even gave up his own supply of tobacco to her). The medium went into a state of mild dissociation in her usual manner—by heavy breathing. The familiar entered. First of all he cursed the thief. Then he said that as yet he had found no indications of who it might be, but that he would go and search—giving details of places he proposed to visit. If he found anything he would send a message by the medium's grandchildren to our servants. Despite all this spirit activity, how-ever, neither thief nor property were ever found.

Sometimes the Tikopia were more practical. After one theft from us of some tins of meat very early in the morning, the thief fled unseen. We awak-ened and watched, but he did not return. At dawn our neighbours and some other people assembled, expressing their shame at the theft having taken place in their locality. One man whooped three times to express the general feelings of outrage—his action was approved by the crowd. Another man examined the area for footprints and found some which he identified by their partial imprint as those of a running man, obviously the thief. A suggestion was then made that we should get Pa Panapa to come and identify the footprints.[1] The footprints were examined by numerous people and identified broadly as those of a young man—though others said those of an elderly man. It was generally agreed that they were not those of a woman. Pa Panapa arrived, examined the footprints and excluded some as not being those of the thief. He discussed the points of the others, but kept any identification to himself—if indeed he had made any. Then he went away. Only later I learned from him the name of the person he had identified. He had not wished to make the name public at the time, and seeing me surrounded by so many people he had slipped away. His identification appeared reasonable to me, though I could not be sure if it was on the basis of the footprints or only a shrewd guess from his general knowledge. Since so much time elapsed and suspicion was not proved, we took no action. Of course I made some recompense to Pa Panapa for his trouble, as was customary.

In 1929, treatment of a thief who was identified varied according to circumstances. He might be reproved, as was Pa Tekara a generation later. I was told in 1929 that if a man observed another in the act of stealing something from a garden, he would talk angrily to the offender, upbraiding him. Then the man was allowed to go, leaving behind him the goods which he had taken. The offender would not be struck, it was said. Sometimes identification of a thief was followed up by the owner of the goods who went and demanded either their return or compensation for their loss.[2] If a thief was seen in the act and identified but not actually caught, no further action was necessarily taken against him, if it was only food which he had stolen. He was talked about, and this public knowledge was up to a point his punishment. In June 1929 a lad was caught stealing yams in the orchard of a prominent man of Matautu. One of the neighbours going through the cultivations observed someone digging, and knowing it was not the owner, threw a stone at him. The lad looked up and bolted. He stayed in his house for a couple of days ashamed. When he came out, he and his friend, the son of the man from whom he had stolen, sat together as usual in the oven house, but they did not talk to one another; they were embarrassed since each knew that the other knew the facts. The sanction of public scorn was invoked also anonymously where a thief had not been identified. A dance song might be chanted to pour ridicule upon him. Public opinion might be invoked against him in another way by the use of sorcery. In such cases the action was more of a relief to the aggrieved owner than a punishment for the thief. The thief might not even know that sorcery had been invoked, yet since illness and misfortune could

[1] The ability of this man to read footprints had been mentioned to me in 1929, and it was interesting to see that his skill was still recognized a generation later (*v. We, The Tikopia*, p. 18).

[2] see *Primitive Polynesian Economy*, p. 320.

X

be attributed retrospectively to sorcery, it might have had some effect as a potential sanction.

Despite the fact that I was told that a thief caught in the act would not be beaten, I think that there were occasions on which he might be struck in hot blood by the aggrieved owner. This might well happen if the offender were known as a persistent thief. If a man got the reputation for persistently stealing, then he might be chased away from his home to settle elsewhere in the island. In an extreme case, it is said, he might be ordered off to sea. I was told in 1929 of one case of a man who was so ordered away, not because of his own thefts but because he had persistently incited other people to steal and hand over the proceeds to him. I was told also of another type of punishment. If a man was caught thieving in an orchard, he might be tied to a tree and his hair cut off by the aggrieved owner. This would cause the man great shame, and he would hide in his house. People hearing this would go and raid his orchards, taking coconuts and food from them in compensation for his depredations on their property. Such a public shame might in itself lead the man to put off to sea.

In 1952, songs publicly chanted to revile unknown thieves were much less common than in 1929. This seemed to be an indication, not of any change in public policy or opinion, but a reaction of greater intensity to famine conditions which made the jesting mood of song seem inapplicable, and any restraining effects of it most unlikely. Thieves when caught were reproved, often insulted, and later, when conditions worsened they were sometimes violently assaulted. Where possible, they were made to yield up their booty. Treatment of identified thieves, however, had some modifications. One was that the possibility of sending a persistent thief out to sea in a canoe with the likelihood of his perishing was much less feasible. It was not that public opinion had softened in regard to this type of punishment, but that the stronger influence of the external Government had made it clear that such a punishment did not now properly lie solely within Tikopia jurisdiction. For this reason, Tikopia chiefs in particular proposed from time to time that persistent known thieves should be taken away by Government or, in particular, should be recruited as labour abroad. By 1952, although the notion of jail (calaboose) was used by the Tikopia as a general threat, they did not seem to have regarded this as realistically very applicable. In particular, they had no conception of specific periods in jail varying according to the specific character of offences.

Another set of attitudes arose through the growing realization, as the famine developed, that theft had become clearly a matter of public policy and could no longer be left to individual treatment. This manifested itself in three ways: attempts to prevent theft by public watch; attempts to forestall it by imposing rules on the general public; and measures of punishment in which the public character was emphasized more deliberately than before, as a deterrent.

Initial measures of prevention took the form of patrols to safeguard cultivations at night by catching, identifying or at least scaring away thieves.

Towards the end of May 1952, one of the most prominent *maru* of Taumako, Pa Ngarumea, fulminated against theft in a public assembly. Then he took to going on watch, carrying a borrowed electric torch, in order to see if he could catch food thieves. As time went on, patrolling increased. Towards the end of July, the Ariki Tafua sent four men in patrols of two at a time to guard the cultivations of Rakisu, and a few days later, after a conference of young men in Potu sa Taumako, some of them went out to patrol the cultivations. Such efforts met with little success; the cunning of the thieves was too great. Later, Spillius recorded that more stringent measures were introduced, including rules to control the behaviour of people in their access to cultivations. To promulgate and discuss these rules, the advice of the public assembly (*fono*) was used. This meant a formalization of Tikopia agricultural behaviour far greater than had been known hitherto.

About the same time the techniques of punishment were also given more formalization. In June 1952 I had asked the Ariki Taumako what, in olden days, happened to a persistent thief. Was he sent off to sea in a canoe (as I had been told in 1929)? He said no—the man was bound up to a post with sinnet cord and left there for some time until he had changed his mind ('until his mind had been replaced'). This punishment was obviously related to that of tying to a tree, and seemed to me at the time to be outmoded. But later, as the public indignation against continued theft grew, it was revived not only as the traditional punishment for incorrigible thieves but also as the penalty for all persons convicted of stealing. A large stake was driven into the sand of the beach, the offender stood up to it and then his or her wrists were lashed to it with cord. According to the severity of the offence and the degree to which the person was regarded as a hardened offender, the period at the stake varied from a day to a week. Food and drink were allowed according to circumstances. Execution of the punishment was done mainly by the principal *maru*. This punishment was carried out only in Ravenga where the influence of paganism and of traditional institutions was stronger than on the other side of the island, and the temper of the leading men fiercer. In all, Spillius recorded about fifty cases in which a thief was so punished.[1] This harsh measure of the stake was supported by the Tikopia public. Chiefs and other responsible men wished to provide a deterrent against the thefts which threatened the general integrity of the Tikopia social and general economic system. Ordinary people appeared to find this public exposure of an identified offender a catharsis for their anger at their own losses, and for possible guilt and shame at their own undiscovered stealing. The punishment of the stake was partly the physical discomfort and privation. But to a much greater measure it was the shame of public exposure and of being subjected to the taunts and jibes of neighbours and friends.

According to Spillius, other types of punishments were also introduced though not used to the same degree. One was the assignment of 'punishment

[1] J. Spillius, *op. cit.* p. 19. Spillius is preparing for publication a detailed analysis of the *fono* institution as part of a general account of political and social affairs in Tikopia in 1951/53.

fatigues'—repairing paths or doing domestic work under the eye of some person of status who could assume responsibility for the offender's good conduct. Another measure, by analogy with an official punishment elsewhere, was public beating of an habitual offender. Despite initial public acceptance of this, however, beating in practice was not carried out. It eventuated that such an assault on a person in cold blood was quite alien to Tikopia modes of behaviour.

Comparison of 1952 with 1929 showed that in ordinary circumstances social control of theft by the Tikopia was relatively ineffective. The various kinds of sanctions, including the general diffused actions of public disapproval, and the specific action of banishment of an habitual offender at the risk of his life, were not sufficient to block theft, especially of food, when there was general acute hunger. When theft occurred, Tikopia procedures were not adequate to identify a thief when he had not been discovered on the spot. There was no organized method of collecting evidence in a systematic way. Measures for detection of a rational kind, and also more irrationally, dependence upon divination or other spirit aid, were haphazard and their efficiency was at a very low level. Measures of punishment were relatively unorganized and left largely to the aggrieved owner of the stolen property. Techniques of prevention of further theft were only weakly developed. There were no adequate means of dealing with any mass movement, such as occurred when a whole boatload of sweet potatoes and coconuts was pilfered (pp. 276–7). Moreover, the Christian ethic was of no avail in such an acute situation. Christians and pagans alike stole food in their need.

Yet the general crisis of the food shortage provided a test of the strength as well as of the weakness of the Tikopia system of social control. The developing circumstances in 1952/3 showed how the Tikopia did finally cope with their problem. The stark exigencies of advancing famine drew forth harsher and more highly organized methods of dealing with theft. At a very early stage the leaders of the community recognized theft as a problem of public policy, not merely individual loss. The existing structure, however, did not give them the power to bring home this recognition and the accompanying inferences for action to the general body of the public until the crisis reached a high level. It was necessary to develop a further more appropriate structure, the organized public assembly, not new but revived on traditional foundations, to give the leaders the necessary power. In this development, the presence of a galvanic modernized young Tikopia, Robinson Vakasaumore, was an important factor.[1] But Vakasaumore owed much of his influence to his traditional status as a *maru*, and he was supported and influenced by other men of status among the Tikopia. Even if he had not been on the island, some other solutions would probably have been found. Here then was the development of a quasi-legal institution to meet a severe threat to the integrity of a society which valued its way of life sufficiently to submit, in the last resort, to rigorous controls to preserve it.

[1] The presence of a sympathetic anthropologist, Spillius, helped to prevent violence and probably facilitated the formal solution.

Conformity among Tikopia Christians

How did Christianity as such stand in the general field of social control? I have shown that in the crisis of famine its precepts proved of little power. But in some other respects it had great force.

Membership of the Christian body carried with it certain obligations more specific than those applying to other, pagan members of the general Tikopia society. Conduct as a Church member involved conformity to a special set of rules which, if broken, resulted in the offender being subjected to Church discipline. On the whole, despite the failure of many Tikopia to follow the Christian ethic in matters of truth, honesty and loving-kindness, most of them did obey the more concrete injunctions, such as those relating to monogamy or non-support of pagan religious rites. I consider now some of the implications of Church membership from the point of view of social control, with particular reference to treatment of offenders.

The main means of Church discipline used in Tikopia were: private and public rebuke; refusal of baptism or marriage; banishment from the Church for a period; and in the case of a Mission teacher, removal from office. Action in regard to these matters was discussed at periodic assemblies (weekly in 1952) of Mission teachers under the leadership of the priest, who had by far the most powerful voice in decisions.

With a priest as active as Pa Pangisi, private rebuke was a sanction very often used, both in 1929 and in 1952. Many sinners responded to his upbraiding and critical arguments; and many other people quoted his objections as the reason why a certain course of action was not pursued. Public rebuke, however, appeared to be very rare.

Refusal of baptism, or of marriage, was a sanction sometimes used, the former especially to mark that the parents of a child were not in a state of grace. The priest explained to me one day that he had just baptised six infants, but had sent away the parents of another infant. The husband and wife were agnatic first cousins (of Mapusanga or Orokofe lineage). The priest had told me that the child was the product of an unlawful marriage. I asked whether he operated by Tikopia custom or by Church custom in this. He answered, 'the latter'. But when I said that as far as I knew the marriage of first cousins was not barred by Europeans he then said that he was following Tikopia custom.[1] The priest stated that the young couple would be allowed back to Church and the baptism would take place when they had repented of their attitude. This was not so illogical as it may seem since their union had been due to the pregnancy of the girl, and had taken place long not before the birth.

Banishment from the Church was of two grades known officially as the

---

[1] The Mission refused marriage to certain categories of persons not conforming to Church rule; I do not know that there was any uniform practice regarding marriage of persons barred by native rule though licit by Church rule. Bishop J. M. Steward noted that marriage with a deceased wife's sister or husband's brother or with a divorced person is not contrary to native custom, though it was contrary (at the time he wrote) to Church rule. See his *Hints on District Work*, Melanesian Mission Occasional Papers, No. 4, Guadelcanar, 1920, p. 20.

Greater and the Lesser Excommunication. According to the rule of the Mission, the pronouncement of the Greater Excommunication was the duty of the Bishop alone. That of the Lesser Excommunication might be a matter for the priest, though it had to be reported in due course to the Bishop. In Tikopia, where the Bishop was in such rare contact with his flock, practically all cases of banishment have been presumably those of the Lesser Excommunication. One year was the usual period of expulsion for serious wrongdoing.

The two offences in particular which drew expulsion from the Church in Tikopia were adultery and attendance at the dances or other rites of Uta.

Fornication as such, though a matter of rebuke, was not necessarily a reason for expulsion. The sexual affairs of the unmarried, frequent enough among Christian young people in 1928/9, did not appear to have diminished in volume by 1952, to judge from gossip and from confidences. Their frequency and the difficulty of getting specific evidence were such that the priest had apparently forborne any attempt at stringent, specific control. Only in the case of a pregnancy was action taken. Then the Mission teachers took upon themselves a role which traditionally was that of the woman's brothers in Tikopia. They endeavoured to force her to confess the name of her lover, and they then tried to induce the guilty pair to marry. Several cases of this occurred during our stay.

Adultery by a married person went against Tikopia moral codes in the way in which sex relations between the unmarried did not. While traditionally adultery of a married man with an unmarried girl gave rise to scandal, that of a married woman was an outrage. Though, as far as I have noted, no case occurred during our stay, both these were offences for which Communion would be refused and repentance demanded of a Tikopia Christian.

A special category of adultery by Christian standards was polygyny which was, of course, licit in traditional Tikopia custom. The priest stated to me in 1952 that he allowed a polygynist to return to the Church, but only after he had put away one of his wives. This was consistent with his disciplinary rules of a generation before, but appeared to be more rigorously enforced with the growth of the Christian body. A Christian who committed adultery to the extent of actually taking his paramour to live openly with him and his wife —though married by Tikopia custom—was hardened in sin. Of the three such cases in 1952 of Tikopia polygynists (cf. p. 205), two of the men and five of the women were Christians. An example was Kasoavae of the lineage of Vainunu. He was baptised by the name of Ellison—taking the priest's name—and later reverted to paganism. He married a daughter of Pa Nukutauo, and then six months later he married her elder sister also. Both sisters were called Nau Rangitaukena in accordance with the house name he had taken—not by different house names as would have been more usual. Both women who, too, had been baptised, lived in the one house with their husband. I talked with the women, who seemed very content. I asked 'Is it good?' One of them replied 'Yes, it is good.' Here their brother-in-law, who was present, added 'It is not wrong. Look at my daughters in Fatumaru.' (These were twins, also married polygynously.) This husband had deserted the Church before he married, so no sanction could be taken against him. But one of his sons, a boy of about three years, had been refused baptism by the priest. For a long time the women had not gone to Church but to the pagan rites in Uta. Recently, however, one of them had begun to go to Church again and had apparently been allowed to do so by the priest—probably not in recognition of the marriage but as a move in recalling all parties to an appreciation of their sin.

Associated with breaches of Christian *mores* was the removal of Mission teachers from office, since it was commonly for allegations of improper sexual conduct that they were set aside. Several cases were well attested, including one of a prominent teacher who made an unmarried girl pregnant; after some years of banishment (presumably by the Greater Excommunication) and purging his offence, he was readmitted to office. Even the priest himself, by 1952, had not escaped the tongue of scandal, though it was impossible to say whether the story was authentic. (He was said to have taken advantage of a sleeping girl when he took refuge in a house from a shower of rain. The girl concerned was said to have insisted on the truth of her story, but the Church authorities evidently believed the priest's denial and no action was taken.) The internal jealousies among the Mission body themselves, however, were shown by the belief among Christian Tikopia that the setting aside from office of some Mission teachers by the priest was largely due to his and his sons' fear that their status might be challenged. Here was a tendency to reinterpret the structure of the Christian leadership in terms of Tikopia local politics.

The other great offence incurring expulsion from the Church was attendance at the pagan religious rites. This offence occurred in 1928/9, but mainly among young men who were attracted by the dancing of Uta, let their hair grow long and automatically put themselves out of Church for the season until a gift to the priest and a profession of repentance allowed them readmission. By 1952 the issue had become somewhat different. Not many young people risked expulsion from the Church to dance at Uta, though my old friend, Fakasingetevasa, told me that some, including himself and his sister, had earlier followed my example and attended the rites. At this later date it was rather the deliberate act of elder men who abandoned the Church and went to Uta to support their chief in the face of the dwindling attendance at the kava performances, and of wives supporting their husbands. I have noted about ten cases of men and a dozen of women who thus abandoned the Church for paganism. But there were others who in varying degrees supported their chief by food at the more secular aspects of the rites, such as preparing the oven. For the most part, this was tolerated by the Mission teachers. A prominent *maru* of Taumako, Pa Motuata, indeed went rather further, but in doing so traded on his political status and his seniority. Support to the chiefs given by the custom of assisting in the refurnishing of sacred temples finally, however, came under challenge from the Church until it was given a political interpretation.[1]

[1] Spillius, *op. cit.*

The gift to the priest referred to earlier as one of the features involved in a return to the Church may be classified theoretically from several points of view. From the Church point of view it was in the nature of a *thank-offering* for readmission to Communion.[1] It was presumably also a token of *repentance*, a material symbol of a wish for renewed communion in the faith. The Church definitely did not regard the offering as a kind of *fine* for breach of discipline. (In such case, strictly speaking, it would be imposed by the priest in specified amount and collected for the benefit of the common purpose of the Church.) The priest appeared to indicate that a gift was required, but he did not state the amount nor make any formal demand for it. On the other hand, he received it into his own possession—he did not, as far as I know, add it to Church funds, but this would have been difficult in the absence of any monetary medium. The Tikopia used the Mission term *alenga* (a Mota word conventionally translated as bounty or offering). It seemed to be regarded by them not as a fine but as a form of *compensation* to the priest for readmission and a kind of personal *gift of propitiation* to him. It was from these points of view that the pagans also saw it; the old Ariki Kafika indeed described it in effect as 'buying one's way back into the Church'. He said 'It is their exchange for the Church. They give and exchange with the priest, and then go to Church. Its name is the *alenga*. Mats are opened and they go and carry one to him with its accompaniments, bark-cloth and food.' What I have translated as 'exchange', he termed '*tauvi*', the conventional Tikopia term for a transaction in which there may be haggling and which nowadays is used for the purchase of an object with money.

In general it may be said that Church discipline in Tikopia by 1952 was fairly systematic and, through the organization of teachers, fairly thorough as regards all the major aspects of Church obligation on the material and formal side.

But the discipline had its drawbacks. A peculiar development which did not specifically relate to Church rules, but which might have been associated with them, was the behaviour of adolescent and young mature girls. At times some of these girls went into an odd state known as *karekare iri*. They went about with vague looks, did not speak even when spoken to, and pointed with a finger to food or to a water bottle to indicate their wants. They might go to the side of the house and break off sugar cane which grew there, to eat like children. They tended to go about in groups, and one girl in this state alone tended to go and look for similar companions. As a group they might gather in one district and move off to another, or go up to the orchards on the mountainside, plucking coconuts irrespective of ownership and taking them home to eat. They might go about with sticks, slashing from side to side. Usually other people did not interfere with them, because if frustrated they might snatch up stick or stone and fight. If hit hard they did not cry, but fought on silently until made to run by superior force, or until their opponent was driven off. But they did not fight one another; they behaved like bond-

[1] *The Primary Charge of the Right Reverend John M. Steward, Bishop of Melanesia,* Norfolk Island, 1919, p. 14.

friends. Moreover, their working capacity was not impaired; they were 'not lazy in jobs'. They went to the orchards and collected food for the household, they filled water bottles and they did other ordinary tasks as they were bid quite efficiently.

I did not myself identify any cases of this phenomenon, although some were seen later by Spillius. The above description was given me by Pa Fenuatara with his usual care. When I questioned him as to its origin, he said that it was something 'of modern times'. He characterized it as 'a madness of the Church alone'. According to him only Christian girls were affected. He said that it occurred in Lent, near Easter, that it lasted four to five days and then was over. The Mission teachers, he said, did not know how to cope with it; they apparently ignored it. It is possible, of course, that here Pa Fenuatara was projecting on to the Christian youth his opposition to their elders' faith. But his circumstantial description and subsequent observations by Spillius made this unlikely.

Some interesting questions arise about this. Firstly, the name was unrevealing. According to Pa Fenuatara it was a metaphorical one, referring to an excrescence on tree trunks—a wartiness. Another possibility given was that it referred to the swivelling motion of the fans (*iri*), which these girls carried when they danced, and which they turned, *karekare*, in elaborate stylized gestures in a very vigorous way. An alternative name for this condition appeared to be 'speaking nonsense' (*muna vare*), but this term was also applied generally to anyone who was incoherent in speech.

What was the reason of this condition? The girls themselves apparently described it (afterwards) in terms reminiscent of descriptions of mystical experience elsewhere. They said that the onset of the attack was their sight of a small cloud, like fog or smoke, descending with a whirling motion. This cloud alighted on their forehead between the eyes and penetrated the skull, which then felt very heavy. Sometimes too they became possessed by spirits. 'Folk gather all this by listening to the talk of the girls,' said Pa Fenuatara, 'but we don't perceive the cloud.' This condition has obvious links with other forms of mild dissociation in Tikopia, in which a part of the body feels heavy, after some pseudo-physical experience, and the subject then behaves abnormally. In a general way, too, the external symptoms of mutism, tendency to aggression, and gregariousness, all suggest a form of adolescent self-protection. They seem to involve some reversion to infantilism as a kind of over-compensation against authority.

There are other special features. The idealogy of the injection of the 'cloud' from outside had analogies with the more mature explanations of spirit mediums. This linked also with the fact that some of the girls did apparently actually become dissociated and spoke in a way in which mediums did. But the sex and the timing were also significant. The fact that this phenomenon appeared to concern only young females reaching puberty probably meant that psycho-physical changes of maturing womanhood gave a greater predisposition to group responses of this kind. One cannot assert that suggestibility was greater among Tikopia women than among men at this period, but the sexual changes probably operated in general with more force, and so rendered them more liable as a category to affections of this kind.

The fact that my informant attributed this phenomenon to Christian girls only was probably significant, though not quite in the way in which he meant it. By 1952 there were very few adolescent young women who were still pagan. Moreover, even among the Christians it was not suggested that all were subject to this affection. But in a broader way the implication was probably correct. Christianity in Tikopia had not only tended to alter the moral evaluation of conduct in many fields, it had also introduced some new moral burdens. Some of those affected most acutely the conduct of the young. In particular, the custom of free sexual relations between the unmarried, formerly regarded as natural and looked at quite leniently, was now stigmatized. The young did not observe the Mission code, but at a stage when a girl became nubile and was beginning to think of sexual adventures, the resentment of the priest and teachers against such adventures might well complicate her judgment and introduce an element of strain or of guilt into her thinking on these matters. As regards the alleged occurrence of the phenomena in the Lenten period, if true[1] this might be correlated with the fact that it was the period when Church authority and ideology were brought to one of their highest points of the year, and in particular reacted upon the young very adversely by the prohibition of dancing. To Tikopia youth without cinemas or other forms of mass amusement except games, this lack of dancing was a very heavy deprivation. Again, then, one can see how a group reaction of young women could be channelled into overt expression most easily in this period. The description of the body condition as 'heavy' may be particularly significant because this was a common feature of Tikopia descriptions of dissociated states. But even although it might have been a derived description, it did fit in quite well with an attitude of mild depression in a period officially laid down as one of abstinence and deprivation.

In general, review of Tikopia social control as affected particularly by the Church shows a high degree of conformity as regards the more specific, more checkable religious and social practices, but a low conformity in the more general, less checkable actions of lying, thieving and pre-marital sex relations. Moreover, the degree of conformity obtained appears to have been not without strain.

The Character of Tikopia Sanctions

I have now compared the system of values, rules and procedures in various major fields of social control in Tikopia in 1929 and in 1952. I want now to discuss the operations of sanctions for control more generally.

The concept of *sanction* has two senses, allied but distinct. In one sense it refers to those measures for social action which are brought into operation in response to the act of an individual. These measures may be of re-enforcement and approval, they may be of check and disapproval, or they may remedy

---

[1] Suggested translation of *karekare iri* by reference to dancing indicates that the condition might last beyond the Lenten period or occur outside it.

that which has already been done. The other sense of sanction is that of *potential* social effect—a person refrains from an action or is encouraged to act by his recognition of the probable consequences. Yet such consequences may be only an inference. The sanction may never be called upon. If then its consequences are inferred, not demonstrated, statements about the force of the sanction must be somewhat uncertain. On the other hand, if the consequences, while negative or repressive, yet are in fact very frequently operative, it may be asked to what extent they really act as a check? Can they be said really to constitute a sanction if they do not inhibit action? A kind of shuttle interpretation then tends to be given in which the probable significance of a sanction is inferred from its results in action elsewhere, and its results in action are judged partly by reference to the occasions on which it is assumed that fear of such results has inhibited breach of the rule.

The difficulty of being very definite about the precise implications of sanctions is illustrated by adultery. As I have noted, recorded cases of adultery by married women in Tikopia were rare in 1929, and I noted no case in 1952. How far the infrequent breach was due to conformity to any one of the various sanctions it is very difficult to say. Fear of the sanction of retaliation by an aggrieved husband might operate in some cases where a woman might be tempted to break the rule. But to judge by public opinion, the moral view that a married woman must be respected may have been far more important. With this was linked the sanction of public opinion. In Tikopia villages public observation of visits to dwellings is very easy, and fear of public scandal might have been a powerful force in restraining liaisons in village areas. But this would have not applied so easily to a liaison in the orchards. On the other hand, as far as incentive to adultery by a man was concerned, the existence of other sources of sex satisfaction in polygyny and in resort to unmarried women may well have been relevant. Since there were so few cases of adultery by married women, one cannot sort out the sanctions of greatest weight with any confidence.

In some spheres this dilemma may be resolved in part by a study of the operations of sanctions over time. It could be seen, for example, in the reactions of Tikopia to measures for controlling theft. In the earlier stages of the food shortage it appeared that public disapproval and private retaliation were ineffective as sanctions. Obedience to the rules was not common, and the application of more stringent sanctions was resented. As the general effects of breach of rule were observed and felt personally, however, public disapproval became more vocal and, combined with organized official exposure, became a real deterrent. The tendency to conformity then grew in all but a hard core of habitual offenders. One is justified then in regarding the sanctions that developed as of real validity in controlling behaviour in regard to food supplies.

Sanctions have been classified in many ways. For convenience in this immediate Tikopia context, they may be referred to in terms of moral, economic, ritual and physical sanctions.

Comparison has shown that in the moral field there was no significant change over a generation in the sanctions of approval and disapproval. In particular the sanctions of public opinion operated in 1952 in similar conventional Tikopia patterns as in 1929. Economic sanctions also—such as the withdrawal of co-operation and assistance by kin—were of the same general order. Ritual sanctions however had undergone much alteration. In all the discussions about the incidence of theft in 1952, there was practically no reference to the effectiveness of any sanction of a ritual order. Tikopia men of rank seemed to have abandoned almost entirely any resort to sorcery or allied means of punishing offenders, and there was no evidence that would-be thieves were inhibited in any way by the beliefs which some of them undoubtedly still held in such supernatural powers. The public displays of coconut fronds which formerly were intended to signify a ritual protection were, by 1952, almost completely a form of social protest. On the other hand, in this field the ritual sanctions of Christianity did not seem to make much difference. Theft was rife, among Christians as well as pagans, and there was no evidence that churchgoing and honesty were to be connected. More generally, however, the sanctions of the traditional pagan religion had lessened considerably between 1929 and 1952, and those of Christianity had tended to strengthen. In some respects the widening of the split between the two religions offered a field for manoeuvre so that an individual, by moving from one system to another, could avoid to some extent the implications of the ritual sanctions of both.

Physical sanctions in Tikopia in 1929 could be of three kinds: (i) *unorganized personal action* where an affronted individual himself retaliated upon the offender; (ii) *organized unofficial action* where a group of people, including the affronted person or acting on his behalf, proceeded against the offender for retaliation or restitution, but without seeking the view of responsible men of rank, in particular, their chief; (iii) *organized official action* where an executive officer took action against the offender on the instructions of a chief, or acted with a general recognition that it would have the support of the chief if required. In 1952, physical sanctions of retaliation and restitution operated much as before. But whereas in 1929 they were relatively unorganized or at least were unofficial, towards the end of 1952 the sanction of retaliation, in particular, had become systematized and elaborated into a quasi-legal mechanism. Involving physical action publicly approved and carried out by properly accredited representatives of the community, it had passed over into the category of official deterrent punishment.

It has often been said that in the last resort law represents the exercise or potential exercise of physical force by organized legitimate political authority. While empirically this can be so, it must be clear that the exercise of such force can never be entirely automatic. Between those who employ it and those who order it to be employed there must be, if not some consensus of view, at least some common recognition of objectives. The person who actually employs the physical force to compel offenders to conform or to undergo punishment, if he himself is not in agreement with the ends of social control must at least concede that the carrying out of these ends promotes his own private objectives. At some point refusal is always open to him as a potentiality, as theoretically possible. Hence, in considering social control from the point of view of the exercise of physical force, one has also to consider what is the nature of the power which permits the exercise of this force. This issue is particularly relevant in discussing social change in Tikopia, where the prime holders of power, the chiefs, did not themselves use physical force to compel their wishes, but left this function to their executives.

While in a few cases fear of crude physical force by an executive officer or other man of rank did operation as a sanction, for the most part that force itself could be called upon only in co-operation with or when backed by public consensus, either mobilized or diffuse. Hence, any description of Tikopia sanctions in terms of force capable of being exercised by the political authority can be only a partial analysis. In this sense there had been by 1952 no fundamental change in the system of Tikopia social control. Even the most active and most feared executives used their power by delegation from the body politic of Tikopia. This body politic was composed of two major entities, the chiefs who were its spokesmen and the mass of the people whose adherence to a policy was recognized as essential in the long run if that policy was to be successful.

This is brought out most clearly by contrasting the Tikopia situation in 1952 with that in other islands in the Western Pacific. In most of these other islands the ultimate authority was exercised by an alien administration actually on the spot or able without difficulty to reach the spot. In many cases this administration used as its agents men who were not members of the community in which the control was exercised. Hence, for their force to be effective, they did not necessarily need the consensus of the local community—though in most cases they did their best to obtain it. As compared with Tikopia, they operated in a sphere of ideology primarily external to the community. As yet in 1952/3 Tikopia had no alien resident officials. Over a long range the Tikopia were governed by their respect for external sovereignty. But except for sporadic and very temporary contacts, the external authority of the Solomon Islands Administration was not in direct touch with Tikopia affairs. Hence, for the most part the force used by the Tikopia authorities was exercised in relation to their own community attitudes and interest.

Over the generation the same kinds of social agencies for implementation of sanctions had tended to operate. In particular, these were: on the one hand the chiefs and their executive officers; the officials of the Church; and on the other hand the family; the peer group; the lineage; the bilateral kin group. I have already indicated some changes in the relative weight exercised by the chiefs and by the Church. Family, peer group and kin group seemed to be after a generation of much the same influence as before.

But granting this overall community of sanctions, it would seem that the immediate social unit for the implementation of sanctions had become more circumscribed over the generation. This is not an impression which I can document at all clearly. In 1929, as in 1952, the lineages did not tend to be involved as corporate structural groups to any great extent in matters of social control. In a dispute between members of two different lineages over land or in an affair over a woman, individuals who were involved in any threat to public order could generally count on the support of their lineage members. If a man offended a chief, then members of his lineage might take the initiative in offering apology in compensation. But the lineage tended to be mobilized only for disputes or transactions where there was no offender; where an offence had been committed, it was the offender's immediate agnatic kin alone who tended to be involved. The lineage as such was not necessarily concerned at all. The head of the lineage might manifest some concern and take some initiative to rectify matters. But there was no equivalent of a lineage court and no responsibility was put upon the lineage head by normal social obligations. Yet in general it seemed that there was a tendency in 1929 for larger sets of lineage members to act together in many issues than was the case in 1952.

To some extent this may have been due in 1952 to the exigencies of famine which, as explained earlier (p. 83), tended to atomize the social units and, for example, lead brothers to look to their own resources against those of their siblings. But it may also have been due in part to a more restricted distribution of imported property. Although much of this was dispersed to other members of kinship units and also for political reasons to the chiefs, it did seem that a greater tendency existed for such property to remain with the immediate receivers of it. Sanctions in regard to the propriety of sharing through the kinship unit seemed to have weakened to some degree, and linked with this may well have been a weakening of kin support.

As regards internalization of sanctions, it is difficult to speak, but my impression was that in 1952 standards of right and wrong were no less nor no more recognized by individuals than in 1929. The field of actions and the social relations to which they were applied had altered to some extent with change in social and economic circumstances. The temporary migration of young men to work abroad, for example, was the object of stronger and more extended sanctions than at the earlier period—more pressures to go abroad were evident. In this sense these young men in 1952 had internalized as conditioning elements for their behaviour a set of sanctions not operative on men of their own age group to the same degree a generation before. On the other hand, the ability to conceptualize issues, objectives and the operations of sanctions, and the workings of conscience, seemed superficially to be much of the same order in 1952 as in 1929.

In one respect some change was becoming perceptible—that is, the degree to which actions of an individual were judged as such and not in terms of his social position. I have spoken in this chapter of punishment and not of justice. The reason for this is that to the Tikopia the two concepts are by no means equivalent. To us in our own society a lack of equivalence is due to one of two elements: the possibility of wrong identification of the offender so that the punishment is misplaced; or a lack of balance between magnitude of punishment and magnitude of offence. This is also the case with the Tikopia, who recognize false accusation or wrong identification of offenders very clearly. They also sometimes think that a punishment has not fitted the crime. But there is something more. The Tikopia have a view which, if expressed very generally and abstractly, is in common with that held by some sections of our society: that punishment, of any physical kind at least, is not really appropriate at all to some kinds of offenders. It is not that they regard the offender as being sufficiently punished by his own conscience, for the idea of a person's own moral sentiments turning against himself is one which they do not ordinarily express. Nor is their differentiation among kinds of offenders restricted to that which we often make, e.g. between juveniles and adults, or between people of unsound and sound mind. They do recognize differences in responsibility for actions and, despite whatever they may do in the heat of the moment, they are often willing to concede special treatment to the socially weaker category. But they have in addition another criterion which is fundamentally different to that of modern Western justice. Through the centuries, justice in the West has succeeded in separating responsibility for action and treatment of offence from social status. Rich man and poor man, duke and commoner, must be treated alike according to their deeds. This is at least the theory of justice.

The Tikopia in fact, though they do not put it like this, take an opposite view. To them what is proper treatment for a commoner who has committed an offence, is not necessarily appropriate for a man of rank who has committed the same type of action. In other words, they take an integral, not an atomistic, view of the actions of an individual. They judge these actions in the whole context of status relations and social activities, not in the immediate context of an offence and its punishment. Hence, an action by a member of one of the weaker categories, say a child of a commoner, which offended a chief might be punished quite harshly. On the other hand, a similar action by the child of a chief against a commoner would be likely to be excused. This is not quite so high-handed or illiberal as may appear at first sight. The Tikopia convention is that people of rank in general do not commit offences such as theft. In ordinary times this is largely true. People of rank are expected to be the guardians of public order, not breakers of it. On the other hand, the fact that most of them are tolerably well off in lands means that they are apt to be not under the same pressures as some commoners. Moreover, their rights over goods are apt to extend by custom more widely than those of commoners. Hence, an accusation of theft is to a considerable degree incompatible with the expected behaviour of a person of rank. The structure of the society then tends to inhibit its leaders from putting themselves into positions where they would be subject to punitive sanctions.

I have spoken of these matters in the historic present because differentiation of social control according to social status seemed to have been built into Tikopia society, in 1952 as it was in 1929. But the exceptional circumstances of the famine did appear to have introduced some modification in this general attitude. The convention that members of chiefly lineages do not steal was shown beyond all public doubt not to be correct. The general food shortage was so severe that people of rank gave way to their hunger and stole. This was commented upon by Tikopia as worthy of note. It was also publicly proclaimed that if members of chiefly lineages were discovered as thieves, they would suffer the same fate as anyone else. There was thus some confusion of categories ordinarily maintained. There was also a definite tendency to link the privileges of men of rank more closely with their obligations. If they did not adhere to their obligations, then they must suffer loss of privilege. In this way it appeared that there was a possibility of a radical change coming about in the Tikopia system of social sanctions, a levelling process of justice as regards traditional class differentiation.

The overall social unit in which the sanctions were operative seemed in 1952, as in 1929, to be still the Tikopia community as a whole. Though split partly along religious lines and partly in terms of district and clan allegiance, the people of the island still represented a closely-knit society, very conscious of the unity of their structure and of their community values.[1] In the extremity of the famine, each of the two districts and each of the two parties associated with Christian and pagan chiefs respectively, followed essentially the same traditional pattern of institutionalized ways of dealing with the crisis. Despite suspicion, disagreement and occasional lack of co-operation, on the whole the chiefs as leaders of their people did succeed in maintaining a common front on matters of public policy affecting the control of their people.

Summary

To sum up the situation in the sphere of social control in Tikopia after a generation, one may say that in 1952, as in 1929, the community had a strong respect for human life, property and social order. These values continued to be expressed in the same linguistic categories and supported by similar rules and procedures, with sanctions for maintaining proper relations in much of these major spheres. On the other hand, there had been some change in the balance of sanctions, in particular as regards those stemming from the Church on the one hand and the traditional pagan religion on the other. The area of conformity had also changed in certain directions. The major changes consisted of:

(a) A greater pressure on external sanctions upon Tikopia through the recognition by the people of a closer, more clearly defined interest of the British Solomon Islands Protectorate Government in the Tikopia social order; linked with this were increased facilities for the external administration to take action in cases of breach of that order.

(b) Increased support of a more formal kind for the chiefs as against other elements in the society; they began to emerge as the definitely recognized instruments of Government in the enforcement of order.

(c) A tendency to narrow down to some extent the role of the lineage as a social unit involved in the operation of sanctions, with some weakening of obligation upon more distant agnatic kin.

[1] This community solidarity has probably been intensified by the complete conversion of the pagan Tikopia to Christianity.

(*d*) More formalization (perhaps only temporary) of sanctions against some specific offences, primarily theft.

(*e*) More overt recognition of offences such as theft as being offences against the community and not against individuals alone.

But all this had taken place in a field of action which remained essentially Tikopia, blending traditional institutions with modern innovations.

A few more general conclusions may now be drawn. Tikopia is an example of a community which has had a *differential* application of sanctions. Not only has the principle of ignoring the trivial (*de minimis non curat lex*) been in vogue. Another principle, which might be phrased as *de maximis non licet lex*, the non-validity of the law as it concerns the greatest personages, has also been applied. This is another example of the general position of the flexibility of sanctions. So far from custom being automatic in its operation, as Hartland and others used to argue, it might be held that the less highly developed the form of government of a community, the less automatic are the sanctions in operation. Moreover, as the Tikopia material has shown, it may be very important for there to be *alternative* sanctions available. For example, a Tikopia who has been robbed has a number of alternatives open to him. He may make search for the thief and seek restitution or direct physical retaliation; he may seek retaliation indirectly either by sorcery or by public song; he may seek none of these, but content himself with public protest either in violent cursing or in a quiet setting-up of a token of his loss. He takes whichever procedure seems to be most appropriate according to circumstances—and included in these circumstances may be his judgment as to the social status of the person whom he conceives to be the thief. Again, the sanctions may be *mixed* in their application; more than one may be put into operation. It is important to realize that sanctions affect other parties than the offender, and they may often serve in a negative way, by reducing the area of action. For example, if a sanction of punishment be applied, it may affect the situation of the punisher adversely by bringing in its train counter-action. Hence, one sanction may inhibit the action of another, and the upshot will be the resultant of several forces of different kinds in a dynamic inter-relation. The conception of offence, followed by sanction, followed by restoration of equilibrium, is far too simple. There is need in our examination of social control for *structural analysis* to isolate the major types of social relation involved, and classify the types of sanction which may come into operation. There is also need for *organizational analysis* to study the inter-relation of these principles in any given case, to show the extent to which the sanctions are congruent or in conflict and how, in the light of principles of accommodation and economy of effort, status involvement and responsibility, the situation is resolved.

Y

CHAPTER XI

Processes in Social Change

This book is a study of a brief period in the history of a social system. Tikopia had changed between the time of earliest European contact and the time when I first saw it in 1928/9; it has continued to change since I left in 1952. But this period of a generation in the lives of its inhabitants was probably more significant for the form of the social system than any which preceded it for a long time. I am not referring here to the effects of famine—this was only one episode in a recurrent cycle of natural disasters. But the modernization of the social system as exemplified by the incorporation into it of the recognition of the use of money, by the acceptance of a wide range of new foods and other consumer goods, by the radical alterations in the religion of the people and, above all, by the acceptance of the view that a section of Tikopia society could live abroad, seemed to be of critical importance.

Scope and Validity of Generalization

In discussing social change in Tikopia I have had constantly to ask myself— is this analysis systematic as well as historiographic? From the Tikopia material can one see an illustration of a stage in social development of small-scale isolated communities? Can one also use the data for some demonstration of processes of social change at a more abstract level? I hope in this chapter to indicate some of these broader implications.

In seeking such comparability some basic questions have had to be faced. I trust I have been successful in disentangling the long-term trends from the short-term accidents of history—as, for example, the separation of the effects of regular population increase from those of sporadic hurricane and famine. But how far will any such general set of ideas about changes in a community of this kind represent the true nature of what has happened and may happen again—or how far is it a personal view by the observer? Do his statements not merely express his own verbal idiom but embody, perhaps in concealed form, his own scheme of values about the course and ends of change?

I think that few anthropologists would deny that certain aspects of their work are interpretative rather than reportorial. They are interested at certain points in passing judgment on the value of the experience rather than on mere objective comment. Their interest in social process is bound up with some view as to the relation between alternative social processes and preferred ways of life. There must always be some temptation to smuggle in as statement of event what in fact is primarily expression of opinion. But this tendency must not be overstressed. Even in the spheres of religion or politics, where the analyst's predilections are likely to be strongest and most subtly interwoven with his observations, the degree of objective analysis by anthropologists seems to have remained high. Responsibility for this rests largely on their discipline, training in which combines use of a common set of theoretical concepts with constantly improving agreed standards of field observation. Hence, the anthropologist tends to have a lively awareness of the implications of social action in terms of a generally recognizable frame of social structure and social values.

Yet there is still need to make more explicit some of the basic assumptions used in such studies. For instance, some of the difficulty in handling the concept of social change has been the implicit use of the basic assumption of homeostasis, that societies are in essence self-regulating systems. On this basis forces making for disequilibrium have been treated as of minor and temporary significance. For example, consider the traditional relation between the African or Polynesian chief and his people expressed, say, in his administrative authority over land resources. The people work for the chief at his behest, and a substantial proportion of the income obtained flows through his hands. Much of it is disbursed again to the people. By one set of assumptions all these relations are regarded as those of process in equilibrium, the chief's privileges and income being conceded by his people as fair return for his exercise of public functions of value to them. Yet by another set of assumptions these relations may be regarded as 'feudal', springing from the chief's autocratic control of land and, because of lack of alternatives open to the people, amounting to exploitation of them. Still another set of assumptions of an intermediate kind—to me more preferable—is that a system of reciprocity is in operation, income and privilege being matched against public service, but that unless the system receives constant supervision the balance may incline strongly in favour of either party. The system may turn into exploitation of the people by too heavy concessions by them to their chief. Or the people may exploit the chief by drawing so largely on his time and energy for supervision and responsibility for public affairs that he may have in effect no private life. On the whole, the system tends to incline in the former direction because of the greater efficiency with which force is normally exercised when authority lies with a single individual than if it is dispersed among many. But for relations between chief and people to continue effectively corrective action may have to be taken periodically by one side or the other. Moreover, the relationship is not necessarily perpetuated in the same form generation after generation; it may change its emphasis. Changes in external circumstances, such as the opening up of a new market for crops or for labour may alter the balance. If the chief controls the channels of distribution he may build up his private wealth. But if it is labour-power itself and not a product that is exported, the chief may lose control of his people. Again, the system of exploitation may change towards one of reciprocity through the imposition of new moral and legal controls involved by the entry of a new political ideology.

Each of these assumptions tends to give the analysis a different character.

Each suggests different criteria for estimation. Any concept which would regard work for the public good as being capable of being offset against material income demands careful consideration of ways of estimating intangible as well as tangible assets, and also ways of distinguishing and comparing the judgement of people on such matters. Any assumption of a system of reciprocity which can operate continuously only under check demands consideration of mechanisms of social control and their efficacy. Notions of the effects of opening a new market or introducing a new political ideology demand consideration of degrees of perceptiveness and responsibility, as well as methods of estimating these. In other words, the type of general assumption taken tends to condition the type of data sought for and systematized. Yet in an honest perceptive study of modern type some attempt will be made to isolate and study all these various criteria so that in the long run the precise nature of the basic assumptions made is less important than the detailed manner in which their implications are examined.

Concepts of Structural and Organizational Change

Discussions on social change are mainly concerned with structural change, that is, with alterations of the principles with which a society is operated, the framework upon which its social relations are constructed. Different definitions of social structure have involved differences in the idea of what constitutes structural change. To Ginsberg, for example, a change in the size of a society, for instance a contraction in the size of the domestic unit, is a change in social structure.[1] Strictly speaking, it would seem that a change in the size of a society, in the size of the family or the domestic unit, are not in themselves changes in social structure though they will probably be of major significance as bases or as indicators for such changes. More evident examples of change in social structure are forms of social re-alignment—a change in the form of a kinship unit, such as the breakdown of a joint family system into a system of individual families, or a change in the authority pattern in a household from mother's brother to father of children. Such changes mean alteration in the character of the social system.

There is, however, another aspect of social change, which I have termed *social movement*. This is an alteration not in principle but in detail, where the position of individuals or groups in the social system have altered but the character of the system as such is not affected. One example of this is given by the processes of *social replacement*[2] in, for example, succession to chieftainship. The succession of a new Tikopia chief brings a new set of persons into the roles of mother's brother and sister's child to the reigning chief, involving reorientation of the activities of the patrilineal descent groups which the

[1] Morris Ginsberg, 'Social Change', *British Journal of Sociology*, vol. 9, 1958, pp. 205–99. For definitions of social structure, cf. Raymond Firth, *Elements of Social Organization*, pp. 28–35; 'Social Organization and Social Change', *Journal Royal Anthropological Institute*, vol. 84, 1954, pp. 1–20; S. F. Nadel *The Theory of Social Structure*, 1957.

[2] The Tikopia recognize this figuratively by the expression '*a tupuranga ku siaki saere*', generations take one another's place in succession—the idea expressed being of persons walking along in file.

chief represents. The structure of chieftainship and of kinship, their values and their obligations, have not altered; but relations between specific persons and groups in the system have altered. Other examples (analysed in Chapter VII) are change of residence, which involves new neighbour relations; or a marriage, which creates new affinal ties. Again, there may be *social multiplication*, as when a decision to split sub-lineage land may give rise to new sub-lineage segments. Such social changes may have been in direct response to major pressures of the society as a whole, in particular pressures of population on the means of subsistence. From another point of view they can be regarded as the collective product of the behaviour of individuals. Seen as a pattern, though only after quantitative examination, this behaviour may be regarded as part of the 'covert' structure of the society.

The study of such social movement is important from two points of view. As I have demonstrated (Chapter VII), the systematic record of such social movement can give indices of continuity and replacement significant for an understanding of a history of the society over a period. Again, the distinction between social movement of personnel and/or social change of a structural order is not easy to draw formally, especially since if a time factor be involved change in one respect may almost inevitably lead to change in the other. In structural change one is concerned with alterations not only in the personnel of social units and in the position of these units *vis-à-vis* one another, but with the nature of the units themselves. One is concerned not with the different persons who have come to fill social roles, but with the disappearance of former roles and the emergence of new ones. Yet the replacement of some persons by others and an alteration in the size and position of social units may lead to further alteration in the nature of these roles and units. Without forcing the distinction too strongly, one can for ordinary purposes conceive of some changes as being primarily *structural* in character and others as being primarily *organizational*. Yet as I have shown, the relations between these may be intimate.[1] The case of Tikopia seems to demonstrate how organizational change may lead to structural change.

At this point it is appropriate to consider the notion of structural change itself a little further. Here it is convenient for some purposes to draw a distinction between a structure of ideals, a structure of expectations and a structure of action. The *structure of ideals* represents the 'pure' statements of the optimum character of the society—what it is held that members of the society ought to do and to have, and how they should be constituted as an entity. In particular, this includes what would be ordinarily called the principles of moral law, but pursued into areas and obligations not usually covered by such a concept in Western eyes as, e.g. in behaviour towards inanimate objects or natural forces. The *structure of expectations* represents the 'anticipated' form of the society—what it is held that members of the society are most likely to do, in particular the degree to which they are most likely to fulfil their obligations and the forms their co-operation will probably take. The *structure of action* represents the 'actual' form of the society as seen

[1] Raymond Firth, *op. cit.*

by the external behaviour—the contemporary alignment. It comprises what members of the society are observed to do in fact, which is often very distinct from what they think they ought to do, and from what they have been expecting themselves to do.

For a community in the situation of Tikopia in 1952, these different aspects seem to alter at different rates. Social change is made possible by alteration in the external circumstances. With this may be associated a modification in patterns of expectations, and closely followed by modification in the patterns of social action. The ideals of the community may not be seriously affected for a long time. But the position is complex. The expectations which develop are unlikely to be equally satisfied owing to the unequal command of resources in the hands of different sectors of the community. Moreover, the structure of action is likely to be affected in ways not foreseen by any members of the community at the time when the initial moves take place. The potentials for social change exist in the expansible character of the wants of the members of the society; the actualities of social change depend on where the control of resources lies and on differential responses to the new opportunities. These actualities also depend on implications—in part unexpected, in part even imperceptible—of the striving to achieve the new expectations. The unevenness in the endowment of different sectors of the society, or in the specific character of their traditional roles, means that in the new situation some sectors will be able to forge ahead and others will drop behind, as regards what they can offer or control. Change in social relations between members of the different sectors will then occur. But apart from this, new courses of action once begun will have necessary consequences; social changes may occur which no one would have sought, even for sectional advantage.

In this certain basic types of motivation seem operative—status involvement, interest in basic compensation for transfer of good or service, interest in economic maintenance and betterment, interest in securing for the next generation of offspring the advantages obtained. These are often expressed in concrete terms.

A Critical State in Tikopia Society

In summary, what had happened in Tikopia between 1929 and 1952? In the terms I have indicated earlier, most of the changes in social alignment and social roles that I noted in Tikopia in 1952 as compared with 1929 were still organizational rather than structural in character. The basic forms of local grouping, descent grouping, kinship and marriage, rights over property, chieftainship, ritual practices and religious beliefs (both pagan and Christian) were essentially the same as a generation before. Even the various reactions to the apparent population pressure had not radically affected the nature of the society—for instance, the Tikopia had not adopted any increased specialization of labour, a result of common occurrence elsewhere.

Yet by 1952 something of fundamental importance had happened to Tikopia society. It had reached a condition from which one felt it would be difficult for it to retreat. How can this be expressed in more formal terms?

In essence it may be said that the organizational changes so far were on the verge of taking structural effect. What especially had happened may be described as alterations in the relative magnitudes of social affairs and alterations in the patterns of expectation.

In terms of magnitude, changes of significance had occurred particularly in two spheres. In the economic field the magnitude of exchange of Tikopia products and service with the outside world had greatly increased, and as a part of this alteration a new magnitude, measurement of transactions in monetary terms, had come to be recognized by very many Tikopia. In the religious sphere, while the system of pagan ritual still existed in 1952 and was carried on with most of its former elaboration and by the same types of units, the relative magnitudes of the pagan and Christian congregations had radically altered. Whereas, a generation before, pagans and Christians each comprised roughly half of the island society, by 1952 pagans had been reduced to about one-third of their earlier total and to about one-seventh of the total community. Not only that—important defections of key men from the pagan ritual had necessitated substitute activities on the part of the faithful; and most significant, young people had left paganism in increasing numbers for the Church. Structurally, in terms of the general framework, the situation was much as it had been; organizationally, the balance had been radically altered.

As regards patterns of expectation, these had altered considerably in both the economic and the political field. In the economic field there had been a great enlargement of the consumers' horizon, both as regards an increase in the types of goods recognized and in the concept of their more immediate availability. The opening of a fairly regular labour market was linked with this as providing hitherto unrealizable opportunities. It also offered fresh expectation of diversified and new kinds of employment hitherto beyond the reach of Tikopia young men. In the political field there were signs of a development of regular Government interest from a mere assertion of sovereignty and remote control to a much more specific wish for the creation of administrative mechanisms, operating in fairly close touch with Government representatives. By 1952, neither headmen nor courts were immediately envisaged in Tikopia. But there had been definite signs of the underpinning of the position of the chiefs by administrative action and conversely of Government requirement from the chiefs of some more specific responsibility for the conduct of Tikopia affairs. All of this meant that Tikopia actions could be governed not only by the internal state of affairs in Tikopia, but also by expectations of how affairs in the external world might react upon the Tikopia situation. Linked with this were other types of expectation. No action had occurred in regard to the Government's preliminary exploration of the idea of migration of a section of Tikopia population to another island. But this ideas was available to the Tikopia, and could be taken up by them as the pressure of circumstances seemed to warrant. In the field of the social services, the Government seemed to have no plans for education for the Tikopia. But on the medical side some relief was being obtained by them, in particular through the stationing of a Native Dresser on the island, and the possibility of hospital and other assistance existed. Thus, though the form of social roles and the structure of social units had still been preserved in Tikopia, the society seemed on the threshold of more radical change because of the implications of the ideas they had already accepted. Thus, in terms of a static analysis, Tikopia social structure had hardly altered, but from a dynamic analysis, there had been very significant change. Now this may be put in another form.

In Tikopia society of 1952 the structure of ideals seemed to be very much as it had been a generation before. Tikopia people still seemed to think of Tikopia as a strongly unified society with a social alignment and customs which they highly valued and with institutionalized symbolic and practical leaders, the chiefs, to whom they gave deep allegiance. Ideally, they wanted to combine life on Tikopia with a richer use of Western goods within their range of knowledge and capacity to utilize. Their structure of action also was largely the same. It had altered, somewhat, in the economic field. There had been a significant shift in the relations of production owing to the enlistment of large numbers of men, especially the younger men, for wage labour abroad, with all the consequences that this involved. Yet, occupationally this was true of only a fraction of the people and only for a fraction of their working life. The distributional norms had changed a little, perhaps more pervasively. But in general, traditional Tikopia modes of production, distribution and exchange were still followed. What above all had changed was, as I have indicated, the structure of expectations. Not that patterns of response to obligation had changed—people still expected the traditional kinds of service from others. But they expected to be able to do better for themselves than heretofore. There was now much more scope for new ideas of what, as Tikopia, they could reasonably expect to obtain from their increased contact with the Western world. This was a series of expectations which, once aroused, could not easily be suppressed.

This separation of structures of ideals, expectations and action is, of course, only an heuristic device. Empirically, these elements though not amorphous are conceived with very differing degrees of clarity and cohesion by different members of a society. Again, they are fairly closely related. Both the structure of ideals and the structure of expectations contribute to the structure of action, since members of the society, as part of their actual behaviour, daily continue to construct and revise their patterns of expectation and pattern of ideals. Moreover, their expectations may be formed of a mixture of ideals and more cynical observation of action; and their actions may be guided partly by the need to safeguard against what they expect others will do. At the operational level of the anthropologist's enquiry, therefore, it may not be possible to separate out these different components clearly enough to see them in independent movement.

Nevertheless, in a somewhat crude way one can see how expectations held and expressed by some sectors of the Tikopia society, e.g. its young men, might at a certain stage differ substantially from those of another sector.

Traditionally, Tikopia young men had an occupational expectation differing little from that of their seniors; since 1952 their paths can diverge widely. In the new occupational structure there is also the possibility of further variation. To some young men labour abroad is still an interim period before they return to routine agriculture at home. Others look to make for themselves a career in quite new skills as a permanent source of income, with new domicile accordingly. According to their earning power in this external labour market so have Tikopia a corresponding capacity for matching performance to ideals at a new level.

The attitude of the young men may not only affect their own behaviour, but draw in their train the expectations and actions of other members of the society who have become increasingly dependent upon them for realization of their wants. In the Tikopia of 1952 some of the younger men in particular seemed to have a fairly clear mental map of what they wanted to have and to do. The only saleable resource of any magnitude the Tikopia had for the outside world was labour, and it was clearly only the younger men who could supply this. Their immediate ideals and expectations were fairly clear and their actions were directed strongly towards this end. While with older men and with women there was some lack of clarity, the willingness of some of the younger men to take fairly drastic action to secure what they wanted involved these other social categories of people also in their wake.

But the results may not be entirely as foreseen.

The processes at work can be seen in part as questions of control. In the Tikopia island community, traditionally the norms of social obligation have normally kept the control of a man's productivity and of his income within the hands of his seniors. When a man goes abroad to work, the control of his productive powers passes right away from his seniors—his chief, his father, his elder married brother—to his employer, and his foreman; and the control of his income passes into his own hands. The seniors are deprived of a large part of income control; what they receive from the overseas labourer accrues to them not by right but as a gift, a privilege. In the overseas labour system the stay-at-home seniors cannot even check what amount of income the labourer receives. Hence their realization of their ideals and expectations—certainly as regards Western goods—will come to depend more and more on the discretion of their juniors, whereas traditionally the situation was reversed. This is a situation the elders almost certainly have not anticipated.

The structure of the descent group system is also likely to be affected. With the resort of many young men to overseas labour the close correlation between lineage, land holding and income from agriculture will tend to weaken. With his growing dependence on income from labour abroad a man will no longer need the same resource of lineage land, and so if he wishes he can free himself from much of the former control of his behaviour in the interests of his lineage. His conformity to lineage affairs now becomes optional rather than mandatory. With an alteration in the occupational structure comes an alteration in the structure of sanctions for conduct, and possibly a weakening of descent group ties.

Z

From another point of view a broadening of the basis of responsibility must follow. Decisions of communal import—about use of labour power, institution of new techniques such as speaking of English, and policy in external relations—will now come to be made as much by younger men as by their elders. There will be a split in the handling of decisions and a sharing of responsibility for community affairs. Traditionally, there was the normal successional shift from one generation to another; now there will come to be an age-grade shift as well. This must be so when the rewards for entrepreneurship and supervision are removed from the local elders and taken over by external agencies.

Such processes, including alteration in the structure of control and of responsibility, are irreversible so long as relations with the external market continue. They also raise very serious problems for the future of the society.

Viability of the Tikopia System

In summarizing the social changes that occurred in Tikopia over a generation and examining their implications, I have tried to keep close to the social reality. Tikopia superficially is a social laboratory of a simple kind in which the separate factors of social change can be identified and their effects perceived. The crude facts of its situation are of undoubted significance—its small size, its isolation, its poverty of resources by modern standards and the relative homogeneity of its population. The separate influences of commercial contact, Mission proselytization and governmental interest can be identified almost in personal terms. Yet even here it is difficult to disentangle precise social effects due to one or other of the external influences. One thing, however, is clear and that is the lack of alternatives offering to Tikopia in the economic field have tended to condition their receptivity to political and economic influences.

From this point of view a basic question which must face many of the small Pacific island communities is that of their economic viability. As their contact with modernization grows, their people are developing wants beyond the capacity of their local resources to satisfy. The magnitude of their technological and economic system is too small to allow them to continue as relatively self-sufficient units. Unless they are to receive a permanent subsidy from outside they are likely to be faced, therefore, by problems of either exporting some of their people as labour resources to gain higher incomes elsewhere or of reducing the level of their wants below those which they know are being satisfied in similar communities. This prospect seems to me one which needs to be viewed much more realistically than it often is nowadays.

How does this bear upon the viability of the Tikopia social system? For a generation or so to come the Tikopia may well benefit from expanding income, but this process may not last. Can they then maintain the integrity of their social system unimpaired?

The magnitude of a social system is not absolute. While governed to a very large extent by the demographic position and by the nature of the physical resources available to the society, both the complexity of its structure and the level of its wants are yet matters which can be determined to some extent by the people themselves. Their continued acceptance of a new religion, as well as their willingness to make an economic system suffice for their wants, lie in the last resort with them.

In the past, the small physical scale of Tikopia has been not deterrent to the creation of a more elaborate social scale by minute sub-division of the social spacing. Men who have a 'town house' and a 'country house' only a few yards apart, or to whom 'banishment' may mean a simple but highly significant movement to another district only half a mile away, have not been inhibited by physical scale from amplifying their social system and deriving rich satisfactions from micro-social relations. But in predicting certain kinds of change as very probable, one assumes that even in such a remote and isolated society as Tikopia, people will in fact want to behave as far as possible like the other people whose technology and consumption schedules they wish to accept. Hence the coming of modernization to the Tikopia may involve the loss of their sense of the social significance of small-scale movement. From our Western point of view, this may be termed a gain in perspective, but from another point of view it may be regarded as a loss of sensitivity in the social system.

There is a further point. In a small-scale community such as Tikopia, with its great isolation, the people have had great limitations in their technical knowledge as compared with the more sophisticated world. Expansion of their technical universe has tended to enlarge their perspective. But in such circumstances their perspective as regards human relations may not have substantially changed. In their own social universe, Tikopia experience of human relations has been very considerable and their comment on such relations has been sensitive, pithy and not at all unsophisticated. Hence an expansion of their social and technical universe may not add appreciably to the subtlety of their understanding of human relations and their knowledge of the ways to manipulate them. It may even give rise to some lack of confidence and uncertainty.

Anthropologists have learned that very small-scale societies of one or two thousand people have not only complex personal relationships among their members, but also a complex formal structure. This may be very different from the structure of other small societies, even in very similar geographical environments. On the other hand, such structures tend to have a fairly high degree of integration. I have shown that in Tikopia the integration of the society was not merely an anthropologist's abstraction, but was an overt notion, with moral connotations, among the more thoughtful of the Tikopia themselves. Granted this integration, and bearing in mind the small size of Tikopia, one sees the difficulties of the 'survival' of the social system. There can be no pockets of untouched culture among the Tikopia as, for example, it has been possible to find in areas of New Guinea. Such small-scale structures are apt to be highly inflexible; when subjected to external pressures they crumble and break down rapidly into either relatively amorphous sub-societies or become merged with the wider structures with which they have been brought into relation.

True, I have shown that this has not so far been the case with the Tikopia. Their social structure did become modified in various ways owing to the pressures from external forces. But there was, even over the generation between my visits, a surprising degree of differentiation or variation in type of social relationship, practice and belief among Tikopia. Their personal responses to these external pressures were markedly differential, specifically in regard to their reception of an alien religion. In this differential acceptance of change, two sets of factors stood out. One was the alignment of change or resistance to it in terms of status interest, both of individuals and of groups. The other was the linkage of the social positions taken up with moral criteria. The various parties to differentiation in the religious field had moral reasons of varying kind to justify the position each took.

The Tikopia social system demonstrated an unequal flexibility in different aspects. In the field of technology, the Tikopia soon abandoned their traditional shell tools, probably a century before I ever saw them. They took on Western consumer goods rapidly. But they were slow to adopt money as a medium of exchange and store of values. They retained their economic system to a very large degree, partly because they had no alternative resources and partly because it was so deeply intertwined with their system of social services. When, however, an alternative resource as regards the employment of labour presented itself, they enlarged their system of production immediately to take advantage of this. However, after a century of Mission contact and pressure, they finally lost completely their pagan religious system —that is on its formal structural side. This meant that they altered their symbolic frame for the interpretation of experience and that, in particular, their lineages lost their ritual individuality (and their ritual leaders) while keeping their social and economic individuality. It was notable, however, that their chiefs, who had been the leading pagan priests, continued to survive in their secular roles. The chiefs entered baptism as chiefs and the aura of taboo which continued to surround them related in part to the recognition of their traditional religious functions.

In the selectivity shown by the Tikopia one can see the importance of shared experiences and perceptions. As regards the Tikopia traditional symbolic frame of religious belief and practice, there was no sharing of experience with Europeans and no common perception of utility. The pagan religion accordingly succumbed. But the Tikopia shared with Europeans a common perception of the relative efficiency of steel tools. They also shared to a considerable extent a common view of the impressiveness of ceremonial and of the political value of chiefs, and these have survived. It is very interesting to see how the Tikopia, less than two thousand strong, have been able to impose their social values on visiting Europeans. This is particularly notable in the European acceptance of their chieftainship. Even the Bishop of Melanesia has written as follows when he was presented to the Ariki Tafua. 'Walking up to him, I made a deep bow and presented my gifts to him (every visitor must bring a gift for each of the Chiefs). As one must never turn one's back on a Chief, I backed away until out of his immediate presence.'[1] The Tikopia then have succeeded in convincing Europeans in the Tikopia milieu of the significance of their political hierarchy.

In the political field of Tikopia can the chiefs continue to survive? Their effective powers of life and death have virtually been lost, not only to the Government by surrender of their power of punishment, but also to the Mission by surrender of their standard of moral judgment as to the propriety of values. Earlier I was inclined to think that the importance of the ritual sanctions for their power would militate against their survival when they turned to Christianity. But they still control the lands of the island in theory and to a considerable extent in practice. Moreover, since they have tended to become the 'chosen instruments' of Government for administration, in the new situation they have a role supported by the external power. But the basis of their survival really rests elsewhere. The Government selection was not arbitrary in this community. From the point of view of the Tikopia people, they must have some representatives in dealing with the external power, and there is no doubt that in the existing Tikopia ideology the chiefs are their proper representatives, entitled by popular view to speak for the community as a whole. Their importance lies to a very large extent in their function of crystallizing and giving sanction to the decision-making roles in the community. The Tikopia responses to external influences, whether of the labour market, of Government intervention or of Mission proselytization, have not been individually free and competitive. They have not even been simply family or lineage responses. They have been guided by the political structure in which the chiefs exercised conjoint, centralized authority. Such decisions of individuals have been determined to a large extent, limited and framed, by the decisions of the chiefs. This has not meant simply automatic conformity. I have given enough evidence to show how great has been the range of variation in the response of Tikopia individuals to the new circumstances. But in the last resort the decisions of individuals have been taken within the whole framework of which the chiefs have been the prime representatives. In a broad sense, chieftainship is an integral character of the Tikopia social system.

It is probable, therefore, that as one very important symbol of the integrity of Tikopia society the chieftainship will long survive. What of other characters of the Tikopia social system?

Cyclical Character of Social Change
In common with other anthropologists, I have tended to see the development of such small-scale Oceanic and analogous communities as likely to be of cyclical form.[2] In general, such a cyclical conception involves the recognition

---

[1] From 'The Bishop's Log', December, 1956, in the *Southern Cross Log*, March, 1957, p. 14.

[2] See Raymond Firth, *Primitive Economics of the New Zealand Maori*, 1929, Chap. 14; F. M. Keesing, *The South Seas in the Modern World*, 1941, pp. 78–80; R. Thurnwald, *Black and White in East Africa*, 1935, pp. 376–7; A. P. Elkin, 'Reaction and Interaction: Food-Gathering, People and European Settlement in Australia', *American Anthropology*, vol. 53, vol. 53, 1951, pp. 164–86; Ernest Beaglehole, *Social Change in the South Pacific*, 1957, pp. 11–126.

of: (*a*) an early stage of exploration and acceptance of Western ideas and materials; (*b*) an attempt at integration of these into the local system, without realizing the full consequences; (*c*) a growing perception of the difficulties, strains and disappointments resulting from this and a reaction, of disillusionment or even of a violent rejective character; (*d*) some broader attempt at reintegration at a more realistic level. Many variants of these processes have been recognized, but in general their cyclical character seems to be borne out.

It will be clear from my analysis in this book that the Tikopia social system in the generation between 1929 and 1952 was at a stage in the cycle when acceptance of Western materials and values was active, and indeed enthusiastic. Broadly speaking, the attitude of the Tikopia towards the new economic, political and religious elements introduced to them was of a positive kind and they were willing to alter their social relationships in many respects in order to take advantage of their opportunities. On the other hand, they were not in a position to see the implications of many of their actions and to estimate the structural modifications which would almost certainly be required in their society if they were to pursue their objectives consistently. Evidence of dissatisfaction with some of the new developments, especially in the religious sphere, was to be seen. This was rather disquiet at disturbance of an old-established order than perception of the inevitable costs of the establishment of a new order. But such disillusioned appreciation would seem inevitable during the next generation, and some hard choices will have to be made before a relatively stable adaptation to modern conditions can be found. This will be so especially if the Tikopia are to have a considerable section of their people living and working elsewhere as a permanent settlement (p. 69), with much higher income and much easier access to Western goods and Western institutions.

That the cyclical presentation of social change in such communities is historically accurate is not the result of any innate character of the process of social change itself. It arises primarily from the character of modern industrial technology. This is, to all intents and purposes, irreversible and has elaborate social correlates, for its effective use. To take advantage of even the peripheral aspects of modern industrial technology, as the Tikopia have set themselves to do, means a radical alteration in the patterns and allocation of work, in the distribution of incomes and in the command over capital. It means also recognition of a legitimacy of wider overseas relationships which are necessary if the new economic patterns are to be pursued. If the gains from modern industrial technology are no longer available, its social concomitants cannot at once be modified. Reversion to traditional ways is no longer possible. Changes in avenues of employment and patterns of occupation have meant a loss of traditional skills, forms of association and values which cannot be recreated.

The Tikopia seem set on a path which in analogous cases has resulted in changes of the following order:

(1) There is a tendency for corporate kin groups of the larger unilineal type to lose coherence and jurisdiction. While they may retain their nominal

structure, effective social relationships tend to move outside them in regard to property rights, marriage roles and economic obligations. Alternatively, special measures, very often involving legislative sanction, are necessary to retain them as functionally operative groups.

(2) There is a tendency for wealth and status relations to become more highly diversified. This process is apt to take place differentially at different generation levels.

(3) The traditional authority system tends to alter. On the one hand there is an orientation towards an external source of authority arising from the need of a small-scale community to draw upon external sources of power and wealth. On the other hand, this reflects also the interest of an external political organization in the administration of the affairs of the small-scale community—partly because the external power has an investment of economical or social capital therein. The traditional authority system may also be modified through the creation of new rules linked with the interpretation of new values or the distribution of new resources.

(4) There is a tendency for the local 'particularistic' religion to become attenuated and finally to disappear as a systematic structure. With this goes a shift from traditional religious leaders to new religious leaders.

(5) In the long run there is a tendency for a small-scale community to behave in many respects as a sector of a larger community. Yet the concept of 'assimilation' as one of complete incorporation does not hold. The tendency is for the local community to absorb economic, political and religious elements from the outside and to relate these to the wider external structures, but to retain many local cultural elements—types of food, styles of sleeping and greeting, recognition of group symbols and interests. These local elements may be regarded as simply group differentials or they may be adhered to defensively because of their expression of group individuality. From this point of view, what the members of a local community normally seek is *participation*, not assimilation.

Trends of Development

I have presented Tikopia society at two time periods for which first-hand observation of a systematic order is available. The changes recorded, therefore, refer to documented, historical events, and not to hypothetical experiences. At the same time, attempts to provide generalizations of a sociological order and not merely a historical record have necessitated some sequence-reading of the meaning of the events observed beyond the period of observation. Comparison of the Tikopia social system of 1952 with that of 1929 has seemed to indicate that the events described form part of more general trends in social change.

An economist would probably describe these events in terms of a concept of development or economic growth. In general, the changes which a small-scale backward economy such as that of Tikopia tends to undergo when the forces of modernization are brought to bear more directly upon it can be regarded economically as of a developmental order, in that they lead initially to a rise in per capita income and to some increased capital formation. Politically too, the more effective and direct incorporation of the local system of social control into the administrative framework of large-scale Government may also be regarded as developmental through its increase in complexity. From the point of view of the increase in social service facilities, especially in medical and educational fields, the change may be described as progressive.

From the point of view of an analysis of the social system, the progressive developmental aspect is by no means so clear. Tendencies to a closer delimitation of individual and small group rights in land, to the disappearance of special statuses such as those of ritual elders, and to modification in patterns of ceremonial exchange, are not so obviously to be classed as social development. In the field of moral and religious values and institutions, the issue is also debatable. Those who accept the ideology of a universalistic religion naturally regard the change to it from a local religion as development. But the content of the change is complex, with many traditional elements retained. Broadly, the concept of development can be applied to any increase in efficiency and control over means, in terms of given ends. This can include recognition of ability to handle an increasingly complex organization by which control of the means can be more effectively secured. In such terms, the Tikopia may be said to have undergone some process of social development in that in the generation between 1929 and 1952 they did succeed in working out ways of taking advantage of the new and wider opportunities presented to them.

Social anthropologists have often tended to treat the subject of social change in small-scale societies as if it were mainly degenerative, as if the breakdown of the structure of authority and the large-scale kinship groups provided less effective ways of satisfying wants than before. But they have also begun to see that just as important is the creation of new social structures and the emergence of new social values with a novel content and a fresh symbolic character, with new elites arising to give a personal meaning to such values. Yet such new integration may not follow a consistent course. I have already questioned whether the levels of consumption towards which the Tikopia seemed to be striving in 1952 are likely to prove attainable to them with their existing resources, and whether in the long run an economic viability of the kind they desire is possible to them without a radical break-up and reconstitution of their society.

My aim in this book has been the study of social process, not simply of differences in pattern. I have shown the structure of Tikopia society at two periods and have indicated that in some major respects it remained unaltered over a generation, while in others it was substantially modified. I have pointed out how social movement occurred under the stimulus of demographic variation and economic pressures, directly expressed in terms of accepted and shared values. I have shown how the structural changes were related to increased opportunities of attaining ends which were valued by the Tikopia. I have defined particularly the nature and range of these values and shown how the Tikopia have exercised their choice among the various alternatives and have decided upon courses of action. Their choices have not been free, but have been limited by their environmental resources, by the structure of their society, and by the symbols in which their traditional values have been expressed. Tikopia decisions have had implications in their social organization—they have involved the manipulation of social relationships and changes in the social position of persons. In this whole sphere of choice and decision, I have shown the extent of Tikopia personal variation in the perception of the nature of the situation and in the acceptance of responsibility for it. But one of the most marked characteristics distinguishing the Tikopia of the mid-twentieth century from the Tikopia of the beginning of the century is the degree to which they have surrendered the ultimate responsibility for their values. From now on, both in the political and in the religious field, they have handed over the ultimate decision as to what values and courses of action are good to authorities whom they themselves now recognize as legitimate in lands far afield. The implications of this have still to be worked out by them.

SOME GENERAL IMPLICATIONS

Apart then from being an analysis of a sector of Tikopia social history, this book may have a certain predictive value as an aid to the understanding of the directions in which further social change may go. It may help us to foresee what may happen to the Tikopia, and it may also to a limited degree help us to foresee what may happen to other small oceanic societies which as yet have had little contact with the Western world.

But it may also have some more general implications. Some of these are retrospective—my analysis of the detailed workings of the processes of change in Tikopia does, I think, help to throw some light on the way in which these processes have operated in the history of other Polynesian societies over the past century or so. More generally still, the analysis may have helped to indicate the manner in which the broad forces of change stand in relation one to another. Tikopia is a highly structured society with its integrative values well developed. Yet the forces of individual enterprise and status interest are continually seeking new expression and enforce change. When the opportunities offered by external contact are relatively few, internal movements in the society—in change of residence, change of occupation and succession to authority—have had only minor structural consequence. But when external opportunities widen in pursuit of their individual expression, the changes which people make in their residence and in their occupation, and in their succession to authority, enlarge the orbit of their social actions and may have structural implications of major consequence. What the example of Tikopia shows is that even in a very small-scale society such as this, processes of social change are complex. There is no simple determinism. The changing forces of the environment and forces of production, including the changing structure of the technological system, have clearly been of great importance. But so also have been the forces involved in the system of social allocation. All of these have operated, together with conceptual and decisional elements of individual and group behaviour, in a field where alternatives for choice have always been possible. The existence of such alternatives, including those between material and symbolic satisfactions, renders it impossible for any social analysis to predict more than in a very tentative way the future history of a society.

Index

Acculturation, 19

Adelaide, HMS, 41

Adultery, 302, 310, 326, 331

Adze, 26, 32, 36, 106, 107–8, 124, 129, 130, 137, 139, 142, 143, 144, 145

Agriculture, 51–76, 154–80, 185, 259; tables and plan, 173–5, 178; *v*. also Land

Alenga (offering), 128

Allen, C. H., 254n

American, US Forces, 42

Anuta, 32, 36, 37, 38n, 43, 44, 49, 73, 90, 109, 166, 197, 251, 274, 275

Applied Anthropology, 28; *v*. also Government

Ariki Fangarere, Plate VI A, 95; in 1929, 137, 158, 281; in 1952, Christian, 271, 301, 315; pagan, 62, 81, 99, 139, 153, 273, 274, 276; chieftainship split, 221, 280–3; on sub-lineages, 246–8

Ariki Kafika, Plate V A, 33, 36, 37n, 38n, 47, 67, 80, 82, 88, 91, 92, 94, 96, 99, 109, 124, 141, 159, 163, 165, 169, 193, 204, 241, 245, 256, 260, 263, 268, 269, 270, 272, 275, 290, 305–6; canoes, 137; on food shortage, 56, 62, 95, 156; on hurricanes, 56; on labour recruitment, 274; ritual decision, 276

Arika Tafua, Plate VI B, 36, 38n, 100, 169, 207, 221, 222, 258, 306; in 1929, 136, 169, 170, 207, 263, 279n; in 1938/51 (Pa Rangifuri), 129, 169, 170, 193, 204, 266, 267, 279–80; in 1952, 43n, 74, 91, 99, 103, 104, 129, 136, 151, 263, 264–5, 278, 281, 282, 292, 323; house, 191; labour relations, 117, 119, 123, 271–5; land encroachment, 170–1, 235

Ariki Taumako, Plate IV B, 196, 207, 221, 222, 266n, 278; in 1929, 87, 186, 206, 228, 288; in 1952, 26, 54, 56, 64, 81, 92, 95, 99, 102, 104, 108, 129, 137, 148, 169, 204, 205, 291, 292, 316, 319; lands, 164–5, 237; on labour recruitment, 124, 271–6; on land rights, 70, 158, 167, 171–2, 179; on *maru*, 293; on theft, 92, 318, 319, 320, 323; rite of reintegration, 226–8, 91

Aristotle, on oligarchy, 256

Arofa (sympathy), 304

Aru (levy), 159

Authority, 66, 77, 78, 218, 251, 252, 256, 263, 264, 271, 279, 281, 297, 339, 340, 351, 352; *v*. also Chiefs, *Maru*

Banks islands, 38, 39, 49

Bark-cloth, 31n, 33, 43, 44, 48, 72, 108, 130, 131, 139, 140, 141, 144, 145, 147, 153, 227, 314

Barter, *v*. Exchange, Trade

Barwell, ship, 32

Bond-friendship, 45, 152, 267, 321

Burial, 185, 190, 196–7, 250, 304, 311; *v*. also Funeral

Bushart, Martin, 32

Camera, owned by Tikopia, 26, 111

Canoe, 26, 31, 39, 107, 112, 114, 131, 182, 277; building, 44, 129, 139–40, 167; capital, 48, 75, 130, 134–7; census, 25, 134; expulsion by, 287–8, 322, 323; flight by, 24, 307, 309; model, 113, 142, 146; ownership, 164, 236, 238; sacred, 95, 134–6, 239–40, 241, 250, 269, 271, 316; voyaging, 38, 45, 53, 116, 117, 118, 262, 273, 310

Capital, 75, 106, 128–37, 153, 156, 164, 255, 351

Census, canoes, 25, 134; property, 187; sociological, 24, 25, 114, 192–212; village, 189